WORKING IN THE CONTEXT OF AUSTERITY

Challenges and Struggles

Edited by
Donna Baines and Ian Cunningham

BRISTOL
UNIVERSITY
PRESS

First published in Great Britain in 2021 by

Bristol University Press
University of Bristol
1-9 Old Park Hill
Bristol
BS2 8BB
UK
t: +44 (0)117 954 5940
e: bup-info@bristol.ac.uk

Details of international sales and distribution partners are available at bristoluniversitypress.co.uk

© Bristol University Press 2021

British Library Cataloguing in Publication Data
A catalogue record for this book is available from the British Library

ISBN 978-1-5292-0867-2 hardcover
ISBN 978-1-5292-0869-6 ePub
ISBN 978-1-5292-0868-9 ePdf

The right of Donna Baines and Ian Cunningham to be identified as editors of this work has been asserted by them in accordance with the Copyright, Designs and Patents Act 1988.

Cover design: Liam Roberts
Front cover image: DavidCallan / iStock

Bristol University Press uses environmentally responsible print partners.

Printed and bound in Great Britain by CPI Group (UK) Ltd, Croydon, CR0 4YY

FSC
www.fsc.org
MIX
Paper from
responsible sources
FSC® C013604

We would like to dedicate this book to all those impacted by austerity, and all those working to create a more just and equitable future.

Contents

List of Figures and Tables

Figure

Tables

List of Contributors

Mimi Abramovitz, City University of New York, US

Pat Armstrong, York University, Canada

Donna Baines, University of British Columbia, Canada

Alina M. Baluch, University of St Andrews, UK

Helen Blakely, Cardiff University, UK

Ian Cunningham, University of Strathclyde, UK

Steve Davies, Cardiff University, UK

Patrick Gunnigle, University of Limerick, Ireland

Philip James, Middlesex University, London, UK

Eva Jendro, University of Strathclyde, UK

Jonathan Lavelle, University of Limerick, Ireland

Wayne Lewchuk, McMaster University, Canada

Juliet MacMahon, University of Limerick, Ireland

Caroline Murphy, University of Limerick, Ireland

Mike O'Brien, University of Limerick, Ireland

Pauric O'Rourke, Limerick Institute of Technology, Limerick, Ireland

Michelle O'Sullivan, University of Limerick, Ireland

Geraldina Polanco, McMaster University, Canada

Jill Rubery, University of Manchester, UK

Lorraine Ryan, University of Limerick, Ireland

Dora Scholarios, University of Strathclyde, UK

Kendra Strauss, Simon Fraser University, Canada

Tom Turner, University of Limerick, Ireland

Niels van Doorn, University of Amsterdam, Netherlands

Feng Xu, University of Victoria, Canada

Doug Young, Edinburgh Napier University, Edinburgh, UK

Jennifer Zelnick, Touro College Graduate School of Social Work, US

Acknowledgements

The editors gratefully acknowledge the contributions of the authors and their goodwill in meeting tight deadlines. On behalf of the authors and ourselves, we would also like to thank the research participants who contributed their experience and insights to our research. We would also like to thank Paul Stevens, Senior Commissioning Editor, Bristol University Press, Caroline Astley, Senior Editorial Assistant, Liam Roberts, cover design, the Bristol University Press team and our anonymous reviewers. Many thanks also to Judith Oppenheimer for her copy-editing of the typescript. Finally, we would like to thank our families for putting up with us and sharing our commitment to a better world.

PART I

Introduction

1

Understanding Austerity: Its Reach and Presence in the Changing Context of Work and Employment

Donna Baines and Ian Cunningham

Let me put it very forcefully: No large economy has ever recovered from an economic downturn through austerity. It's not going to happen in the United States, and it's not going to happen in Europe. (Joseph Stiglitz)[1]

Introduction

This introductory chapter sketches out some of the major debates concerning austerity, neoliberalism and work. Given the international content in this volume, austerity debates are sketched in broad strokes rather than being specific to national contexts. Austerity is viewed as a set of interwoven policies aimed at reducing public debt and expenditure, increasing consumer taxes and purportedly stimulating economic well-being through corporate tax cuts and support for private business. Since the 1970s, austerity policies have been closely associated with neoliberalism, a set of policies and processes that valorize the private market as the solution to all social and economic problems and seek to reduce or eliminate social entitlements and public provision (Harvey,

2007; Evans and McBride, 2017). Austerity policies are underscored by neoclassical economics assertions that cutting public budgets and reducing government debt will generate 'confidence' and a return to growth and prosperity during difficult economic times (Blyth, 2013, p 3).

The current wave of austerity policies stems from the aforementioned neoliberal economic consensus that pervades developed economies, albeit in an uneven way. The current iteration of austerity, rather than its ongoing presence as an integral part of neoliberalism (Pierson, 1998; Clarke, 2017), was triggered by the global financial crisis (GFC) of 2007–08. Neoliberalism's emphasis on creating freedom of capital and lifting restrictions on international finance (Harvey, 2007) led to the financial 'light touch' regulation that governed the US sub-prime and other national housing markets. The financial crisis that followed the collapse of these housing markets threatened the entire global economy (Lethbridge, 2012). The initial government responses in 2008–09 were fiscal stimulus packages, which increased government borrowing and levels of debt, and simultaneously prevented deep and lasting recessions.

The second stage of crisis involved governments taking the opportunity of crisis to reduce the real and purportedly high accumulated levels of debt created by the GFC and previous decades of social spending (Mendoza, 2014; Stiglitz, 2014; Evans and McBride, 2017). Stimulus was replaced by measures to contract public expenditure to the point where global gross domestic product (GDP) fell between 2010 and 2011 (Ortiz and Cummins, 2013). At the level of policy and economy, McBride (2018) argues that there are three interlinked components to this current phase of austerity: (1) fiscal consolidation through balanced budgets (generally spending cuts rather than revenue increases); (2) restructuring of the public sector (devolution, downsizing, marketization, privatization and public-private partnerships) and structural reform of social policy programmes (changes to disability, eldercare and healthcare programmes; the erosion of pensions and elimination of early retirement policies; and the reduction of employment benefits and other social welfare supports); and (3) the flexibilization of labour markets and lowering of production costs through wage caps and cuts (McBride, 2018, p 4). It is primarily the latter two components and the precarity and insecurity they bring in relation to work that will be explored in this volume, although the first component sets the stage for and reinforces the other two components.

In examining component (2), and based on recent Organisation for Economic Co-operation and Development (OECD) data, Table 1.1 highlights how employment security measured by the percentage of permanent employees in the workforce has seen limited change during the era of austerity. Table 1.1 highlights OECD and EU averages, and change in

Table 1.1: Change in proportion of workers in permanent employment (%)

Country	2011	2019
Australia	94.4	94.7
Canada	86.3	86.7
Germany	85.5	87.5
Ireland	89.8	90.0
Netherlands	87.1	78.5
United Kingdom	93.8	94.5
United States	–	–
EU	85.6	85.5
OECD average	88.2	88.3

Source: OECD (2019a)

countries that are the subject of chapters in this book. Overall, the OECD average of the proportion of employees in permanent jobs has increased slightly, while decreasing in the EU. Among the countries highlighted in the table, only the Netherlands has witnessed a significant decrease, although there has been an increase among other member states in relation to vulnerable groups such as women and the young (OECD, 2019a).

At the same time, sectors vulnerable to austerity policies have been subject to restructuring and job losses. It was the case that, at the start of governments' fiscal consolidation programmes, 80 per cent of OECD countries were implementing or planning to implement plans to 'rightsize' their public sector workforce, and/or reductions in salaries to reduce compensation costs (OECD, 2019a, 2019b). This would include freezes on recruitment, and also redundancies. Table 1.2 outlines restructuring regimes in countries featured in this volume. It illustrates how the UK and the US were more easily placed to rapidly engage in downsizing. The most common approach to downsizing is to target layers of managers, so increasing their precarity, but also increasing insecurity for front-line, non-management employees in a number of ways (highlighted in this volume) through inadequate supervision and the erosion of career development opportunities.

There have, however, been changes in the participation in specific forms of precarious and insecure employment. The financial crisis and austerity have led to workers experiencing under-employment and not receiving enough hours to make a living, with the proliferation of part-time, casual and zero-hours contract work. Economies hardest hit by the crisis have been slow to recover in terms of providing adequate hours to their working populations, with young workers and women more vulnerable (OECD, 2019a).

Table 1.2: Restructuring plans and leaving conditions for public sector employees on open-ended/permanent contracts, 2010

Country	Yes, with an allowance for employee	Potential relocation to other jobs	Attractive voluntary leave allowances	Attractive early retirement policies
Australia	✓	✗	✗	✗
Canada	✓	✓	✗	✗
Germany	✗	✗	✗	✓
Ireland	✗	✗	✓	✓
Netherlands	✗	✓	✗	✗
United Kingdom	✓	✓	✓	✓
United States	✓	✓	✓	✓

Source: OECD (2019a)

In the case of under-employment, OECD studies reveal further data according to gender, outlined in Table 1.3. Women are still more likely to be under-employed than men (8 per cent, as compared to 3.8 per cent) (OECD, 2019a). At the same time, unlike the percentage of the female workforce in part-time work, the proportion of men working shorter hours has increased across the OECD and EU and in most countries highlighted in this volume, indicating that, as for women, men may increasingly become employed in conditions where they are unable to work sufficient hours to meet all of their material needs (OECD, 2019b). Moreover, it is the case that, for many, taking on part-time work is involuntary (OECD, 2019a).

Table 1.3: Part-time employment as percentage of female and male employment

Countries	Female		Male	
	2009	2018	2009	2018
Australia	38.2	37.5	13.2	15.0
Canada	27.2	25.8	12.0	12.2
Germany	38.3	36.6	7.9	9.3
Ireland	37.4	32.8	11.0	10.5
Netherlands	59.9	58.0	17.0	19.2
United Kingdom	23.5	17.6	10.8	11.4
United States	38.7	36.4	–	–
EU	27.4	26.5	7.0	8.0
OECD average	26.1	25.4	8.8	9.4

Source: OECD (2019b)

OECD data also points out that, although there are individual country differences across member states, the number of hours worked per year per person in employment (including part-time work) fell from 1,750 in 2011 to 1,734 by 2018) (OECD, 2019a. Under-employment has also grown more rapidly among those countries hit hardest by the GFC, such as Ireland, Spain, Greece and Italy, by an average of 6.2 percentage points, which is 1.1 percentage points higher than the OECD average (OECD, 2019a).

The aforementioned flexible work practices, including casual and zero-hours contract work and under-employment, have emerged as a consequence of employers changing working patterns to accommodate shifts in customer demand: demands that become more acute among employers following economic crisis (OECD, 2019a). Moreover, job stability (the length of time individuals spend in their current job) has decreased. This is particularly so for younger or older workers with lower levels of education, who are also more likely to be under-employed (OECD, 2019a).

The rise in zero-hours contracts or casual work has been less consistent across OECD states. A quarter of Australia's workforce are casual workers, with over half having no guaranteed hours. The Netherlands reports on-call work as the fastest-growing form of flexible work. In the UK, 3 per cent of the workforce reported being on a zero-hours contract, and 5.3 per cent of Ireland's workforce report they are on variable hours.

Salary cuts have come in the form of pay freezes and suspension of automatic length-of-service or performance bonuses. Future increases in pay would be linked to efficiency gains or market rates, and attention would turn to the bargaining relationship with recognized unions (OECD, 2012).

Although austerity has long been the reality for large portions of the global South (Clarke, 2017), a lively debate exists in the literature as to whether austerity is an enduring aspect of neoliberalism in the global North or a new stage that gained hegemony following the 2008 GFC. A decade before the GFC, Pierson (1998) argued persuasively that austerity policies were a permanent feature of neoliberalism, with citizens constantly reminded by governments and the corporate sector that social programmes are too expensive and government debt is an abomination and an insupportable burden on present and future populations. However, in the post-2008 period austerity policies deepened significantly, even in countries that did not experience recession, such as Canada and Australia, suggesting that the GFC provided a convenient moment in which to further consolidate neoliberalism's hold on society (McCann, 2013). The ideology that there is no alternative to neoliberalism and austerity justified the eventual roll-back of various Keynesian-like stimulation packages that had been implemented to ease the GFC (Peters, 2014; Denniss, 2015).

As well as a set of social, labour market and economic policies, austerity is a persuasive ideological frame that encourages sacrifice and lowered expectations from working people and average citizens, with the promise of improvements at some undefined point in the future. Evans and McBride (2017, p 13) argue that the ideology of austerity also involves blame transfer: 'from the private sector that caused the crisis to the public sector, and from the public sector to the populace'. They also note a tendency for citizens to blame themselves or other less 'worthy' individuals, accepting pain and unmet needs as necessary for long-term improvement (see also McCann, 2013; Clayton et al, 2015; Hayes and Moore, 2017). Clarke and Newman (2012) refer to similar processes as the alchemy of austerity, in which governments secure consent to austerity and lowered expectations, in large part through unfounded claims that austerity revives struggling economies and better times are just down the road.

Hitchen (2016, p 102) argues that the lived experience of austerity is best understood through individuals' overlapping experiences of constraint and sacrifice, including: anticipating austerity; adapting to austerity; getting on with life; and accepting austerity. Denniss (2015) argues that, also operating at the level of ideology, and largely without solid evidence, austerity asserts the idea that technocratic, financial accounting and market rationalization practices can be applied to all social, economic and workplace problems, generating substantial savings for governments and taxpayers and simultaneously providing better-quality service. As will be discussed in the chapters in this volume, this set of ideas provides a rationalization for why workers in all sectors must consent to job losses, eroded benefits and reduced or no pensions, longer hours, greater precarity, fewer social supports and entitlements and ongoing privatization of services.

Blyth (2013, p 179) notes that although historically austerity has been 'tried and tried again – its application was not found wanting – and it simply didn't work". In large part this is because cutting the public sector eliminates jobs and protections, exerting a downward pressure on other forms of employment, shrinking GDP and further depressing the economy (McGimpsey, 2017; Kahloon, 2019). Criticism of austerity policies has been widespread, including by the International Monetary Fund (IMF) (Ortiz and Cummins, 2013; Geir, 2016), although governments have not stepped back from them in any significant way. This has prompted some authors to note austerity's resilience and capacity to adapt to new conditions and changing social forces (Peck, 2010; Aalbers, 2013; Evans and McBride, 2017). Fraser (2016) asserts that, in the face of growing opposition, neoliberalism has resiliently and strategically adopted some progressive demands in order to co-opt and appeal to its opponents. Progressive human rights demands can be seen to be cynically integrated into individualized funding policies for disability and old-age care that have concomitantly introduced further fragmentation and privatization of care and deepened precarious work for those employed in the care sector (Cunningham and Nickson, 2013; Hussein and Manthorpe, 2014). Other scholars use terms like 'zombie austerity' and 'zombie economics' to emphasize the ways that austerity policies have failed and lost a great deal of public credibility; but, like zombies, neoliberal and austerity policies continue to devour everything in their path and infect others in a pandemic of constraint, degradation of work and perpetually unmet social needs (Krugman, 2010; Peck, 2010; Quiggin, 2012; Mendoza, 2014; Stiglitz, 2014). Finally, austerity is viewed as an opportunistic response to crises and a phase of late neoliberalism in which political and economic institutions continue to be restructured to more closely reflect private market ideology (Aalbers, 2013; Evans and McBride, 2017; Clarke, 2017; McGimpsey, 2017).

Evidence confirms that austerity has widened existing inequalities based on the intersecting social relations of class, gender and race (Durbin, Page and Walby, 2017). Indeed, austerity has been characterized as a highly gendered and racialized phenomenon, with public sector retrenchment producing substantial job losses in relatively better paid and more secure female-majority, race-friendly public sector jobs, such social care, healthcare, education and general services (Blyth, 2013; Cohen, 2013; Peters, 2014; Rubery, 2015). Cuts to public services also generate an increase in the unpaid care and support work that, mostly, women are expected to undertake in the home and community (Daly and Armstrong, 2016; Fraser, 2016). For women, austerity is seen to have multiple impacts that are more acute than for other groups, including loss of income, employment and welfare benefits, and reduced access to public services (Rafferty, 2014; Rubery, 2015). Moreover, these effects can continue long after GDP recovers from recession and can derail or slow improvements in the labour market position of women (Lethbridge, 2012; Durbin, Page and Walby, 2017).

Hard fought-for union and employment policies such as seniority (job retention for longer-term workers), more commonly known as last hired/first fired policies, often mean that female, racialized workers and recent immigrants lose their positions first in austerity-driven downsizing exercises (Thomas and Tufts, 2016). For those remaining in employment, studies show that racialized workers could experience lower average gross earnings, along with worsening poverty levels (Joseph Rowntree Foundation, 2012). Indeed, it has been found that as the GFC gave way to austerity policies, ethnic-minority women and men have fared worse than UK-born white women and men (Joseph Rowntree Foundation, 2012).

Precarious and gig or gig-like employment has arisen in the place of permanent, full-time employment, impacting on jobs in the core economy (Lewchuk, 2017). Ironically, this shift often occurs through state-led social policy initiatives putatively aimed at extending equity and choice, such as the aforementioned personalized funding in the UK, Canada, the US and Europe or the National Disability Insurance Scheme in Australia.

This shift to individualized funding policies and other pro-market social policies dissemble the public sector and are part of what Bach (2016, p 11) refers to as 'the turning point for public sector employment relations'. Once anchoring economies with more secure employment while simultaneously fulfilling its role as a regulator of industrial relations and defender of employment rights, and providing an upward pull on wages and conditions, the public sector now bears 'the burden of adjustment' in light of the GFC and subsequent economic challenges of all kinds (Bach, 2016, p 12). This has had deleterious impacts on public service work, terms and conditions, especially wages, as well as eroding much-needed public services and entitlements. Referring to the UK, but applicable to most national contexts, Bach (2016) notes a continuity of austerity and public sector restructuring since the advent of neoliberalism under Thatcher in the late 1970s. Referring specifically to measures introduced after the GFC, Bach (2016, p 25) notes that 'a narrative of crisis and public sector excess has been used to diminish the size and protective role of the state, withdrawing service provision, encouraging provider diversity and engaging in concerted attempts to demobilise and deprivilege the public sector workforce'.

In terms of public sector retrenchment, Ortiz and Cummins (2013) document 132 countries contracting public expenditures by 2015 (94 developing and 38 high-income countries), with one quarter of these countries undertaking 'excessive contractions' to below pre-crisis expenditure levels. In addition, 98 countries cut or capped public sector wages (74 developing and 23 high-income) and 32 countries (15 developing and 17 high-income) introduced labour flexibilization policies (including revisions on minimum wages, limiting salary adjustments to cost-of-living benchmarks, decentralizing collective bargaining and easing firing and compensation arrangements at the enterprise level) (Ortiz and Cummins, 2013). Ortiz and Cummins (2013, p 19) argue further that 'available evidence suggests that labour market flexibilization will not generate decent jobs; on the contrary, in a context of economic contraction, it is likely to generate labour market "precarization", depress domestic incomes and ultimately hinder recovery efforts' (see also Peters, 2014; Pineault, 2014).

McBride (2018) was quoted earlier, arguing that restructuring of the labour market and flexibilization for employers is a pivotal condition of austerity. Weakened regulation and protections for working people are key conduits for increased flexibilization, enabling the shift from permanent, full-time employment to increased temporary, part-time and casual work (Fudge, 2017), as well as the growth and legitimacy of platform and gig work in domestic labour and care work (for example, Handy, Mopify, AskforTask, AirTasker), taxi work (for example, Uber or Lyft) and delivery (for example, Deliveroo).

Although it seemed that the EU might provide protections for the myriad of temporary, part-time and casual workers within its borders, the literature highlights the diminished force of labour regulation through the social dimension (Heyes, 2013; Hastings and Heyes, 2018). Prior to the financial crash, the EU was increasingly seen as a vehicle for promoting market integration with the social dimension, and subordinating the interests of workers to those of multi-national corporations (Meardi, 2012). EU thinking on employment regulation became influenced by the 'Lisbon Agenda', emphasizing business competitiveness and flexibility (Hyman, 2011). Moreover, the EU's response to the global financial and eurozone crisis was to impose a requirement on member states to balance their budgets, creating a permanent austerity regime. This regime, in turn, led to the EU compelling member states to impose moderation on pay through the diminishment of trade union power, as well as encouraging the deregulation of employment standards and greater flexibility in labour markets (Hyman, 2011; Heyes and Lewis, 2015).

Hepple (2013, p 203) notes that changes in employment regulation and labour protections are the result of governments being 'locked into a model where there is a presumption that regulation interferes with the efficient working of labour markets'. Ironically, at the global level, highly regulated, unfree, migrant labour (where workers are tied to a single employer and must leave their host country if they attempt to change jobs) has also grown with immigration and labour market policy regulating and facilitating this movement of marginalized workers while providing few, if any, protections (Inghammar, 2010; Strauss and McGrath, 2017). This leaves these vulnerable workers exposed to exploitation, workplace violence, serious health and safety concerns and wages that are far below national averages, with little or no recourse or access to remedies (Inghammar, 2010). Some research evidence highlights that the wages and conditions of unfree and migrant workers can act as a downward pull on all wages and conditions as immigration and labour market policy, and employers, normalize third world conditions in high-income countries (Alberti et al, 2013; Strauss and McGrath, 2017).

Although the social state can act as a model employer and provide an upward pull on wages and conditions, neoliberal voices have long called for an end to the putative 'public sector wage premium' (de Quetteville and Scott, 2017; Fraser Institute, 2018). The evidence as to whether public sector employees continue to enjoy higher wages than their private sector counterparts is inconclusive. Using a general equilibrium model, Fernández-de-Córdoba et al (2009) argue that public and private sector wages across the OECD tend to have an upward pull on each other, with increases in one sector precipitating increases in the other. Similarly, despite claims of a large gap, a Canadian study found that public employees are paid only 0.5 per cent more than their equivalent private counterparts, with greater pay equity experienced across the public sector in terms of gender, region and age, particularly in lower-level, female-majority job categories such as cleaners, food-prep workers and clerks (Canadian Union of Public Employees, 2012). The wages and conditions of private sector managers, lawyers, accountants and chief executive officers, who tend to be overwhelming male, continuously outstrip those in the public sector, while sectors, such as retail, that have no obvious public sector comparator find little traction for improvement of wages or conditions (Canadian Union of Public Employees, 2012; Minnick and Rosenthal, 2014).

Growing evidence confirms that public sector declines in wages and conditions act as a serious downward pull on other sectors (Henderson and Stanford, 2017; Bivens and Blair, 2016). For example, in the UK wages in the public sector declined by 17 per cent between 2010 and 2014 (Reed, 2014, p 1) and, overall, wages fell 6 per cent across all sectors (Asthana and Mason, 2017). These declines happen across the economy, in significant part because many private sector businesses depend on government contracts and the spending stimulus from public sector workers for consumer goods, food, housing, transportation, recreation and many others. As Henderson and Stanford (2017) document in Australia, when public spending and public wages are lowered, a general decline reverberates across the economy (see also, Quiggin, 2012; Reed, 2014; McCauley and Lyons, 2015).

There is also substantial evidence that vulnerable organizations are bearing the brunt of national and international austerity measures (Pearson and Sweetman, 2011; Leschke and Jepsen, 2012). In particular, the reverberations of austerity in the public sector are felt keenly in the non-profit or voluntary sector, through the details of funding contracts with the government and decreased funding levels. Successful competitive bids generally involve reducing costs as far as possible in order to appear more efficient than competitors, with the largest cost saving found in wages and conditions. In the context of austerity, non-profit service organizations and their staff argue that they are asked to continually do more with less (Cunningham and James, 2014; Baines et al, 2017). This has increased since the 2008 GFC, with most non-profit services receiving significant funding cuts at a time when working and poor people require increasing support. Extending their reach into the work and the workplace, government contracts tend to stipulate that funded agencies must adopt New Public Management (NPM), competitive performance management and outcome metrics. These mechanisms standardize work practices, erasing many of the harder-to-quantify, open-ended practices such as continuous assessment, community development and ongoing relationship building with service users and communities. Erasure of these practices and routinization of the work makes it easier for employers to replace higher-credential, higher-paid workers with lower-credentialed, lower-paid workers or even unpaid volunteers (Baines with Daly, 2015; Daly and Armstrong, 2016).

Further austerity-related changes in the non-profit sector include government social policy initiatives, such as personalization in the UK and the cash-for-care National Disability Insurance Scheme in Australia, and have led the creation of new, precarious labour markets in which smaller, non-profit, community-based organizations are no longer able to compete and cede the turf to large-scale organizations and international, for-profit chains (Needham, 2011; Cortis et al, 2016; Macdonald and Charlesworth, 2016). In sites of a mixed economy of care, including public, non-profit and for-profit care, financialization and globalization of services have progressed substantially in areas such as eldercare, where economies of scale and an ageing demographic provide a continuous supply of service users as well as substantial opportunities for profit making on a world scale. Weakened regulation and pro-market conditions bolster for-profit providers, taking further ground from public and non-profit providers and rendering the work more temporary and insecure.

Although austerity is experienced as a lived, local experience, it is also a global phenomenon with continuities across national contexts as well as unique aspects based on national and local contexts (Peters, 2014). For example, extensive welfare states have not been typical of the global South. In order to receive credit from the World Bank, countries in the global South with even minimal social states were required to introduce structural adjustment policies (SAPs) aimed at generating savings to apply to government debt (Sahn et al, 1997. SAPs also gutted emerging public sectors and reoriented economies to production for export, rather than meeting local needs. Rather than building states that actively intervene in inequities and economies, austerity, like SAPs, endorses the removal of all but essential police and military services, and a free hand for private business and corporate interests (Harvey, 2007; Peck, 2012). Replicating pro-market policies found in much of the global South under SAPs, although at a slower pace and with much more of a welfare state to reduce, austerity policies in the global North bear a startling resemblance to SAPs in terms of reducing and restructuring welfare states, reorienting economies and privatizing or terminating human services.

Through the shedding of welfare provision and shrinking GDP, SAPs produce workers for the global North. Compelled to replace local employment with often precarious, poorly paid, temporary employment, migrant work is a widespread practice in richer countries, with 'host' countries benefiting from the lack of employment opportunities in countries with SAPs. Under austerity, immigration policies in the global North overlap with weakened employment regulations, permitting corporations in many sectors to hire permanently impermanent migrant workers. Found in areas as diverse as fast food, social care, agriculture, healthcare, delivery and transportation, cleaning and private domestic work, migrant workers enter employment on temporary visas that tie them to a single employer, generally at payment below the minimum wage, with few protections and no opportunity to become citizens or rights-bearing workers.

Challenging austerity

Resistance in the era of austerity can be found among all groups of workers, as will be noted across the chapters in this collection, although the adaptability and ideological dominance of late neoliberalism frequently seems to circumvent or defuse the impacts of strategies undertaken to improve the lives and conditions of working people. Positive policy initiatives such as defeating zero-hours contract legislation in Ireland and New Zealand or implementing living wages in social care in Scotland were strong strategies that, although introduced, produced unexpected outcomes and confirmed the embeddedness and reach of the austerity agenda. In gendered areas of work, such as care work, resistance in the form of unpaid care is undertaken by largely low-waged, female workers in order for them to live in tandem with their personal values and identities as caring people. This resistance is replete with tensions as it extends underfunded services, and makes it appear that austerity is working, while simultaneously critiquing the uncaring society that denies quality and meaningful services to a growing portion of the population (Baines with Daly, 2015). Union and collective strategies, locally and internationally, continue to provide working people with the best defence against austerity policies (Thomas and Tufts, 2016; Evans and McBride, 2017). As Stanford (2015, p 198) notes, even under conditions of strict austerity, working people express a 'creative and stubborn resistance', which they will continue to express 'so long as they hope for a better world'.

Theory

Although the authors in this volume are writing from a number of disciplines, their analyses draw on the tenets of political economy, particularly feminist political economy, which provides a way to link and contextualize the changing dynamics of everyday work with larger policy trends and institutions (Vosko, 2010; Luxton and Bezanson, 2013). Labour Process Theory is also used to clarify similar dynamics. By analysing the organization and conditions of work, Labour Process Theory explores the distribution of power and control between management and workers within the realm of work (Thompson and Smith, 2009; Knights and Willmott, 2016).

Summary of contributions

Part II of the book looks at larger trends and themes within the context of austerity and work, including privatization, precarity and wage stagnation. Although all three of these trends pre-exist austerity, their character is currently more aggressive and hegemonic than in earlier phases of neoliberalism. In Chapter 2, on precarity, Wayne Lewchuk reviews how the growth in precarious employment is changing the nature of most developed economies, particularly under austerity, as well as how it has contributed to the stagnation of wages, the increase in income inequality, the hollowing-out of the middle class and the reshaping family structures as young people delay starting a family due to employment and income insecurity. He draws on the work of precarity scholars who comment on the social costs of precarious employment, including: Standing (2011), who sees precarity leading to a new class structure; Cowen (2013), who paints a bleak picture of society without a middle class; and Hedges (2018), who sees society unravelling.

Writing ethnographically about the growing reality of private sector gig-work, Niels van Doorn (Chapter 3) explores some of the ways that nationally and locally distinct conditions of neoliberal austerity shape how people come to take up work in the platform-mediated gig economies of New York City and Berlin. Focusing on gig workers' experiences with platforms providing domestic cleaning service, van Doorn analyses the experience of four young platform workers and concludes that global institutional phenomena such as 'the gig economy' and 'austerity' have local platform-specific iterations as well as larger global patterns.

In Chapter 4 Ian Cunningham and Phil James highlight widening income disparities under austerity, alongside the diminishing power of collective bargaining. The chapter's focus is on exploring trends in collective bargaining in the EU and North America. In doing so, it identifies a common trajectory in nation-state policies, including a shift towards identifying the GFC as a public debt crisis; blaming trade unions and their members (in particular public sector workers) for crisis; and the introduction of reforms to collective bargaining and union security that are designed to reinforce the deflationary austerity policies of the EU, the US and Canada. However, in the latter case, there will be insights into continuing union resistance to austerity. This is accompanied by an overview of wages and wage equality across these countries.

In their comment on privatization, Pat Armstrong and Donna Baines argue in Chapter 5 that privatization is much more than the process of selling off all or part of public assets. It is also very much about transforming what the population thinks about the public services, about shared responsibility and decision making, about how work should be organized and about who gets to decide on what basis. Their comment illustrates the many forms and variations of privatization and provides further insights into austerity's gendered effects.

Part III of the book presents case studies of various forms of labour and employment under austerity policies and conditions, including: temporary, non-citizen, migrant work; highly gendered and increasingly precarious social care work; under-resourced public sector work; and increasingly managerialized non-profit work. This analysis takes place at a very grounded level, analysing the changing relations and experiences of employment at the level of everyday work, while also drawing on critical literature to link these experiences to larger austerity trends and dynamics. The chapters included in this collection have been chosen for their capacity to illustrate broad trends through key examples from the countries studied. The goal has been to provide an overall narrative of austerity trends, challenges and struggles as well as to generate insights that might be applied usefully to other contexts and comparisons.

Drawing on the experience of a growing group of workers made vulnerable in the austere economy, in Chapter 6 Geraldina Polanco uses qualitative research to sketch the experience of migrant workers in fast-food jobs in Canada. The chapter discusses the immigration and employment policies that produce non-citizen, vulnerable, low-waged workers for the global North. Polanco highlights the vulnerabilities faced by migrant workers and details mobilization strategies for better conditions and protections that, although specific to North America, reflect the distinct needs faced by those with less-than-full citizenship status in globalized, low-waged worksites found in many contexts.

In Chapter 7 Kendra Strauss and Feng Xu use austerity as a lens for understanding diverse processes and argue that the market plays an ambivalent role in austerity discourse at the sub-national level in China and Canada, at the level of policy development and restructuring of the eldercare sector in Vancouver and Shanghai. They review the history of austerity as a discourse, and its relationship to distinct but related discourses of balanced budgets, fiscal prudence and cost containment in Canada, and balanced growth in China. Exploring how fiscal austerity leads to a variety of paths for outsourcing costs and devolving responsibility to non-government actors, they highlight implicit and explicit processes of privatization, resulting in 'varieties of financialization' (Aalbers et al, 2011) with distinct differences and similarities, as well as increasing connections between these 'aspiring global cities'.

In Chapter 8 Eva Jendro and Dora Scholarios examine restructuring in the public services as a policy response to fiscal consolidation pressures. More specifically, the chapter describes rationalization and efficiency gains at several levels, including national, organizational, workgroup and job, in the Fire and Rescue Services in Scotland. The chapter reveals how austerity, in one sense, has moved away from NPM by recentralizing control of services. This 'break' with NPM is in parallel with continuing ideological attachment to values that see public services as wasteful. Restructuring efforts at the various levels, from the national to the job level, were interdependent in order to deliver on the overarching aim of meeting the reduced budget. Front-line staff experienced work intensification and loss of morale. At the same time, high absence levels, recruitment freezes and so on led to problems in achieving projected cost savings.

In Chapter 9 Donna Baines and Doug Young explore the employment impacts of two of the most significant pieces of social policy introduced in Scotland and Australia in the past decade, namely the Social Care (Self-Directed Support) (Scotland) Act 2013 and the National Disability Insurance Scheme Act in Australia (see https://www.ndis.gov.au/

about-us/governance/legislation). Launched in the era of austerity, both policies have been viewed as critical human rights-engaged legislation aimed at improving the social inclusion of marginalized and vulnerable populations. Drawing on qualitative interview data in Scotland and Australia, Baines and Young identify a downward spiral in wages and conditions, and increased privatization, fragmentation, precarity and insecurity, alongside serious concerns about quality of care. The analysis shows no winners, as may be characteristic of social policy introduced in the context of austerity and neoliberalism; instead, the private-market focus and austere funding of these new policies places the human rights of service users in a zero-sum competition with the employment rights of care workers.

Exploring the impact of managerialism on the work of non-profit human service workers in New York City, in Chapter 10 Mimi Abramovitz and Jennifer Zelnick draw on survey data to paint a portrait of a sector that has been deeply restructured to emulate private market relations and processes. The authors argue that austerity and managerialism generate the perfect storm in which austerity cuts resources and managerialism promotes 'doing more with less' through performance and outcome metrics and close management control of the labour process. Closely analysing practices for resistance, Abramovitz and Zelnick conclude that in lower-managerial workplaces, workers had fewer problems with autonomy, a greater say in decision making, less work stress and more sustainable employment, suggesting that democratic control of the workplace is an alternative route to quality, worker engagement and successful outcomes.

Pauric O'Rourke's Chapter 11 explores whether austerity can be interpreted as a continuation of an established neoliberal ideology or as a not-to-be-wasted opportunity that is unique to a particular era in time. Using the case of the Irish Republic, the chapter draws on a qualitative-based empirical study within the sub-sector of Physical and Sensory Disabilities, built around two principal service providers. It explores the extent to which government funding and service level agreements with providers have created the conduit for NPM-orientated thinking and practices, which have conveniently aligned with austerity ideology to enter the Irish non-profit sector and influence how it manages people and work.

The final part looks at workplace resistance under austerity and suggests that it is an uneven project and that solutions are necessarily complex as austerity continues its ideological and policy hold on social life.

In Chapter 12 Alina Baluch explores the implementation of a progressive policy to introduce a living wage to the social care workforce in Scotland during austerity, and during a period where low wage earners are experiencing cuts in public services, stagnant real wage growth and precarious work at the same time as declining union strength. The chapter reveals a number of unintended consequences that have exacerbated austerity-compelled precarity in the sector. These include: rewarding poor payers among social care providers; greater insecurity in market relations between funders and providers; trade-offs between paying a living wage and service quality; providers withdrawing and/or refusing to enter into unsustainable contracts; and questions over whether the increase in hourly rates of pay actually increases the take-home pay of employees.

In Chapter 13 Juliet MacMahon, Michelle O'Sullivan, Lorraine Ryan, Jonathan Lavelle, Caroline Murphy, Mike O'Brien and Tom Turner highlight the resilience and buoyancy of neoliberal and austerity strategies and the difficulties that unions and their allies face in challenging them. They argue that austerity in Ireland ushered in a sharp rise in zero-hours work, or fragmented and variable working time arrangements that were largely exempt from protective legislation. The authors contend that even though a union strategy met with victory in the form of new legislation prohibiting zero-hours contracts, employers found other means to enforce precarious and insecure employment. Closely examining the intersection of austerity and the new regulations, Mahon and her colleagues find that the new legislation has further exacerbated the precariousness of many workers in the Irish context and served to further undermine the Standard Employment Relationship. They argue further that collective bargaining has been the more effective way to curtail precarious types of work, although many precarious workers are not unionized and hence may see more benefit from a fundamental reconceptualizing of the legal taxonomy of the employment relationship to more accurately reflect its fragmented, dispersed realities (Davidov, 2011).

Contending that non-profit/voluntary sector care workers resist in ways that reflect their positioning within the social relations of austerity, the market and the gender order, in Chapter 14 Donna Baines analyses qualitative data collected in non-profit organizations to develop a theorization of unpaid work as lying at a cross roads of self-exploitation and resistance. Using direct quotes from voluntary sector care workers, Baines shows that they assign oppositional meaning to the after-hours work that they do to resist the 'uncaring' of funders and larger society. These workers frequently also develop a shared critical analysis with co-workers and sometimes undertake workplace resistance strategies aimed at improved conditions for each other and service users. Baines argues that these dynamics represent a form of compromise resistance in which the workers express their personal values as ethical people through doing unpaid labour in their paid workplaces.

In Chapter 15 Helen Blakely and Steve Davies draw on interviews undertaken as part of a research study carried out with UNI Global Union (the Global Union Federation for unions representing workers in private sector service industries) to explore new forms of unionism in the context of advanced austerity and neoliberalism. This chapter analyses three case studies (in each of Romania, the Dominican Republic and the US) in sectors that have been hostile to unionization and that unions have traditionally found hard to organize. These unions successfully undertook activities including new forms of social movement and community-based unionism that have no immediate or obvious 'pay off', and activity that secured collective bargaining agreements and transformative increases in membership. These activities represent a broadening of union purpose and effective strategies in the face of the growing precarity, fragmented workforces and globalization of work in the context of austerity.

In the afterword (Chapter 16), Jill Rubery challenges us to think critically about a new robots-are-taking-over mythology that is emerging to replace the austerity mythology that unrestrained, perfectly functioning markets are offering an alternative to state welfare systems. The austerity mythology argued that debt was the pivotal problem for governments to wrestle down, and that markets should take over responsibilities from the state, shifting responsibility to the average person to self-provide or meet all their needs through wage employment or unpaid labour. Providing a low-tax regime to businesses would incentivize them to expand employment and to entrepreneurially take new risks and offer job opportunities for all, as long as workers were not selective about wages, work, conditions or hours. However, we are now told that robots will replace humans in most jobs and that we all will soon be unemployed. As Rubery points out, the gutting of social supports and entitlements under austerity and neoliberalism means that those thrown out of work will quickly become destitute, and social unrest is likely to follow. To avoid this dire scenario, Rubery calls for a major rethinking of social policies and employment, drawing on Nancy Fraser's (2012) gender-equity model, wherein breadwinning and care-giving responsibilities are shared across society, with the support of strong social programmes in which employment is protected and regulated in the interests of working people.

Note
[1]   https://www.rollingstone.com/politics/politics-news/the-price-of-inequality-interview-with-joseph-e-stiglitz-51549/.

References

Aalbers, M.B. (2013) 'Debate on neoliberalism in and after the neoliberal crisis'. *International Journal of Urban and Regional Research*, 37(3): 1053–7.

Aalbers, M.B., Engelen, E. and Glasmacher, A. (2011) '"Cognitive closure" in the Netherlands: Mortgage securitization in a hybrid European political economy'. *Environment and Planning A: Economy and Space*, 43(8): 1779–95.

Alberti, G., Holgate, J. and Tapia, M. (2013) 'Organising migrants as workers or as migrant workers? Intersectionality, trade unions and precarious work'. *The International Journal of Human Resource Management*, 24(22): 4132–48.

Asthana, R. and Mason, A. (2017) 'Damning government report shows depth of public sector pay cuts'. *The Guardian*. https://www.theguardian.com/society/2017/jul/03/damning-government-report-shows-scale-of-public-sector-pay-cuts. Accessed 19 July 2019.

Bach, S. (2016) 'Deprivileging the public sector workforce: Austerity, fragmentation and service withdrawal in Britain'. *The Economic and Labour Relations Review*, 27(1): 11–28.

Baines, D. with Daly, T. (2015) 'Resisting regulatory rigidities: Lessons from front-line care work'. *Studies in Political Economy*, 95: 137–60.

Baines, D., Cunningham, I. and Shields, J. (2017) 'Filling the gaps with unpaid, formal and coerced work in the nonprofit sector'. *Critical Social Policy*. http://journals.sagepub.com/doi/abs/10.1177/0261018317693128.

Bivens, J. and Blair, H. (2016) 'A public investment agenda that delivers the goods for American workers needs to be long-lived, broad, and subject to democratic oversight'. *Economic Policy Institute Newsletter*, 8 December. https://www.epi.org/publication/a-public-investment-agenda-that-delivers-the-goods-for-american-workers-needs-to-be-long-lived-broad-and-subject-to-democratic-oversight/. Accessed 1 July 2020.

Blyth, M. (2013) *Austerity: The History of a Dangerous Idea*. New York: Oxford University Press.

Canadian Union of Public Employees (2012) *Battle of the Wages: Who Gets Paid More, Public or Private Sector Workers?*, https://cupe.ca/battle-wages-who-gets-paid-more-public-or-private-sector-workers. Accessed 19 July 2019.

Clarke, J. (2017) 'Articulating austerity and authoritarianism: Re-imagining moral economics?' In: Evans, B. and McBride, S. (eds), *Austerity: The Lived Experience*. Toronto: University of Toronto Press, 20–39.

Clarke, J. and Newman, J. (2012) 'The alchemy of austerity'. *Critical Social Policy*, 32(3): 299–319.

Clayton, J., Donovan, C. and Merchant, J. (2015) 'Emotions of austerity: Care and commitment in public service delivery in the North East of England'. *Emotion, Space and Society*, 14 (1): 24–32.

Cohen, M. (2013) 'Neo-liberal crisis/social reproduction/gender implications'. *University of New Brunswick Law Journal*, 64: 234.

Cortis, N., Young, A., Powell, A., Reeve, R., Ho, K. and Ramia, I. (2016) *Australian Charities Report 2015*. Sydney: Centre for Social Impact and Social Policy Research Centre. http://dx.doi.org/10.4225/53/59a4b308998bc

Cowen, T. (2013) *Average is Over: Powering America Beyond the Age of the Great Stagnation*. New York: Penguin.

Cunningham, I. and James, P. (2014) 'Public service outsourcing and its employment implications in an era of austerity: The case of British social care'. *Competition & Change*, 18(1): 1–19.

Cunningham, I. and Nickson, D. (2013) 'Public Sector Austerity, Personalisation and the Implications for the Voluntary Sector Workforce'. www.ccpscotland.org/wp-content/uploads/sites/3/2014/02/Public-Sector-Austerity-personalisation-and-the-voluntary-sector-workforce.pdf. Accessed 23 July 2019.

Daly, T. and Armstrong, P. (2016) 'Liminal and invisible long-term care labour: Precarity in the face of austerity'. *Journal of Industrial Relations*, 58(4): 473–90.

Davidov, G. (2011) 'Re-matching labour laws with their purpose'. In: Davidov, G. and Langreille, B. (eds) *The Idea of Labour Law*. Oxford: Oxford University Press, 179–80.

de Quetteville, H. and Scott, P. (2017) 'Are public sector workers really so badly paid?' *The Telegraph*. https://www.telegraph.co.uk/news/2017/09/12/public-sector-workers-really-badly-paid/. Accessed 23 July 2019.

Denniss, R. (2015) 'Spreadsheets of power', *The Monthly*, April: 28–32.

Durbin, S., Page, M. and Walby, S. (2017) 'Gender equality and "austerity": vulnerabilities, resistance and change'. *Gender, Work and Organisation*, 24(1): 1–6.

Evans, B. and McBride, S. (2017) 'Austerity: The lived experience'. In: Evans, B. and McBride, S. (eds), *Austerity: The Lived Experience*. Toronto: University of Toronto Press, 3–16.

Fernández-de-Córdoba, G., Perez, J. and Torres, J. (2009) *Public and Private Sector Wage Interactions in a General Equilibrium Model*. Working Papers Series. Madrid: Banco de Espana.

Fraser, N. (2012) *Can Society Be Commodities All the Way Down? Polanyian Reflections on Capitalist Crisis*. Fondation Maison des Sciences de l'homme No 18. www.msh-paris.fr/en/news/news/article/can-society-be-commodities-all-the-way-down-polanyian-reflections-on-capitalist-crisis/.

Fraser, N. (2016) 'Capitalism's crisis of care'. *Dissent*, 63(4): 30–37.

Fraser Institute (2018) *Comparing Government and Private Sector Compensation in Ontario, 2018*. https://www.fraserinstitute.org/studies/comparing-government-and-private-sector-compensation-in-ontario-2018. Accessed 19 July 2019.

Fudge, J. (2017) 'The future of the standard employment relationship: Labour law, new institutional economics and old power resource theory'. *Journal of Industrial Relations*, 59(3): 374–92.

Geir, B. (2016) 'Even the IMF now admits neoliberalism has failed'. *Fortune*. https://fortune.com/2016/06/03/imf-neoliberalism-failing/. Accessed 23 July 2019.

Harvey, D. (2007) *A Brief History of Neoliberalism*. Oxford: Oxford University Press.

Hastings, T. and Heyes, J. (2018) 'Farewell to flexicurity? Austerity and labour policies in the European Union'. *Economic and Industrial Democracy*, 39(3): 458–80.

Hayes, L. and Moore, S. (2017) 'Care in a time of austerity: The electronic monitoring of homecare workers' time'. *Gender, Work & Organization*, 24(4): 329–44.

Hedges, C. (2018) *America: The Farewell Tour*. New York: Simon & Schuster.

Henderson, T. and Stanford, J. (2017) *False Economies: The Unintended Consequences of NSW Public Sector Wage Restraint*. Sydney: Centre for Future Work.

Hepple, B. (2013) 'Back to the future: Employment law under the Coalition government'. *Industrial Law Journal*, 42(3): 203–23.

Heyes, J. (2013) 'Flexicurity in crisis: European labour market policies in a time of austerity'. *European Journal of Industrial Relations*, 19(1): 71–86.

Heyes, J. and Lewis, P. (2015) 'Relied upon for the heavy lifting: Can employment protection legislation reforms lead the EU out of the jobs crisis?' *Industrial Relations Journal*, 46(2): 81–99.

Hitchen, E. (2016) 'Living and feeling the austere'. *New Formations*, 87: 102–18.

Hussein, S. and Manthorpe, J. (2014) 'Structural marginalisation among the long-term care workforce in England: Evidence from mixed-effect models of national pay data'. *Ageing & Society*, 34(1): 21–41.

Hyman, R. (2011) *Trade Unions, Lisbon and Europe 2020: From Dream to Nightmare*. LSE 'Europe in Question' Discussion Paper Series, No. 45, London: London School of Economics.

Inghammar, A. (2010) 'The employment contract revisited. Undocumented migrant workers and the intersection between international standards, immigration policy and employment law'. *European Journal of Migration and Law*, 12(2): 193–214.

Joseph Rowntree Foundation (2012) *Monitoring Poverty and Social Exclusion 2012*. York: Joseph Rowntree Foundation.

Kahloon, I. (2019) 'Use – and abuses – of austerity. Economists revisit an unsettled economic policy'. *Harvard Magazine*. https://harvardmagazine.com/2019/01/austerity-when-it-works-giavizzi-alesina-favero. Accessed 17 July 2019.

Knights, D. and Willmott, H. (2016) *Labour Process Theory*. London: Springer.

Krugman, P. (2010) 'When zombies win'. *New York Times*, 19 December 2010. https://www.nytimes.com/2010/12/20/opinion/20krugman.html. Accessed 17 July 2019.

Leschke, J. and Jepsen, M. (2012) 'Introduction: Crisis, policy responses and widening inequalities in the EU'. *International Labour Review*, 151(4): 289–312.

Lethbridge, J. (2012) *Impact of the Global Economic Crisis and Austerity Measures on Women*. Public Services International Research Institute, University of Greenwich, London.

Lewchuk, W. (2017) 'Precarious jobs: Where are they, and how do they affect well-being?' *The Economic and Labour Relations Review*, 28(3): 402–19.

Luxton, M. and Bezanson, K. (2013) *Social Reproduction: Feminist Political Economy Challenges Neo-Liberalism*. Montreal: McGill-Queens Press.

Macdonald, F. and Charlesworth, S. (2016) 'Cash for care under the NDIS: Shaping care workers' working conditions?' *Journal of Industrial Relations*, 58(5): 627–46.

McBride, S. (2018) 'Eight things the crisis taught us about austerity'. *The Monitor*, Ottawa: Canadian Centre for Policy Alternatives. https://www.policyalternatives.ca/publications/monitor/eight-things-crisis-taught-us-about-austerity.

McCann, L. (2013) 'Reforming public services after the crash: The roles of framing and hoping'. *Public Administration*, 91(1): 5–16.

McCauley, I. and Lyons, M. (2015) *Governomics: Can We Afford Small Government?* Melbourne: Melbourne University Press.

McGimpsey, I. (2017) 'Late neoliberalism: Delineating a policy regime'. *Critical Social Policy*, 37(1): 64–84.

Meardi, G. (2012) *Social Failures of EU Enlargement: A Case of Workers Voting with Their Feet*. Abingdon: Routledge.

Mendoza, K.A. (2014) *Austerity: The Demolition of the Welfare State and the Rise of the Zombie Economy*. New York City: New Internationalist.

Minnick, K. and Rosenthal, L. (2014) 'Stealth compensation: Do CEOs increase their pay by influencing dividend policy?' *Journal of Corporate Finance*, 25: 435–54.

Needham, C. (2011) *Personalising Public Services: Understanding the Personalisation Narrative*. Bristol: Policy Press.

OECD (2012) *Public Sector Compensation in Times of Austerity*, Table 2.1. https://dx.doi.org/10.1787/9789264177758-en. Accessed 22 March 2020.

OECD (2019a) *Employment by Permanency of the Job: Incidence*. https://doi.org/10.1787/data-00297-en. Accessed 22 March 2020.

OECD (2019b) *Labour Force Statistics 2019*. https://doi.org/10.1787/g2g9fb3e-en. Accessed 22 March 2020

Ortiz, I. and Cummins, M. (2013) *The Age of Austerity. A Review of Public Expenditures and Adjustment Measures in 181 Countries*. IMF World Bank Meetings Proceedings, May. Washington, DC. http://siteresources.worldbank.org/CSO/Resources/FromArabRevolutionstoGlobalAusterityby Ortiz.pdf. Accessed 17 July 2019.

Pearson, R. and Sweetman, C. (2011) *Gender and the Economic Crisis*. London: Oxfam. https://oxfamilibrary.openrepository.com/handle/10546/121671. Accessed 17 July 2019.

Peck, J. (2010) *Constructions of Neoliberal Reason*. Oxford: Oxford University Press.

Peck, J. (2012) 'Austerity urbanism'. *City*, 16(6): 626–55.

Peters, J. (2014) 'Neoliberalism, inequality and austerity in the rich world democracies'. In: Baines, D. and McBride, S. (eds), *Orchestrating Austerity: Impacts and Resistance*. Halifax: Fernwood Press, 50–64.

Pierson, P. (1998) 'Irresistible forces, immovable objects: Post-industrial welfare states confront permanent austerity'. *Journal of European Public Policy*, 5(4): 539–60.

Pineault, E. (2014) 'Neoliberalism and austerity as class struggle'. In: Baines, D. and McBride, S. (eds), *Orchestrating Austerity: Impacts and Resistance*. Halifax: Fernwood Press, 91–104.

Quiggin, J. (2012) *Zombie Economics: How Dead Ideas Still Walk Among Us*. Princeton, NJ: Princeton University Press.

Rafferty, A. (2014) 'Gender equality and the impact of recession and austerity in the UK'. *Revue de l'OFCE*, 133: 335–61.

Reed, H. (2014) 'Lifting the cap: The economic impact of increasing public sector wages in the UK'. London: Unison. https://www.unison.org.uk/content/uploads/2014/05/On-line-Catalogue223292.pdf. Accessed 19 July 2019.

Rubery, J. (2015) 'Austerity, the public sector and the threat to gender equality: Geary Lecture 2014'. *The Economic and Social Review*, 46(1): 1–27.

Sahn, D.E., Dorosh, P. and Younger, S.D. (1997) *Structural Adjustment Reconsidered: Economic Policy and Poverty in Africa*. Cambridge: Cambridge University Press.

Standing, G. (2011) *The Precariat: The New and Dangerous Class*. London: Bloomsbury Academic.

Stanford, J. (2015) *Economics for Everyone: A Short Guide to the Economics of Capitalism*. London: Pluto Books.

Stiglitz, J.E. (2014) 'Europe's austerity zombies'. *Project Syndicate*, 26: 26.

Strauss, K. and McGrath, S. (2017) 'Temporary migration, precarious employment and unfree labour relations: Exploring the "continuum of exploitation" in Canada's Temporary Foreign Worker Program'. *Geoforum*, 78: 199–208.

Thomas, M. and Tufts, S. (2016) '"Enabling dissent": Contesting austerity and right populism in Toronto, Canada'. *The Economic and Labour Relations Review*, 27(1): 29–45.

Thompson, P. and Smith, C. (2009) 'Labour power and labour process: Contesting the marginality of the sociology of work'. *Sociology*, 43(5): 913–30.

Vosko, L.F. (2010) *Managing the Margins: Gender, Citizenship, and the International Regulation of Precarious Employment*. Oxford: Oxford University Press.

PART II
Trends and Themes

2

The Age of Increased Precarious Employment: Origins and Implications

Wayne Lewchuk

Introduction

We are only beginning to appreciate the full societal impact of the shift to monetarism and the ideas of the Chicago school of economics. In line with monetarist ideas, Paul Volker, the US federal reserve chairman, moved to tighten monetary supply and push up interest rates to stamp out inflation in 1979 (often referred to as the Volker Shock). This set in motion changes that spelled the end of the era of the Standard Employment Relationship (SER) in both the US and Canada (Cooper, 2017) and the rise of neoliberal austerity policies. The social compromise that allowed workers to bargain collectively and to rely on the state to fill at least some of the gaps in the social wage would gradually unravel. In the intervening four decades a new set of rules and norms have emerged, regulating the relationship between employers and employees. This chapter explores why employment rules and norms took the form they did, the prevalence of precarious employment in the labour market today and the social implications of what this chapter labels as the era of Increased Precarious Employment.

The employment norms associated with the era of Increased Precarious Employment represent one component of a broader shift to a neoliberal form of social organization. Neoliberalism is defined here as a form of social organization where individuals are free to contract, where outcomes are disciplined by the market (Harvey, 2005) and where the role of the family in providing for its members is emphasized over the role of state welfare (Cooper, 2017). Neoliberalism has redefined 'common sense' around the role of the state and the rights of individuals. In the process, it has remade institutions such as the employment relationship, and many of the values held by individuals (Brown, 2015; Kotsko, 2018). This chapter will argue that the increased prevalence of less secure employment has as much to do with the ideological shifts embedded in the neoliberal and austerity discourse as it does with rational responses to economic forces.

For many workers, particularly white men who were the greatest beneficiaries of the post-1945 social compromise, employment has become less secure and less rewarding. Since 1979, real wages have stopped growing for most workers. The risks of injury and illness, unemployment and old age are increasingly borne by workers (Cappelli, 1999; Hacker, 2006). Many employers have abandoned their role in training workers, preferring to seek the skills they need on the open market rather than relying on internal job ladders. Unions are viewed as toxic by a growing cohort of business leaders. Even in countries like Canada, which prides itself on its public health system, its old-age security benefits and its public education system, an increasing share of the costs of these services are borne by individuals as governments adopt austerity policies and either delist services or privatize them. If we are to believe surveys of employers, the use of less secure employment is likely to increase in the immediate future (Manyika et al, 2011; OECD, 2019).

This chapter is organized into three sections: the first reviews the factors that led to the transition from the SER and the forces that shaped the employment relationship in the era of Increased Precarious Employment. The second section examines debates over how to measure the prevalence of the precarious workforce; and section three reviews the impact of precarious employment on households, families and communities. The latter will be done by summarizing the findings of the Poverty and Employment Precarity in Southern Ontario (PEPSO) research group (Procyk, Lewchuk and Shields, 2017). The PEPSO project, which began surveying workers in precarious employment in 2011, provides an in-depth understanding of what it is like to live in a neoliberal society based on austerity and precarious employment. It is a cautionary tale (PEPSO, 2013; 2015; 2018).

From security to precarity: how new is precarious employment?

As we learn more about the forces leading to the current era of Increased Precarious Employment, two things are becoming clear. First, the employment insecurity that many workers are experiencing today is not new. Since the end of feudalism in Europe, employment insecurity has been a core characteristic of capitalist labour markets, and it is the period from 1945 to 1979 that stands out as different. Second, while the move away from the SER was fuelled by globalization and other structural economic shifts since the 1970s, the precise form the post-SER labour market was shaped by social actors who were weakly motivated by these broader structural forces. It was not inevitable that the post-SER employment relationship took the form it did. The new employment relationship norms rest on a narrow ideological base about the rights of labour in a market economy.

One of the earliest researchers to draw links between the post-1980 labour market and earlier norms was Quinlan (2012). He argued that the insecurity many workers experience today was the norm for most workers a hundred years ago, when employment was insecure, paid few benefits and could end with no warning. A more recent investigation by Van Arsdale (2016) argues that precarious employment and temporary employment agencies have a much longer history and were essential to the transition from feudalism to capitalism. He argues: 'The employment agency concept is not the product of the contemporary global economy. Privately operated for-profit employment agencies rose with the birth of investment capitalism in England where they played a critical role in its evolution' (Van Arsdale, 2016, p 57).

The first recorded employment agency was established by Théophraste Renaudot in France in 1630 and existed at the intersection of the established feudal labour market that regulated employment through a master–servant framework and the emerging free labour market that allowed employers and workers to contract at will. The idea that workers could engage with prospective employers on a one-to-one basis was a radical departure in employer–employee contracting. Renaudot not only created a space where workers and employers could find each other, he also administered healthcare and provided loans and education to those in need (Van Arsdale, 2016, p 60).

Employment agencies became a feature of many 18th- and 19th-century European labour markets. Within a short period of time they became for-profit private institutions that focused on bringing workers and employers together, while jettisoning most of the public welfare roles originally envisioned by Renaudot's Bureau d'Adresse. They provided workers with insecure jobs on terms that favoured employers. They demanded payment for their services and sent workers to short-term jobs that kept them in poverty and coming back to the agency for more work (Van Arsdale, 2016, pp 76–7). The reputation of employment agencies became increasingly tarnished. As labour markets in North America developed, for-profit, temporary employment agencies were established on the North American side of the Atlantic. They played a leading role in managing the slave-labour market of the American South and the integration of European immigrants to North America.

The research by Quinlan and Van Arsdale reinforces our appreciation of how unique the era of the SER was in the larger context of the history of capitalist labour markets. While the insecurity that many workers experience today is not new, the rules and norms of employment in the current period are unique, and hence it is important to understand the forces that shaped the post-SER labour market.

It has become clear how critical was the visible hand of social actors representing temporary employment agencies, major American consulting firms and corporate lobby groups in shaping business and public thought. Their actions helped to construct the ideological basis for the post-1980 labour market and, more recently, the expansion of employment precarity and austerity policies. Much of their effort took place before globalization and financialization became major concerns and, as such, they were not motivated mainly by the need to respond to these changes. They either had a narrow self-interest in promoting less-secure employment or had normalized insecure employment as they themselves were temporary contract workers. For temp agencies, promoting temporary employment increased the profits of temp agencies. For consulting firms, promoting insecure employment was rational, given that most consultants were already employed as temporary employees of consulting firms. Corporate lobby groups were motivated by a new ideology of the rights of labour under neoliberalism, fuelled by earlier temp agency campaigns and their own concern over their shrinking share of economic output. As a result, as pointed out by Harvey (2005), neoliberalism, despite its promises, has not unleashed a new era of increased productivity and wealth creation for all. It was never about economic efficiency. Like austerity, it was about reducing the conditions, expectations and entitlements of workers and poor people.

In the decades following the Second World War, a consensus emerged among leading business people and politicians regarding the advantages of a new, more stable form of capitalist organization associated with more secure forms of the employment relationship and state support for those unable to find secure employment. The post-1945 search for economic stability was fuelled by the economic crisis of the 1930s, the horrors of the First and Second World Wars and the demand by workers who had sacrificed so much for a better world. For those in positions of power, both within the state and within the corner suites of leading corporations, it appeared that failure to heed these demands could very well lead to the fall of capitalism. They had only to look at Russia and China as examples of what might be if they failed to act.

The leaders of major American corporations, who were nearly unanimous prior to 1939 in their opposition to trade unions and collective bargaining, took a different position after the war. Kotz (2017) points to the role of the Committee for Economic Development (CDC), the leading voice of big business after the war, in promoting a different vision of the employment relationship. He concluded that by 1948 there was a general consensus among business leaders in support of collective bargaining, Keynesian macro policy and the government provision of social welfare programmes (Kotz, 2017, pp 53–5). As late as 1964 the CDC published a report that argued, 'Workers should be able to form unions of sufficient power to represent them effectively in negotiations with employers that affect the terms and conditions of their employment' (Kotz, 2017, p 56).

Hence was born the era of 'Monopoly Capitalism', the company 'man' and the SER, at least for white men. For workers, this vision was formalized in the Treaty of Detroit in the 1950s as General Motors and the UAW (United Auto Workers) reached a consensus on who was to run the factories (management) and how the proceeds were to be shared, with labour being guaranteed annual wage increases reflecting annual productivity improvements and recognition of their right to bargain collectively. Kotz (2017) describes this as the era of regulated capitalism while Harvey (2005) refers to it as an era of 'embedded liberalism'. Unions were accepted, the role of the state in supporting those left behind by capitalism was legitimated and firms generally opted not to compete on price. Family well-being was based on the male breadwinner wage, female caregiver household and heterosexual relationship norms (Cooper, 2017). Less privileged households without a high-wage male breadwinner would be sustained by state welfare. In 1965 even the National Association of Manufacturers was advocating that 'Private employee benefit plans with their inherent flexibility to adapt to the almost infinite requirements of employees and employers should be encouraged to grow and prosper within a favorable government policy climate' (quoted in Hacker, 2006, p 45).

However, while this consensus was being implemented by employers and the state in the 1950s and 1960s, other voices were articulating a different vision of the rights of workers and the proper form of the employment relationship. Hatton's (2011) study of the rise of temporary employment agencies exposed the very visible hand of temp agencies during this period in advocating a different employment relationship from that advocated by the CDC. Agencies like Manpower and Kelly Girl conducted sophisticated campaigns to legitimate the role for temporary employment agencies as labour market intermediaries. They framed workers as liabilities, best employed in short-term contracts, supplanting an earlier view that workers were assets and best employed in permanent, long-term contracts. In Hatton's view, 'By the mid-1980s, the cultural battle between the asset model and the liability model of work had, for the most part, been won. Workers were generally considered profit-limiting liabilities rather than profit-boosting assets' (Hatton, 2011, p 82).

Hatton points out that while the temp agency sector represents a small component of the labour market in North America, this is not reflective of its impact on labour markets overall. 'Temp industry campaigns thus penetrated not only the economy but also the economy of ideas' (Hatton, 2011, p 10). Hatton notes that:

> The temp industry provides American employers with convenient, reliable tools to turn 'good' jobs into 'bad' ones (and bad jobs into worse ones). But the temp industry has operated on another, equally important level – the cultural arena, where battles over 'common sense' about work and workers take place. The temp industry's high-profile campaigns have had a powerful impact on the cultural battlefield, helping establish a new morality of business that did more than sanction the use of temps; it also legitimated a variety of management practices that contributed to the overall decline in Americans' work lives. (Hatton, 2011, p 2)

In his assessment of the agency campaigns, Hyman (2018, p 52) concluded that the goal was to 'convince managers that no one had a right to job security. The decision to use or not to use temps was not only about costs, but about beliefs – beliefs about the proper organisation of the labour force.' The validity of temp agency claims that temp employment was in the long-run interest of employers was, and remains, questionable. Ton (2014) argues that employers and economic efficiency would benefit from a return to more stable, long-term employment.

The era of regulated capitalism and the SER reached maturity in the late 1970s. The post-Second World War economic boom was fading, and the mass fatalities of the two world wars and the economic collapse associated with the Great Depression were distant memories. The economic models adopted by the Soviet Union and China were looking like less of a threat to capitalism. Inflation and wages continued to rise, despite increases in unemployment. The share of income going to the top 10 per cent of income earners had fallen by half since the end of the war. To a growing number of business leaders, the post-Second World War social compromise was broken.

Leading business groups began reversing their support for unions and employment security and adopting a view of the employment relationship that mirrored the interpretation favoured by the temp agencies. In the US the Business Roundtable, an organization limited to corporate chief executives (CEOs), was formed in 1972 and played a key role in articulating this new vision of employment rights. What began as a call for 'better balance in labor–management relations' quickly developed into a call to significantly weaken labour (Kotz, 2017, p 69). Support for Keynesian policies and an adequate social welfare system was replaced by a call for government austerity, giving birth to neoliberalism. The role of the family in assuring the welfare of its members was to be re-emphasized, while the role of state social welfare was to be reduced (Cooper, 2017). This new agenda was taken up by a growing number of right-wing organizations funded largely by the Koch brothers (MacLean, 2017). Hyman (2018, p 290) concluded: 'The reframing of work from permanent to temporary was ideological.'

In response to the crisis facing leading American corporations in the early 1970s, senior management called in consultants employed by leading consulting firms such as McKinsey and the Boston Consulting Group to reorganize and re-energize their firms. Most of the workers employed by these consulting firms were themselves on temporary employment contracts. Hence it is not surprising that they viewed it as perfectly normal to fix what ailed large American companies by imposing a similar labour–management model to the one they worked under, a model laced with short-term thinking and temporary employment structures. Traditional champions of stability, the long-term vision of corporate success and the SER, such as General Electric, AT&T and Hewett Packard, were asked to become lean and nimble, to subject themselves to market discipline and to reallocate capital to its most productive use so as to maximize shareholder value. In the process, a growing number of workers moved from long-term employment and a SER to something less secure. Not all workers became, or are likely to become, gig workers or contract workers. However, virtually all, from the CEO to the person sorting the mail, became more insecure and temporary under this new vision of American capitalism. Hyman concluded that during the 1980s, 'In place of long-term investment and stable workforce, the new ideal for American firms was short-term returns and flexible labor' (Hyman, 2018, p 6).

The increased role of finance as a source of profits made it easier for employers to be less concerned about the long-run, or even short-run, interests of their employees. Appelbaum (2017) points to how financialization makes workers who produce goods less critical to profitability. As a result, employment for most workers becomes more precarious. She wrote:

> As workers and the production process becomes less central to the firm's financial success, investing in employees' skills or paying higher wages to ensure their cooperation becomes less important to the firm's financial success. Cost containment via work intensification, subcontracting, and a range of low-wage alternative work arrangements becomes more attractive as a means of increasing profit margins. (Appelbaum, 2017, p 6)

One result of this new focus on lean organization and flexible staffing was the rise of the Fissured Workplace documented by Weil (2014). Major US firms became shells of their former selves as they shed (fissured) key responsibility to small firms along extended supply lines. These small firms operated in more competitive sectors of the economy, which further weakened labour's bargaining power and contributed to stagnant earnings, heightened health and safety risks and increased employment insecurity.

Several studies suggest that this new model of economic organization has significantly changed key metrics regarding economic performance. Appelbaum (2017) notes how the extension of supply chains has increased wage inequality between workers with similar skills and characteristics employed by different firms. She points to the different bargaining power of firms along extended supply chains and their ability to capture a share of total value added by the supply chain. Smaller and weaker firms do not get their fair share of the value added, and this is then passed on to their workers in the form of lower wages and less-secure employment, despite the qualifications they bring to the labour market.

Several major banks, including the Bank of Canada, have explored the relationship between the spread of precarious employment and the failure of wage rates to increase despite historically low rates of unemployment (Bracha and Burke, 2018; Duca, 2018; Kostyshyna and Luu, 2019). These studies indicate that labour market changes associated with the increase in precarious employment, gig work, informal employment and non-standard employment have disrupted the traditional relationship between low rates of unemployment and high rates of wage growth (Bracha and Burke, 2018, p 12).

While temp agencies and prominent consulting firms were reorganizing companies around models of less-secure employment, government policy makers, particularly in the US, were dealing with how to support families that were not benefiting from the SER. During the 1960s and 1970s the approach was to improve welfare programmes, including efforts to introduce public health benefits in the US and even discussion of a guaranteed annual income during the Nixon presidency (Cooper, 2017, pp 37–43). In the US this effort floundered on the predominance of racialized families among those excluded from the SER. Concerns were voiced that providing social insurance to racialized families, many of whom were already struggling, would result in what is known as moral hazard and more of the very outcomes that social insurance was supposed to reduce. With the election of Ronald Reagan as US president in 1980, the emphasis turned to making families responsible for their members' well-being. This shift was compatible with the spread of austerity-embedded neoliberal values, which argued that freedom to contract with minimal state regulation and greater market discipline would make everyone better off. As will be shown later, the shift to less-secure forms of employment associated with austerity and neoliberalism has made an increasing number of families unable to provide for the welfare of their members at the very time when neoliberals were arguing that the family needed to become more self-reliant and less reliant on state welfare.

Structural factors such as globalization, financialization and the declining share of output claimed by the top 10 per cent of individuals in the economy clearly fuelled the end of the era of the SER, but what replaced the SER was not predetermined by these shifts. As we learn more about this transition, it has become clear that increased employment precarity was not a simple response to economic forces and that cultural shifts in what seemed to make 'common sense' played a significant role. This was driven by social actors with a vested interest in promoting less-secure employment relationships. This suggests that the era of Increased Precarious Employment was not inevitable and that the end of this era will, at least in part, be a result of a shift in culture and common sense, back to a world where employment security is seen as a right of workers and advantageous to society.

How to measure the precarious workforce, and how large is it?

Measuring the size of the precarious workforce is hampered by the lack of historical data and the lack of an agreed measurement standard. The

US Bureau of Labor Statistics (BLS) began collecting data on 'contingent' forms of employment only in 1995, fully two decades after most analysts believe the transition from the era of the SER began. Statistics Canada followed the US example in 1997 when they started asking workers annually if they were employed on a contract with a fixed end date, including employment that was seasonal, temporary, term or casual.

Doogan (2001) and Choonara (2019) have pointed out that the seismic shifts in attitudes to labour and the employment relationships discussed in the first section of this chapter have not generally been reflected in the post-1995 data collected by the BLS or by Statistics Canada, nor in that collected by other national statistical agencies. The BLS provides occasional estimates of the numbers of workers in job categories that it considers as precarious through the Contingent Work Supplement (CWS) of the Current Population Survey (CPS). Ignoring the lack of data from the critical decades of the 1980s and 1990s, it is now recognized that the data collected by the BLS and Statistics Canada may underestimate the significance of the changes underway (Abraham et al, 2018; Katz and Krueger, 2019). The BLS focuses on primary jobs or modes of employment (the job in which one works the most hours) and hence misses precarious work undertaken as a side job. It is estimated that nearly 70 per cent of Uber drivers are not captured by the BLS because they also hold full-time jobs. Both the Canadian and the US data focus on work done in the previous week and, given the irregular nature of precarious employment, many precarious workers are likely excluded from these reports when they are out of work. A third problem is the challenge that workers have in self-identifying the nature of their employment relationship, particularly during a period of change. Katz and Krueger concluded: 'The basic monthly CPS and CWS instrument may have difficulty capturing changes in the incidence of casual or intermittent work in the United States because of respondent reporting errors that are likely to be exacerbated during a period of changing work relationships' (Katz and Krueger, 2019, p 3).

Several central banks have begun measuring the prevalence of precarious employment as a result of the recent failure of wages to rise in both the US and Canada despite historically low rates of unemployment. They focus on the prevalence of informal work, defined as work through online websites, side jobs or other informal work.[1] In 2013 the Federal Reserve Bank of Boston began their Survey of Informal Work Participation. This survey measured participation in informal employment over a longer period than the last week used by both the BLS and Statistics Canada. Bracha and Burke (2016, pp 1–2) concluded that, as of 2015, 20 per cent of non-retired US adults were participating in some type of informal paid work and 55 per cent had participated in informal paid employment in the previous two years, which represents an increase from 40 per cent in 2013. The Bank of Canada conducted a similar exercise in 2018. They reported that 30 per cent of Canadian adults engaged in some form of paid informal employment in 2018. This number rises to 66 per cent if one includes those who gain income by selling goods or renting property (Kostyshyna and Luu, 2019, p 3).

A significant weakness of both the BLS data and the Statistics Canada data, and even that collected by central banks, is that they focus on the form of the employment relationship. Are you in full-time employment, a temporary agency worker or self-employed? These are relatively crude measures of insecurity. Agency work can be relatively permanent, while some 'permanent' full-time employment can be relatively insecure. Weil (2014) pointed out that the spread of employment across extended supply chains and the fissuring of employment can lead to jobs that are described as permanent having many of the features of less-secure employment.

The existing research on measuring the prevalence of precarious employment makes clear the need for a more expansive definition of precarious employment than simply workers in jobs with precarious forms, such as working through a temp agency. To fully appreciate the depths of the transition from the era of the SER, what are needed are measures that capture workers in degraded forms of permanent full-employment that fall far short of the wage, benefit and security norms of the SER.

There are several ongoing efforts to develop more nuanced and continuous measures of employment insecurity that go beyond simply measuring the form of the employment relationship (see Vosko, 2006; Vives et al, 2010; PEPSO, 2018; Puig-Barrachina et al, 2014; Bohle and Quinlan et al, 2015; Gallie et al, 2017; McCann and Fudge, 2017). One of the more intriguing approaches is by McCann and Fudge (2017), who suggest a multidimensional model of unacceptable forms of work. Their approach integrates two strands of thought on what makes employment precarious. One is the characteristics of the relationship itself. The second is the legal and social context in which the work is done and who it is being done by, a point first made by Vosko (2010). For instance, employment that does not provide benefits will be experienced as more precarious in jurisdictions that lack public healthcare benefits. Likewise, racialized workers might experience different types of employment insecurity differently than white workers.

The PEPSO research group developed two indicators of employment security. The Employment Precarity Index (EPI) is a continuous index made up of ten indicators. It is scored from zero (high security) to 100 (high precarity). The questions that make up the EPI can be found at www.pepso.ca and include questions on income security, scheduling uncertainty, employment insecurity and benefits. Because the EPI is a continuous measure, using it to define who is and who isn't in precarious employment is arbitrary. PEPSO used the convention of using the 2011 data to define four cut-points that divided the sample into four more or less equal categories of employment (Secure, Stable, Vulnerable, Precarious).

A second indicator was developed to measure the prevalence of workers in a SER. To be in a SER, respondents had to indicate that they were in a permanent full-time position, had one employer, expected the job to last at least 12 months and received some benefits other than just a wage or salary.

Between 2011 and 2017, PEPSO conducted three waves of surveys in the Greater Toronto and Hamilton region. A total of 10,360 randomly selected individuals completed one of the surveys. To be included in the survey, individuals had to have worked for pay in the previous three months and be between the ages of 25 and 65. The remainder of this chapter reviews some of the key findings. The reports based on these three surveys can be found at www.pepso.ca.

How precarious employment affects individuals, households and communities

PEPSO's first report, *It's More than Poverty*, provided an insight into the prevalence of precarious employment and its impact on individuals and their households. It offers a much more nuanced picture of the social impact of precarity relative to that available from official sources. In the three waves of surveys, just under 50 per cent of the sample defined themselves as working in a SER. The average EPI score for workers in a SER was significantly lower than for those not in a SER.

Table 2.1 reports the forms of the employment relationship of those in the precarious category. Not surprisingly, workers employed through temp agencies, on short-term contracts and the self-employed are prevalent in the category. Perhaps more surprising is that over one-fifth of the category is made up of individuals who reported that they were in permanent full-time employment. Racialized workers were over-represented in the precarious category and under-represented in the secure category. Men and women were equally likely to be found in the precarious category, while women were marginally over-represented in the secure category, a sign of the depth of the loss of manufacturing employment in the

Table 2.1: Form of employment relationship for those in the precarious category (%)

Temporary employment agency	8.9
Casual/short term	16.2
Fixed contract 1 year or more	4.4
Self-employed	33.4
Permanent part time	15.2
Permanent full time	21.9

Source: PEPSO, 2013; 2015; 2018

region being studied. Workers aged 25 to 34 were over-represented in the precarious category; however, over 40 per cent of this category were aged 45 to 65.

PEPSO's first report shed light on the income differentials between workers in secure and precarious employment. Individuals in precarious employment earned barely half the amounts earned by those in secure employment. Households of at least two people, where at least one person was in precarious employment, earned less than three-quarters of earnings reported by households with at least one person in secure employment. While the household income differential narrowed, as compared to the individual differential, it was still significant. This suggests that a family structure of one person in secure employment and a second earner in a less-secure employment, which is often suggested in discussions of the standard employment era, may be less prevalent in the era of Increasing Precarious Employment. A major source of this differential is differences between individuals in secure and precarious employment and the prevalence of their partner working for pay and the quality of their employment. In households with at least one person in precarious employment the partner is more likely to be not employed, to work part time or to be in a precarious form of employment, and less likely to be in permanent full-time employment.

PEPSO's first report revealed the social cost of precarious employment for households and families, an issue that is investigated further in subsequent reports. Nearly half of all households with at least one person in precarious employment reported that their employment situation interfered with personal or family life – double the rate reported by households with someone in secure employment. Over three-quarters of households with at least one person in secure employment reported that anxiety over their employment situation rarely or never interfered with personal or family life. This was true for just over half of households with at least one person in precarious employment.

PEPSO also examined whether income acted as a buffer against some of these anxieties. The sample was divided into a secure group, combining the secure and stable categories discussed earlier, and an insecure group, combining the vulnerable and precarious categories. Three family income categories were created, <$50,000, $50–100,000 and >$100,000. By crossing the two employment security categories with the three household income categories, six income employment security categories were created.

The results (Table 2.2) indicate that household income does act as a buffer against anxiety about employment interfering with personal or family life, but that it has the most effect for very high earning households. However, within each income category, households with at least one person in insecure employment were substantially more likely to report employment anxiety than households with at least one person in secure employment. Perhaps the most surprising result from this data is the depth of middle-income employment insecurity anxiety. Over 40 per cent of households with at least one person in insecure employment living in a middle-income household reported that employment insecurity interferes with personal or family life. The prevalence of employment anxiety among this group was even greater than that reported by households with at least one person in secure employment and with a low household income. These results suggest that while employment insecurity affects household life most frequently in low-income households, it also creates anxiety for households at all income levels.

PEPSO's second report, *The Precarity Penalty*, explored the issue of income stress. Less than half of individuals in precarious employment reported that they were able to keep up with their bills and financial commitments in the last 12 months, as compared to three-quarters of individuals in secure employment. Over one-third of individuals in precarious employment were concerned about meeting their financial

Table 2.2: Anxiety about employment situation interferes with personal or family life (%)

Secure/high income	27.4
Insecure/high income	33.8
Secure/middle income	31.0
Insecure/middle income	42.9
Secure/low income	37.9
Insecure/low income	52.9
Total sample	36.5

Source: PEPSO, 2013; 2015; 2018

THE AGE OF INCREASED PRECARIOUS EMPLOYMENT

obligation in the next 12 months, as compared to less than 10 per cent of individuals in secure employment. Over one-third of individuals in precarious employment reported being concerned about maintaining their current standard of living in the next 12 months, as compared to less than 5 per cent of individuals in secure employment.

Precarious employment also has an impact on individuals starting relationships or starting families. Workers aged 25–34 in precarious employment were five times more likely to have delayed forming a relationship than were workers in secure employment, and more than twice as likely to have delayed having children.

PEPSO's first survey in 2011 and third survey in 2017 bracket a period of substantial employment growth in the Greater Toronto and Hamilton labour market. PEPSO's third report, *Getting Left Behind*, explored what this meant for the overall level of employment security and the impact on workers with different characteristics. The number of workers in SERs increased from 50.2 per cent in 2011 to 55.9 per cent in 2017. There was a small drop in the number of workers in permanent part-time employment. The number of workers in precarious forms of employment on short-term contracts, employed through temp agencies or own-account self-employed remained the same. Despite the improved labour market, the prevalence of less-than-very-good mental health increased from 29.3 per cent in 2011 to 33.4 per cent in 2017. The prevalence of anxiety interfering with personal and family life was unchanged.

To discover more about how workers with different characteristics experienced the growth in employment, the sample was divided into eight categories based on gender, race and having a university degree. White men and women with a university degree and racialized men with a university degree were all more likely to be employed in a SER in 2017, as compared to 2011. No other category of worker reported a statistically significant change in the prevalence of having a SER, despite the growth in employment.

EPI scores revealed a similar pattern. White men and women with a university degree and racialized men with a university degree all reported lower EPI scores, representing improved employment security. The average improvement was an 18 per cent reduction on their scores in 2011. All other categories reported smaller reductions in EPI scores, none of which was statistically significant.

The net result of these changes was that the improvements in employment security resulting from an improved labour market were mainly captured by groups of workers who were already the most secure in 2011. In 2011, white men with a degree were 9 per cent more likely to be in a SER than were racialized women without a degree. In 2017 the difference increased to 22 per cent. In 2011, racialized women without a degree had EPI scores that were 28 per cent higher than those of white men with a degree. In 2017, racialized women without a degree had EPI scores that were 50 per cent higher.

Conclusion

This chapter has offered an explanation of the rise of precarious employment, stressing the importance of ideological shifts regarding the rights of workers, shifts whose roots were in the 1950s and 1960s. This new vision became a reality only in the 1980s and 1990s as globalization, financialization and the share of output captured by the wealthiest in society declined, undermining the era of the Standard Employment Relationship. In reporting on the impact of insecure employment and austerity on households, the chapter has exposed the contradiction between austere neoliberal policies' promotion of family responsibility for maintaining household well-being while at the same time fuelling a shift from the SER to less-secure employment. The changes to the employment relationship associated with austerity and neoliberalism make it more difficult for families to fulfil their role within the neoliberal paradigm.

Finally, this chapter has discussed the challenges in measuring the prevalence of precarious employment. It has pointed to the limitation of indicators based on the form of the employment relationship and the need for a more nuanced set of measures that capture the declining quality of employment of workers in both precarious and non-precarious forms. It could be argued that employment in the age of Increased Precarious Employment is much like employment in any other era of capitalism other than the immediate post-1945 decades. For the majority of people, employment is insecure, lacks full benefits and often does not pay enough to sustain a full standard of living. While the era of Increased Precarious Employment differs from the era of the SER in that more workers fall into the less-secure bracket and all types of employment in general are less secure, the difference relative to capitalism's 400-year history should not be exaggerated.

Note
[1] To see the full list of types of employment included under informal paid activities see SCE-SIWP I, December 2013, question 29. https://www.newyorkfed.org/microeconomics/databank.html.

References

Abraham, K.G., Haltiwanger, J.C., Sandusky, K. and Spletzer, J.R. (2018) 'Measuring the gig economy: Current knowledge and open issues'. NBER Working Paper #24950.

Appelbaum, E. (2017) *What's Behind the Increase in Inequality?* Washington, DC: Center for Economic and Policy Research.

Bohle, P., Quinlan, M. et al (2015) 'Health and well-being of older workers: Comparing their associations with effort–reward imbalance and pressure, disorganisation and regulatory failure.' *Work & Stress*, 29(2): 114–27.

Bracha, A. and Burke, M.A. (2016) *Who Counts as Employed? Informal Work, Employment Status, and Labor Market Slack.* Federal Reserve Bank of Boston Current Policy Perspectives, 2018 Series, No 16-29.

Bracha, A. and Burke, M.A. (2018) *Wage Inflation and Informal Work.* Federal Reserve Bank of Boston Current Policy Perspectives, 2018 Series, No 18-2.

Brown, W. (2015) *Undoing the Demos: Neoliberalism's Stealth Revolution.* New York: Zone Books.

Cappelli, P. (1999) *The New Deal at Work: Managing the Market-Driven Workforce.* Boston: Harvard University Press.

Choonara, J. (2019) *Insecurity, Precarious Work and Labour Markets: Challenging the Orthodoxy.* Switzerland: Palgrave Macmillan.

Cooper, M. (2017) *Family Values: Between Neoliberalism and the New Social Conservatism.* New York: Zone Books.

Doogan, K. (2001) 'Insecurity and long-term employment'. *Work, Employment and Society*, 15(3): 419–41.

Duca, J.V. (2018) *Inflation and the Gig Economy: Have the Rise of Online Retailing and Self-Employment Disrupted the Phillips Curve?* Working Paper 1814. Federal Reserve Bank of Dallas.

Gallie, D., Felstead, A., Green, F. and Inanc, H. (2017) 'The hidden face of job insecurity'. *Work, Employment and Society*, 31(1): 36–53.

Hacker, J.S. (2006) *The Great Risk Shift: The Assault on American Jobs, Families, Health Care and Retirement and How You Can Fight Back.* Oxford: Oxford University Press.

Harvey, D. (2005) *A Brief History of Neoliberalism.* Oxford: Oxford University Press.

Hatton, E. (2011) *The Temp Economy.* Philadelphia, PA: Temple University Press.

Hyman, L. (2018) *How American Work, American Business, and the American Dream Became Temporary.* New York: Viking.

Katz, L.F. and Krueger, A.B. (2019) *Understanding Trends in Alternative Work Arrangements in the United States*. Working Paper 25425. Cambridge, MA: National Bureau of Economic Research.

Kostyshyna, O. and Luu, C. (2019) *The Size and Characteristics of Informal ('Gig') Work in Canada*. Staff Analytical Note 2019-6. Bank of Canada.

Kotsko, A. (2018) *Neoliberalism's Demons: On the Political Theology of Late Capitalism*. Stanford, CA: Stanford University Press.

Kotz, D.M. (2017) *The Rise and Fall of Neoliberal Capitalism*. Cambridge, MA: Harvard University Press.

MacLean, N. (2017) *Democracy in Chains: The Deep History of the Radical Right's Stealth Plan for America*. New York: Penguin Books.

Manyika, J., Lund, S., Auguste, B., Mendonca, L., Welsh, T. and Ramaswamy, S. (2011) *An Economy that Works: Job Creation and America's Future*. McKinsey Global Institute.

McCann, D. and Fudge, J. (2017) 'Unacceptable forms of work: A multidimensional model'. *International Labour Review*, 156(2): 147–84.

OECD (2019) *OECD Employment Outlook 2019: The Future of Work*. Paris: OECD Publishing.

PEPSO (Poverty and Employment Precarity in Southern Ontario) (2013) *It's More than Poverty: Employment Precarity and Household Well-Being*. Toronto: United Way of Greater Toronto and McMaster University.

PEPSO (2015) *The Precarity Penalty: The Impact of Employment Precarity on Individuals, Households and Communities – and What to do about It*. Toronto: United Way of Greater Toronto and McMaster University.

PEPSO (2018) *Getting Left Behind: Who Gained and Who Didn't in an Improving Labour Market*. Toronto: United Way of Greater Toronto and McMaster University.

Procyk, S., Lewchuk, W. and Shields, J. (2017) *Precarious Employment: Causes, Consequences and Remedies*. Halifax, Canada: Fernwood Publishing.

Puig-Barrachina,V., Vanroelen, C., Vives, A., Martínez, J., Muntaner, C., Levecque, K., Benach, J. and Louckx, F. (2014) 'Measuring employment precariousness in the European Working Conditions Survey: The social distribution in Europe'. *Work*, 49: 143–61.

Quinlan, M. (2012) 'The "pre-invention" of precarious employment: The changing world of work in context'. *The Economic and Labour Relations Review*, 23(4): 3–24.

Ton, Z. (2014) *The Good Jobs Strategy: How the Smartest Companies Invest in Employees to Lower Costs and Boost Profits*. Boston, MA: New Harvest.

Van Arsdale, D. (2016) *The Poverty of Work: Selling Servant, Slave and Temporary Labor on the Free Market*. Chicago: Haymarket Books.

Vives, A., Amable, M., Ferrer, M., Moncada, S., Llorens, C., Muntaner, C., Benavides, F.G. and Benach, J. (2010) 'The Employment Precariousness Scale (EPRES): Psychometric properties of a new tool for epidemiological studies among waged and salaried workers'. *Occupational and Environmental Medicine*, 67(8): 548–55.

Vosko, L. (ed) (2006) *Precarious Employment: Understanding Labour Market Insecurity in Canada*. Montreal and Kingston: McGill-Queen's University Press.

Vosko, L.F. (2010) *Managing the Margins: Gender, Citizenship and the International Regulation of Precarious Employment*. Oxford: Oxford University Press.

Weil, D. (2014) *The Fissured Workplace: Why Work Became So Bad for So Many and What Can Be Done to Improve It*. Cambridge, MA: Harvard University Press.

3

Stepping Stone or Dead End? The Ambiguities of Platform-Mediated Domestic Work under Conditions of Austerity. Comparative Landscapes of Austerity and the Gig Economy: New York and Berlin

Niels van Doorn

Introduction: the austerity of domestic labour platforms

How to do more with less? This is, essentially, austerity's onerous question. Its default answer, in turn, has been to defer, download and outsource the burden of being overtasked and cash strapped. As Peck (2012, p 632) notes, 'austerity is ultimately concerned with offloading costs, displacing responsibility; it is about making *others* pay the price of fiscal retrenchment' (emphasis in original). These 'others' are, frequently, marginalized communities of colour and the low-income urban neighbourhoods they inhabit. Cities, to quote Peck again, are 'where austerity bites' as it 'operates on, and targets anew, an already neoliberalized institutional landscape', but does so in a highly uneven manner (Peck, 2012, pp 629, 631). What Marxist-feminist scholars have referred to as the 'crisis of social reproduction' or, more narrowly defined, the 'crisis of care' is thus experienced differently depending on what urban household one belongs to (Fraser, 2016; Hester, 2018). In the face of enduring cuts to publicly provisioned social reproductive services and a 'post-Fordist sexual contract' that expects women to excel both as mothers and as entrepreneurial professionals (Adkins, 2016), white middle-class households have increasingly turned to the market to outsource their reproductive tasks (Gutiérrez-Rodríguez, 2010). As formal and informal markets for domestic work expand, they not only generate income opportunities for working-class minority and migrant households but also intensify their social reproductive challenges (Gutiérrez-Rodríguez, 2010). Moreover, it has been extensively documented how such feminized and racialized reproductive labour is highly precarious, un(der)-regulated and subject to exploitation by employers and labour market intermediaries alike (for example, Glenn, 1992; Ehrenreich and Hochschild, 2003; McGrath and DeFilippis, 2009). It is within this historical and socioeconomic setting that this chapter considers the market entrance of a new type of 'intermediary': the on-demand domestic work platform.

Digital platforms amplify existing power dynamics and inequalities while introducing technologies and techniques that produce qualitatively new arrangements, conditions and experiences of work, generally referred to as gig work. Whereas I have elsewhere focused on the historically gendered and racialized techniques that render platform-mediated domestic work invisible and devalued (Van Doorn, 2017), here I examine how formally self-employed domestic workers negotiate the engineering of their visibility, agency and income opportunities on two home-cleaning platforms – Handy and Helpling. As Ticona and Mateescu (2018) have shown with respect to the care industry, platforms use metrics such as ratings and reviews in combination with profiles and background checks to construct individualized forms of visibility that serve to market care workers to potential clients, 'displaying specific qualities of workers in standardized and comparable ways' (Ticona and Mateescu, 2018, p 4394). While these techniques are intended to foster trust on the clients' side, the dynamically hierarchical display of 'an abundant and always-available pool of workers' presents a novel market interface that may nevertheless exacerbate the deeply unequal power relations that have historically marked domestic work (Ticona and Mateescu, 2018, p 4394; Hunt and Machingura, 2016). At the same time, platform companies are less compelled to ensure the institutional/legal visibility of their 'care professionals' as formally employed workers, to the extent that most companies identify as labour-market intermediaries that match supply and demand, rather than as employers or employment agencies. Although they provide clients and workers with tools for documenting worked hours, processing payments and/ or calculating taxes, and despite framing the formalization of a largely informal sector as one of their main value propositions to both clients and policy makers, platforms managing care and other domestic work strategically refrain from enforcing the norms and requirements of formal employment (Ticona and Mateescu, 2018). Instead, they dissolve the formal employment relation into a nexus of private contracts and user agreements (Tomassetti, 2016).

Accordingly, I argue that domestic labour platforms engage in *selective formalization*, or a set of business practices that formalize some aspects of the gig while perpetuating and sometimes aggravating certain conditions of informality that have long characterized domestic labour. These practices structurally benefit the platform and its clients, while disempowering workers, who are expected to carry all the (administrative, fiscal and legal) burdens of a formal labour relation but receive few of its benefits. Previous studies have shown that the boundary between formal and informal employment is not as sharp as it may initially seem and that labour platforms exploit this ambiguous terrain by technical and legal means (Ticona and Mateescu, 2018; Fudge and Hobden, 2018; Moore, 2018; Flanagan, 2019). For example, Moore (2018, p vi) notes that the negative characteristics of informal work are prevalent in large parts of the gig economy, where work is under-regulated, frequently unprotected, usually 'does not guarantee minimum wage', 'does not offer income security', 'runs a high risk of discrimination' and offers no occupational health standards or career-enhancing educational prospects (see also Adamson and Roper, 2019). In this precarious setting, gig workers run a higher risk of being subjected to psychosocial violence that can take the form of 'isolating people, manipulating reputations, withholding information, assigning tasks that do not match capabilities and assigning impossible goals and deadlines' (Moore, 2018, p 2). Likewise, in her historical analysis of domestic labour market intermediaries in Australia, Flanagan concludes that digital platforms have instigated a 'paradigm shift' in worker control 'from one of *dyadic* to *structural* domination' (Flanagan, 2019, p 65, emphasis in original). Whereas domestic workers have historically worked under informal conditions of dyadic domination, which requires obedience to an individual employer, today's domestic labour platforms enforce a semi-formalized regime of structural domination where workers can leave a household when they please while remaining captured by a platform-engineered 'market system' that 'provides the primary mechanism for worker discipline' by setting opaque and non-contestable 'rules of the game' (Flanagan, 2019). Echoing the previously mentioned authors, Flanagan (2019) argues that such discipline is achieved primarily through platforms' extensive and often punitive surveillance capacities as well as their use of unilateral ranking and rating systems that operate 'as a kind of "memory" that is held by the entire market' rather than by individual employers (Flanagan, 2019, p 66).

What this study adds to the literature on gig work, and specifically to the still understudied topic of platform-mediated domestic labour (Ticona and Mateescu, 2018), is a cross-national comparative analysis of how nominally self-employed cleaners in New York City (NYC) and Berlin negotiate these conditions of structural domination and selectively imposed informality. Critically, I understand structural domination not as a totalizing arrangement but, rather, as a pressured space that leaves just enough wiggle room for people to improvise changes and switch gears, if not directions and destinations. What matters here is how 'structural domination' − as an abstract category with descriptive and evaluative currency insofar as it is derived from concrete impediments and inequalities − is articulated on specific platforms operating in particular urban labour markets populated by low-wage workers whose dependency on and approach to platform labour vary considerably. Similarly, as Baines and Cunningham write in Chapter 1 of this volume, austerity is at once 'a global phenomenon with continuities across national contexts' and a 'lived, local experience'. While I will briefly mention some national and urban austerity policies, this chapter is primarily concerned with how the logics of austerity are scaled down to the everyday practices of platform companies and gig workers.

One reason why austerity policies have seen such a widespread − if uneven − uptake across nations and regions is because they not only scaffold a political and socioeconomic project of retrenchment but also have a strong moral dimension (Muehlebach, 2016). In the words of Baines and Cunningham, again, austerity persuades as 'an ideological frame that encourages sacrifice and lowered expectations from working people and average citizens, with the promise of improvements at some undefined point in the future'. In certain ways, as I will show, platform labour satisfies austerity's moral imperative to a tee: it is a form of sacrificial labour that pulls itself up by its own bootstraps in the hope that the hard work and risk taking will pay off, either by turning the gig into a sustainable occupation or by buying enough time to transition into something better. Yet it will also become clear that labour platforms can enter people's life as a gift, making them feel like they have won the lottery. For while it is true that the gig economy's business model is predicated on austerity logics, to the extent that its two central tenets are risk offloading and continuous accounting, platform companies are also notorious for burning through massive amounts of venture capital in their quest to achieve scale. The immediate impact of this pursuit on many gig workers has been one of relative – and *short-lived* – splendour, as they eagerly collect sign-up bonuses and enjoy initial payouts higher than any previously received wage. Platform labour's link to austerity is thus not a straightforward matter, as it is rife with ambivalence and contradictions.

The remainder of this chapter is structured into three sections. The next section situates Handy and Helpling in the socioeconomic context of two of their main markets, respectively NYC and Berlin, which both have been at the vanguard of 'austerity urbanism' (Peck, 2012). It also provides a brief overview of the research design. The following sections then offer an ethnographic account that relays the experiences of this chapter's two protagonists: Kenny, an African American Handy Pro; and Kostas, a Greek Helpling cleaner. The third section reflects on these experiences and offers some concluding remarks.

Situating the platforms

Handy in New York City

New York City's extensive welfare infrastructure became the target of politicians and bankers in 1975, when a major fiscal crisis nearly resulted in municipal bankruptcy (Phillips-Fein, 2017). The far-reaching austerity measures imposed by the financial sector to teach public officials a lesson in fiscal responsibility radically remade New York City. A year before Clinton's 1996 Personal Responsibility and Work Opportunity Act, Mayor Giuliani's Work Experience Program had already forced unemployed New Yorkers off the city's welfare rolls and into poorly remunerated public sector jobs (Krinsky, 2007). The city's income and wealth inequality ballooned and has since only continued to grow, resulting in an exceedingly polarized environment where a massive low-wage service sector caters to a class of highly paid white-collar professionals (Ehrenreich and Hochschild, 2003). This sector is sustained by the precarious labour of predominantly African American and Latinx workers whose low wages are frequently subsidized by food stamps and other forms of public 'work support' that bolster low-road labour practices (Dickinson, 2016). Domestic services constitute a large and growing industry within the city's broader low-wage sector, composed of formal and informal markets where immigrants and women of colour seek work that is typically isolated and 'only partly covered by core employment and labour laws' on federal and New York State levels (McGrath and DeFilippis, 2009, p 74). While exclusion from such laws was redressed when the New York Domestic Workers Bill of Rights passed the state legislature in 2010, after a six-year grassroots campaign (Burnham and Theodore, 2012), its enforceability remains a serious issue and (putatively) self-employed workers are exempt.

This exemption from statutory labour laws is likely to be the reason why Handy classified its cleaners (which the company calls 'Professionals' or 'Pros') as independent contractors when it entered the NYC market in 2012, and why it continues to lobby the state legislature to pass a Bill that would legally cement this status (Pinto et al, 2019). Now operating in over 450 locations in the US as well as some cities in Canada and the UK,[1] Handy markets its extended range of home services as affordable and reliable to potential customers while highlighting 'great pay', a 'flexible schedule' and 'easy payments' as reasons to become a Pro.[2] Noting that it 'is not an employer, but simply connects independent service professionals with customers', it charges a 'trust and support fee' for this matching service but also takes a significant cut (20–50 per cent, depending on the source consulted)[3] from each booking. Meanwhile, the payment NYC Pros receive is structured into four rolling tiers – $15, $17, $20 and $22 – that each come with a specific target regarding the number of jobs completed and average customer rating over a 28-day period.[4] All Pros have a basic profile showing their average rating, jobs completed, reviews and an optional photo, but they can also purchase a Premium account for $8 per week that allows them to add biographical information and a Premium badge – among other privileges.[5] Finally, the company deploys an elaborate system of disciplinary fees that 'are easy to incur, can be hard to avoid, and seriously destabilise the income streams [...] cleaners are trying to establish and maintain' (Van Doorn, 2018).[6]

Between February and September 2018, I conducted 22 semi-structured interviews with Handy cleaners in NYC.[7] Participant recruitment was challenging, due to the isolated and hidden nature of domestic cleaning, and happened mostly online (on Craigslist, Facebook and LinkedIn), where possible augmented through snowball sampling. Interviews took place in public places and lasted between approximately 50 and 150 minutes. The participant sample consisted mostly of women (15) and African Americans (15), with African American women making up the largest contingent (10), followed by African American men (5). The sample further included two white men, two white women, two Latina women and an Asian American woman. Participants were not consistently asked to disclose their age, but most were in their 20s and 30s.

Helpling in Berlin

At the start of the 21st century, Berlin's economic downturn converted into a fully fledged fiscal crisis as it became apparent that the city's Senate had allowed a large public banking consortium to 'engage in dubious real estate speculations and almost go bankrupt in 2001' (Bernt et al, 2013, p 127). In what came to be known as the 'Berlin banking scandal', the Senate decided to bail out the consortium and thereby created an 'extreme budgetary emergency' that 'permanently changed the framework of Berlin's urban politics' by legitimizing enduring austerity measures and privatizations aimed at reducing the city's enormous deficits (Bernt et al, 2013, p 16). It was in this austere urban environment that the far-reaching federal 'Hartz reforms' were rolled out between January 2003 and January 2005, aiming to reduce unemployment and welfare dependency. While these workfare reforms did reduce national unemployment rates, they also increased income inequality and job insecurity by deregulating temporary and non-standard work arrangements – generating high volumes of publicly subsidized low-wage jobs – while leaving the core labour market untouched (Chih-Mei, 2018). Although Berlin's income and wealth inequalities are benign compared to NYC's, the city thus also experienced an intensification of labour market dualization that has been compounded by rapid gentrification and exploding rents (Bernt et al, 2013).

Having reinvented itself as Europe's rising tech and creative industries hub, Berlin annually attracts (tens of) thousands of foreign young professionals.[8] When failing to land a job in their field, these hopefuls either return home or join the ranks of other labour migrants and refugees whose 'outsider' status and lack of German-language skills drastically reduce their income opportunities and push them into precarious, often informal occupations such as home cleaning. As in the US, domestic work in Germany is characterized by informality and is mainly performed by immigrant women – in this case predominantly from Eastern Europe, Asia and Latin America (Lutz and Palenga-Möllenbeck, 2010; Trebilcock, 2018). While, officially, domestic workers are included in most of the nation's labour laws (one notable exception being occupational health and safety regulation), and Germany ratified the International Labour Organization's Decent Work for Domestic Workers Convention in 2013, there are 'inconsistencies and paradoxes between the *official welfare state policy* on domestic work and the *unofficial reality* of a feminized work sector which lacks rules on workers' and clients' protection' (Lutz and Palenga-Möllenbeck, 2010, p 420, emphasis in original). Similar to the situation in NYC, the lack of regulatory oversight and enforcement, combined with the rise of self-employment, in this sector fuels these inconsistencies (Lutz and Palenga-Möllenbeck, 2010).

Helpling, founded in Berlin in 2014, has thrived under these conditions and publicly promotes its platform as an antidote to Germany's large 'black market' in domestic services (Höhne, 2017), while accelerating the self-employment trend by classifying its cleaners as independent contractors. Active in over 200 cities in ten countries across three continents, Helpling's operations vary (slightly) per country. In Germany, the company promotes its platform to cleaners by highlighting 'complete flexibility' with respect to work scheduling, the presence of a 'personal point of contact' and the ability to 'determine your own price'.[9] Whereas Helpling started out with a set hourly wage (€11 in its Berlin market), it switched to cleaner-determined rates in 2018 – likely to avoid potential misclassification lawsuits. Although its commissions vary per market and type of service, the company takes between 25 and 33 per cent from the amount a Berlin-based customer pays for a cleaning. The platform encourages cleaners to add personal information to their profile, which otherwise includes one's hourly rate, average rating, reviews, number of jobs completed and one's 'verification level' (contingent on the submission of a business licence and proof of a police check). Customers can either browse profiles and select a preferred number of cleaners directly or let Helpling make the match. To reduce cancellations and increase cleaners' 'reliability', the platform used to deploy a Performance Score, but this score has been discontinued and from May 2019 Helpling – mimicking Handy – switched to a disciplinary fee system for cleaners and customers who transgress its rules.

In the period between October 2018 and June 2019, I conducted 25 semi-structured interviews with Berlin-based Helpling cleaners. Participant recruitment again happened mostly on Craigslist, Facebook and LinkedIn, but snowball sampling played a bigger role in Berlin. Interviews took place in public places and lasted between approximately 60 and 140 minutes. Save for one German cleaner, the participant sample consists solely of migrants who came to Berlin to pursue education, work and/or asylum. The sample particularly reflects the large population of young Chileans and Argentineans who reside in the city on a one-year 'working holiday' visa and sign each other up for Helpling (n = 10). Other cleaners came from various Southern/Eastern European countries, Brazil, India, Syria, South Africa and Nigeria. Men (13) slightly outnumbered women (12) in the sample, which deviates from the gender distribution within Germany's overall domestic worker population but reflects how digital platforms have made cleaning work more palatable to migrant men.

As the next section demonstrates, drawing on Kenny's and Kostas's stories,[10] both platforms can function as vital lifelines for minority and migrant workers who find themselves in difficult circumstances. However, as they spend more time working through these platforms, it becomes clear that the companies governing them do not have cleaners' best interests in mind. Faced with deteriorating and increasingly punitive working conditions in which platform companies offload various forms of risk while continuing to extract rent from each service transaction, cleaners like Kenny and Kostas repeatedly have to figure out how to respond. Although small acts of resistance and risk absorption allow them to remain active on the platform, its engineered inequities and enforced austerity also motivate cleaners to experiment with informal work arrangements made possible by the platform but taking place beyond its control. Whereas such experimentation appeals to someone like Kenny, who sees a world of entrepreneurial opportunity, for Kostas it rather forms a gateway to another life, one relieved from the burdens of being a domestic cleaner.

A much-needed resource: Kenny's story

Kenny says he can defend Handy all day long if he has to. The way he sees things, "you gotta think on Handy's end" because they are a smart company that allows you to make good money as long as you work hard. Kenny is an African American man in his mid-40s who grew up in Brooklyn but now lives in a remote part of Queens that is still affordable, which means that he has to travel about 90 minutes to get to Manhattan, where most of his clients live. It's a lot of travel time each day, for which he is not compensated, yet he doesn't really mind because the trains are relatively cheap as long as you stay within the five boroughs. He is good at his job, as can be gleaned from the 4.8 rating and glowing reviews on his profile, which he is quick to refer to when discussing his work experiences over the past two years. Handy entered his life at an opportune moment and helped him get back on his feet, something for which he remains deeply grateful. Nearly three years ago, he "got into trouble" at home and his girlfriend at the time put him out. Suddenly homeless, he decided to check into a shelter because he didn't want to burden his friends. There he was told that he needed to be working if he wanted to get overnight passes or support with his housing search, which is when he remembered his ex-girlfriend – and mother of three of his seven kids – telling him about Handy. The problem was that, as she had warned him, they "don't take felons", and Kenny had spent 18 months in prison for a felony conviction in the past. This is why he first turned to Uber Eats and Postmates as a quick way to make money for the shelter contribution and child support, doing food delivery for about two weeks until shelter management informed him that app-based food delivery did not constitute a 'real job' because it had no set hours. At the end of his rope, he decided to try his luck with Handy and, to his surprise, the company took him on board.

The 'onboarding' process, as gig companies call it in order to avoid the appearance of hiring workers, was quick and smooth: "You don't meet nobody at Handy," Kenny says, and he was pleasantly surprised that he only had to answer five easy questions about cleaning situations. "Once you pass the test then they tell you to download the app and then they'll be like 'Hey take some jobs because we gonna need some money from you'." While he, for unknown reasons, was not charged the usual background-check fee, Handy did send him a starter kit with cleaning supplies for which they took $50 out of his first pay cheque. When asked if he thinks the company should have given him these supplies, Kenny gives me a smile communicating amused incredulity and brings up his independent contractor status as if this should nip the discussion in the bud: of course *he* is responsible for these costs, just like he's responsible for his own healthcare insurance. This situation doesn't worry him though, as he is still on Medicaid – despite officially exceeding the income cap – and at least he can always count on Handy to give him work: "Like, when you first look at the app and then they say you're good, they show you work! You can get to work, get paid and get money in your pocket." Starting at $15 an hour, he quickly managed to work himself up to the $20 tier and is keen on staying there. Kenny feels like he's got it made: "It's the best thing that's ever happened to me [...] I mean you've got your freedom, you do what you do, you meet new people, I'm out here talking to you, having lunch." Compared to his previous jobs, Handy offers him an unprecedented sense of freedom and control over his own schedule. When a cleaning falls through he can even go home early and "indulge" in some weed, without having to worry about getting fired over a urine test – something he always had to be vigilant about during his days as a customer service representative. Ultimately, "it's the cash and the flexibility" that make this platform such a great opportunity for him.

While he loves this work, Kenny acknowledges that there's quite some risk involved in operating via Handy's platform and he has, over time, found ways to either hedge against this risk or absorb it in an attempt to turn it into a new business opportunity. He has noticed how more clients appear to be frustrated with Handy or previous cleaners these days, how they frequently cancel or try to reschedule at the last minute, how some try to scam their way to a free cleaning, and how Handy usually sides with the client rather than with its Pro in cases of dispute. These experiences have taught him the importance of taking screenshots. Because "Handy has to see it to believe it", Kenny's phone is loaded with screenshots ready to be attached to e-mails providing evidence for his claims, activities and whereabouts. This practice is essential because Handy regularly deletes job documentation from the app. Kenny was once fined for a 'no show' even though he was 15 minutes early and called the disgruntled client on the number that was left on a note outside when communication via the app didn't work. Wanting to prove his communication attempts, he turned to his app, only to find that Handy had already deleted the job information: "But I had his number still, that I called on my cellphone. So I erased all my other contacts, like all the people I had called, and sent them the thing [screenshot] saying 'Hey I called the guy and he did not want your service'." After much hassle back and forth, Handy finally retracted the $50 fine and since then he's been meticulously screenshotting his jobs.

Nevertheless, screenshots cannot protect him against all the risks that are unevenly distributed on Handy's platform. When Kenny accepts a new client, he usually has little information regarding the size of the home or the cleaning specifications, as clients are not required to share these details. In practice this means that he is often confronted with a workload that exceeds his booked time and with 'extras' (that is, tasks with an additional charge) that weren't requested through the app. Instead of asking clients to add such extras so that he can be properly reimbursed or just declining these tasks, he has an alternative strategy: "Another Pro may say they need the money or something. I don't need nothing, I just need your repeat business, we good." Kenny is willing to absorb the risk offloaded on him by Handy and take small financial hits as long as this "investment" pays off in the long run. Not only does a portfolio of repeat clients offer a steadier income stream, it also reduces the risk and stress inherent to dealing with new clients: "I just don't want to have to be searching for jobs every day because that gets frustrating." As Kenny and his peers know, labour platforms may lower transaction costs on the demand side, yet this often happens at the expense of those supplying the commoditized labour. Faced with rising costs, they seek to create a stable routine and/or to shift their transactions (back) to the informal economy that shields them from platform surveillance and rent seeking.

Kenny's livelihood depends on his cleaning work, which he considers not just his job but a "career" despite how "people talk shit" about him cleaning toilets. Given that Handy has played such a formative role in this career, I was surprised when I heard him dismiss the company as "nothing but that stupid platform". I think this remark reflects how he was trying to make himself less dependent on Handy's platform, which he now approached as merely a lead generator that connects him to new clients but otherwise mostly extracts value (in the form of commissions) rather than adding it. "At this point," he told me, "I am riding with them because I could take all their customers. Like I have two, three outside that I got through Handy." He never solicits his clients directly, but has started mentioning how much Handy takes from each transaction, and when they show interest he suggests a better deal for both parties. One technology that really helps his "side hustle" is Cash App, a mobile payment service that he uses as a financial interface between him and his private clients, who usually "don't like cash". He, on the other hand, loves cash, and Cash App comes with a debit card that he uses to cash out after clients have transferred the money via the app. Handy, which knows how important daily payments are for many of its Pros, also initiated an instant cash out option, but it charges $3 per transaction – too much, if you ask Kenny.

Still, he uses the option frequently, just like he continues to work with Handy as long as he's "getting the better end of the deal". For him, this means being able to make a decent living while enjoying his freedom, maintaining his regulars but increasingly adding private clients to his portfolio because this keeps the expensive middleman out. Otherwise, the distinction between formal and informal work is not that clear in Kenny's world, which is largely due to Handy's selective formalization of the job. While it adds a digital payment system, standardized performance metrics and work documentation tools, it also systematically erases this documentation, and its metrics render the working conditions of its Pros highly insecure. Furthermore, while it issues a 1099 tax form to all Pros earning over $600 per year, it doesn't offer tax information or enforce payment. This suits Kenny well, as he's trying to stay under the radar of the Internal Revenue Service now that his child support contributions for two of his children have ended and he's finally making good money. "Nobody digs into my money mess with Handy," he says, and when I mention the possibility of a tax audit his response – while tongue in cheek – made my heart sink: "I mean, I am probably going to jail at some point [pauses]… at least things are good on Handy's end."

A stopgap measure: Kostas's lament

Although Helpling does not deploy a tiered wage system for its cleaners, like Handy, it still enforces wage discipline. It does so by engineering an evaluative infrastructure generating what could be called a 'customer public sphere', in which clients are *collectively* empowered to compare cleaners' profiles based on ratings, reviews and prices, in order to establish the best value for their money (cf. Kornberger et al, 2017; Ticona and Mateescu, 2018). I emphasize 'collectively' here because this arrangement does not just serve the individual client but empowers all members of the 'customer class' – that is, the structurally advantaged side of Helpling's marketplace – insofar as it aggregates pertinent market information that can be consulted and contributed to by everyone belonging to this class (cf. Flanagan, 2019). Moreover, this information is also available to cleaners themselves, prompting vigilance and making price-based competition much more prevalent on Helpling than in informal home-cleaning markets whose distributed interfaces haven't been centrally configured in favour of the demand side. Just ask Kostas, a 28-year-old Greek man who had come to Berlin two years previously for an extended holiday after finishing his degree in interior architecture and had – often reluctantly – stuck around after getting involved with someone. Like many young migrants in Berlin, he soon found out that the city's living costs are high while the chances of finding decent work are slim when you do not speak German. Faced with limited options and realizing that his financial situation was getting dire, he took a friend's advice and signed up with Helpling. Although he acknowledges that the platform has offered him quick and easy access to money, he increasingly resents the high commission the company charges on each job he completes. He also feels frustrated by certain changes to the platform since he's been active, particularly when cleaners began to be able to set their own rates:

> 'When I started the job I made €11 [per hour], but if you are new in the job you don't know how much cleaners charged before. Even if you [charge] €9 it's okay because you don't know how the market works in Berlin. So you can ask for less money. But if I am working in the company for more than a year and I have really good reviews …'

With a 4.8 rating and over 400 completed cleanings, Kostas feels like he should be able to charge more than newcomers. But because Helpling allows cleaners to set their hourly rate (after commission) as low as €7.50,[11] he fears a race to the bottom in which more cleaners will feel compelled to decrease their rates in order to stay competitive in an environment where high ratings and good reviews are the norm rather than the exception. In this sense, the 'evaluative inflation' on the platform forces cleaners to compete on price instead of quality, in a market for labour that may be less fungible than food delivery but is nonetheless routinely subject to commoditization. Kostas believes that Helpling should raise its wage floor and do more to discourage new cleaners from charging less than €11. Not only have the costs of living gone up, he argues, but you also have to take into account that you have to pay for your own insurances as a self-employed cleaner, which is something Helpling doesn't sufficiently bring to people's attention. When I note that the platform at least offers price recommendations based on 'cleaners with similar profiles', he counters that these recommendations are exactly the problem because they show how low a lot of people are willing to go. In other words, rather than operating purely in a prescriptive manner, this device is at once *descriptive* of segmented price-setting behaviour and *performative* insofar as it influences this very behaviour: if you set your rate below the recommended margins you may get more work (Espeland and Sauder, 2007).

Besides the price-setting system, Kostas thinks that Helpling's Performance Score (which at the time purported to measure cleaners' quality, reliability and communication) also contributes to the degradation of working conditions on the platform. Before its implementation he could cancel a client 48 hours in advance without repercussions, but now any cancellation lowers the score on the metric of reliability, and if that drops below a certain threshold his account could be temporarily blocked. He doesn't just experience this new measure as an infringement on his freedom to call in sick or protect himself from bad clients, but also finds it offensive because he believes that his quality or reliability cannot *and should not* be measured in such an impersonal way. To him, the score rather measures Helpling's lack of trust in its cleaners and its eagerness to please its customer base. Performance scores, reviews and starred ratings offer control to clients while putting more pressure on cleaners to keep up their metrics and keep down their prices, in order to appeal to the all-seeing eye of Helpling's prudent customer class. In this setting, Kostas is happy that his regular customers offer a measure of protection against the growing work insecurity induced by the platform.

Since his arrival in Berlin, Kostas has been depending on a European travel insurance to cover any healthcare costs that he might incur, although he is not quite sure how much it actually covers or if it covers him while working in people's homes. He went with this option because he's not able to afford the notoriously expensive German health insurance for freelancers, which is why he wants Helpling to contribute to its cleaners' insurance costs. This is just one of his many grievances with the company, which by now he cannot wait to leave because he feels that "they don't give a shit about you". Still, he continues to work through Helpling because he likes his regulars and he needs the money. He has also noticed that many German clients are hesitant to break Helpling's rules by taking him off the platform, and they don't realize that the company takes a cut from his wages. On a couple of occasions clients did solicit him with a reasonable offer, however, which he gladly accepted because it's more money in his pocket and he does not think he needs the platform anymore (echoing Kenny). While it has given him market access, it has provided nothing in terms of income or social security, and it ultimately even ruined this market for him. There was a time when he still had the good faith and energy to work on earning the trust of his platform-mediated customers, but these days Kostas feels tired. He is tired not just of Helpling but of cleaning work more generally, of Berlin and of living in Germany. His heart yearns for Athens and he really wants to work in a field where he can put his degree and skills to good use. While he realizes the difficulty of finding a job back in Greece, given the present circumstances, he also wonders how hard it can be compared to his experience in Berlin. At least he speaks the language there.

Although he's still on the platform, Kostas acts like he already checked out. In contrast to Kenny, he has nothing good to say about the cleaning platform he has used for nearly two years: "If it wasn't Helpling, it would have been another platform or something more creative. I can't feel grateful for Helpling because I'm doing all the work." While doing all this work, he allowed himself to fall "into the hole of Helpling", which he now regrets. He just got too comfortable in this hole, which shielded him from Berlin's disappointing labour market prospects, but now he is determined to pull himself out of it and move on with his life.[12]

Discussion and conclusion

In the context of an 'acute confluence of austerity, diminishing public welfare, and fragmentation of formal employment' (Thieme, 2018, p 529), domestic labour platforms like Handy and Helpling can offer an important economic lifeline to vulnerable labour market 'outsiders' such as minorities and migrants. Yet what initially constitutes a stepping stone or stopgap opportunity eventually becomes – or threatens to become, if one doesn't continue to step up – a dead end. In cities where, for many inhabitants, 'crises become unexceptional, and where coping with uncertainty is normalized' (Thieme, 2018, p 530), these outsiders develop a 'hustle' at once enabled and thwarted by platforms that constantly experiment with labour-market governance and segmentation while operating on the cusp of formality and informality (cf. Van Doorn and Velthuis, 2018; Ravenelle, 2019). Improvisation, in this sense, comes from both sides, although information asymmetries and other data-driven instruments of structural domination regularly give domestic labour platforms and their customers the upper hand (Flanagan, 2019). Moreover, the previous section demonstrated that the opportunities and challenges of platform labour are unevenly distributed and some workers are better positioned than others to absorb the risks/costs attendant to platform companies' selective formalization of the labour relation and process.

Kostas initially perceived Berlin less as the origin of Greece's post-crisis suffering and more as a destination imbued with the possibilities of a temporary reprieve. His dismissive attitude toward Helpling and platform-mediated domestic work stems as much from his educational and professional trajectories in Greece – co-constitutive of his gendered class identity – as from his imagined prospects in Berlin or another European city. After all, as a European citizen Kostas is more mobile than non-EU migrants or refugees (Könönen, 2019), especially given that he doesn't have any dependents to care for: if Berlin doesn't work out, he can always return home or try again elsewhere. So, while he occupies an outsider status on Berlin's labour market, primarily due to his struggles with the German language, Kostas has accumulated enough 'human capital' to treat Helpling as little more than a stopgap that holds him over until he finds something better. In this position of relative privilege, the costs and insecurities of platform-governed self-employment are reluctantly accepted as a passing burden, such as when Kostas relies on his cheap travel insurance as a provisional healthcare solution. Conversely, Kenny's reliance on Medicaid is less of a provisional solution and more of a protracted predicament. Likewise, his job mobility is restricted, due to his criminal record, while his kids will need his support for years to come. For Kenny, faced with limited funds and mobility, New York is closer to destiny than destination. He has to roll with the punches and has more to lose – but also more to gain – than Kostas, which explains his entrepreneurial approach to domestic cleaning and his readiness to build on what Handy has made available. However, it is exactly what Handy is *not* making available, namely a formal set of resources that can support and educate Kenny as well as other precarious independent contractors with respect to tax compliance, that threatens to eventually disrupt his entire livelihood. Beyond individual biographies and labour-market trajectories, the long history of institutional racism and mass incarceration of African Americans in the US positions Kenny as a de facto outsider in his own country despite his formal citizenship, intensifying his vulnerability to Handy's selective formalization of his labour.

Finally, on a more general note, to emphasize that platform labour is primarily migrant and minority labour matters insofar as it recalibrates the parameters for a critical discussion about how and to what extent 'the gig economy' exerts a downward pull on labour conditions and erodes the norms, standards and protections scaffolding 'regular employment' (for example, Daugareilh et al, 2019). While certainly not denying such dynamics, I believe that claims regarding the degradation of labour by gig platforms tend to mobilize a comparative frame of reference that has little bearing on the everyday circumstances of many gig workers and indeed is increasingly belied by the practices and logics of neoliberal labour-market governance. It is evident that we did not have to wait until the advent of gig platforms to witness the decline of the standard employment relation in various sectors, or the massive expansion of low-wage, insecure jobs (for example, Crouch, 2019). Platforms, as amplifiers, have a structural tendency to accelerate and scale the labour-market dynamics and arrangements that have been over four decades in the making, thereby crystallizing existing problems now subjected to a resurgence of public scrutiny that is often too narrowly focused on platform culpability. Although this scrutiny is justified and useful, it is equally justified and useful to scrutinize our own assessments and aspirations with respect to platform labour. Are we expecting this type of work to be better than traditional forms of precarious work just because it is governed by a platform? When we judge platform labour to be 'degraded', what do we compare it to (Doussard, 2013)? As I have shown, for minority and migrant workers whose experience with and short-term prospects for finding a 'decent' job with proper protections and pay are minimal at best, gig work can present a provisional step *up* rather than down. Yet I have also demonstrated how working conditions and income opportunities on the platform tend to deteriorate over time, suggesting that labour degradation is more salient as a problem internal to platforms – as companies seek scale and profitability – than in comparison to other industry actors. Moreover, the broader point is that nobody should have to choose between a rock and a hard place. Instead of raising our norms and expectations solely with respect to platform labour, we should collectively raise the bar on non-standard work and social security in post-welfare societies by organizing and legislating for higher wages, broader protections, more enforcement capacities and a robust, redistributive social safety net. This would present 'gig economy' companies with a new status quo: either follow suit or close shop following a worker exodus.

Notes

[1] See https://www.handy.com/locations.

[2] See, respectively, https://www.handy.com/services/cleaning-service and https://www.handy.com/apply.

3   In 2015, Handy claimed that it charges 'about 20 per cent on the average booking' (see https://slate.com/business/2015/07/handy-a-hot-startup-for-home-cleaning-has-a-big-mess-of-its-own.html). However, numerous Handy Pros claim this percentage is usually much higher, as can be gleaned from browsing their reviews on Indeed: https://www.indeed.com/cmp/Handy/reviews?ftopic=paybenefits.

4   See https://prohelp.handy.com/hc/en-us/articles/217290407-Payment-tiers.

5   See https://prohelp.handy.com/hc/en-us/articles/115011938868-Pro-Premium-Accounts.

6   See https://prohelp.handy.com/hc/en-us/articles/217287967-What-are-fees-.

7   This research is part of a five-year project entitled Platform Labor, funded by the European Research Council. It investigates how digital platforms are transforming low-wage labour, social reproduction and urban governance in post-welfare societies, zooming in on NYC, Amsterdam and Berlin. For more information about the project, see https://platformlabor.net.

8   See https://www.berlin.de/sen/wirtschaft/en/about-us/artikel.458761.en.php.

9   See https://www.helpling.de/anmelden.

10   In order to do justice to the richness and complexity of cleaners' experiences with these platforms within the given space constraints, I have opted to zoom in on one cleaner per city. I have selected these two cleaners because their socioeconomic backgrounds and experiences are in many ways representative of the total sample of cleaners interviewed in each city. Although the majority of the cleaners interviewed in NYC were female, Kenny's narrative aptly represents the entrepreneurialism, lack of better job opportunities and childcare responsibilities that were prevalent themes in the interviews and in informal conversations I had in this city. Meanwhile, Kostas's experience as a well-educated Greek migrant in Berlin is representative of the relatively large share of highly skilled migrant men (and women) who work through Helpling in this city, and of their disassociation with the role of domestic cleaner.

11   Helpling has since raised the minimum rate to €10 per hour in Germany.

12   A few months after this conversation, Kostas informed me that he and his boyfriend were moving back to Athens to pursue new job opportunities there.

References

Adamson, M. and Roper, I. (2019) '"Good" jobs and "bad" jobs: Contemplating job quality in different contexts'. *Work, Employment and Society*, 33(4): 551–9.

Adkins, L. (2016) 'Contingent labour and the rewriting of the sexual contract'. In: Adkins, L. and Dever, M. (eds), *The Post-Fordist Sexual Contract: Working and Living in Contingency*. Basingstoke: Palgrave Macmillan, 1–28.

Bernt, M., Grell, B. and Holm, A. (eds) (2013) *The Berlin Reader: A Compendium on Urban Change and Activism*. Bielefeld: transcript Verlag.

Burnham, L. and Theodore, N. (2012) *Home Economics: The Invisible and Unregulated World of Domestic Work*. Report commissioned by the National Domestic Workers Alliance (NDWA), New York.

Chih-Mei, L. (2018) 'Are labour market reforms the answer to post-Euro-crisis management? Reflections on Germany's Hartz reforms'. *European Review*, 26(4): 738–54.

Crouch, C. (2019) *Will the Gig Economy Prevail?* Cambridge: Polity Press.

Daugareilh, I., Degryse, C. and Pochet, P. (2019) *The Platform Economy and Social Law: Key Issues in Comparative Perspective*. Working paper of the European Trade Union Institute (ETUI).

Dickinson, M. (2016) 'Working for food stamps: Economic citizenship and the post-Fordist welfare state in New York City'. *American Ethnologist*, 43(2): 270–81.

Doussard, M. (2013) *Degraded Labor: The Struggle at the Bottom of the Labor Market*. Minneapolis, MN: University of Minnesota Press.

Ehrenreich, B. and Hochschild, A.R. (eds) (2003) *Global Woman: Nannies, Maids, and Sex Workers in the New Economy*. New York: Henry Hold & Company.

Espeland, W.N. and Sauder, M. (2007) 'Rankings and reactivity: How public measures recreate social worlds'. *American Journal of Sociology*, 113(1): 1–40.

Flanagan, F. (2019) 'Theorizing the gig economy and home-based service work'. *Journal of Industrial Relations*, 61(1): 57–78.

Fraser, N. (2016) 'Contradictions of capital and care'. *New Left Review*, 100: 99–117.

Fudge J. and Hobden C. (2018) *Conceptualizing the Role of Intermediaries in Formalizing Domestic Work*. ILO working paper: Conditions of Work and Employment Series No 95. Geneva: International Labour Organization.

Glenn, E.N. (1992) 'From servitude to service work: Historical continuities in the racial division of paid reproductive labor'. *Signs: Journal of Women in Culture and Society*, 18(1): 1–43.

Gutiérrez-Rodríguez, E. (2010) *Migration, Domestic Work and Affect: A Decolonial Approach on Value and the Feminization of Labor*. London: Routledge.

Hester, H. (2018) 'Care under capitalism: The crisis of "women's work"'. *IPPR Progressive Review*, 24(4): 343–52.

Höhne, V. (2017) 'Wir Bekämpfen den Schwarzmarkt'. *Die Tageszeitung*, 4 February. https://taz.de/Helpling-Gruender-Benedikt-Franke/!5377514/.

Hunt, A. and Machingura, F. (2016) *A Good Gig? The Rise of On-Demand Domestic Work*. Working Paper No 7 of the Overseas Development Institute (ODI), London.

Könönen, J. (2019) 'Becoming a "labour migrant": Immigration regulations as a frame of reference for migrant employment'. *Work, Employment and Society*, 33(5): 777–93.

Kornberger, M., Pflueger, D. and Mouritsen, J. (2017) 'Evaluative infrastructures: Accounting for platform organization'. *Accounting, Organizations and Society*, 60: 79–95.

Krinsky, J. (2007) 'The urban politics of workfare: New York City's welfare reforms and the dimensions of welfare policy making'. *Urban Affairs Review*, 42(6): 771–98.

Lutz, H. and Palenga-Möllenbeck, E. (2010) 'Care work migration in Germany: Semi-compliance and complicity'. *Social Policy and Society*, 9(3): 419–30.

McGrath, S. and DeFilippis, J. (2009) 'Social reproduction as unregulated work'. *Work, Employment and Society*, 23(1): 66–83.

Moore, P. (2018) *The Threat of Physical and Psychosocial Violence and Harassment in Digitalized Work*. ILO working paper. Geneva: International Labour Organization.

Muehlebach, A. (2016) *The Moral Neoliberal: Welfare and Citizenship in Italy*. Chicago: University of Chicago Press.

Peck, J. (2012) 'Austerity urbanism: American cities under extreme economy'. *City*, 16(6): 626–55.

Phillips-Fein, K. (2017) *Fear City: New York's Fiscal Crisis and the Rise of Austerity Politics*. New York: Macmillan.

Pinto, M., Smith, R. and Tung, I. (2019) *Rights at Risk: Gig Companies' Campaign to Upend Employment as We Know It*. National Employment Law Project (NELP) report. New York: NELP.

Ravenelle, A.J. (2019) *Hustle and Gig: Struggling and Surviving in the Sharing Economy*. Oakland, CA: University of California Press.

Thieme, T.A. (2018) 'The hustle economy: Informality, uncertainty and the geographies of getting by'. *Progress in Human Geography*, 42(4): 529–48.

Ticona, J. and Mateescu, A. (2018) 'Trusted strangers: Carework platforms' cultural entrepreneurship in the on-demand economy'. *New Media & Society*, 20(11), 4384–404.

Tomassetti, J. (2016) 'Does Uber redefine the firm? The postindustrial corporation and advanced information technology'. *Hofstra Labor and Employment Law Journal*, 34(1): 1–78.

Trebilcock, A. (2018) 'Challenges in Germany's implementation of the ILO Decent Work for Domestic Workers Convention'. *International Journal of Comparative Labour Law and Industrial Relations*, 34(2): 149–76.

Van Doorn, N. (2017) 'Platform labor: On the gendered and racialized exploitation of low-income service work in the "on-demand" economy'. *Information, Communication & Society*, 20(6): 898–914.

Van Doorn, N. (2018) 'Late for a job in the gig economy? Handy will dock your pay'. *Quartz at Work*, 3 October. https://qz.com/work/1411833/handy-charges-fees-to-its-workers-for-being-late-or-canceling-jobs/.

Van Doorn, N. and Velthuis, O. (2018) 'A good hustle: The moral economy of market competition in adult webcam modeling'. *Journal of Cultural Economy*, 11(3): 177–92.

4

Trends in Collective Bargaining, Wage Stagnation and Income Inequality under Austerity

Ian Cunningham and Philip James

Introduction

The purpose of this chapter is to explore the impact of the Global Financial Crisis (GFC) and austerity on collective bargaining and wage outcomes internationally. It takes as the starting point for its analysis the argument advanced in Chapter 1 that the current wave of austerity policies stems from a neoliberal economic consensus that has pervaded developed economies and emphasizes free markets, the removal of rigidities to capital and shrinking the state. That is a philosophy that in policy terms is the antithesis of one supportive of trade unions and collective bargaining, which are themselves under this ideology seen as impediments to markets and economic growth (Harvey, 2007). The chapter therefore adopts a perspective that sees the GFC and austerity as providing a convenient point from which to further consolidate neoliberalism's hold on society (McCann, 2013) and simultaneously undermine one of the chief forms of resistance – trade unions and collective bargaining.

The first part of the chapter focuses attention on exploring trends in collective bargaining in the EU and North America (US and Canada) in the post-GFC period. In doing so, it identifies a common trajectory in nation-state policies that encompasses a shift towards identifying the GFC as a public debt crisis; the blaming of trade unions and their members (in particular public sector workers) for the crisis; and the introduction of reforms to collective bargaining and union security designed to reinforce deflationary austerity policies. The chapter's second part then examines trends in wage growth and equality since 2008 and discusses the factors influencing them and the extent to which they can be viewed as a product of the neoliberal-informed economic policies and reforms adopted in response to the crisis.

Changes to collective bargaining in the EU

Institutional context of collective bargaining in the EU under austerity

Since 2000 there have been significant social, economic and political policy shifts that have fundamentally challenged the status of collective bargaining in the EU. Policies associated with a neoliberal agenda that view unions and collective bargaining as sources of rigidities in the market have been central to this change as the EU has focused on the neoliberal free market agenda of labour-market flexibility and downward pressure on terms and conditions to sustain economic growth (Waddington, Muller and Vandaele, 2019). This process of change received support from EU enlargement and the move towards economic and monetary union (EMU). In the former case, enlargement meant the accession to the EU of new Eastern European members with limited traditions of collective bargaining. In the latter, EMU emphasized reducing public debt, limited social convergence criteria across the bloc, failed to establish a mechanism to coordinate fiscal policy and stressed the importance of moderating wage growth (Waddington et al, 2019).

The EU had no legal basis on which to directly intervene in the wage-setting arrangements of nation-states. Yet the move towards economic and monetary union, and the creation of the euro presented challenges to collective bargaining. EMU's deregulatory ethos and measures to facilitate the 'four freedoms'[1] led to pressures for wage moderation as competition between member states intensified. At the same time, member states of the eurozone lost sovereignty over macro-economic tools that allowed them to deal with shocks and economic imbalances, such as devaluation of their currencies. This loss, in turn, led to the increasing importance of wage moderation as a source of internal devaluation in order to reduce costs and deal with significant economic adjustments, while the EU's emphasis on deficit reduction imposed a discipline over public sector pay rises (Waddington et al, 2019). It should nevertheless be noted that prior to austerity the European Council had regularly called for wage moderation and decentralized collective bargaining arrangements as policy moved in a neoliberal direction (Schulten and Muller, 2015).

EU countries vary in the extent to which they use centralized, multi-employer bargaining. Some states operate highly centralized arrangements, others more intermediate arrangements (centralized and enterprise) and those that are largely decentralized to the business unit (Delahaie, Vandekerckhove and Vincent, 2015). The EU's call for decentralization therefore involved support for a move away from the former type of arrangements and towards the latter. This advocacy reflecting a belief that such decentralization was key to making employment relations more responsive to the needs of managerial efficiency, labour-market conditions and unit performance (Winchester and Bach, 1999).

Austerity brought an intensification of these challenges to collective bargaining within the EU (Delahaie et al, 2015; Waddington et al, 2019). New governance mechanisms have emerged under austerity that have led to the curtailment of EU states' discretion over economic policy choices. Led by EU institutions, such as the Commission and the European Central Bank (ECB), and the International Monetary Fund (IMF) (the Troika), this policy shift has been labelled the 'new European economic governance' (Schulten and Muller, 2015). The objective of this governance regime is for member states to accept fiscal restraint, cost competitiveness and downward flexibility in terms of wages and a reduced influence of national collective bargaining arrangements (Leisink and Bach, 2014). The rationale for this type of intervention was the EU's decision to tackle its debt crisis through encouraging public sector cuts that would have an immediate impact on collective bargaining and wages that make up a significant aspect of public sector expenditure (Schulten and Muller, 2015). The new governance model therefore sees wages (specifically cuts and flexibility) as a key variable in creating the conditions for economic growth (Pond and Jacob, 2014).

EU intervention has included non-binding measures in the form of Country Specific Recommendations as part of the framework of the European Semester, which is a yearly cycle of European economic policy coordination made up of preventative measures and sanctions on states for non-compliance (Schulten and Muller, 2015; Hermann, 2014). Further measures included the EU Stability and Growth Pact, the Europe 2020 strategy and the 2011 Euro Plus Pact, which called for the close monitoring of wages and wage-setting arrangements. These arrangements included all eurozone members being allowed a maximum 9 per cent increase in unit labour costs within a period of three years (12 per cent for those outside the eurozone), backed by the risk of financial sanctions for those countries not complying (Schulten and Muller, 2015). Furthermore, the DG ECFIN Report on 'Employment and Social Developments in Europe 2011' recommended decreasing automatic extensions of collective agreements, decentralization of collective bargaining and the promotion of measures to reduce the wage-setting power of trade unions (European Commission, 2012).

Declines in coverage and the decentralization of collective bargaining

The outcomes for collective bargaining across the EU were significant. Against the policy background just outlined, the coverage of collective bargaining (defined as the proportion of employees having their terms and conditions determined by collective negotiations) declined through a combination of job losses and reforms. Countries such as Cyprus (54 per cent to 45 per cent), Greece (83 per cent to 40 per cent) and Portugal (84 per cent to 75 per cent) suffered significant declines in coverage, as did accession states from Eastern Europe, such as Romania (98 per cent to 35 per cent), Slovenia (92 per cent to 65 per cent) and Slovakia (40 per cent to 30 per cent). Only in Finland did coverage increase, from 85 per cent to 89 per cent, between 2000 and 2015. Indeed, the Nordic (Sweden, Denmark and Finland) countries more generally fare better in terms of coverage, reaching 80 per cent and over (Waddington et al, 2019).

Despite some cases of decentralization of collective bargaining before the GFC, with the UK being the most far reaching prior to austerity, multi-employer bargaining remained dominant in the EU. Austerity, however, brought greater pressure for reform. This was particularly so in the case of countries, such as Cyprus, Greece, Hungary, Ireland, Latvia and Portugal, that had to seek financial assistance from the Troika through the European Stability Mechanism and/or from the IMF. This assistance was available only on condition that these countries met demands for reforms of collective bargaining (Schulten and Muller, 2015). Specifically, under pressure from the Troika, Greece and Ireland undertook major restructuring of collective bargaining in favour of decentralization. In Ireland's case, this involved abandonment of national bargaining in 2009 (Keune, 2015). Collective bargaining in Romania via the Social Dialogue Act 2011 was subject to reform by a centre-right government, without any parliamentary debate, and led to the abolition of the national agreement for the private sector (Waddington et al, 2019). Radical decentralization also occurred in Italy as a direct result of ECB intervention (Meardi, 2012).

Further weakening of national multi-employer bargaining has encompassed the removal of extensions in a number of countries (Greece, Portugal, Romania and Hungary), that is, provisions in agreements concluded between one or more employer organizations and trade unions whereby they can be made applicable to an entire sector or region. Other changes have included countries (Estonia, Greece and Spain) removing the 'after effect' regulations to collective agreements, including stipulations that the conditions of a deal continue to apply after it has expired, so encouraging employers to negotiate a new one (Hermann, 2014).

Yet further developments have involved the undermining of the 'favourability principle', or the social advantages attained at multi-employer level take precedence over any inferior content at company level. In Spain and Portugal their collective bargaining system experienced reforms that reversed this principle so that priority was given to company agreements on basic wages. At the same time, there was a clause in each of these changes that allowed employers and trade unions to renegotiate the 'favourability principle' (Delahaie et al, 2015). Accompanying decentralization and these other trends has been a reduction in the scope of agreements, that is, the range of issues that are subject for negotiations (Muller, Vandaele and Waddington, 2019).

Analysis of bargaining outcomes across the EU also reveals the reinforcement of wage moderation, downwards renegotiation of existing agreements, pay freezes and cuts, or below-inflationary increases. Moreover, following the economic crisis in 2009, collectively agreed wage increases in the EU were volatile. Wage growth was low: 1.7 per cent in 2010, but increasing to 2.0 per cent in 2011 and 2.2 per cent in 2012. In 2013, however, the growth of wages slowed down again with a growth rate of 1.8 per cent, before then increasing again (Bernaciak et al, 2014).

More narrowly, and unsurprisingly, given the focus on deficit reduction, public sector pay reforms have been adopted by at least 18 out of the 27 EU member states. Cuts by EU states in terms and conditions have involved bypassing traditional collective bargaining and have been undertaken over several cycles of wage setting. These reforms have further been accompanied by cuts, freezes or below-inflationary increases in statutory national minimum wages (NMW) (Bernaciak et al, 2014). In the latter case, for example, reforms led to the reduction of the NMW in Greece and Ireland (later reversed) by 22 per cent and 12 per cent, respectively. Pensions have also been expected to be more sustainable, leading to the raising of retirement ages in line with life expectancy rates (Hermann, 2014). Even member states relatively untouched by the financial crisis, such as Poland and the Czech Republic, have implemented public sector austerity measures in terms of pension reforms and restructuring and job losses (Bernaciak et al, 2014).

The above measures meant significant cuts to wages. In Portugal, public servants' wages and salaries were frozen, overtime payments were reduced by 50 per cent, holiday and Christmas payments suspended, alongside an increase in working time (from 35 to 40 hours weekly) without compensation, and cuts to pension rights. Similar patterns emerged in Greece, with cuts in wages, deterioration in holiday benefits, an increase in the working week from 37.5 to 40 hours without a proportional pay rise and reductions in trade union power and the scope of collective agreements (Rocha, 2015).

It is of note that some countries experienced assaults on collective bargaining both prior to and during austerity, as well as falls in union membership. This was the case in Germany, Hungary and the Netherlands. For example, Germany's 'Harz reforms' led to some erosion and fragmentation of collective bargaining, through local deals that deviated from nationally agreed industry standards (Lehndorff, 2009). Austerity then exacerbated these trends, with a decline in the coverage of sectoral bargaining and works councils, and evidence of the erosion of the dual system (Addison et al, 2017). Moreover, the use of 'opening' or hardship clauses in collective agreements to allow companies to undercut national deals is increasingly common in Germany (Keune, 2015). In a similar vein, Germany suffered a percentage fall in density of 5.3 points in the ten years prior to 2013 (OECD and Visser, 2016).

Austerity has, then, added to long-standing trends in union decline. In this regard, the UK provides a particularly graphic example. Since the 1980s, collective bargaining in the UK has been subject to an ideologically inspired assault on trade union influence and power (Hyman, 2018), with the result that collective bargaining is now a minority practice. Collective bargaining coverage fell 40 percentage points between 1980 and 2016 (Waddington et al, 2019). The five Workplace Employment Relations Studies (WERS) between 1980 and 2011 illustrate how much of this decline was prior to austerity. Overall, 70 per cent of employees were covered by collective bargaining in 1980, but this declined to 23 per cent by 2011. Private sector coverage has stagnated for some years at 16 per cent, but between 2004 and 2011, public sector coverage also fell from 68 per cent to 44 per cent (Kersley et al, 2006; Wanrooy et al, 2013). Moreover, the influence of multi-employer and national collective bargaining in the UK declined from the 1980s as employers sought to make their own arrangements that reflected broader macro-economic policy changes such as the privatization of state industries and attempts to link pay to local performance and productivity conditions, meet local recruitment and retention needs and undermine union influence and ability to strike (Brown, Bryson and Forth, 2009).

Austerity in the UK added to this assault, with the Cameron-led governments targeting public sector workers. In particular, the 2010–15 Conservative–Liberal Democrat coalition oversaw the following:

- public sector union membership falling by 209,000, to 3.6 million in 2016;
- recommendations to decentralize bargaining to make it more reflective of local labour-market conditions;
- greater outsourcing of public services to make union organizing more challenging;
- wage freezes announced without any consultation;
- limits on paid time off for representatives to undertake their union duties;
- increased pension contributions and raising of pension age;
- limited scope of pay review bodies to recommend pay increases, raising questions about their independence (National Health Service [NHS]);
- reform of incremental pay-progression arrangements seen as 'antiquated' and 'unfair' – thereby, as in the teaching profession, increasing the emphasis on performance-based progression (Bach, 2016).

In addition, the second Cameron administration tightened the legal requirements on unions when undertaking strike ballots in 'important public sector services' (schools, fire service, NHS) by requiring strike calls to be supported by at least 40 per cent of all eligible voters in order for them to receive legal support and hence protection (Darlington and Dobson, 2015).

Processes of change in union membership and collective bargaining can, however, be noted to have varied, in terms of both their nature and scale. The impacts of the GFC and austerity have therefore varied significantly. In this regard, commentators have drawn distinctions in the level of union decline between coordinated market economies, which offer more state protection for unions, and liberal market economies, in which union security arrangements are weaker and neoliberal trends stronger, with decline being noted to have been generally lower in the former (Schnabel, 2013).

Local government collective bargaining

The institutional resilience of collective bargaining in the public sector has also been more specifically challenged by austerity at the level of local government (Glassner and Keune, 2012). In what some have labelled a 'blame avoidance' strategy by central government, working conditions and collective bargaining in local government across the EU have particularly suffered during austerity as states have passed on a significant proportion of cuts to this tier of governance (Leisink and Bach, 2014; Pond and Jacob, 2014). A study of seven EU states, for example, found that countries that experienced high exposure to the crisis in public debt put greater pressure on local governments. Cuts to local government finances have been implemented in several ways, including by reductions in income provided from the central state and restrictions on their own tax-raising powers (Leisink and Bach, 2014).

At the same time, a combination of factors means that there has been variation in the exposure of local governments and their collective bargaining arrangements to such challenges at member state level. Variations include differences in exposure to the GFC and austerity cuts among nation-states; differences in commitment to accompanying market-based public sector reform initiatives, as well as the political complexion and hence philosophies of national and local governments; and the balance of powers (and discretion) subsisting between central and local governments (Bach and Bordogna, 2013; Leisink and Bach, 2014). In the latter case, for example, there have been cases (France, Italy, Hungary and the UK) where established local arrangements have been bypassed by unilateral action by central government to impose wage freezes.

Studies into the impact on local government (Bach and Stroleny, 2014; Leisink and Bach, 2014; Roche and Teague, 2015) do not paint a picture of either collective bargaining or trade unions in complete retreat but, rather, one where the latter are placed in a position of adopting highly defensive 'concession bargaining'. This involves bargaining wherein unions accept declines in terms and conditions, perhaps on a temporary basis, in exchange for enterprise and employment security (Roche and Teague, 2015; Muller et al, 2019). The nature of these exchanges has varied. For example, a study in Ireland showed the adoption of modes of concession bargaining ranging from highly cooperative forms to those characterized by minimal engagement with unions (Roche and Teague, 2015).

Gender impact

There is insufficient space here to do full justice to the gender impact of austerity on collective bargaining and women's employment experiences. The European Women's Lobby Group in a study of 13 European countries found that austerity had a disproportionate impact on women, including perpetuating existing inequalities and causing new ones (Briskin, 2014). The Fawcett Society (2012) identified a 'triple jeopardy' where women lose services, lose the jobs providing these services and are then responsible for the resulting unpaid caring work. There is, however, an additional jeopardy for those remaining in work, from the burden of declining job quality. For example, studies have highlighted worsening job quality for women in low-paid, part-time work (Warren and Lyonette, 2018), as well as work-life balance initiatives increasingly having to embrace 'business case' rationales in order to maintain employer commitment (Lewis et al, 2017).

Occupations such as home care work, overwhelmingly staffed by women, are especially vulnerable to degradation under austerity. The crisis of underfunding in adult social care leads to stringent controls on labour costs. Here, austerity drives increased time-monitoring in care provision and the rationing of home care workers' pay through penalties for late arrivals and non-payment of travel time. Such rationing is accompanied by the intensification of labour and removal of autonomy over work. Care quality also suffers, as such monitoring undermines the opportunity for relationships to flourish between workers and service users (Hayes and Moore, 2017).

A comparative study of women's employment experiences in the UK and Spain found that in the latter austerity meant that women experienced either unemployment or being trapped in temporary jobs. In the former, women faced exposure to job insecurity and threats to pay and conditions from the squeeze in public expenditure. These trends are in the context of reduced collective bargaining protection, employment protection and regulation, weakened unemployment benefits and stalled or reduced care services (Lopez-Andreu and Rubery, 2018).

As well as the aforementioned evidence of austerity leading to the degradation in women's employment conditions, it is also seen as undermining organizational efforts to achieve equality targets. In the UK, a study by the TUC (2012) found that austerity was providing an excuse for employers to not commit to or to avoid equality targets. The same study revealed how individual unions also reported a difficult bargaining climate around equality issues. This difficult climate is further highlighted in a study of the implementation of the UK's 2007 gender equality duty (GED) in local authorities. This duty introduced a legal requirement on all public authorities to have due regard to the need to eliminate unlawful discrimination and harassment on grounds of sex and to promote equality of opportunity between men and women. The economic crisis led to the authorities in the study undertaking organizational restructuring that impacted significantly on the work of equalities teams, including the closure of two out of five units. Moreover, members of the aforementioned teams felt that equality was not seen as an organizational priority during austerity, and had to increasingly reflect a business case (Conley and Page, 2018a). However, this business case had its limits, as austerity was seen to intensify the contested politics of equality as programmes such as the GED clashed with 'the red tape challenge' of the UK Coalition government (Conley and Page, 2018b).

Effective resistance to the above by women can be difficult, as trade union campaigns can continue to reflect old tensions between class and gender politics. Trade unions can be essentially class focused, and feminist or intersectional agendas are underdeveloped even during austerity (Cullen and Murphy, 2017). Moreover, there are restraints on women's activism to offset the impact of austerity and raise their concerns within anti-austerity groups such as trade unions. These limitations in large part reflect the time constraints on women brought about by their caring responsibilities (Craddock, 2017).

Yet there is evidence of resistance to austerity and its accompanying pressures to push women back into the home and leave those in work in more precarious employment and degraded conditions. Studies have revealed a continued commitment among women to employment and career trajectories, as they remain in the labour market (Lombardo, 2017; Lopez-Andreu and Rubery, 2018). Successful resistance is not wholly due to the impact of collective bargaining, however, but also attributed to other social movements (Craddock, 2017; Lombardo, 2017). At the same time, other research highlights the continued importance of workplace activists such as trade union representatives in challenging austerity and its impact on women by framing conflict in such ways that build a collective identity (Granberg and Nygren, 2017).

North America, austerity and collective bargaining

The US

Corporate interests have been pushing back against unions and collective bargaining in the US since the Reagan era. The assault on unions during this period contributed to a fall in the private sector unionization rate from 25 per cent in 1975 to just 7 per cent at the start of the GFC (Abramovitz, 2012). Much of the consequent reform of collective bargaining and erosion of union rights has been directed at the public sector (Collins, 2011). This focus reflects the fact that while there remain whole groups of workers and individual states that remain non-unionized, particularly in the South, union density in the sector is approximately 40 per cent, and hence considerably higher than in the private sector (Cantin, 2012; Rose, 2012).

Commentators are raising concerns regarding the opportunity that austerity has brought to those with anti-union sentiments to roll back this comparatively favourable public sector union position (Cantin, 2012; Rose, 2012, Peck, 2014). Recent attacks during austerity are seen to reflect long-standing political hostility to unionism and collective bargaining from within the US's modern conservative movement (Cantin, 2012) that has been voiced, among others, by the Manhattan Institute, the McIver Institute, the Heritage Foundation, the Tea Party-supporting Koch Family Foundation and the Walton Family Foundation (Wal-Mart) (Collins, 2011).

The financial crisis opened up opportunities for conservatives to advocate for fiscal discipline, downsizing and privatization. Central to this advocacy were anti-state narratives that shifted the blame for the GFC away from the private banking sector and Wall Street to federal and state governments and other public organizations, and their workforces, unions and clients (Peck, 2014). Initially, for federal employees, there was a two-year pay freeze, introduced at the beginning of austerity (Rose, 2012). Subsequent actions have been concentrated within individual states, with some choosing to pursue anti-union measures with vigour. Local governments experienced fiscal crises as they faced restrictions on running deficits and local tax-raising powers. In total, state spending reductions from increasing federal cuts amounted to $291 billion over the period 2008–12, while revenues from increased taxes and fees totalled $101 billion. During this period, it was unsurprising therefore that cities entered into bankruptcy (Peck, 2014).

Rather than blame the years of industrial decline, labour unions, their members (especially in public sector) and collective bargaining became the focus of much of the blame for the financial problems of states and individual cities (Peck, 2012; 2014). Public sector unions were accused of being responsible for substantial government deficits resulting from demands for exorbitant salaries and pensions. Public sector workers were also portrayed as lazy and privileged, as compared to their private sector counterparts, and labelled the new 'labour aristocracy', despite evidence indicating that US public sector workers are under-compensated by 5 per cent relative to comparable private sector workers (Cantin, 2012; Rose, 2016). These anti-union campaigns served the purpose of creating divides across public and private sector workforces, citing the latter as making excessive sacrifices since the advent of the GFC, and at a time when the private sector safety net in the US had collapsed (Devinatz, 2012).

In cities such as San Bernadino and Vallejo, anti-union rhetoric and campaigns led to the downsizing of unionized employees, the removal of health benefits for workers, the cancelling or restructuring of union agreements and the cutting of pension entitlements (Peck, 2014). In the 2010 mid-term elections, Republicans were elected in states such as Wisconsin and Michigan on promises to reduce the salaries and benefits of public sector workers (Devinatz, 2012). Consequently, public sector unionism in Wisconsin was subjected to an unprecedented assault by Governor Scott Walker. Wisconsin possessed a higher degree of unionization, as compared to the rest of the US public sector, with 50 per cent membership density, as compared to 40 per cent (Collins, 2011). The state had suffered considerable deindustrialization, and public sector jobs provided far more stability than what was on offer in the growing private service sector. Many households in Wisconsin had a public sector worker in residence and relied on the accompanying health and retirement benefits (Collins, 2011). It was against this background that Walker's Budget Repair Bill, as well as introducing stringent cuts to services, removed the right to bargain for large swaths of public sector workers, day care workers and home helpers, removed bargaining rights over issues such as pensions and health benefits, limited future pay increases to rises in inflation, required annual votes to maintain union certification, prohibited automatic payroll deductions of union dues, removed the right to arbitration and imposed restrictions on the right to strike (Collins, 2011; Rose, 2013). With regard to the certification measures, recertification elections had to occur every year and would have to gain the votes of 51 per cent of the membership for the union to remain a bargaining agent. The irony of this case was that Wisconsin was the first state to ever extend collective bargaining rights to public sector workers and, at the time the changes were announced, did not have a deficit in its current budget, and its long-term budget deficit was not significantly higher than that of the rest of the country (Collins, 2011; Cantin, 2012).

Ohio attempted to follow suit with similar proposals to Wisconsin's, but they were eventually defeated in a referendum. Similar defeats were experienced in Alaska, Colorado, Connecticut and Iowa (Cantin, 2012). Yet, legislators in 43 states in total presented bills to modify public employee bargaining in some significant way, including ending public worker collective bargaining; reducing the amount of dues that could be taken from members' salaries; reducing political activities and contributions; limiting the topics on which public sector unions could bargain; capping public employees' pay and pay increases; increasing pension contributions and/ or health insurance premiums; and increasing public workers' retirement age (Rose, 2013). For example, in New Jersey, bargaining rights were limited, alongside considerable reductions in pension benefits, while wage freezes and unpaid leave were introduced in states such as New York and Connecticut (Devinatz, 2012; Rose, 2013). In a similar vein, in Idaho a bill was passed that banned 12,000 teachers from negotiating over their pay and conditions (Cantin, 2012), and Indiana introduced a 'right to work law' that allowed workers to gain the benefits of union contracts without having to join them. In combination, these and other changes led to the proportion of US workers who were union members falling to a 97-year low in 2012, of 11.3 per cent of the US workforce (Pollin, 2013).

Commentators have highlighted how the impact of the above has fallen disproportionately on women in the US, especially given that they form a majority of public sector programme recipients, public service workers and union members. In the case of public sector services, hardest hit have been reproductive health services, prevention of domestic violence, sexual health, Planned Parenthood, food subsidies, care for the elderly, childcare, Medicaid, Medicare and education and training. Cuts in services also denied women access to public sector jobs – traditionally seen as an important route for upward mobility for white women and people of colour. Women formed 57.2 per cent of the public workforce at the time of the recession in 2008. However, they lost the majority (63.8 per cent) of the 578,000 jobs cut in the public sector between June 2009 and October 2011. These job losses further denied women a greater opportunity than they would have in private organizations to secure benefits such as pensions and healthcare (Abramovitz, 2012). The attacks on unions from state governments in the US have also fallen disproportionately on women, given that 61 per cent of unionized women – but only 38 per cent of unionized men – worked in the public sector. Furthermore, the aforementioned removal of collective bargaining rights has fallen on overwhelmingly female-occupied roles such as teaching, while those of men (firefighters and police) have remained intact (Abramovitz, 2012).

Canada

Prior to austerity, Canada's federal and provincial governments enjoyed a period of balanced and budget surpluses in public expenditure (Rose, 2016). This favourable financial position was seen to be partly reached through persistent hard bargaining with public sector unions over pay increases. Canada's unions and collective bargaining rights had also been subject to attacks. These moves were part of a series of pre-GFC neoliberal policies that found favour across Canada's entire political spectrum and that encompassed tight public sector budgets and the liberalization of markets (Rose, 2016).

Canada's experience of the GFC was not as harsh as the US and Europe's, as the country did not experience a subprime mortgage crash or as dramatic a fiscal crisis. Despite this context, and an initial stimulus package during recession, governments at federal and provincial levels decided that the neoliberal recipe of reduced public expenditure was the way to promote economic growth and recovery. This programme of reform included five-year targeted deficit-reduction plans. Contained in these plans were commitments to no additional funding for wages. As a result, pay increases had to be linked to cost savings and productivity gains. The federal government further introduced the Expenditure Restraint Act, which established limits or caps on annual wage increases for a five-year period. Governments were further reluctant to increase taxes, imposing pressure for savings on public sector workers (Rose, 2016).

Provincial governments in Canada are responsible for delivery of public services such as health, education, social assistance and social services, and are therefore at the front line of cuts and accompanying reforms to collective bargaining. Ontario is the country's most populous province and is a useful case to illustrate austerity's impact. In 2010 the province's government introduced the Open Ontario Plan, which called for greater competitiveness through reducing what was claimed to be bureaucracy and 'red tape' from environmental and labour standards. The proposals were accompanied by reductions in personal and corporate income taxes and plans to privatize public assets. The aim was to eventually shrink the public sector as a proportion of GDP from 19.2 per cent to 15.5 per cent by 2017–18. The 2010 Public Sector Compensation to Protect Public Service Act introduced a two-year wage freeze for 300,000 non-unionized public sector workers. In addition, representatives of almost three-quarters of a million unionized public sector workers were asked to take part in a social dialogue process with a view to agreeing to a two-year 'voluntary' wage freeze. Collective bargaining was further undermined by a refusal by the provincial government to fund costs associated with collective agreements. Wage freezes were further implemented in the municipalities/ cities of Ontario on public sector workers, especially women. At the same time, public sector chief executives and other managers were excluded from these measures, so that they continued to receive performance-related pay bonuses (Evans, 2011; Fanelli and Thomas, 2011).

As in the US, there were efforts to persuade the non-unionized to resent what were portrayed as the privileged positions of unionized public sector workers. Pensions were central to such efforts to divide public and private sector workers. For example, in Ontario, 78 per cent of public sector workers were in a defined pension plan, in contrast to 25 per cent of private sector employees (Evans, 2011). Again, this diminution of rights to collective bargaining and the benefits of public sector work fell on unionized women, as they make up the majority of union members in Canada (Evans, 2011).

Austerity and pay inequality and stagnation

Internationally, the post-2008 period, and the policies of austerity encompassed within it, have been marked by three earnings-related trends (International Labour Organization, 2018): first, the presence of low nominal wages growth; second, a widespread growth in wage inequality; third, the occurrence of declines or very limited rises in real wages. Each of these trends is briefly mapped in this section and attention paid to the factors that have contributed to them and, more particularly, to the role that has been played by austerity-driven expenditure cuts and labour-market reforms.

With regard to the first of the above-identified trends, the first two columns of Table 4.1 provide Organisation for Economic Co-operation and Development (OECD) figures for the growth of annual changes in annual nominal wages for its 35 member countries for the periods 2000–07 and 2008–16. As can be seen, with just a few exceptions, increases in the latter period are notably lower. In addition, in only Chile, Estonia, Iceland and Lithuania do the averages in this period stand at 4 per cent or higher. In short, the post-2008 period has for the most part been marked by declining and low nominal wage growth.

The last two columns of Table 4.1 present essentially a same picture in relation to changes in real annual earnings over the two periods. Indeed, in only two countries, Chile and Poland, are they shown to have grown by 2 per cent or more from 2008 to 2016. Such statistics therefore add (broader-based) weight to the argument that within the EU, prior to the GFC, most countries experienced real-wage increases, while under austerity the opposite has been the case (Schulten and Muller, 2015).

Turning to the issue of wage inequality, movements in this are commonly measured through two ratios that compare earnings, respectively, at the 90th and 10th percentiles and the 90th and 50th ones. Machin (2016) examined both ratios for 19 OECD countries that had relevant data for 2000 and 2013 and found that both ratios had risen in 15 of them. His analysis further highlights how real-wage stagnation has occurred alongside rising wage inequality in countries like the US, Germany and the UK, and further confirms the point made earlier regarding weak real-wage

Table 4.1: Annual average wage changes, 2000–16

	Nominal		Real	
	2000–07	**2008–16**	**2000–07**	**2008–16**
Australia	4.2	2.9	1.3	0.6
Austria	2.8	2.3	0.8	0.4
Belgium	2.5	1.7	0.1	0.3
Canada	3.5	2.6	1.7	1.2
Chile	4.9	7.0	1.3	2.7
Czech Republic	6.9	2.4	4.6	1.1
Denmark	3.4	2.7	1.5	1.1
Estonia	13.2	4.2	8.1	1.4
Finland	3.4	2.4	1.8	0.5
France	3.0	1.7	1.1	1.0
Germany	1.6	2.3	0.2	1.1
Greece	5.7	−1.7	2.6	−2.2
Hungary	10.9	2.9	4.3	0.1
Iceland	7.8	5.0	5.1	0.0
Ireland	5.9	1.2	2.4	1.2
Israel	1.8	2.3	0.2	0.5
Italy	3.1	1.2	0.4	−0.1
Japan	−0.8	−0.2	−0.1	0.0
Korea	5.6	2.7	2.5	0.5
Latvia	16.5	3.9	8.9	2.7
Lithuania	9.8	4.0	8.2	1.3
Luxembourg	3.8	1.8	1.4	0.7
Mexico	7.8	3.6	2.3	−0.7
Netherlands	3.5	1.8	1.0	0.7
New Zealand	4.3	2.3	2.5	0.8
Norway	4.7	3.6	2.8	1.3
Poland	4.8	3.8	1.2	2.0
Portugal	3.4	0.6	0.0	−0.4
Slovak Republic	8.9	3.2	3.6	1.7
Slovenia	8.0	2.1	3.0	0.9
Spain	3.3	1.8	−0.1	0.7
Sweden	3.5	2.7	2.2	1.3
Switzerland	1.9	0.5	−0.1	0.6
United Kingdom	4.1	1.7	2.7	−0.3
United States	3.8	2.2	1.5	0.7

Source: Blanchflower (2019)

growth more generally. At the same time, more recent analysis undertaken by Blanchflower (2019) in respect of 24 countries indicates that the post-2008 period has not been universally marked by rising inequality. Thus, earnings dispersion between the 90th and 10th percentiles was found to have risen in nine countries, fallen in 14 and remained unchanged in France.

Rising inequality at the general level, it must be noted, has clear implications for that existing between men and women. This is for the simple reason that, as a result of labour-market segmentation, as well as the under-rewarding of female-dominated occupations, women are overly represented in low-paying parts of national economies (International Labour Organization, 2018). Indeed, they tend to also be overly represented in public sector employment, and hence exposed to austerity-driven pay policies encompassing pay freezes or limited rises.

If attention is more specifically focused on the UK, the picture to emerge from the presented statistics points to both low nominal wage growth and declining real wages, with it being additionally estimated by Blanchflower (2019, p 35) that real wages in 2019 were 5 per cent below their 2008 level. Meanwhile, on the basis of the analyses of Machin and Blanchflower, it appears that wage inequality has risen to some extent since 1980 but, as a result of changes in the National Minimum and Living Wages, has declined a little since 2008. A complex range of somewhat overlapping factors have been identified as contributing to the three wage trends discussed earlier, both since the onset of the GFS and, at times, before it. In discussing the rise in inequality in the US, for example, Stiglitz (2013) has drawn attention to how government policies and actions have played a central role in creating the market dynamics that have acted over the longer term to drive down labour conditions. In doing so, he has observed that

> The most important role of government, however, is setting the basic rules of the game through laws such as those that encourage and discourage unionization, corporate governance laws that determine the discretion of management, and competition laws that should limit the extent of monopoly rent. (Stiglitz, 2013, p 72)

The analysis of post-2008 trends cannot then be understood, as Stiglitz highlights, without attention being paid to wider and longer-term processes that have supported the development of an institutional environment serving to weaken the labour-market power of workers (and their unions) and strengthen that of employers. There is no doubt that the macro-economic policies pursued over the period since the crisis and the associated cutbacks in public sector expenditure have played an important role.

The decision internationally to quickly reverse the fiscal stimuli that were initially provided at the onset of the GFS has been widely acknowledged to explain the slowness of the economic recovery that has followed (see Blanchflower and Skidelsky, 2011; Wolf, 2011). This, in turn, has clearly served to limit the scope that existed for rises in wages, particularly given that the slow growth has occurred against a background within which the share of wages in national income has tended to decline in developed economies since the 1980s (New Economics Foundation, 2014), along with a decoupling of movements in wages and productivity (Machin, 2016; International Labour Organization, 2018). At the same time, trends in individual countries have varied, reflecting the differing economic dynamics within them. In the case of the UK, for example, according to Blanchflower (2019, pp 60–5), the decline in real-wage growth has been influenced, among other things, by such factors as an appalling post-2008 productivity performance that has been influenced by low levels of investment, increased reliance on the recruitment of low-paid and less-productive workers, a collapse of private sector unionization, a rise in labour supply towards the lower end of the labour market and significant labour-market slack stemming from the existence of a substantial level of underemployment. The net effect of these according, to Blanchflower has been a decline in the bargaining power of workers that, according to work by Blundell and colleagues (Blundell et al, 2014), has meant that:

> workers are likely to have lower reservation wages than in the past and seem to attach more weight to staying in work (because their expected time to find another job is longer than in the past) than on securing higher wages and are thus willing to accept lower wages in exchange for holding onto their jobs. (Blanchflower, 2019, p 65)

This is not to argue, however, that austerity-driven public sector pay freezes and restrictions, along with labour market-influencing reforms, have not exerted an important influence. In the case of the UK, for example, an analysis undertaken by the Office for National Statistics (2017) revealed that, as a result of a pay freeze from 2011 and the subsequent limiting from 2013 of pay rises to an average of 1 per cent, inflation generally outpaced public sector pay growth over the period from 2011. In addition, on the basis of like-for-like comparisons of mean pay per hour, it is shown that in 2016 public sector workers earned 1 per cent less per hour than their private sector counterparts, whereas in 2010 they had earned 4 per cent more.

There are also good grounds for arguing more generally that cuts to welfare benefits, along with the types of reforms detailed earlier in regard to the coverage and structure of collective bargaining arrangements, are likely to have exerted a significant influence. Thus, in an analysis of the determinants of male wage inequality in 11 OECD countries, Koeniger et al (2007) found its level to be negatively influenced by union density, the strictness of employment protection law, unemployment benefit duration, unemployment benefit generosity and the size of the minimum wage. They further found that about a fifth of the percentage change in wage inequality in the US and the UK over the period 1973 to 1998 could be explained by changes in these labour-market institutional measures.

More narrowly, there is ample evidence, particularly from the US and UK, that negative shifts in wage inequality and real wages have been associated with (but not wholly determined by) declines in union membership and collective bargaining coverage. Machin (2016) reports findings, for example, that show for the period 1980–2013 significant associations between falls in real wages and union collective bargaining coverage at the state level. Mishel (2012), meanwhile found the erosion of collective bargaining coverage to explain between one quarter and one third of the growth in wage inequality in the US between 1973 and 2007, while Card et al (2004) similarly found unions to systematically reduce variances in wages in the US, Canada and the UK over the period 1983–2001. Such findings also more generally exist alongside more general, 'consistent evidence … that overall earnings dispersion is lower where union membership is higher and collective bargaining more encompassing and/or more centralised/coordinated' (OECD, 2014, p 160), and further evidence that declines in union density have been the main factor leading to falls since the 1980s in the share of wages in national incomes (New Economics Foundation, 2014).

Discussion and conclusion

This chapter has revealed that across the developed world mechanisms of wage determination and their outcomes have been the subject of three overlapping and mutually reinforcing sets of developments. The first has been the pursuit of fiscally restrictive economic policies that have held back economic growth and recovery over the post-GFC period. The second has been the reform of wage-setting institutions through the placing of restrictions on the role of unions and collective bargaining in setting pay. The third has been almost universal downward trends in trade union membership, in both absolute and density terms and influence. Together, these changes, it has been noted, explain in large part why, in general, real-wage growth has been low (or declining) and wage inequality has been rising.

The nature and significance of the changes occurring in each of these areas have, however, varied across countries, as have the dynamics between them. Such variations have also existed alongside marked differences in domestic labour markets more generally, notably with regard to the degree of labour-market slack that exists and therefore the balance of power existing between buyers and sellers. These variations and differences in turn can be seen to lend weight to analyses that point to the need to recognize that, while the broad direction of policy travel has embodied a marked degree of commonality internationally, countries have exhibited differences with regard to the nature of the reforms they have introduced and the outcomes that have flowed from them.

More specifically, the chapter has lent weight to perspectives that accord recognition to the fact that although there has been a convergence around a neoliberal agenda (Baccaro and Howell, 2017), promoted by, among others, the EU Troika (Hermann, 2014), neoliberalism takes on many local forms and generates uneven outcomes (Peck, 2014). Its analysis therefore echoes those of authors who have raised doubts regarding the notion of a universal neoliberal trajectory and instead identified a more nuanced picture of divergence in European industrial relations flowing from variations in the strategies of institutions and actors, and their capacities to act as countervailing forces pushing against the neoliberal approach (Dolvik and Marginson, 2018). It has been found, for example, that national-level collective bargaining structures do not have the same capacity to resist intensified competition, financialization and the shift to service sector economies. In line with this, it has been found that countries with multi-employer bargaining structures and strong trade unions that can sustain the security of collective bargaining are better able to more actively resist such pressures (Muller et al, 2019). Meanwhile, it has been noted that countries not subject to bailouts from the Troika or IMF, such as Italy and Spain, have maintained a greater degree of discretion that has been shaped by the extent to which governments have been influenced by centre-left ideas (Picot and Tassinari, 2017).

More widely, the chapter has further lent weight to analyses that highlight how such divergences arise due to countries starting from different points, including with regard to the application of the principles of neoliberalism (Peck, 2014); variation in the degree of their exposure to the GFC and austerity; the distribution of power and resources between institutions and actors, as well as their varying capacities to act as countervailing forces pushing against austerity; the capacity of international institutions such as the EU and the IMF to shape collective bargaining in nation-states; and the ideologies predominant within individual nation-states (Frege and Kelly, 2013).

The three lines of change identified at the start of this section can furthermore be noted to not only contribute to an understanding of why wage growth has been poor and wage inequality has been increasing, but to simultaneously point to areas in which action is required if these trends are to be reversed. It is striking, for example, not to say remarkable, that studies undertaken by both the IMF and the OECD, long-term proponents of labour flexibility and deregulation, have drawn attention to the connection between declining union membership and collective bargaining coverage and rising wage inequality, and, in doing so, have effectively pointed to the detrimental effects of their own policies in this regard (OECD, 2011; Jaumotte and Buitron, 2015; Keune and Tomassetti, 2016).

Note

[1]   The 'Four Freedoms' were introduced under the original Treaty of Rome 1957 and involve the free movement of labour, the right of establishment, provision of services and the free movement of capital across EU member states.

References

Abramovitz, M. (2012) 'The feminization of austerity'. *New Labor Forum*, 21(1): 30–9.

Addison, J., Texeira, P., Pahnke, A. and Bellman, L. (2017) 'The demise of the model? The state of collective bargaining and worker representation in Germany'. *Economic and Industrial Democracy*, 38(2): 193–234.

Baccaro, L. and Howell, H. (2017) *Transformation: European Industrial Relations*. Cambridge: Cambridge University Press.

Bach, S. (2016) 'Britain: Contracting the state: public service employment relations in a period of crisis'. In: Bach, S. and Bordogna, L. (eds), *Public Service Management and Employment Relations in Europe*. London: Routledge, 136–63.

Bach, S. and Bordogna, L. (2013) 'Reframing public service employment relations: The impact of economic crisis and the new EU economic governance'. *European Journal of Industrial Relations*, 19(4): 279–94.

Bach, S. and Stroleny, A. (2014) 'Restructuring UK local government employment relations: pay determination and employee participation in tough times'. *Transfer*, 20(3) 343–56.

Bernaciak, M., Gumbrell-McCormick, R. and Hyman, R. (2014) *European Trade Unionism: from Crisis to Renewal?* Brussels: European Trade Union Institute.

Blanchflower, D. (2019) *Not Working: Where have all the Good Jobs Gone?* Princeton and Oxford: Princeton University Press.

Blanchflower, D. and Skidelsky, R. (2011) 'Cable's attempt to claim Keynes is well argued – but unconvincing'. *New Statesman*, January.

Blundell, R., Crawford, C. and Jin, W. (2014) 'What can wages and employment tell us about the UK's productivity puzzle?'. *The Economic Journal*, 124(576): 377–407.

Briskin, L. (2014) 'Austerity, union policy and gender equality bargaining'. *Transfer*, 20(1): 115–33.

Brown, W., Bryson, A. and Forth, J. (2009) 'Competition and the retreat from collective bargaining'. In: Brown, W., Bryson, A., Forth, J, and Whitefield, K. (eds), *The Evolution of the Modern Workplace*. Cambridge: Cambridge University Press, 22–47.

Cantin, E. (2012) 'The Politics of Austerity and the Conservative Offensive against US Public Sector Unions, 2008–2012'. *Relations Industrielles*, 67(4): 612–30.

Card, D., Lemieux, T. and Riddell, W. (2004) 'Unions and wage inequality'. *Journal of Labor Research*, 25(4): 519–62.

Collins, J. (2011) 'Theorizing Wisconsin's 2011 protests: Community-based unionism confronts accumulation by dispossession'. *American Ethnologist*, 39(1): 6–20.

Conley, H. and Page, M. (2018a) 'The good, the not so good and the ugly: Gender equality, equal pay and austerity in English local government'. *Work, Employment and Society*, 32(4): 789 –805.

Conley, H. and Page, M. (2018b) 'Revisiting Jewson and Mason: The politics of gender equality in UK local government in a cold climate'. *Gender, Work and Organisations*, 24(1): 7–19.

Craddock, E. (2017) 'Caring about and for the cuts: A case study of the gendered dimension of austerity and anti–austerity activism'. *Gender, Work and Organisation*, 24(1): 70–82.

Cullen, P. and Murphy, M.P. (2017) 'Gendered mobilizations against austerity in Ireland'. *Gender, Work and Organizations*, 24(1): 83–97.

Darlington, R. and Dobson, J. (2015) *The Conservative Government's Proposed Strike Ballot Thresholds: The Challenge to Trade Unions*. London: Institute of Employment Rights.

Delahaie, N., Vandekerckhove, S. and Vincent, C. (2015) 'Wages and collective bargaining systems in Europe during the crisis'. In: Van Guyes, G. and Schulten, T. (eds), *Wage Bargaining under the New European Economic Governance: Alternative Strategies for Inclusive Growth*. Brussels: European Trade Union Institute (ETUI), Brussels, 61–92.

Devinatz, V. (2012) 'The attack on US public sector unionism in the age of austerity'. *Labour Law Journal*, 63(1): 5–21.

Dolvik, J.E. and Marginson, P. (2018) 'Collective wage regulation in Northern Europe under strain: Multiple drivers of change and differing responses to them'. *European Journal of Industrial Relations*, 24(4): 321–39.

European Commission (2012) *Employment and Social Developments in Europe 2011*. European Commission. Directorate-General for Employment, Social Affairs and Inclusion, Brussels.

Evans, B. (2011) 'The politics of public sector wages: Ontario's social dialogue for austerity. *Socialist Studies*, 7(1/2), Spring/Fall: 171–90.

Fanelli, C. and Thomas, M.P. (2011) 'Austerity, competitiveness and neoliberalism redux: Ontario responds to the great recession'. *Socialist Studies*, 1(2), Spring/Fall, 141–70.

Fawcett Society (2012) *The Impact of Austerity on Women*. www.fawcettsociety.org.uk/wp-content/uploads/2013/02/The-Impact-of-Austerity-on-Women-19th-March-2012.pdf.

Frege, C. and Kelly, J. (2013) 'Theoretical perspectives on comparative employment relations'. In: Frege, C. and Kelly, J. (eds), *Comparative Employment Relations in the Global Economy*. London: Routledge, 8–26.

Glassner, V. and Keune, M. (2012) 'The crisis and social policy: The role of collective agreements', *International Labour Review*, 151(4): 351-375.

Granberg, M. and Nygren, K. (2017) 'Paradoxes of anti-austerity protest: Matters of neoliberalism, gender, and subjectivity in a case of collective resignation'. *Gender, Work and Organisation*, 24(1): 56–68.

Harvey, D. (2007) *A Brief History of Neoliberalism*. Oxford University Press, Oxford.

Hayes, L. and Moore, S. (2017) 'Care in a time of austerity: The electronic monitoring of homecare workers' time'. *Gender, Work and Organisations*, 24(4): 329–43.

Hermann, C. (2014) 'Structural adjustment and neoliberal convergence in labour markets and welfare: The impact of the crisis and austerity measures on European economic and social models'. *Competition and Change*, 18(2): 111–30.

Hyman, J. (2018) *Employee Voice and Participation: Contested Past, Troubled Present, Uncertain Future*. London: Routledge.

International Labour Organization (2018) *Global Wage Report 2018/19: What Lies Behind Gender Pay Gaps*. Geneva: International Labour Organization.

Jaumotte, F. and Buitron, C. (2015) *Inequality and Labour Market Institutions*. IMF Staff Discussion Note. https://www.imf.org/external/pubs/ft/sdn1514.pdf.

Kersley, B., Alpin, C., Forth, J., Bryson, A., Bewley, H., Dix, G. and Oxenbridge, S. (2006) *Inside the Workplace: Findings from the 2004 Workplace Employment Relations Survey*. London: Routledge.

Keune, M. (2015) 'The effects of the EU's assault on collective bargaining: Less governance capacity and more inequality'. *Transfer*, 21(4): 477–83.

Keune, M. and Tomassetti, P. (2016) *Wage (In)equalites and Collective Bargaining in Germany, Italy, the Netherlands, Slovakia and the UK*. https://moodle.adaptland.it/pluginfile.php/28248/mod_resource/content/1/newin_final_report.pdf.

Koeniger, W., Leonardi, M. and Nunziata, L. (2007) 'Labor market institutions and wage inequality'. *Industrial and Labor Relations Review*, 60(3): 340–56.

Lehndorff, S. (2009) *Before the Crisis, and Beyond: Collective Bargaining on Employment in Germany*. Geneva: International Labour Office.

Leisink, P. and Bach, S. (2014) 'Economic crisis and municipal public service employment: Comparing developments in seven EU member states'. *Transfer*, 20(3): 327–42.

Lewis, S., Anderson, D., Lyonette, C., Payne, N. and Wood, S. (2017) 'Public sector austerity cuts in Britain and the changing discourse of work–life balance'. *Work, Employment and Society*, 31(4): 586 –604.

Lombardo, E. (2017) 'The Spanish gender regime in the EU context: Changes and struggles in times of austerity'. *Gender, Work and Organization*, 24(1): 20–33.

Lopez-Andreu, M. and Rubery, J. (2018) 'Austerity and women's employment trajectories in Spain and the UK: A comparison of two flexible labour markets'. *Economic and Industrial Democracy*, doi: 10.1177/0143831X18760988.

Machin, S. (2016) 'Rising wage inequality, real wage stagnation and unions'. *Research in Labor Economics*, 43: 329–54.

McCann, L. (2013) 'Disconnected amid the networks and chains: employee detachment from company and union after offshoring'. *British Journal of Industrial Relations*, 52(2): 237–60

Meardi, G. (2012) 'Employment relations under external pressure: Italian and Spanish reforms in 2010–12'. Paper presented at the International Labour Process Conference, Stockholm, 27–29 March.

Mishel, L. (2012) *Unions, Inequality and Faltering Middle-Class Wages*. Washington, DC: Economic Policy Institute.

Muller, T., Vandaele, K. and Waddington, J. (2019) 'Conclusion: Towards an endgame'. In: Muller, T., Vandaele, K. and Waddington, J. (eds), *Collective Bargaining in Europe: Towards an Endgame: Volume III*. Brussels: European Trade Union Institute, 625–67.

New Economics Foundation (2014) *Working for the Economy: The Economic Case for Trade Unions*. London: New Economics Foundation.

OECD (Organisation for Economic Co-operation and Development) (2011) *Divided We Stand: Why Inequality Keeps Rising*. Paris: OECD.

OECD (2014) *OECD Employment Outlook 2014*. Paris: OECD.

OECD and Visser, J. (2016) ICTWSS data base (Institutional Characteristics of Trade Unions, Wage Setting, State Intervention and Social Pacts, 1960–2010), version 3.0, Amsterdam Institute for Advanced Labour Studies, Amsterdam.

Office for National Statistics (2017) *Is Pay Higher in the Public or Private Sectors?* https://www.ons.gov.uk/employmentandlabourmarket/peopleinwork/earningsandworkinghours/articles/ispayhigherinthepublicorprivatesector/2017-11-16.

Peck, J. (2012) 'Austerity urbanism: American cities under extreme economy'. *City*, 16: 621–50.

Peck, J. (2014) 'Pushing austerity: State failure, municipal bankruptcy and the crises of fiscal federalism in the USA'. *Cambridge Journal of Regions, Economy and Society*, 7: 17–44.

Picot, G. and Tassinari, A. (2017) 'All of one kind? Labour market reforms under austerity in Italy and Spain'. *Socio-Economic Review*, 15(2): 461–82.

Pollin, R. (2013) *Austerity Economics and the Struggle for the Soul of US Capitalism*. Working Paper Series, No 321. Political Economy Research Institute, University of Massachusetts, Amherst.

Pond, R. and Jacob, C. (2014) 'Countering European economic policies through meaningful European social dialogue on local and regional government'. *Transfer*, 20(3): 445–53.

Rocha, F. (2015) 'The new EU economic governance and its impact on the national collective bargaining systems'. *EPSU Collective Bargaining Conference 2015*, Brussels, 13 January.

Roche, W.K. and Teague, P. (2015) 'Antecedents of concession bargaining in the great recession: evidence from Ireland'. *Industrial Relations Journal*, 46(5): 434–45.

Rose, J. (2013) 'Austerity blues: public sector bargaining rights in the United States and Canada'. *Labour Law Journal*, 64(4): 189–97.

Rose, J. (2016) 'Constraints on public sector bargaining in Canada'. *Journal of Industrial Relations*, 58(1): 93–110.

Schnabel, C. (2013) 'Union membership and density: Some (not so) stylized facts and challenges'. *European Industrial Relations Journal*, 19(3): 255–72.

Schulten, T. and Muller, T. (2015) 'A new European interventionism? The impact of the new European economic governance on wages and collective bargaining'. In: Lehndorff, S (ed), *Divisive Integration. The Triumph of Failed Ideas in Europe – Revisited*. Brussels: European Union, 331–65.

Stiglitz, J.E. (2013) *Selected Works of Joseph E. Stiglitz: Volume II: Information and Economic Analysis: Applications to Capital, Labor, and Product Markets*. Oxford: Oxford University Press.

Waddington, J., Muller, T. and Vandaele, K. (2019) 'Setting the scene: Collective bargaining under neoliberalism'. In: Muller, T., Vandaele, K. and Waddington, J. (eds) *Collective Bargaining in Europe: Towards an Endgame: Volume I*. Brussels: European Trade Union Institute, 1–32.

Wanrooy, B., Bewley, H., Bryson, A., Forth, J., Freeth, S., Stokes, L. and Wood, S. (2013) *Employment Relations in the Shadow of Recession: Findings from the 2011 Workplace Employment Relations Study*. Basingstoke, Hampshire, Palgrave Macmillan.

Warren, T. and Lyonette, C. (2018) 'Good, bad and very bad part-time jobs for women? Re-examining the importance of occupational class for job quality since the 'great recession' in Britain'. *Work, Employment and Society*, 32(4): 747–67.

Winchester, D. and Bach, S. (1999) 'The transformation of British public service employment relations'. In: Bach, S., Bordogna, L., Della Rocha, G. and Winchester, D. (eds) *Public Service Employment Relations in Europe: Transformation, Modernization: Transformation, Modernization or Inertia?* Abingdon: Taylor & Francis, 22–55.

Wolf, M. (2011) 'How austerity has failed'. *New York Review of Books*, 11 July.

5

Privatization, Hybridization and Resistance in Contemporary Care Work

Pat Armstrong and Donna Baines

Clarke (2017, p 23) argues that, rather than a wholly new project, austerity is 'assembled anew in specific times and places, but in ways that draw on or at least try to mobilize – older stocks of knowledge and sentiment'. Privatization is one of these older stocks of knowledge and sentiment that have yet to be wholly actualized in most developed countries (Starr, 1987). Clarke (2017, p 26) argues further that it is helpful to think about the present as 'the accumulation of failure: failed, stalled, or incomplete hegemonic projects that try to combine economic, social, and political restructuring with the securing of popular consent to that project'. Privatization can be viewed as an incomplete hegemonic project, and a central aspect of neoliberalism that austerity has revisited with enthusiasm, once again trying to win popular consent to reduce and remove public entitlements and services. Although little evidence has been produced to back the claim, neoliberals have long argued that privatization provides cost savings, efficiency and greater accountability through increased competition and consumer choice (Yarrow, 1986; Kamerman and Kahn, 2014). These arguments have resurfaced boldly in the post-2008 global financial crisis (GFC) and current iteration of austerity.

Although privatization is often thought of as a singular phenomenon, this chapter will identify seven forms of overlapping and interwoven privatization. In the current era of austerity, privatization has been able to extend its reach through these integrated processes and, in some cases, operate almost by stealth as an overarching ideological force that legitimizes private market relations in places where it once would have been thought to be contrary to a public sector ethic of entitlement and equity. This is a growing dynamic across many public and non-profit/voluntary services and organizations. Services and assets are privatized in their entirety, as well as piece by piece through the contracting out of various aspects of the organization such as human resources management, cleaning, security, management itself, specialists, consultants and the use of temporary workers hired through for-profit agencies. As Armstrong et al (1997) argued earlier in the era of neoliberalism, among political economists, private and public are increasingly not viewed as 'dichotomous, readily separable entities. Rather, the nature, and representation, of either private or public are constantly being constructed not only by states and by the search for profit, but also by the individual and collective struggles of citizens' (Armstrong et al, 1997, p 3).

This chapter will briefly discuss seven forms of privatization in the provision of long-term residential or nursing home care for older people in Ontario, Canada and in the UK. Although differences exist, the examples we present are broadly representative. We use this example because of the existing high demand for care for older adults, which is anticipated to increase in the light of shifting demographics in the global North, and because this public service illustrates austerity effects and processes that apply to many contexts and settings. We also use this example to underscore gendered and racialized effects, as 80 per cent of the workers are women, as are the majority of nursing home residents, volunteers and family visitors (Armstrong and Armstrong, 2019). The workforce is also increasingly racialized in many jurisdictions, including in Canada, where one third of the workers identify as women of colour (Armstrong and Armstrong, 2019), including migrant care workers who are regulated under the same immigration legislation discussed in Chapter 6 in this collection.

This chapter introduces the seven forms of privatization and analyses them in order to expose their ideological, neoliberal nature and to provide ways to resist the kind of mystification that undermines democratic control. The chapter ends with examples and discussion of resistance.

Seven forms of privatization

1: Privatization of ownership

When people think about privatization, they often think about private ownership. Nursing homes in much of the global North have been a mix of public, non-profit/charitable and for-profit ownership (Healy, 2002; Choiniere et al, 2016). Historically, in Canada, most of the for-profits have been small homes owned by families or professionals, although, as is discussed in Chapter 7, large, multinational, financialized, for-profit chains are now the dominant forms of for-profit nursing homes. Today these four types of nursing homes are all funded at provincial level through the same formula, regardless of ownership. However, the competitive bidding process, combined with the complexity of regulations in relation to making bids and operating nursing homes, favours the large international chains that now dominate in this sector. These chains are increasingly global in reach (see Chapter 7) and are prepared to quickly sell, move or close nursing homes in the interests of profit making. As such, they have no connection to the communities in which the homes are based, nor to the residents or employees, placing quality and continuity of care in jeopardy.

Similarly, in the UK, the business failure in 2019 of two major nursing home chains, Southern Cross and Four Seasons Healthcare, left 31,000 residents at risk of losing their homes and care, and left thousands of employees without work (Armstrong and Armstrong, 2019; Rowland, 2019). Currently, around 30 per cent of nursing homes in the UK are owned by overseas investors who view them as a source of profit making and who, as Rowland (2019, p 2) argues, 'view them as assets for extracting large sums in the form of interest payments, rent and profit'. Rowland argues further that, 'As things stand, the rights of hedge funds and private equity investors to extract rent and profit from the care home sector are given greater priority than the rights of older people to a secure home at the end of their lives' (Rowland, 2019, p 3). In addition to the stress and insecurity introduced into the lives of those living in nursing homes, as will be discussed in point 6, the privatization of nursing home care to overseas, financialized chains simultaneously off-shores decision making and precludes democratic input or control.

In response to the significantly higher numbers of verified complaints and scandals in for-profit homes, governments, especially in North America and the UK, have introduced increased regulations, inspections and reporting mechanisms (Lloyd et al, 2014; Harrington et al, 2016). This additional regulation creates more complex bureaucracy and less choice for workers, and makes it difficult for smaller nursing homes to remain in compliance and in operation. Due to economies of scale, large firms have systems in place to deal with bureaucracy, and this gives them an advantage in terms of contract compliance, or at least the appearance of contract compliance. It also makes it is easier for them to handle attempts to limit their negative practices and places them at an advantage in competitive bidding processes.

As is discussed later (point 4), many non-profit, charitable and municipal homes contract out many in-house services to private companies. These services are often central aspects of the organization, such as dietary, laundry, cleaning, security, human resources and even entire management teams. Organizations also frequently sub-contract with private, temporary nursing and care-worker agencies to fill unexpected gaps in staffing and scheduled vacancies such as annual leave and statutory holidays. These many forms privatization within the auspices of public and non-profit nursing homes blur the lines between for-profit and non-profit, making it more and more difficult to assess the impact of profit taking or to determine the differences between private, non-profit and public, because they are increasingly intermeshed. Thus, privatization becomes a familiar and ever-present aspect of nursing home operations and care delivery.

2: Privatization of costs

A second form of privatization relates to costs. The example of Ontario is instructive in terms of how costs are quietly transferred to the individual. In Ontario, the government sets the rates that nursing home residents pay for their accommodation. The rates are set in this way so that admission can be largely based on care needs rather than on ability to buy. A private room costs more, but a basic room should be within the reach of even the poorest Canadians in receipt of old-age benefits and entitlements.

However, nursing homes can and do charge additional fees for services like physiotherapy, transport to services, laundry, activities and so forth, creating inequities between residents, and privatizing costs. Moreover, an increasing number of families pay for private care workers to provide care for their loved one within the nursing home, supplementing the increasingly tightly quantified and largely medical care provided to residents, and making up for the lack of staff to provide social care. This dynamic is another process of privatizing costs and creating inequalities between residents. It is also a process of normalizing the growing inequity that accompanies privatization, as the services listed are viewed as 'extras' rather than essentials and thus are not entitlements but available only to those with the ability pay. As Evans and McBride (2017) note, austerity is a mechanism for lowering expectations and encouraging the population to accept lean services rather than to demand full entitlement. In this case, privatization works hand in glove with austerity to foster the acceptance of inadequate resources and people's adaptation to them (see Hitchen, 2016; Clarke, 2017).

3: Privatization by stealth: the failure to provide enough spaces in publicly funded care

The real differences in cost shifting from the public to the private sector comes from another form of privatization, the failure to provide enough spaces in publicly funded care, or a process that has been called privatization by stealth (Macarov, 2003). As Macarov (2003, p 71) explains, privatization 'is sometimes attained not by outright sales but by deliberately allowing services to run down, by erecting barriers to access, by withholding information and by making receiving benefits so difficult and demeaning that the public has little alternative but to turn to the private sector'. When insufficient services are available in the public and non-profit sector, service users are produced for the private market (Baines, 2004b). The shortage of beds in the public and non-profit systems also results in less employment opportunities in these systems relative to those available in the private sector. Thus, care workers are also produced for the private nursing homes, shifting the workforce from public sector wages and conditions to the lower-waged, increasingly precarious and less desirable conditions found in private sector nursing home employment.

Some nursing homes in Ontario have waiting lists of up to three years, forcing those who can afford the costs into what are usually called retirement homes (Health Share Services Ontario, 2017). Waiting lists and waiting times are expected to grow significantly in coming years (D'Mello, 2019). These retirement homes are mostly owned by for-profit chains and can cost as much as three times more than a nursing home, without providing any nursing care as part of that cost. Women account for 80 per cent of nursing home residents, and the costs charged by retirement homes are well beyond the reach of many women or anyone earning the minimum wage (Armstrong and Armstrong, 2019). Given the shortage of public and non-profit nursing home beds (producing clients and workers for the private sector), and the guaranteed government payment, private retirement and nursing homes are a very attractive investment for for-profit companies.

4: Privatization of management: the application of for-profit management strategies to non-profit and public homes

Another form of privatization that is almost as invisible as privatization by stealth is the application of for-profit management strategies to the remaining non-profit and public homes. Rather than committing to the public good or equity, management models such as New Public Management (NPM) apply business principles and business means to organizing non-profit and public sector care work (Evans et al, 2005). The application of private market models such as NPM to social care spheres such as nursing homes is a clear example of Denniss's (2015) argument that, in the era of austerity, governments have accepted the unproven tenet that technocratic, financial accounting and market rationalization practices can resolve existing social, economic and organizational challenges and, in the process, can generate considerable cost savings. In sync with the private market logics of cost rationalization and profit making, NPM tends to standardize care work, with the goal of improving cost efficiency and overall effectiveness (Evans et al, 2005). Standardization permits work to speed up, with care workers required to follow tightly scripted and ordered tasks and to document the meeting of performance targets and outcome metrics (O'Neill, 2015). Baines (2004b) characterizes this change in the public/non-profit ethos as pro-market/non-market, as the services more closely align with private market values and practices, further extending the market's reach and legitimacy in areas of life where it once would have seemed abhorrent. The services remain nominally non-market in that, although they rationalize with an eye to continually cutting costs, they do not produce a surplus or profit.

These shifts in how the work is performed and measured to be successful (in meeting targets and outcome measures, rather than in building open-ended, hard-to-quantify, care relationships) simultaneously set the conditions wherein workers have less and less space in which to build and sustain care relationships with residents and feel compelled to undertake unpaid work in order to complete their care tasks and maintain their sense of personal and professional integrity (for further discussion of this, see point 5) (Baines and Daly, 2015). Standardization implies a standard patient as well as a standard worker, neither of which applies in care. Employers expect workers to provide care labour beyond their paid hours, and workers often expect the same from themselves. The expectation is gendered, mirroring the naturalized view of women as endlessly caring, regardless of pay or conditions. This unpaid care work is simultaneously a form of resistance against the uncaring of the employer and the larger society (Baines, 2004a; 2016). Workers' responses to this form of privatization represent a complex, gendered process of adapting to austerity through self-sacrifice in the hopes of better times at some undefined point in the future (Hitchen, 2016).

5: The privatization of responsibility: responsibilization and the shift from public paid work to unpaid work

Another form of privatization relates to responsibilization, or shifting the responsibility and the work from the public paid sector to the unpaid work of care workers, family and community members – work that in all three cases is usually taken on by women (Budlender, 2010). In terms of the unpaid work of workers in the nursing home, as Baines (2004a, 2016) has explained, the female-majority workers take on unpaid work to make up for the gaps in care resulting from underfunding and tightly Taylorized work (see also Daly and Armstrong, 2016). The standardization of work under NPM generally speeds it up and focuses almost exclusively on tasks related to basic biomedical rather than social care, leaving little room for the open-ended processes and relationships that most people view as the bedrock of care (Hussein and Manthorpe, 2014). Workers frequently argue that they undertake unpaid work in their workplaces because they want to live in tandem with their personal and professional values of care and feel that they have to 'give back' and do 'those little extras' for the residents (Baines, 2016), which frequently includes hair washing, manicures, walks outdoors, the purchase of toiletries such as shampoo, reading aloud, playing card or board games and listening to stories of past lives, hopes and losses. In the past, these tasks were generally seen as aspects of paid work in nursing homes, but they are now excluded from fast-paced, task-based, outcome-documented work days. Nursing homes frequently expect this and other unpaid work from their staff, claiming that they could not make them go home even if they wanted to (Baines, 2016).

As Daly and Armstrong (2016) have shown, the retreat of the state has meant that family members and friends are expected to help nursing home residents eat, to clean their clothes, to brush their teeth, to take them for walks and to 'volunteer' to do all kinds of work for other residents. Noting the growing prevalence of nurses undertaking unpaid care work for family members in institutional settings and in their own homes, St-Amant et al (2014) argue that this is a professionalizing of unpaid familial care as women in the caring professions are asked to provide the care no longer provided by the state. In addition, as discussed earlier, an increasing number of families are hiring private care workers to work with their family members in nursing homes. Here too, most of the low-wage, precarious, usually informal care work falls to women, and most often to immigrant and/or racialized women.

6: *The privatization of decision making*

A sixth form of privatization relates to decision making. In the context of austerity and neoliberalism, more and more decision making takes place behind closed doors at the level of government or within private businesses on which there is no requirement for transparency or shared decision making (Evans and McBride, 2017; Giroux, 2018). The public is frequently denied information on services paid for from the public purse, on the grounds that confidentiality is necessary to ensure competition among the corporations and, allegedly, to ensure that austere funding is spent in the best way possible. Private companies, then, are completely free to exclude the public from any form of decision making, and instead to privately decide the content and quality of the services provided. As is confirmed by an extensive literature, this removal and delimiting of public participation and elected officials in decision making is an additional aspect of the erosion of liberal democracy (Vázquez-Arroyo, 2008; Jessop, 2016; Clarke, 2017; Evans and McBride, 2017; Giroux, 2018). As already mentioned in point 1, this erosion takes on new dimensions in the privatization of nursing home care to overseas, financialized chains, as it outsources decision making and further removes it from any form of democratic input or control, instead leaving decision making in the so-called invisible hand of the market.

7: *The privatization of service: service users as consumers and individual choice based on the ability to buy*

Finally, there is the shift in discourse that moves society away from a notion of shared responsibility, democratic decision making and the idea that the public sector operates according to a logic of service to all. Instead, citizen-service users become citizen-consumers (Clarke, 2007) and individual choice based on the ability to buy becomes the common-sense notion of care. In nursing homes, this logic deepens inequities, with those with the ability to pay able to access needed services that are seen as 'extras', such as physiotherapy, dental care, laundry and dry-cleaning options, activities and excursions outside the nursing home, menu choices and so forth. As noted previously, it also includes the capacity of nursing home residents or their families to hire private care workers to supplement tightly rationed nursing home care. Although this aspect of privatization has a long history (Armstrong et al, 1997; Clarke, 2007), it is resurrected and finds new salience in today's austere context of underfunding, rigidly rationalized work processes and reduced scope for democratic input or participation.

Resistance and conclusion

Although the first form of privatization discussed in this chapter, private ownership, is commonly thought to be the only or main form of privatization, austerity analyses can be more incisive and specific, with a greater awareness of the complexity and multiplexity of the forms of privatization operating within formerly public and non-profit spaces. Although privatization and austerity have been an ongoing presence through the various phases and stages of neoliberalism, Clarke (2017, p 21) argues that earlier versions of austerity did not seem 'to carry the symbolic political charge of the current deployment'. Bach would likely agree, as he has argued that the current round of austerity represents 'the final straw for public sector restructuring' (Bach, 2016, p 11). Operating in tandem with the radical downsizing and degradation of the public sector are the seven forms of privatization discussed in this chapter. In terms of the illustrative example (nursing home care) analysed here, all seven forms of privatization are active, although there is no evidence that costs to governments decline under for-profit ownership, nor that services improve (Hussein and Manthorpe, 2014). Indeed, substantial evidence suggests the reverse seems to be the case (Lloyd et al, 2014; Choiniere et al, 2016), and it is clear that money going to profit is not going to care.

In the example discussed in this chapter, gendered effects were clearly present in the impacts on female-majority workers, volunteers, residents and family care givers. The observation that privatization has gendered effects echoes earlier research that concluded that austerity itself is also highly gendered (Rafferty, 2015; Rubery, 2015). The gendered effects of privatization seem inseparable from the hegemonic project of reassembling failed or incomplete economic, social and political restructuring projects (Clarke, 2017), and the general lowering of expectations and acceptance that there is no alternative to the market and neoliberalism.

However, there is resistance in the sphere of care for older people, and some of it has been successful. For example, in Norway a coalition of community organizations and unions has been successful not only in preventing further privatization of ownership but also in reversing some of it. They achieved this through old-fashioned education strategies, including education about the differences among forms of ownership, and especially between small, individually owned homes and those owned by corporations. Their campaign needed slogans and short messages as a way into the debate and as a way of educating the broader public. It gathered simple stories and easy-to-understand arguments that provided concrete examples to show the consequences of this transformation in ownership. The purpose was to change the discourse and to create a new space by clearly distinguishing among forms of ownership. The campaign developed a new term, 'welfare profiteers', and used it successfully in election campaigns

On a smaller and more local scale, an Ontario home had contracted out the food provision to Aramark, a US-based multinational corporation. The home was part of a public complex that included a hospital and medical clinics. Although the kitchen remained on the premises and some staff kept their jobs, the pay and benefits declined, and so did the quality of the food. Combined resistance from the unions, family and resident councils as well as from the hospital board was successful in bringing the food services back in-house, and now the kitchen is winning awards for quality. In another Ontario example, a regional council decided to oppose privatization by constructing their own public, sustainable alternative. The council built a complex that included a nursing home, apartments for assisted living and an apartment building for independent living. Charging somewhat below market rates to those in the apartment building allowed the council to cross-subsidize provision, while offering a wide range of services and amenities to everyone. Staff were unionized and decision making was transparent.

So, the message is clear. Although privatization can seem to be an unstoppable aspect of austerity and neoliberalism, resistance, involving all those involved in the care endeavour, can be an effective strategy to halt or reverse privatization, even against huge, international, financialized nursing home chains. While all seven kinds of privatization are detrimental to nursing home care and other forms of human services, the message is don't mourn – organize.

References

Armstrong, H., Armstrong, P. and Connelly, M.P. (1997) 'Introduction: The many forms of privatization'. *Studies in Political Economy*, 53(1): 3–9.

Armstrong, P. and Armstrong, H. (2019) 'Privatizing care: Setting the stage'. In: Armstrong, P. and Armstrong, H. (eds), *The Privatization of Care: The Case of Nursing Homes*. New York: Routledge, 4–19.

Bach, S. (2016) 'Deprivileging the public sector workforce: Austerity, fragmentation and service withdrawal in Britain'. *The Economic and Labour Relations Review*, 27(1): 11–28.

Baines, D. (2004a) 'Caring for nothing: Work organization and unwaged labour in social services'. *Work, Employment and Society*, 18(2): 267–95.

Baines, D. (2004b) 'Pro-market, non-market: The dual nature of organizational change in social services delivery'. *Critical Social Policy*, 24(1): 5–29.

Baines, D. (2016) 'Moral projects and compromise resistance: Resisting uncaring in nonprofit care work'. *Studies in Political Economy*, 97(2): 124–42.

Baines, D. and Daly, T. (2015). 'Resisting regulatory rigidities: Lessons from front-line care work'. *Studies in Political Economy*, 95(1): 137–60.

Budlender, D. (2010). 'What do time use studies tell us about unpaid care work? Evidence from seven countries'. In: Budlender, D. (ed), *Time Use Studies and Unpaid Care Work*. New York: Routledge, 23–67.

Choiniere, J.A., Doupe, M., Goldmann, M., Harrington, C., Jacobsen, F.F., Lloyd, L., Rootham, M. and Szebehely, M. (2016). 'Mapping nursing home inspections & audits in six countries'. *Ageing International*, 41(1): 40–61.

Clarke, J. (2007) 'Citizen-consumers and public service reform: At the limits of neoliberalism?' *Policy Futures in Education*, 5(2): 239–48.

Clarke, J. (2017) 'Articulating austerity and authoritarianism: Re-imagining moral economics?' In: Evans, B. and McBride, S. (eds) *Austerity: The Lived Experience*. Toronto: University of Toronto Press, 20–39.

Daly, T. and Armstrong, P. (2016) 'Liminal and invisible long-term care labour: Precarity in the face of austerity'. *Journal of Industrial Relations*, 58(4): 473–90.

Denniss, R. (2015). 'Spreadsheets of power'. *The Monthly*, April, 28–32.

D'Mello, C. (2019) '"It will get worse": Ontario faces long-term health care crunch'. *CTV Toronto News*. https://toronto.ctvnews.ca/it-will-get-worse-ontario-faces-long-term-health-care-crunch-1.4662243. Accessed 31 October 2019.

Evans, B. and McBride, S. (2017) 'Austerity. The lived experience'. In: Evans, B. and McBride, S. (eds) *Austerity: The Lived Experience*. Toronto: University of Toronto Press, 3–16.

Evans, B., Richmond, T. and Shields, J. (2005) 'Structuring neoliberal governance: The nonprofit sector, emerging new modes of control and the marketisation of service delivery'. *Policy and Society*, 24(1): 73–97.

Giroux, H.A. (2018) *Terror of Neoliberalism: Authoritarianism and the Eclipse of Democracy*. London: Routledge.

Harrington, C., Armstrong, H., Halladay, M., Havig, A.K., Jacobsen, F.F., MacDonald, M., Panos, J., Pearsall, K., Pollock, A. and Ross, L. (2016) 'Comparison of nursing home financial transparency and accountability in four locations'. *Ageing International*, 41(1): 17–39.

Health Share Services Ontario (2017) 'Long-term care wait times and waitlists'. https://hssontario.ca/important-links/long-term-care-wait-times-and-waitlists. Accessed 31 October 2019.

Healy, J. (2002) 'The care of older people: Australia and the United Kingdom'. *Social Policy & Administration*, 36(1): 1–19.

Hitchen, E. (2016). 'Living and feeling the austere'. *New Formations*, 87(87), 102–18.

Hussein, S. and Manthorpe, J. (2014) 'Structural marginalisation among the long-term care workforce in England: Evidence from mixed-effect models of national pay data'. *Ageing & Society*, 34(1): 21–41.

Jessop, B. (2016) 'Territory, politics, governance and multispatial metagovernance'. *Territory, Politics, Governance*, 4(1): 8–32.

Kamerman, S.B. and Kahn, A.J. (eds) (2014) *Privatization and the Welfare State*. Princeton, NJ: Princeton University Press.

Lloyd, L., Banerjee, A., Harrington, C., Jacobsen, F. and Szebehely, M. (2014) 'It is a scandal! Comparing the causes and consequences of nursing home media scandals in five countries'. *International Journal of Sociology and Social Policy*, 34(1–2): 2–18.

Macarov, D. (2003) *What the Market does to People: Privatization, Globalization, and Poverty*. Atlanta: Clarity Press.

O'Neill, L. (2015) 'Regulating hospital nurses and social workers: Propping up an efficient, lean health care system'. *Studies in Political Economy*, 95(2): 115–36.

Rafferty, A. (2015) 'The UK recovery, austerity and economic "rebalancing": Implications for women's employment'. *Travail, genre et sociétés*, 33(1): 149–56.

Rowland, D. (2019) 'Corporate care home collapse and "light touch" regulation: a repeating cycle of failure'. British Politics and Policy at LSE blog. https://blogs.lse.ac.uk/politicsandpolicy/corporate-care-homes/. Accessed 15 July 2020.

Rubery, J. (2015). 'Austerity and the future for gender equality in Europe'. *International Law Review*, 68(4): 715–41.

St-Amant, O., Ward-Griffin, C., Brown, J.B., Martin-Matthews, A., Sutherland, N., Keefe, J. and Kerr, M.S. (2014) 'Professionalizing familial care: Examining nurses' unpaid family care work'. *Advances in Nursing Science*, 37(2): 117–31.

Starr, P. (1987) 'The limits of privatization'. In: Hanke, S. (ed), *Prospects for Privatisation. Proceedings of the Academy of Political Science*, 36(3): 124–37.

Vázquez-Arroyo, A.Y. (2008) 'Liberal democracy and neoliberalism: A critical juxtaposition'. *New Political Science*, 30(2): 127–59.

Yarrow, G. (1986) 'Privatization in theory and practice'. *Economic Policy*, 1(2): 323–64.

PART III

Case Studies of Austerity in the Private, Public and Nonprofit Sectors

6

Non-Citizenship at Work: Labour Flexibility Behind the Counter in Western Canada

Geraldina Polanco

> How one is identified shapes how one is positioned within global capitalism. The accumulation of capital continues to take place through the social and legal differentiation of labour. (Sharma, 2006, p 29)

Immigration laws operate as increasingly central instruments of discipline and control, with significant impacts on how work is organized (Anderson, 2010) and how access to substantive rights is granted or denied. Many countries have revived 'guest worker' schemes because they are said to promote mutually beneficial outcomes,[1] yet labelling the subjects of these schemes 'temporary migrant workers (TMWs)', 'foreign workers', or more generally 'non-citizens' contributes to profound vulnerabilities for migrants at work. This chapter analyses the role of immigration controls in furthering labour flexibility and worker vulnerability in Canada and the way that this flexibility and vulnerability dovetail with austerity.

Non-citizenship is an uneven and contingent category, with social locations amplifying or ameliorating a migrant's experience of precariousness (Fudge and Tham, 2017, p 4). Research shows that high-end migrant professionals and consultants generally do not experience significant disadvantage as non-citizens; however, this designation does disadvantage those who are differentiated as low-skilled 'non-citizens' (Sharma, 2006; Goldring and Landolt, 2013). Indeed, 'state-defined legal status categories establish configurations of rights for people occupying these categories' (Bosniak, 2006, p 3), and the rights of those positioned as outside their boundaries are rationed or limited, including rights at work and in the labour market (Anderson, 2010). In addition to a normative political discourse that criminalizes migrants and/or sees them as problems to be 'managed' (Munck, 2008), regulations governing work and citizenship increasingly intersect, generating new and compounding insecurities, with the form of labour precarity depending on the specific immigration controls and labour regulation. This chapter explores how features of a new labour regime in Canada in the era of austerity, and the increased presence of 'temporary migrant workers' in the quick-service restaurant industry, promote increased labour flexibility and exacerbate migrant workers' vulnerability. Migrant workers face unique challenges, distinct from those of their domestic counterparts, and with their growing presence in low-wage Canadian worksites, the need to organize at the intersection of work and citizenship has become an urgent project.

Canada's Temporary Foreign Worker Program and the diversification of fast-food worksites

Canada is widely regarded in the global imagination as a country of permanent migrant settlement. In reality, however, Canada has a long history of patrolling its nation-state boundaries along social lines and relying on temporary labour schemes to address purported labour-market pressures. Moreover, while Canada once used to grant permanent residency to the majority of those who migrated to its land (with notable exclusions that are discussed later), it is no longer as 'welcoming' or generous in extending permanent residency status.[2] This is particularly the case in recent years with the expansion of its Temporary Foreign Worker Program (TFWP).

Canada's TFWP, an umbrella programme that encompasses all temporary labour migration to Canada, was introduced in 1973. Historically, the programme was leveraged to fill positions in the top tiers of the labour market, including for doctors, engineers, and university professors. Those recruited in such high-skilled streams have generally enjoyed institutionalized pathways to transition from temporary to permanent status. In contrast, for 'low-skilled' occupations, the TFWP has primarily been reserved for the agricultural and domestic caregiving sectors. These streams are marked by notable exclusions and restrictions from formal membership in the polity. Agricultural workers have been recruited through the Seasonal Agricultural Workers Program (SAWP) since 1966, while domestic caregivers have been streamed through the Live-in Caregiver Program (LCP), the Caregiver Program and now the Home Child Care Provider Pilot and Home Support Worker Pilot since 1992, 2014 and 2019, respectively.

A pronounced shift occurred in 2002 when Canada introduced what is popularly referred to as the 'Low-Skilled Pilot'. In this new stream, employers who can establish a labour need can recruit workers transnationally as temporary contract labour for any occupation classified as 'low-skilled' under the federal government's National Occupation Classification System. Despite the programme's slow start (in 2002, only 2,145 workers were recruited under the Low-Skilled Pilot), by 2007 it had grown in popularity as a way to secure staff in a host of occupations – as hotel cleaners, manual labourers, food-counter attendants and so on (ESDC, 2014). Indeed, as Figure 6.1 and Table 6.1 show, there has been a steady increase in 'lower-skilled' workers labouring under this stream, such that by 2012 they were outpacing those working under Canada's long-standing Live-In Caregiver Program. While a 2014 moratorium on the food services sector abated these flows,[3] in December 2016 the moratorium was lifted. Continued lobbying efforts suggest that, once the policy environment becomes more favourable, Canada will once again see a steady increase in workers recruited to fill a host of low-waged occupations. Viewed over time, then, there has been a steady increase of people in Canada with less than full citizenship status working in the bottom tiers of the Canadian labour market.

The increased presence of migrant workers with less than full citizenship status – what Goldring and Landolt (2013) refer to as 'precarious legal status' – is a prime example of the broader shift to precarious work, wherein risk has been consistently downloaded from employers onto individual workers, to the benefit of corporations and capital accumulation (Anderson, 2010). The growing reliance on migrant workers is also entirely consistent with the shift towards austerity in Canada. An austerity agenda aims to reduce public expenditures and expectations while simultaneously increasing government support for private business. This often entails cuts to social entitlements and the public provisions available to the polity (Chapter 1, this volume). Legally defining migrant workers as 'non-citizens' (and hence as not belonging to the nation-state) advances this austerity agenda, as these workers are often denied access to many publicly funded support systems that are otherwise available to citizens and permanent residents (McLaughlin and Hennebry, 2013). Publicly funded immigrant settlement services, for example, are key to the integration

Figure 6.1: Low–wage flows

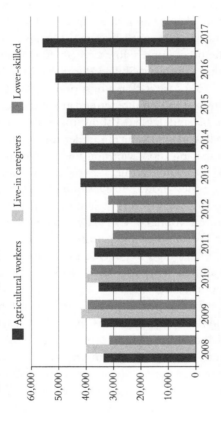

Table 6.1: Temporary migrant workers with labour–market impact assessment

Labour stream	2008	2009	2010	2011	2012	2013	2014	2015	2016	2017	Total	%
Agricultural workers	33,586	34,512	35,352	36,883	38,255	41,878	45,243	46,802	50,934	55,569	419,014	41.34
Live–in caregivers	39,982	41,719	39,651	36,488	28,494	24,057	23,239	20,457	16,880	11,676	282,643	27.88
Lower–skilled	31,528	39,359	38,104	29,863	31,820	38,638	40,924	32,010	17,987	11,805	312,038	30.78
Total	105,096	115,590	113,107	103,234	98,569	104,573	109,406	99,269	85,801	79,050	1,013,695	

Data source: IRCC (2017)

of newcomers but often formally denied to those labelled temporary, and have increasingly borne cuts to funding under federal and provincial austerity policies.

The social constitution of temporary migrant flows and the accompanying weakened regulations and protections are important dynamics in the reorganization of globalized worksites. Research shows that the shift towards temporary, low-wage labour schemes is associated with increasingly gendered and racialized flows (Trumper and Wong, 2010; Wang and Zong, 2014), with low-skilled flows starting to outpace high-skilled flows in Canada. By the end of 2016, there were only 20,334 high-skilled workers with a valid work permit in Canada, compared to 30,590 in the low-skilled category (IRCC, 2016). With respect to the racialized nature of flows, from 2007 to 2016 the top two countries of citizenship for those with temporary work permits in Canada were the Philippines and Mexico, except in 2015, when Guatemala slightly outpaced Mexico by 645 workers. Women have also tended to be concentrated in low-skilled occupations; in 2016, only 4,458 female workers in Canada were on a valid work permit in a high-skilled occupation on 31 December, compared to 12,762 women with valid work permits in a low-skilled occupation (IRCC, 2016).

Fast-food flows reflect these broader trends. As my research has documented, in Canada's two most western provinces (British Columbia and Alberta), Canada's leading fast-food corporation, Tim Hortons, sought to recruit almost 75 per cent of its temporary migrant workforce from the Philippines, with Mexico and India as the distant runners-up at approximately 4 per cent each (Polanco, 2016; 2017). These new flows are altering work and employment conditions in the quick-service restaurant industry, and, consistent with austerity agendas, are further weakening regulations and protections and leading to increased precarity.

Fast-food work in a neoliberal economy

'McJobs' are said to represent everything that is wrong with low-wage, service sector work (Schlosser, 2002, p 4). Employment in the bottom tiers of the service economy is generally part-time, low-status and low-wage, with few employment benefits and significant insecurity (Newman, 2000; Royle and Towers, 2002). Fast-food restaurants are among the most poorly remunerated niches in the economy; only migrant farm workers consistently earn lower hourly wages in the US (Royle, 2010, p 254). Unionization rates in fast-food sites are low, and there are limited prospects for upward mobility (Reiter, 2002). High surveillance, extreme routinization of the labour process, employee scripting, and a fast pace of work guided by the principles of Taylorism and Fordism typify a day behind the counter. The work is boring and repetitive, and employees have limited control over the labour process (Royle, 2010). Even for those fortunate enough to secure full-time employment (which is in itself rare), most still live on or near the poverty line (Allegretto et al, 2013). Moreover, while fast-food work is often portrayed as an opportunity for entry-level staff, in many cases it entraps a wide range of working people in poverty; they are working for survival, not just extra spending money. Not surprisingly, staff turnover in this sector is notoriously high, with some scholars citing levels from 150 to 400 per cent (Leidner, 1993; Reiter, 2002; Schlosser, 2002). In other words, only those with few other options in the labour market work in fast-food restaurants.

With the sector's poverty-level wages and poor working conditions, fast-food employers have long drawn from vulnerable segments of local labour markets to staff their worksites. Depending on the local context, the social constitution of the workforce might vary, to include women, youth, (recent) immigrants, inner-city residents, racialized people and ageing populations (Newman, 2000; Royle, 2010). In some regions of the US, workers with undocumented status often fill such positions, while in regions like Canada it is youth, ageing women and recent immigrants, more so than migrant workers, who make up a large proportion of the urban fast-food workforce. In regions where migration is scarce, the workforce is notably less racialized and might include more youth, students, women or ageing populations. Irrespective of their specific qualities, it is those with few other options in the labour market who make up the bulk of fast-food workers. This suggests that a marginalized, domestic labour force is available to employers, although some, like Tim Hortons, may prefer a migrant workforce. These dynamics are discussed further later in the chapter.

While mobile industries like manufacturing have long 'gone global' by decentralizing and respatializing the labour process to the global South in the pursuit of profits (Collins, 2003; Salzinger, 2003), this has generally not been considered feasible for 'immobile' occupations. Instead, employers in grocery stores and fast-food establishments have drawn from marginalized segments of local labour pools to staff their worksites. With the inclusion of the Low-Skilled Pilot in Canada's TFWP, employers in previously 'immobile' sectors can now figuratively 'relocate' to global labour pools and recruit migrant workers through transnational importation. Multinational corporations like McDonald's and Tim Hortons take advantage of the TFWP to resolve long-standing human resource challenges (such as high turnover and the perceived limited motivation of workers), using it as a business model to meet corporate ends. They are 'going global', recruiting from countries like the Philippines and Mexico through a state-regulated temporary migrant worker programme. Employers have thus been able to secure a relatively permanent workforce, with their preferred worker qualities, at domestically low wages (Polanco, 2016; 2017). Under the terms of their visas, migrant workers have no or little mobility, thus creating a stable workforce in a sector with notoriously high turnover.

Fast-food organizing and the challenge of non-citizenship behind the counter

The fast-food sector is widely recognized as among the most poorly paid, low-status, fast-paced, boring and at times dangerous employment niches, with minimal fringe benefits and low union representation. Significant efforts have thus been made to organize workers in this employment niche, especially as the number of people constituting the ranks of the working poor continues to grow. As Chun (2009, p 1) contends, 'low-paid service workers – many of whom are immigrants, people of color, and women – demonstrate that building power from the margins is not only possible but *pivotal* to the future of workers and their collective organizations in the twenty-first century' (emphasis in original). Given the sheer number of those employed in what is now a predominantly service (and not manufacturing) economy, it is no longer possible to overlook these workers in favour of organizing more privileged segments of the working class. It is also vital to think through what 'workers and their collective organisations' might look like. Indeed, while unions once regarded women, recent immigrants and racialized populations as 'unorganizable', the future of the labour movement now depends on the ability to mobilize these segments of the workforce and organize creative initiatives.

Efforts to organize workers in fast-food restaurants over the decades have often involved unionization drives, with limited and varying levels of success. Reiter (2002) and Clark and Warskett (2010) report on such efforts across Canada. While some gains have been made (such as in British Columbia, Ontario and Quebec with KFC, White Spot, Swiss Chalet and Robin's Donuts), unionizing in restaurants has been an uphill battle, with limited long-term gains. For instance, Canada boasted North America's first McDonald's union, in Squamish, British Columbia, but in 1999 the workers voted to decertify their union before the first contract was ever negotiated (Zeidler, 2019). Tim Hortons, the largest fast-food chain in Canada, boasts 4,613 Canadian locations (Sagan, 2018) but has only approximately a dozen unionized locations. As Royle (2010) has documented, part of the challenge in organizing these worksites is that many multinational fast-food corporations employ an aggressive strategy of 'union suppression' to keep their labour costs down. As Royle describes:

> the last forty years is littered with unionization struggles, many of which have failed or have had little effect on the business ... Fast-food chains are adept at using a variety of union busting techniques, which usually involve a combination of legal action, flying squads of managers, buying out contracts and/ or harassment and intimidation of union supporters. (Royle, 2010, p 257)

Head offices of fast-food corporations widely pursue the 'carrot strategy' to counter unions: they promise to improve pay and working conditions in anti-union meetings and sometimes even hold employee parties to win over staff. If the carrot does not succeed, then the stick is employed: 'sympathizers are harassed and intimidated ... They have their hours shortened or denied, they have their shifts changed to times when they cannot work, and/or they are given unpleasant duties to fulfil' (Royle, 2010, p 258). As Reiter (2002, p 40) concludes, 'the combination of a well-resourced employer opposition, enterprise based labour law that privileges large workplaces and a ... workforce with high turnover mean that organizing fast-food workers in Canada is still an uphill struggle'. Nevertheless, there have been some victories in organizing drives, including a second KFC/Taco Bell location in Winnipeg in 2015 (Winnipeg Sun, 2016), a Tim Hortons restaurant in Canora, Saskatchewan in 2018, and two Winnipeg Tim Hortons restaurants in 2017 (CBC, 2017).

Given the limited successes and ongoing challenges of organizing fast-food worksites, recent innovative strategies have been implemented in North America to mobilize workers across worksites. The most notable of these strategies is Fast Food Forward, an organizing effort funded and led by the Service Employees International Union and supplemented by other unions. Its goal is to unionize all fast-food restaurant employees in New York City, with a secondary objective of securing a $15 minimum wage and promoting dignity and respect for low-waged workers nationally. Fast Food Forward operates as a worker centre where worker committees plan initiatives, including a number of fast-food strikes, supported by union organizers. The first strike of fast-food workers, in 2011, has subsequently led to nationwide walkouts in over 150 cities, including in chains like Burger King, Taco Bell, McDonald's and Wendy's. Because corporations use union suppression at local restaurants to counter unionization efforts, the hope for initiatives like this is that unionizing a whole sector rather than a single worksite will make it more difficult for employers and corporations to union-bust individual restaurants. Since its inception a number of gains have been made, including wage increases for 22 million workers nationwide and scheduling rights for workers in New York City. Schedules for these workers must now be produced at least two weeks in advance, workers must have at least 11 hours between shifts (unless they opt to work additional shifts) and employers cannot require workers to be 'on-call' without pay. If employers make schedule changes, they face penalties ranging from US$10 to US$75 per change (Szekely, 2017). These gains grant some stability for workers in insecure jobs, allowing them to know their working hours in advance and, in turn, their anticipated pay. However, few workers have been formally unionized through this initiative, and a sector-wide union has yet to materialize.

These mobilization efforts reflect the power of low-waged workers and offer a range of possibilities for promoting improved conditions, yet for migrant workers it is essential that we consider the vulnerabilities generated specifically through temporary labour schemes. Although precarious work shapes the experiences of almost all fast-food workers, migrant workers are uniquely vulnerable to a range of control mechanisms and employer violations. They are also directly segmented into the worst occupations in the labour market. These vulnerabilities must therefore be specifically addressed in organizing efforts.

The classification of 'migrant worker' is not an inherently vulnerable designation; TMWs are *made* vulnerable through the interplay of immigration controls and labour regulations (Anderson, 2010). One way that immigration controls do this is through the precarious legal status they confer to migrant workers, which limits workers' ability to resist employment violations on the job or to seek better employment elsewhere. The 'tied' nature of employment contracts (that bind TMWs to their employers) often denies migrant workers the ability to circulate freely in the labour market, meaning that in practice they are 'unfree' and can become indentured to a potentially abusive employer (Strauss and McGrath, 2017). TMWs are made 'disposable' in the sense that their right to live and work in Canada is directly related to their temporary employment; dismissal can be tantamount to repatriation back to the sending country, which translates into workers' widespread hesitation to stand up for their work and employment rights (Binford, 2009; Fudge and MacPhail, 2009). This hesitation and vulnerability feed the trope of the supposedly superior 'work ethic' associated with migrant workers who are more willing to withstand abuse and employment violations or who perform a more industrious and hard-working subjectivity than domestic staff (Barber, 2008; Harrison and Lloyd, 2012). Employers of TMWs often commit a host of labour violations, such as paying migrant workers less than their domestic counterparts, withholding overtime pay, committing wage theft and using incorrect classification systems (also a form of wage theft) (Sharma, 2006; Choudry and Smith, 2016). Migrant workers also tend to experience a broad range of on-the-job health violations, which are more typical of sectors that staff with TMWs (Preibisch and Hennebry, 2011).

Research has shown that employers who rely on TMWs can be significantly choosier in their recruitment of workers (Preibisch, 2010). Temporary labour schemes allow employers to select the workforce that they believe embodies the ideal characteristics for capital accumulation in their specific occupation and destination (Polanco, 2017), recruiting staff along lines such as sex, nationality and age – a practice that is often illegal in the host-country context but perfectly normative in many developing countries. As Preibisch (2010, p 406) puts it, capital uses labour-market flexibility to ensure a vulnerable and compliant workforce. In today's age of contracted borders, more sending states are vying to staff international labour markets, while comparatively fewer host countries are willing to receive them. Sending states thus become complacent, devaluing their citizens or placing them in dangerous employment contexts in order to secure global contracts (Rodriguez, 2010; Polanco, 2019).

Given this broad context, it is not surprising that TMWs in the restaurant sector in Canada employ a range of organizing and resistance strategies beyond unionization drives. Indeed, while scholars have widely noted the rampant employment violations that TMWs face, the institutionalized vulnerability of TMWs means that such violations often go unheard of or unchallenged, at least in a traditional organizing sense. Some highly visible cases have emerged, though, including class-action lawsuits and public shaming exercises against bad employers and the Canadian government. These strategies have generally been employed when it appears that there is nothing left to lose (such as when deportation or repatriation seems imminent) or when migrants hope that public pressure will alter conditions in their favour. For example, in January 2011, 77 TMWs, supported by Migrante British Columbia, filed and eventually won a class-action lawsuit against a Denny's restaurant. A settlement of CAN$1.3 million was reached in 2015, due to confirmed allegations that the employer was not living up to the conditions specified in the employment contract: workers had been required to pay $6,000 to recruiters, they did not receive the full-time hours of pay promised under the contract, they did not receive overtime pay and air travel expenses were never reimbursed. Similar lawsuits have been pursued by other food-service TMWs, including a class-action lawsuit by Mexican TMWs who were employed in a Tim Hortons restaurant in Dawson Creek, British Columbia. According to allegations, the employer had crammed four TMWs into cramped living conditions and charged them above market value for the rent. He was also accused of confiscating their passports and threatening to fire them when they objected to the terms of their employment.

Alongside class-action lawsuits, there have been productive 'public shaming' exercises that seek to protect migrant workers' well-being by appealing to the government and general public. One such case was that of Maria Victoria Venancio, a TMW from the Philippines who was recruited to Edmonton, Alberta to work in a McDonald's restaurant. One day while cycling to work she was hit by a car; the accident left her quadriplegic. As she could no longer work as a food-counter attendant, her employer felt that he could no longer employ her, and the Canadian government sought her deportation. As a result of organizing efforts by local community groups, most notably Migrante Alberta and Migrante Canada, in July 2015 she was granted an open work permit and the right to stay in Canada for two years, and at the end of this period she was ultimately granted permanent residency status in Canada.

Such cases demonstrate the creativity and resilience that TMWs use in their organizing for better rights, with the support of community groups and allies. Migrant and low-waged workers do not take their exploitation passively; they are active agents in organizing for improved conditions. However, while these conspicuous examples of resistance in the food services sector are important, they do not resolve the quotidian and unique vulnerabilities faced by migrants in the Low-Skilled Pilot.

Precarious labour migration regime

In addition to general patterns of vulnerability associated with temporary labour schemes, different programmes employ distinct sets of immigration controls that condition workers' vulnerabilities in the labour process and beyond. In Canada's Low-Skilled Pilot, many fast-food workers recruited to Canada desire permanent residency in Canada, yet, unbeknown to many, they must navigate a hyper-precarious and employer-initiated process to transition from temporary to permanent status. This uniquely ambiguous, insecure and employer-led labour/migration regime renders migrants inherently vulnerable to a host of violations and exploitations – insecurities that *differ* from the institutional regulations organizing agricultural and domestic caregiving flows under the SAWP and Caregiver

Program, for example. The result has been the introduction of a new 'precarious labour migration regime' in Canada (see Polanco, 2016).

As previously discussed, Canada has a long history of recruiting TMWs to address labour-market pressures, but recruiting migrant workers in the bottom tiers of the labour market has generally been confined to two niches: agricultural workers under the SAWP since 1966 and domestic caregivers under the LCP and a host of reconfigured streams since 1992. The Low-Skilled Pilot expanded the scope of occupations potentially covered by low-waged migrant workers, instigating a new globalization of the Canadian labour market. It also marked the introduction of a particularly fraught immigration scheme with regard to prospects for becoming permanent residents.

The mention of permanent residency under a 'guest worker' scheme may seem counterintuitive, given that temporary labour programmes are coveted precisely for their exclusionary dimensions. Indeed, a host of countries have embraced TFWPs precisely because they seek to access labour while simultaneously denying migrants the rights commonly associated with citizenship. Moreover, migrant worker programmes are consistent with broader neoliberal programmes and austerity measures, as the state aims to limit public expenditure and shift risks and costs from employers to workers. As access to many public services requires formal legal membership (such as access to education, employment insurance and old-age pensions), the promise of subjects with limited rights who return home post-contract affords receiving states many cost-saving benefits. Yet limiting access to permanent status is a relatively new practice in Canada. Unlike other Western countries with long histories of limiting access to formal legal status for many within their territory (such as the US), Canada has a long tradition of accepting newcomers with a clear path to permanent residency status. This includes migrants under the Federal Skilled Workers Program (colloquially known as the points system), wherein migrants are assessed and selected for permanent immigration using a range of criteria such as language skills, education, age, work experience, perceived prospects for adaptability and fulfilment of identified labour-market needs. Permanent newcomers have also been accepted under family reunification programmes and business and immigrant entrepreneur streams, as well as under asylum and refugee programmes. Most newcomers who have migrated to Canada – an immigrant-receiving nation and settler-colonial nation-state – over generations have done so with the purpose and (eventual) right to permanent settlement.[4] This even holds true in most cases for TMWPs.

Different TFWP streams offer differing prospects for permanent residency in Canada. For high-skilled workers, options for transitioning from temporary to permanent status have long existed and consist of straightforward institutional pathways. For 'low-skilled' streams such as the LCP and Caregiver Program, there is an institutionalized 'two-step' process for transitioning to permanent residency status (Hennebry, 2010); workers can apply for permanent residency after a period of time in Canada and meeting a set of criteria (including 24 months of continuous employment). While the requirements for transitioning from temporary to permanent status have shifted in recent years, alongside changes to the regulatory framework for domestic caregivers, it is nevertheless *workers* who can apply directly to become permanent residents after meeting a set of requirements.[5] In contrast, the SAWP has consistently and explicitly stipulated that under no condition may workers transition from temporary to permanent residency status.[6] Despite important exclusions and shortcomings, then, with the exception of the SAWP there has generally been a direct and institutionalized process for transitioning from temporary to permanent status, with workers themselves initiating this process. The Low-Skilled Pilot marks a notable departure from this tradition.

Subjects who migrate to Canada under the Low-Skilled Pilot face considerable ambiguity with regard to their prospects for transitioning from temporary to permanent residency status (Polanco, 2016). Unlike the 'two-step' process for domestic caregivers and in contrast to SAWP workers who are explicitly denied the possibility of permanent residency, fast-food workers and other low-waged migrants recruited under the Low-Skilled Pilot must be nominated by their employer under a Provincial Nominee Program (PNP) to transition to permanent residency status. PNPs are immigration programmes wherein employers can nominate a migrant for permanent residency in an occupation defined as being under pressure. This immigration scheme is employer initiated, and employers are under no obligation to nominate a worker. Regulated by Immigration, Refugees and Citizenship Canada (IRCC), Employment and Social Development Canada (ESDC) and respective provincial governments, these programmes are intended to grant mechanisms for individual provinces and territories to address regional labour-market pressures through access to workers in select occupations. In both Alberta and British Columbia (Canada's two most western provinces), food-counter attendant has been an occupation repeatedly listed as under pressure and included under a PNP. Using distinct 'pilot projects', provinces identify sectors and occupations thought to have a labour shortage and then consider employer nominations of selected applicants for permanent residency. The federal government establishes quotas per province (for example, Alberta allowed 6,000 nominations in 2019), and individual provinces stipulate the quotas for select occupations and streams. For food-counter attendants in Alberta, the provincial government has experimented with allowing only one allocation per restaurant, permitting up to a maximum of 20 per cent of a restaurant's migrant workforce and eliminating (and at times reinstituting) the category as an eligible occupation. The result has been competition among workers and significant insecurity for individual migrants seeking nomination under a PNP, creating a new management regime from which to organize labour consent.

In this new precarious labour/migration regime in Canada (Polanco, 2016), the prospect of being nominated for permanent residency and receiving the presumed benefits of Canadian citizenship exerts a strong disciplinary force on workers within their worksites. Because labour migration under the Low-Skilled Pilot and PNP neither 'denies nor facilitates access to legal incorporation ... [it] converts the worksite into a transnational space in which migrants are solicited to compete for employer-nominated citizenship' (Polanco, 2016, p 1342). In turn, employers can leverage people's desires for permanent residency in order to recruit highly coveted workers (namely those who are university educated, young, able bodied, English speaking and motivated) and secure their consent to a flexible employment contract and the poor working conditions that typify employment in the sector. Moreover, as employers have the power to nominate (or not nominate) a worker, subjects must compete to demonstrate how they are 'worthy' of nomination, all to the benefit of capital. In practice, this possible path to Canadian citizenship leads workers to demonstrate enthusiasm in the labour process and even to accept outright employment violations. This acquiescence eases the struggles related to worker control and retention that have long plagued the sector, as workers' TMW status 'ties' them to their worksites, and hopes of permanent residency elicit their consent.

Employers can also circumvent vulnerable segments of the domestic workforce in favour of their preferred global workforce. For example, Tim Hortons employers appear to prefer Filipino TMWs over local workers and those from other countries, such as Mexico (Polanco, 2019). Employers prefer Filipino fast-food workers over Mexican nationals partly due to the workings of the Filipino migration apparatus. Boasting the most sophisticated migration apparatus in the world, the Philippines uses a three-pronged process consisting of researching global labour markets, training workers and marketing their mobility in efforts to outpace other labour-sending states (Rodriguez, 2010). The second prong – training workers – involves configuring components of the state's educational system to produce workers for a range of globally identified in-demand occupations, such as nursing and welding. The state also provides 'pre-departure orientation seminars': mandatory workshops that are officially meant to empower prospective migrant workers with the knowledge to navigate life and employment while overseas, but that critics have argued are largely aimed at socializing workers to be eager and disciplined migrants – the 'ideal migrant subjects' behind the counter (Polanco, 2017). With Filipino migrants socialized to 'be the best' or to perform a congruent 'market-based subjectivity' (Barber, 2008), employers gain access to a highly desirable workforce (often young, English speaking and university educated) in sectors where they have long struggled to secure 'desirable', motivated and committed workers. This both renders migrant workers more 'desirable' to employers than domestic staff, and positions Filipino migrants as more desirable than other global workers, at least for interactive occupations. As documented in a comparison with Mexico (Polanco, 2019), the Philippines has (racially) 'branded' Filipino migrants as preferable, in part by deploying university–educated graduates and those with professional work experience to work in entry-level occupations. This positioning produces tensions and inequalities not only across domestic/'foreign' lines but also among migrant workforces and sending states. Dovetailing with the deregulation characteristic of austerity agendas, the result of these shifts is a 'race to the bottom', as sending states and individual migrant subjects are encouraged to accept weakened regulations and protections to secure global work. Canada's Low-Skilled Pilot reinforces these pressures by exploiting migrant desires for Canadian citizenship to the benefit of capital accumulation.

Centring non–citizenship to resist labour flexibility

States that introduce, expand or reinstate TFWPs benefit from a series of cost-saving regulations that are conducive to capital accumulation. Savings are leveraged through the social and legal differentiation of migrants as 'non–citizens' and the exclusions borne from such classifications. For instance, denying migrants the right to be accompanied by their partners and families and treating them as merely labour – not people – allows states to address purported labour-market shortages without having to cover the costs of social reproduction. This is consistent with austerity projects in which the costs of social reproduction are shifted from the state and the employer to the workers, in this case vulnerable migrant workers and sending states. Guest-worker schemes also provide advantages for employers and private businesses, granting them access to a highly disciplined (read: exploitable), 'just-in-time' workforce that neither employers nor the state have invested in but whose labour they can appropriate. These workers are highly flexible, not only due to labour controls that disenfranchise all low-waged workers but through additional immigration controls that render migrant workers 'hyper-precarious' (Lewis et al, 2015). When guest workers are no longer needed or are deemed 'less valuable' due to ageing or injury, employers and states can dismiss or repatriate them, saving on costs such as healthcare and pensions. In the case of racialized flows, nation-states can also access labour without having to contend with the 'threat' of (racial) diversification borne from long-term integration (Smith, 2013).

Vulnerability is the norm for many low-waged workers, including those employed in fast food, particularly in the context of austerity, yet guest workers face additional vulnerabilities when employed in foreign labour markets. While these vulnerabilities have been extensively documented, it is essential to also consider the specific vulnerabilities that labour flexibility can produce, partly determined by the particularities of different temporary labour schemes. In Canada's Low-Skilled Pilot, a principal vulnerability faced by fast-food migrant workers is the desire for Canadian citizenship and the pressures entailed by an employer-led process for securing permanent residency status. The proliferation of PNPs in Canada has inserted employers directly into the immigration process, empowering them to wield the promise of Canadian citizenship to discipline workers behind the counter through a 'precarious labour migration regime' (Polanco, 2016). Individual sending states also play a role in generating vulnerability under the Low-Skilled Pilot by marketing and preparing worker subjects with a subjectivity that is meant to be agreeable to employers but relies on their willingness to perform docility and accept labour abuse as a normal element of working under transnational contracts (Polanco, 2017). Some countries (such as the Philippines) have perfected their labour-migration apparatus to such an extent that other sending states (like Mexico) come to be viewed as less desirable source countries, at least for interactive occupations like fast food (Polanco, 2019). The result is a transnational landscape wherein fast-food employers have the ability to shop globally for their coveted, preferred workforce, despite the poor working and employment conditions that characterize the sector.

Citizenship, then, should be at the centre of our organizing efforts to resist downward pressures on working and employment conditions and to fight exclusions in the broader society. This is not to suggest that individual organizing efforts should not be pursued at the scale of the shop floor, that specific cases involving migrants should not be fought or that efforts to unionize should be abandoned. Rather, the vulnerability of those with precarious legal status stems directly from social and legal processes that produce 'non-citizens'; thus, in addition to our efforts in worksites and related institutions, we must also focus our struggles on the social and legal realm where 'otherness' is manufactured. Collectively, we must organize against immigration schemes like PNPs that empower employers by inserting them directly into the immigration process, and we must oppose temporary migrant worker programmes that commercialize (im)migrant selection and outsource it to profit-driven actors. It is essential that we educate the public to reject discourses that, as citizens of Western nations, 'we' need to defend ourselves against 'them/Others', who want but a small piece of the shrinking citizenship pie that we enjoy. The revival and proliferation of TMWPs comes at a time of expanding border controls and the criminalization of subjects (particularly those from the global South). Receiving states need to challenge the patrolling of the boundaries of belonging (from which rights often accrue); the quotidian implications of 'othering' those whom we legally define as non-citizens; and the austerity-linked agendas of using schemes like the TMWP to make all workers more vulnerable through the global deregulation of labour markets and retrenchment of public services, rights and entitlements.

Notes

[1] Perceived mutual benefits include access to labour for receiving states, remittances for sending states and higher wages for individual migrants.

[2] This is not to suggest that Canada does not have a long history of immigrant exclusion along lines such as race and gender (see, for instance, Thobani, 2007). Indeed, these exclusions are significant and have formed the foundation of Canada's nation-building project as a white-settler colonial nation-state. However, Canada has increasingly moved away from granting permanent residency status to the majority of newcomers, opting instead to promote more temporary and circular migration patterns.

[3] The moratorium was instituted in April 2014 following allegations that fast-food employers were abusing the Low-Skilled Pilot by sidelining Canadian and permanent resident recruits in favour of TMWs.

[4] There have, however, been notable (gendered and racialized) immigrant exclusions (see, for instance, Thobani, 2007).

[5] This is not to negate the many shortcomings associated with these transitions (including significant backlogs and the introduction of criteria that make it increasingly difficult for domestic caregivers to meet the requirements), but nevertheless workers themselves initiate(d) the process.

[6] This in itself is a classed, gendered and racialized example of Canada patrolling the boundaries of its nation-state, which has been harshly critiqued by many activists and scholars (for example, Smith, 2013).

References

Allegretto, S., Doussard, M., Graham-Squire, D., Jacobs, K., Thompson, D. and Thompson, J. (2013) *Fast Food, Poverty Wages: The Public Cost of Low-Wage Jobs in the Fast-Food Industry*. Berkeley: Center for Labor Research and Education.

Anderson, B. (2010) 'Migration, immigration controls and the fashioning of precarious workers'. *Work, Employment and Society*, 24(2): 300–17.

Barber, P. (2008) 'The ideal immigrant? Gendered class subjects in Philippine–Canada migration'. *Third World Quarterly*, 29(7): 1265–85.

Binford, L. (2009) 'From fields of power to fields of sweat: The dual process of constructing temporary migrant labour in Mexico and Canada'. *Third World Quarterly*, 30(3): 503–17.

Bosniak, L. (2006) *The Citizen and the Alien: Dilemmas of Contemporary Membership*. Princeton, NJ: Princeton University Press.

CBC (2017) 'Workers at 2nd Winnipeg Tim Hortons vote to unionize'. 27 July. https://www.cbc.ca/news/canada/manitoba/winnipeg-tim-hortons-unionize-1.4224200.

Choudry, A. and Smith, A. (2016) *Unfree Labour? Struggles of Migrant and Immigrant Workers in Canada*. Oakland: PM Press.

Chun, J. (2009) *Organizing at the Margins: The Symbolic Politics of Labor in South Korea and the United States*. Ithaca, NY: Cornell University Press.

Clark, D. and Warskett, R. (2010) 'Labour fragmentation and new forms of organizing and bargaining in the service sector'. In: Pupo, N. and Thomas, M. (eds), *Interrogating the New Economy: Restructuring Work in the 21st Century*. Toronto: University of Toronto Press, 235–56.

Collins, J. (2003) *Threads: Gender, Labor and Power in the Global Apparel Industry*. Chicago: University of Chicago Press.

ESDC (Employment and Social Development Canada) (2014) *Overhauling the Temporary Foreign Worker Program*. Table 2: Canada – Entries of temporary foreign worker work permit holders by sub-status 2002 to 2013. Ottawa: ESDC.

Fudge, J. and MacPhail, F. (2009) 'The Temporary Foreign Worker Program in Canada: Low-skilled workers as an extreme form of flexible labour'. *Comparative Labor Law and Policy Journal*, 31: 101–39.

Fudge, J. and Tham, J.C. (2017) 'Dishing up migrant workers for the Canadian food services sector: Labor law and the demand for migrant workers'. *Comparative Labor Law and Policy Journal*, 39(1): 1–28.

Goldring, L. and Landolt, P. (2013) *Producing and Negotiating Non-Citizenship: Precarious Legal Status in Canada*, Toronto: University of Toronto Press.

Harrison, J. and Lloyd, S. (2012) 'Illegality at work: Deportability and the productive new era of immigrant enforcement'. *Antipode*, 44(2): 365–85.

Hennebry, J. (2010) 'Who has their eye on the ball? "Jurisdictional fútbol" and Canada's Temporary Foreign Worker Program'. *Policy Options*, 63: 62–7.

IRCC (Immigration, Refugees and Citizenship Canada) (2016) *Facts and Figures 2016: Immigration Overview – Permanent and Temporary Residents.* Ottawa: IRCC.

IRCC (2017) *Facts and Figures 2017: Immigration Overview – Permanent and Temporary Residents*, Ottawa: IRCC.

Leidner, R. (1993) *Fast Food, Fast Talk: Service Work and the Routinization of Everyday Life.* Berkeley, CA: University of California Press.

Lewis, H., Dwyer, P., Hodkinson, S. and Waite, L. (2015). 'Hyper-precarious lives: Migrants, work and forced labour in the global North'. *Progress in Human Geography*, 39(5): 580–600.

McLaughlin, J. and Hennebry, J. (2013) 'Pathways to precarity: Structural vulnerabilities and lived consequences for migrant farmworkers in Canada'. In: Goldring, L. and Landolt, P. (eds), *Producing and Negotiating Non-Citizenship: Precarious Legal Status in Canada.* Toronto: University of Toronto Press, 175–95.

Munck, R. (2008) 'Globalisation, governance and migration: An introduction'. *Third World Quarterly*, 29(7): 1227–46.

Newman, K. (2000) *No Shame in My Game: The Working Poor in the Inner City.* New York: Vintage Press.

Polanco, G. (2016) 'Consent behind the counter: Aspiring citizens and labour control under precarious (im)migration schemes'. *Third World Quarterly*, 37(8): 1332–50.

Polanco, G. (2017) 'Culturally tailored workers for specialised destinations: Producing Filipino migrant subjects for export'. *Identities: Global Studies in Culture and Power*, 24(1): 62–81.

Polanco, G. (2019) 'Competition between labour-sending states and the branding of national workforces'. *International Migration*, 57(4): 136–50.

Preibisch, K. (2010) 'Pick your own labor: Migrant workers and flexibility in Canadian agriculture'. *International Migration Review*, 44: 404–41.

Preibisch, K. and Hennebry, J. (2011) 'Temporary migration, chronic effects: The health of international migrant workers in Canada'. *Canadian Medical Association Journal*, 183(9): 1033–8.

Reiter, E. (2002) 'Fast food in Canada: Working conditions, labour law and unionization'. In: Royle, T. and Towers, B. (eds), *Labour Relations in the Global Fast Food Industry.* New York: Routledge, 30–47.

Rodriguez, R. (2010) *Migrants for Export: How the Philippines Brokers Labor to the World.* Minneapolis, MN: University of Minnesota Press.

Royle, T. (2010) 'Low-road Americanization' and the global "McJob": A longitudinal analysis of work, pay and unionization in the international fast food industry'. *Labor History*, 51(2): 249–70.

Royle, T. and Towers, B. (2002) *Labour Relations in the Global Fast Food Industry.* New York: Routledge.

Sagan, A. (2018) 'By the numbers: Tim Hortons franchisees and Ontario's minimum wage hike'. 10 September. https://www.theglobeandmail.com/report-on-business/by-the-numbers-tim-hortons-franchisees-and-ontarios-minimum-wage-hike/article37553411/.

Salzinger, L. (2003) *Genders in Production: Making Workers in Mexico's Global Factories*. Berkeley, CA: University of California Press.

Schlosser, E. (2002) *Fast Food Nation: The Dark-Side of the All-American Meal*. New York: Perennial Books.

Sharma, N. (2006) *Home Economicus: Nationalism and the Making of 'Migrant Workers' in Canada*. Toronto: University of Toronto Press.

Smith, A. (2013) 'Pacifying the "armies of offshore labour" in Canada'. *Socialist Studies*, 9(2): 78–93.

Strauss, K. and McGrath, S. (2017) 'Temporary migration, precarious employment and unfree labour relations: Exploring the "continuum of exploitation" in Canada's Temporary Foreign Worker Program'. *Geoforum*, 78: 199–208.

Szekely, P. (2017) 'New York City law gives fast food workers scheduling rights'. *Reuters*, 30 May. https://www.reuters.com/article/us-new-york-fastfood-scheduling-idUSKBN18Q2IR.

Thobani, S. (2007) *Exalted Subjects: Studies in the Making of Race and Nation in Canada*. Toronto: University of Toronto Press.

Trumper, R. and Wong, L. (2010) 'Temporary workers in Canada: A national perspective', *Canadian Issues*, Spring: 83–89.

Wang, Y. and Zong, L. (2014) 'Temporary natives, perpetual foreigners: The secondary status of temporary foreign workers in Canada and structural barriers to their inclusion'. In: Kilbride, K. (ed), *Immigrant Integration: Research Implications for Future Policy*. Toronto: Canadian Scholars Press, 3–20.

Winnipeg Sun (2016) 'Second KFC/Taco Bell Unionizes'. 28 October.

Zeidler, M. (2019) '20 years ago, employees in Squamish, B.C. voted to disband the first McDonald's union in North America'. *CBC News*, 30 June. https://www.cbc.ca/news/canada/british-columbia/20-years-ago-employees-in-squamish-b-c-voted-to-disband-the-first-mcdonald-s-union-in-north-america-1.5195490.

7

What We Talk About When We Talk About Austerity: Social Policy, Public Management and Politics of Eldercare Funding in Canada and China

Kendra Strauss and Feng Xu

Introduction

A decade after the 'global' financial crisis, austerity is still being debated in relation both to post-crisis policy orientations and to longer-term trends since the 1970s (Dunn, 2014; McBride and Baines, 2014; Whiteside, 2018a). It is clear from the significant body of scholarship focusing on Western 'worlds of welfare capitalism' (Esping-Andersen, 1990) that austerity – in the sense of policies that constrain or reduce public spending on social welfare; (re)privatize or (re)commodify welfare state functions, public goods and public assets (including infrastructure) and seek to shrink the 'social state' (Peck, 2013) – is connected both to state responses to the 2008 financial crisis and to longer-run processes and mechanisms. These include capitalist restructuring associated with neoliberalization and with the rise of New Public Management (NPM) as a vehicle for redrawing the boundaries between state and market.

NPM refers to an ideology and policy framework for the management of public finances and the public sector that seeks to embed a managerialist model 'characterized by competitive tendering, strict adherence to legalistic contracts and performance indicators, private-sector business practices, short-term funding and continued calls for efficiency, "more for less", value for money and cost savings' (Cunningham et al, 2017, pp 370–1).

As we argue in this chapter, however, context-specific and relational understandings of austerity and the complex policy mobilities (McCann and Ward, 2012) of NPM require critical attention to how processes play out in particular contexts (Pike et al, 2018). There are common trends, but unevenness also exists at the national and sub-national levels (Baines and Cunningham, 2015). Moreover, the policy diffusion of NPM also goes beyond European and Anglo-American welfare states and – as in countries like Canada and Australia that did not suffer financial crises – has been a convenient driver of reform. This chapter contributes to the literatures on austerity and NPM by comparing two such contexts, focusing on sub-national scales to examine the social care sector in Vancouver, British Columbia (Canada) and Shanghai (China). It does so by using the concept of social infrastructure to connect state-led marketization and outsourcing in the eldercare sector with, on the one hand, the influence of NPM and, on the other, the financialization that has accelerated in the past two decades.

Viewing labour's subordination through the lens of social infrastructure allows for the identification of similarities and differences in strategies designed, to different degrees at different moments, to reduce public spending, open up new terrain for capital, discipline workers and reduce the power of organized labour. At the same time, the Chinese case illustrates that policies enacted under the broad rubric of NPM may have different logics and entail different relations of power and visibility between state actors and private capital or the non-profit sector – which may themselves have different meanings and definitions.

The remainder of the chapter is in three sections. We start with a short discussion of the concept of social infrastructure, followed by an examination of social policy and public management in British Columbia. Although focusing on the period after the turn of the millennium, this period is historicized through a brief examination of the development of public eldercare in the province. We then turn to a similar examination of social policy dynamics and public management in China. We conclude with brief comments on austerity, public management and financialization in the sector in both contexts.

Social infrastructures of labour, and labour as social infrastructure

Infrastructure has become a powerful conceptual lens in geography, sociology, anthropology and cognate social science disciplines, as well as in media, cultural and communication studies, for focusing on relations between social formations and their cultural, technical, material and political manifestations. Indeed, some have claimed that we are in the midst of an 'infrastructural turn' (Shrestha and Yeoh, 2018; Power and Mee, 2019). While there has long been an interest in physical infrastructures, especially in urban theory and urban studies, the infrastructural turn is increasingly oriented towards a broader and more critical understanding of *social infrastructures* (Angelo and Hentschel, 2015; Lo et al, 2015; Addie, 2017).

Like pipes, roads, bridges or fibre optic networks, social infrastructures have typically referred to aspects of the built environment that connect people or provide physical spaces for service provision. Examples are schools, hospitals, day care and recreation centres and nursing homes. In urban theory, these were specifically public urban infrastructures of social reproduction, such as public housing and public libraries. Increasingly, they exist at the intersection of public (state), private and non-profit ownership and management, due to privatization and the proliferation of public-private partnerships (PPPs) in infrastructure financing. What is notable that the *physical infrastructures also stand in for the services and programmes that take place in those spaces.* Childcare, eldercare, education, recreational services and cultural programmes are evoked by the reference to social infrastructures often without any explicit acknowledgement that they depend on *workers*. A school building cannot teach without teachers, a long-term care (LTC) home cannot care without care aides.

Thus, despite the interest in so-called 'soft infrastructures' and the recognition that social infrastructures include, as Addie (2017) writes, 'public services or utilities, [which] may be provided by governmental agencies [and] may also be forged by a diverse array of actors operating at multiple scales – from small-scale cooperatives to transnational organizations – when the state is unable or unwilling to provide them', there is relatively little work that conceptualizes social infrastructures in relation to labour. This absence of an infrastructural labour politics is paralleled in the discourse of infrastructural investment or renewal among politicians in both Canada and China. In Canada in 2016, Justin Trudeau reversed a decade of federal Conservative Party domination with, among other things, a promise to invest in social infrastructure spending. The Liberal government implicitly defined social infrastructure as the physical spaces in which the activities of social reproduction take place, making explicit reference in its election manifesto to affordable housing, seniors' facilities, early learning and childcare centres and cultural and recreational infrastructure. Leaving aside how these social infrastructures were to be funded – as Whiteside (2017) argues, the Liberals' Canada Infrastructure Bank represents a continuation of the logics of PPPs – it was investment in the built environment, not in workers providing services, that underpinned those pledges. In China, building social infrastructure is considered part of the new growth strategy, as laid out in the Chinese Communist Party's 2013 'Third Plenum Blueprint' (*People's Daily Online*, 2013). This Blueprint moves away from a 'high inflationary growth trajectory' and emphasizes the need to 'focus on quality growth' by 'expanding the service sector, protecting the environment ... expanding public services, and reducing poverty' (Lam et al, 2017, p 5).

In both Canada and China, while paid and unpaid labour are foundational to formal and informal infrastructures of care, which are woven into the fabric of urban socio-technical infrastructures, the invisibilization and devaluation of that labour (Strauss and Xu, 2018) means that workers themselves are understood as a cost to be minimized in the calculus of infrastructure investment rather than as an investment that pays social dividends. That the labour of social infrastructures of care is highly feminized, as well as classed and racialized, stands in contrast to implicitly masculine jobs (in construction and engineering) related to infrastructure construction.

Social policy, NPM and the marketization of eldercare in British Columbia

As Davies (2001, p 156) writes in her history of nursing homes in British Columbia (BC), 'Public and political interest in residential accommodation for the elderly has waxed and waned over the course of the 19th and 20th centuries.' This is true of eldercare (also called seniors' care) more broadly. Eldercare is assumed to be the responsibility of families, especially women, and social welfare policies aimed at its defamilialization have been slow to develop and uneven. Where policy and public service provision have evolved to meet clear and pressing needs of older people without support or resources, they have had to shed the associations between institutional facilities and the poorhouse, and between community or homecare and unregulated, low-waged domestic service. That women, who tend to live longer than men and are more likely to be poor in old age, benefit most from the public funding and provision of care for the elderly, and that they are most likely to do the work of providing that care (paid or unpaid), has made it a challenge to sustain the interest of politicians and the general public in this as a social policy arena.

Given that the concept of austerity, or permanent austerity (Evans and Albo, 2011; McBride and Whiteside, 2011), associates fiscal restraint and the shrinking of the welfare state with phases of neoliberalization after the crises of the late 1970s, it is helpful to briefly historicize (despite a relative dearth of research) the 'waxing and waning' of interest in social policy designed to address the care of the elderly in BC. As Davies (2001, p 157) persuasively argues, the shift in attitudes towards institutional eldercare in the post-war period was influenced by changing norms of professionalism, medicalization and middle-class ideals of home and (nuclear]) family as well as by the politics of public spending. Nursing homes in the early and mid-20th century were funded and run by different levels of government (particularly municipal and provincial), by charitable and religious organizations and as private businesses. Davies (2001) documents the associated rise of professional and specialized occupations related to eldercare: not only doctors and nurses trained in geriatric medicine, but social workers, occupational and physical therapists and nutritionists. These fields were highly feminized. As Baines and Armstrong (2019, p 936) note in relation to long-term care, eldercare developed as:

> work that operates within an inverted triangle of hierarchy with historically male doctors at the top, few in number but high in reward and authority; largely female nurses in the middle in greater numbers than doctors but much lower numbers than frontline care workers; and low authority, frontline, quasi-professional or non-professional, female-majority care workers at the bottom of the triangle with the highest numbers of staff, the lowest pay, conditions and authority.

Supplementing institutional care during this period were homemaker services, provided to families with children and individuals unable to manage on their own at home due to a health or social problem (Ryan, 1983, p 7). The creation of the Long Term Care Program in 1978 expanded the provision of homemaker services to include residential homes, and by 1981 public, non-profit and for-profit (proprietary) agencies employed over 6,000 homemakers throughout BC (Ryan, 1983, pp 7–8). By the early 1990s, however, the government was starting to circumscribe the range of services provided by homemakers, even as the shift toward care in the community was gathering pace.

What this short overview suggests is that the history of social policy and social provision of elderly care is more complex than a story of state investment after the Second World War followed by retrenchment and spending constraints during the period of 'roll-out neoliberalization'. While the fiscally conservative Social Credit Party, in power provincially throughout the 1980s, ushered in public spending cuts and rolled back civil and labour rights, with particular impacts on public services like education (Fallon and Poole, 2014), the New Democratic Party (NDP), which was in power during the 1990s, to some extent resisted austerity logics (Isitt and Moroz, 2007; cf. Whiteside, 2018b), including those emanating from the federal level. Thus, the federal austerity policies of the mid-1990s that enacted deep cuts to provincial transfers, starting with the 1995 federal budget (McBride and Whiteside, 2011), did not at first impact overall healthcare spending in BC as dramatically as in many other provinces.

A series of studies by the Canadian Centre for Policy Alternatives has, however, documented how publicly funded home support services and homecare bore the brunt of cuts, which accelerated after the provincial Liberal Party came to power in 2001 (Stinson et al, 2005; Cohen, 2012; see also Cohen, 2006). Access to publicly funded residential care also declined. Between 2001–02 and 2009–10, access to home support services in BC dropped by 30 per cent and access to residential care dropped by 21 per cent (Cohen, 2012, p 11). In other words, the health and social care infrastructures that evolved, albeit unevenly, throughout the 20th century in BC to support older people beyond hospitals and emergency services provided a buffer against cuts to the acute healthcare system when austerity started to bite.

Thus 'permanent austerity' represented by fiscal restraint, and neoliberalism represented by the socialization of risks and the privatization of rewards in the economy, was both an early and late comer to provincial politics in BC (Whiteside, 2018b, p 23). By 2002, however, the provincial government had started to implement policies designed to permanently shrink the social state, discipline labour and open up areas of the public sector and public infrastructure to private capital. The introduction of Bill 29-2002 stripped no-contracting-out and job-security clauses from the collective agreements of health support workers and resulted in more than 8,000 job losses by the end of 2004 (Stinson et al, 2005, p 12), and Bill 37-2004 imposed wage roll-backs on more than 43,000 healthcare workers (Whiteside, 2018b). These bills are often seen as a turning point in the provincial government's approach to health and social services as arenas for marketization, privatization and wholesale assaults on the more militant public sector unions.

As Whiteside (2018b) argues, a longer view of public finances in BC demonstrates that the early 2000s, a period of economic expansion prior to the financial crisis of 2008 – rather than the post-crisis period – was key for the embedding of 'permanent' austerity in BC. Cohn (2008, p 72) further notes impacts of the Liberals' 25 per cent across-the-board cut to income tax: the 'resulting financial crisis was then used as a driver to not only cut government activity but to encourage a re-thinking of what the responsibilities of the provincial state should be and how the public sector should go about meeting these responsibilities'. Austerity in these analyses is not a reaction to crisis or recession, but a political economic project aligned with (but not reducible to) neoliberalization as a political economic process (Peck, 2001; 2013). Feminized, unionized sections of the health and social care sectors were targets of this project and process through public spending cuts, public sector job losses, contracting out, informalization and subsequent reductions in wages and benefits.

As the limited provincial literature on municipal contracting out shows (for example, McDavid and Clemens, 1995), the private and non-profit sectors have always had a role in the provision of 'public' services in BC – including, as discussed previously, social and health services for the elderly. The adoption of NPM in the public sector in BC was, however, a vehicle for several changes documented by Cohn and by Whiteside: the opening up of public services and infrastructures to private capital through the implementation of a programme of PPPs; and the downloading of greater risks and responsibilities related to service delivery to local authorities, while simultaneously constraining their autonomy through balanced-budget regulations. The privatization of public assets and public infrastructure, and the subordination and devaluation of feminized and racialized workers integral to the social infrastructures of labour that provide care, are two sides of the same coin. The state often retains an interest in being 'visible' in the delivery of large public infrastructure projects, such as new hospitals or cancer centres, which matter to voters, while simultaneously claiming efficiency and prudence through cost-cutting measures (often aimed at cheapening labour and weakening unions) that reduce the capacity and resilience of social infrastructures of labour.

Profits can be generated in PPP models only from costing in or transferring risks and by securing assets and/or revenue streams, especially through access to land for (re)development or to privatized or contracted-out services (Cohn, 2008). With marketization and privatization of social infrastructures in BC came financialization in the eldercare sector, especially concentrated in Vancouver, where a boom in real estate asset prices was under way. Private, and more recently finance, capital has flowed into the BC eldercare sector to fill the gaps created by cutbacks to publicly funded services. Liberal policies between 2001 and 2016 enacted 'backdoor' privatization by at least two means: by moving care services from public health facilities like hospitals and residential care homes into private households, where they are provided by workers who may be sub-contracted or privately hired agency workers; and by rationing care so as to expand the private sector for those who can pay. The result, now relatively well documented in BC, has been increased precariousness for workers across multiple dimensions: more part-time and casual work, split shifts and intensified scheduling patterns; understaffing and higher workloads with unpaid overtime; and high rates of injury, violence and harassment (Cohen et al, 2006; Zuberi and Ptashnick, 2011; Chun, 2016). Research by BC's Office of the Seniors Advocate has shown how private sector LTC providers in BC profit by securing public block funding for care provision, based on average unionized wages in the sector, and then understaffing facilities, underpaying workers and co-locating private-pay beds to benefit from publicly funded care hours (Office of the Seniors Advocate, 2020).

The cheapening of labour, including through state re-regulation of labour markets, is a condition of possibility for the realization of profits through both privatization and financialization. LTC has long been a sector of interest for insurance companies, private equity firms and real estate investment trusts. A common strategy of large private LTC chains is to separate their operating nursing homes from their property (real estate assets) and use leaseback arrangements with property companies (Harrington et al, 2017). In addition, private equity firms – especially venture capital firms, growth capital/mid-market buyout firms, and buyout firms – have shown increased interest in the LTC sector (Robbins et al, 2008). In global cities like Vancouver and Shanghai, the interrelationship of real estate and LTC makes residential care particularly attractive, not least because mortgage interest (and in some cases principal) can be expensed to health authorities (Office of the Seniors Advocate, 2020). The result is deals like the acquisition of the company Retirement Concepts (BC's largest private eldercare provider) by the Chinese multinational Anbang Insurance. Large for-profit chains often own and operate a range of related LTC companies, which allows nursing home chains to purchase services from their own related companies to enhance profit taking (Harrington et al, 2017); strategies of assetization and locking in revenue streams thus involve complex corporate arrangements for the separation of functions and ownerships and leasing back of physical infrastructure. These strategies, as Horton (2019) points out in her paper on the financialization of LTC in the UK, involve the devaluation of social infrastructures of labour and care in financialized strategies of accumulation.

Social policy, NPM and the marketization of eldercare in Shanghai, China

Demographic ageing has led to a care crisis in China: who cares, how care is paid for and where care is provided have become critical policy questions. The Chinese government considers social policy to be a crisis-management tool in order to maintain social and political stability, something that sets social policy there apart from its Western counterparts. Historically, eldercare in China had been provided by unpaid labour at home, but after the Chinese Communist Party took power, the state became omnipresent in Chinese people's lives. The state in this period took on social relief work, but only for urban Chinese, and only for those who had the 'three withouts' (*sanwu*): without means of livelihood; without the physical or mental ability to labour; and without anybody legally obligated to provide care. *Sanwu* urban residents were further divided into the elderly, the disabled and orphans. Welfare for these groups was considered government's social relief (*shehui jiuji*), funded through national or subnational government budgets, and administered by civil affairs bureaus. Together with *danwei-* (work-unit) based welfare, which is also called the 'iron rice bowl', these core policies formed the bulk of China's welfare system during the Mao era.

Since 2013, however, the central government has issued directives on ageing to be implemented by subnational governments. Shanghai is considered to be the first municipality to have entered an 'ageing society'. Traditional models of household life and informal provisioning of seniors' care are challenged by the large-scale patterns of internal migration and urbanization of younger adults, as well as by the competitive character of the labour market. In contrast to the (re)privatization of the eldercare sector in Canada and in other Western countries, an eldercare market has had to be created from scratch in the face of the mounting insufficiency of household provision. The process started in the midst of a period of the Chinese government's embrace of NPM initiatives, a development that promotes limited and entrepreneurial government. The creation of PPPs is thus one of the main measures set out in the revised Budget Law (2015) to help subnational governments finance social infrastructure without further accumulating already-high debt (The National People's Congress Net, 2015).

China's initial turn to NPM was not a direct response to retaining public sector policy-making authority amid economic and government-revenue crises by restoring fiscal prudence. Nor is it directly linked to political discourses of austerity. Rather, it has been part of the long-term response to China's internal reform process that, from 1979 on, moved

China from Mao's socialist planned economy to a post-Mao emphasis on marketization, all the while maintaining China's authoritarian political system. Neoliberal ideas such as NPM, adopted in China as a novel mode of governance, circulated and operated in combination with China's pre-existing modes of governance (Xu, 2012).

A major component of the post-1979 reform period was to smash the 'iron rice bowl', starting with reforms to state-owned enterprises. Since 1986, civil affairs bureaus have also undergone reforms: 'society', rather than the state, should be responsible for social welfare, although still under the Party's direction; social welfare shifted from pure relief and charity to client-oriented service in preparation for a return to the job market; and social welfare became focused on social as well as economic or monetary benefits (Su, 2007). In the context of this chapter, the central point is that society and market forces were called on in this reform period to join forces with the state in developing an eldercare market.

Reforming civil affairs was part of post-Mao government reforms: the aim was expressed in the slogan, 'small government, big society'. Society (*shehui*) or the social, a term introduced to China via Japan at the turn of the 20th century, was suppressed during the Mao period. Its re-emergence in the post-Mao era, however, does not indicate a retreat of the state and the re-emergence of some supposedly autonomous civil society. Instead, it points to a 'regrouping' of the state. As Xu (2012, p 15) has argued, 'the state has been re-organising, so as to continue intervening in areas it deems essential, but it leaves areas that now belong to "society" to be handled by "society"'. Furthermore, and in contradistinction to Western patterns, there has been an equally important regrouping of the Party, which continues to assume a role of oversight of both the restructured state and the newly structured civil society.

China's growth-oriented development model, characterized by the comprehensive marketization of virtually all aspects of people's lives, has led to spectacular economic growth since the early 1990s, but it also led to increasing social polarization and rising social conflicts. If not properly dealt with, that polarization and conflict have the potential to undermine the Party's legitimacy in exercising its political and societal monopoly. Ma Kai, the State Councillor and Secretary General of the State Council, explains the state-driven and state-dominant social management as entailing

> the activities to regulate social behaviours, coordinate social relationships, promote social identification, uphold social fairness, solve social problems, resolve social contradictions, safeguard public order, and cope with social risks; these

activities are centred around the imperative to maintain social order, dominated by the government. (BBC, 2010)

These social objects were thus integrally related to China's evolving growth and stability model. An important part of growth-oriented development in the reform period has been driven by land-based and infrastructure-oriented urbanization, because since 1994 subnational governments have had to rely on land for core revenues in China's fiscal decentralization scheme (Strauss and Xu, 2018). Under these circumstances, local government revenues were not able cover local spending obligations. Furthermore, the 1984 Budget Law prohibited local governments from borrowing or falling into debt, echoing balanced-budget imperatives in Western national and subnational regimes.

This growth model was further boosted by the central government's response to the 2008 global financial crisis. That response amounted to a distinctive Chinese policy of institutional counter-cyclical measures (Lam et al, 2017, p 163). In a jointly issued document in March 2009, the People's Bank of China and China Banking Regulatory Commission 'explicitly requested that local governments establish financing platforms. They simultaneously mandated that banks finance the local-government investment projects' (Heilmann, 2017, pp 340–1). Local governments seized the opportunity to set up what were essentially front companies to handle their land-based investment strategies. Local governments handed tax revenue and land-use rights over to these municipally backed companies, and the latter in turn placed these assets in state-owned banks and used them to leverage loans from these institutions. Local governments thus used these financing vehicles to borrow from banks and capital markets to fund physical infrastructure and real-estate development, which 'facilitated a rapid economic recovery, but simultaneously... led to an increasing indebtedness of local governments' (Heilmann, 2017, p 338).

The result was an astonishing wave of infrastructural investment that was widely understood as unsustainable. New-Type Urbanisation (2014–20) has since shifted from land-based and infrastructure-led urbanization to 'human-centred' urbanization – with the aggressive development of social services at its centre. The revised Budget Law (2015) attempts to alleviate subnational governments' burden by financing basic public services through fiscal transfers from national to subnational governments, and by allowing local government to develop bond markets (Lam et al, 2017, p 185). Within this regime, eldercare is now built in as line items (performance bonuses) in subnational government budgets. In line with NPM principles, the central government issued Circular No 96 in 2013, requesting that subnational governments subcontract social service deliveries to 'social forces' (institutions in civil society) to enhance quality and efficiency. Subnational governments have formed PPPs with non-profit social organizations to operate government-owned eldercare facilities, including LTC facilities, day care for seniors, home meal delivery (resembling Western 'meals-on-wheels' programmes), community care facilities and, finally, private eldercare facilities. Even though regulations specify that only non-profit social organizations may deliver social services, not all providers are themselves non-profit: for-profit companies can and do register for non-profit status as well, in order to get around this regulation. Generally, however, government entities give contracts to those that are closest to them, in various formal and informal ways (Jing and Chen, 2012; Teets, 2012; Jing, 2015).

In both Western and Chinese contexts, then, a necessary consequence of NPM is the proliferation of PPPs and other forms of public sector outsourcing: the emergence of 'governing through contract' by way of contracting out. The on-the-ground logics and relations vary, however. An examination of a sample service contract issued by the Shanghai Bureau of Civil Affairs sheds light on these techniques in the Chinese context. In order to ensure that non-profit social groups are brought under direct Party control – a crucial qualification of contracting out – those groups have to register with municipal governments. Providing a social credit number on the sample contract is an illustration of this process: this new all-China policy, currently at the advanced pilot project stage in specific sectors, has served since 2017 as a mechanism for political and ideological control under the Party's leadership, and as a mechanism analogous to a Western financial credit rating or criminal record check. Funds from government are given out in instalments, with checks in place, and the municipal government does not provide subsidies to service agencies but instead provides rewards for achieving desirable results (*yijiangdaibu*). Governing by contract thus instils discipline, but not exactly market discipline.

Financialization, entailing the enhanced role of the financial sector in steering and exercising control over the wider economy, and the prioritization of both markets and quantitative indicators to the detriment of other, more concrete and qualitative markers (Mulligan, 2016), also expresses itself in trends in the governance of social policy areas in China – eldercare provision is no exception. The shifting of debt risk from the central government to local governments, and from the local governments to the semi-autonomous public agencies under their continued control, helps to meet the intense rising demand for large-scale credit while preserving earlier principles that shield core government agencies from unmanageable credit risks. A further feature of the global financialization process is the privatization of debt: the development of such private debt vehicles as reverse mortgages, life insurance policies, LTC insurance in the Chinese market. Finally, PPPs attract private capital, including finance capital, to invest in eldercare infrastructure; the latest central government policies give international investors equal treatment with domestic investors.

Government policy has guided all of these developments. The General Office of the State Council issued the 'Opinion on Promoting the Development of Eldercare Services' (General Office of the State Council, 2019), which came six years after a pioneering 2013 document from the same Office that provided initial policy support for developing the eldercare service sector. The 2019 document provides more concrete measures to facilitate the development of the sector, and is important in requiring key measures for local governments to maintain comprehensive oversight of the emerging local eldercare sector, including provisions that mandate a standard floor of provision for the most vulnerable elderly. But, for present purposes, we highlight its financialization measures: increasing the financing channels for private residential care facilities; encouraging the development of LTC insurance; and increasing 'inclusive finance' for other aspects of eldercare, a term that refers to private familial savings instruments for eldercare provision. These include private accident insurance and private eldercare investment funds (*yanglao mubiaojijin*).

Financialization of the care sector exhibits an important quality that differentiates the latter from other sectors: it enhances the tendency, in the private provision of care, to divorce these services from the human and emotive core of care itself, with crucial implications in a society that is increasingly unable to provide care along classical lines. It is a commonplace of care literature that this tendency has implications for the care recipient. But, as we have argued elsewhere (Strauss and Xu, 2018), eldercare policy has already been marked in both Vancouver and Shanghai by the invisibility to policy makers of eldercare workers themselves. From that invisibility flow a wide range of negative and dehumanizing implications for the very workers charged with providing some of the most intimate forms of care for some of society's most vulnerable members.

In the wider Chinese economy, one further key aspect of financialization bears on this dehumanizing pressure on eldercare workers: the emergence of housing as a key investment field for private individuals. Homes are treated as investments to an even greater extent in China than in most Western countries, especially since the Asian financial crisis of 1998, as the Chinese have long lacked other reasonably reliable investment opportunities for their own retirement. This role that housing plays is important both for upper- and middle-class investors, and for lower-income Chinese, such as peasants, who are often compensated for their lands' expropriation with one or more apartments and who thereby become petty landlords. Because homes are subject to intense speculation that greatly exceeds the price pressures that would result from narrow housing requirements, housing has become increasingly unaffordable for many urban residents and migrants (Teng et al, 2007; He and Wu, 2009; Lin, 2000; Aveline-Dubach, 2013).

Spill-over effects from this reality are becoming highly controversial features of the housing markets in other Pacific-Rim countries, including major cities in New Zealand, Australia and Canada (Vancouver included). But the implications are also crucial for workers in Shanghai itself, including eldercare workers. Over 70 per cent of the eldercare workforce in Shanghai are rural-to-urban migrant women, 40–50 per cent of whom are live-in caregivers, whether at home or in institutions. The rest often rent, each with a few others, in a market that is often prohibitively expensive. More remote housing may be more affordable, but of course involves much longer commutes for a population already working very long hours. Rental market and transportation costs are the two main factors that make live-in work more appealing to migrant workers (personal interview, May 2017). The workforce is comprised both of middle-aged urban women laid off from state enterprises or manufacturing jobs, and local rural women who have lost land and have been recruited to the eldercare workforce. Rural migrant women are more likely to live in; housing investment is thus a crucial trigger in the return of classic domestic service in China, in which social infrastructures of care are reliant on contracted-out eldercare provision.

Conclusion

Both Canada and China are outliers in the post-2008 crisis-response model of austerity. Canada has a longer and well-documented history of austerity budgeting that is connected (but not reducible) to neoliberalization and the shrinking or circumscription of the social state. China has sought to restrain government debt obligations, but this goal is always in tension with the political imperatives of social stability and order and the visibility of the central and subnational state apparatuses. In both cases, social infrastructures play a crucial role in attempts to resolve the tension between fiscal restraints and the capacity of the state to resolve crises of social reproduction that capitalist relations produce.

In this sense, as we have argued, social infrastructure is a crucial lens for focusing on 'variegated austerity' (cf Peck and Theodore, 2007) and its impacts. However, the concept of social infrastructure has been limited by an inadequate theorization of labour: of both social infrastructures *of* labour (as in the case of home care and home support in 'ageing' cities), and of labour's social infrastructures (public assets, the product of working people's struggles for collective social reproduction), which have been the targets of policies aimed at privatization and/or financialization, especially through NPM.

NPM has been a mechanism for the reform of public management in both the Canadian and Chinese contexts, in similar and divergent ways. Governing through contract has been a feature in both cases, but through the establishment of different kinds of market relations: in Vancouver and BC more broadly, the non-profit sector has been squeezed between retrenched but still significant direct state provision of eldercare (in residential and home settings) and an expanding for-profit sector reliant on contracting-out; in China, the 'social forces' mandated by policy encompass non-profit and for-profit players connected to the local state. In both Vancouver and Shanghai, however, financialized capital is increasingly important, in part due to real estate asset price appreciation (which also connects the two cities, and China with Canada). The entry of finance capital through marketization and de facto privatization, especially of LTC, has exacerbated precarity for workers. In this sense, eldercare safety nets are social infrastructures of care *labour* from which profits are extracted through devaluation. In both places that devaluation falls most heavily on the older women, many of whom are migrant workers (rural-to-urban migrants in China) and immigrant workers (first- and second-generation immigrants, many racialized and some former temporary foreign workers, in Canada), on whose labour those infrastructures of care depend.

Acknowledgements

Research for this chapter has been supported by Social Sciences and Humanities Research Council of Canada insight Grant (#435-2016-0872). We also thank Lynn Ng and Katie Gravestock for their research assistance.

References

Addie, J.-P.D. (2017) 'Infrastructure'. In: *International Encyclopedia of Geography* (Editor-in-Chief, D. Richardson; General Editors, N. Castree, M.F. Goodchild, A. Kobayashi, W. Liu and R.A. Marston). Chichester, UK and Hoboken, NJ: John Wiley & Sons, 1–7.

Angelo, H. and Hentschel, C. (2015) 'Interactions with infrastructure as windows into social worlds: A method for critical urban studies: Introduction'. *City*, 19(2–3): 306–12.

Aveline-Dubach, N. (2013) 'Finance capital launches an assault on Chinese real estate'. *China Perspectives*, 2013(2): 29–39.

Baines, D. and Armstrong, P. (2019) 'Non-job work/unpaid caring: Gendered industrial relations in long-term care'. *Gender Work and Organization*, 26(7): 934–47.

Baines, D. and Cunningham, I. (2015) 'Care work in the context of austerity'. *Competition & Change*, 19(3): 183–93.

BBC (2010) 'State Councillor Ma Kai discusses China's social management'. Available at: https://advance.lexis.com/document/?pdmfid=1516831& crid=dd204716-f1e2-44ff-9003-ce45909cae0d&pddocfullpath=%2F shared%2Fdocument%2Fnews%2Furn%3AcontentItem%3A519F-5VW1 -JC8S-C33V-0000000&pdcontentcomponentid=10962&pdteaserkey= sr0&pditab=allpods&ecomp=kb63k&earg=sr0&prid=11a52649-bcab -4ae4-9089-49aa827c4c51 (accessed 19 June 2020).

Chun, J.J. (2016) 'Organizing across divides: Union challenges to precarious work in Vancouver's privatized health care sector'. *Progress in Development Studies*, 16(2): 173–88.

Cohen, M. (2006) 'The privatization of health care cleaning services in southwestern British Columbia, Canada: Union responses to unprecedented government actions'. *Antipode*, 38(3): 626–44.

Cohen, M. (2012) *Caring for BC's Aging Population: Improving Health Care for All*. Vancouver, BC: Canadian Centre for Policy Alternatives BC Office.

Cohen, M., McLaren, A., Sharman, Z. et al (2006) *From Support to Isolation: The High Cost of BC's Declining Home Support Services*. Vancouver, BC: Canadian Centre for Policy Alternatives, BC Office.

Cohn, D. (2008) 'British Columbia's Capital Asset Management Framework: Moving from transactional to transformative leadership on public-private partnerships, "railroad job"?'. *Canadian Public Administration–Administration Publique du Canada*, 51(1): 71–97.

Cunningham, I., Baines, D. and Shields, J. (2017) '"You've just cursed us": Precarity, austerity and worker's participation in the non-profit social services'. *Relations Industrielles–Industrial Relations*, 72(2): 370–93.

Davies, M. (2001) 'Renovating the Canadian old age home: The evolution of residential care facilities in BC, 1930–1960'. *Journal of the Canadian Historical Association*, 12: 155–75.

Dunn, B. (2014) 'Making sense of austerity: The rationality in an irrational system'. *The Economic and Labour Relations Review*, 25(3): 417–34.

Esping-Andersen, G. (1990) *The Three Worlds of Welfare Capitalism*. Cambridge: Polity Press.

Evans, B. and Albo, G. (2011) 'Permanent austerity: The politics of the Canadian exit strategy from fiscal stimulus'. *Alternate Routes*, 22: 7–28.

Fallon, G. and Poole, W. (2014) 'The emergence of a market-driven funding mechanism in K–12 education in British Columbia: Creeping privatization and the eclipse of equity'. *Journal of Education Policy*, 29(3): 302–22.

General Office of the State Council (Guowuyuan Bangongshi) (2019) 'Opinions on promoting the development of pension services' (*guanyu tuijin yanglao fuyu fazhan de yijian*).

Harrington, C., Jacobsen, F.F., Panos, J. et al (2017) 'Marketization in long-term care: A cross-country comparison of large for-profit nursing home chains'. *Health Services Insights*, 10: 1–23.

He, S. and Wu, F. (2009) 'China's emerging neoliberal urbanism: Perspectives from urban redevelopment'. *Antipode*, 41(2): 282–304.

Heilmann, S. (ed) (2017) *China's Political System*. Lanham, MD: Rowman & Littlefield.

Horton, A. (2019) 'Financialization and non-disposable women: Real estate, debt and labour in UK care homes'. *Environment and Planning A: Economy and Space*. doi: 10.1177/0308518X19862580.

Isitt, B. and Moroz, M. (2007) 'The hospital employees' union strike and the privatization of Medicare in British Columbia, Canada'. *International Labor and Working-Class History*, (71): 91–111.

Jing, Y. (2015) 'Between control and empowerment: Governmental strategies towards the development of the non-profit sector in China'. *Asian Studies Review*, 39(4): 589–608.

Jing, Y. and Chen, B. (2012) 'Is competitive contracting really competitive? Exploring government nonprofit collaboration in China'. *International Public Management Journal*, 15(4): 405–28.

Lam, W.R., Rodlauer, M., Schipke, A. et al (eds) (2017) *Modernizing China: Investing in Soft Infrastructure*. Washington, DC: International Monetary Fund.

Lin, G.C.S. (2000) 'State, capital, and space in China in an age of volatile globalization'. *Environment and Planning A*, 32(3): 455–71.

Lo, P.C.L., Anisef, P., Wang, S. et al (2015) *Social Infrastructure and Vulnerability in the Suburbs*. Toronto: University of Toronto Press.

McBride, S. and Baines, D. (2014) *Orchestrating Austerity: Impacts and Resistance*. Halifax and Winnipeg: Fernwood Publishing.

McBride, S. and Whiteside, H. (2011) 'Austerity for whom?' *Socialist Studies*, special issue on Organizing for Austerity: The Neoliberal State, Regulating Labour and Working Class Resistance, 7(1–2): 42–64.

McCann, E. and Ward, K. (2012) 'Policy assemblages, mobilities and mutations: Toward a multidisciplinary conversation'. *Political Studies Review*, 10(3): 325–32.

McDavid, J.C. and Clemens, E.G. (1995) 'Contracting out local government services: The BC experience'. *Canadian Public Administration-Administration—Publique du Canada*, 38(2): 177–94.

Mulligan, J. (2016) 'Insurance accounts: The cultural logics of health care financing'. *Medical Anthropology Quarterly*, 30(1): 37–61.

Office of the Seniors Advocate (2020) *A Billion Reasons to Care*. Victoria: Office of the Seniors Advocate. https://www.seniorsadvocatebc.ca/a-billion-reasons-to-care/. Accessed 10 March 2020.

Peck, J. (2001) 'Neoliberalizing states: Thin policies/hard outcomes'. *Progress in Human Geography*, 25(3): 445–55.

Peck, J. (2013) 'Austere reason, and the eschatology of neoliberalism's End Times'. *Comparative European Politics*, 11(6): 713–21.

Peck, J. and Theodore, N. (2007) 'Variegated capitalism'. *Progress in Human Geography*, 31(6): 731–72.

People's Daily Online (2013) 'CPC plenum, reform blueprint are of great significance to China, world: overseas experts'. http://en.people.cn/90785/8461374.html. Accessed 19 June 2020.

Pike, A., Coombes, M., O'Brien, P. et al (2018) 'Austerity states, institutional dismantling and the governance of sub-national economic development: The demise of the regional development agencies in England'. *Territory, Politics, Governance*, 6(1): 118–44.

Power, E.R. and Mee, K.J. (2019) 'Housing: an infrastructure of care'. *Housing Studies*. doi: 10.1080/02673037.2019.1612038.

Robbins, C.J., Rudsenske, T. and Vaughan, J.S. (2008) 'Private equity investment in health care services'. *Health Affairs*, 27(5): 1389–98.

Ryan, E.B. (1983) *Description and Analysis of Homemaker Training Programs in British Columbia Community Colleges*. Vancouver: University of British Columbia.

Shrestha, T. and Yeoh, B.S.A. (2018) 'Practices of brokerage and the making of migration infrastructures in Asia: Introduction'. *Pacific Affairs*, 91(4): 663–72.

Stinson, J., Pollak, N., Cohen, M. et al (2005) *Pains of Privatization: How Contracting out Hurts Health Support Workers, Their Families, and Health Care*. Vancouver: Canadian Centre for Policy Alternatives, BC Office.

Strauss, K. and Xu, F. (2018) 'At the intersection of urban and care policy: The invisibility of eldercare workers in the global city'. *Critical Sociology*, 44(7–8): 1163–78.

Su, Z. (2007) 'The evolution and the structure of China's social relief under the framework of civil affairs' [Woguo minzhengfulishiye de lishiyanbian jiqi goujian]. *Fujian Forum* [*Fujian Luntan*] (04): 115–19.

Teets, J.C. (2012) 'Reforming service delivery in China: The emergence of a social innovation model'. *Journal of Chinese Political Science*, 17(1): 15–32.

Teng, F., Mitton, C. and MacKenzie, J. (2007) 'Priority setting in the provincial health services authority: survey of key decision makers'. *BMC Health Services Research*, 7: 84. DOI: 10.1186/1472-6963-7-84.

The National People's Congress Net (2015) *New Budget Law: Opening up Legal Guarantee of Modern Budget Construction (Xinyushuanfa: Kaiqi Xiandaiyushuanjianshe de Falu Baozhang)*. http://www.npc.gov.cn/zgrdw/npc/zgrdzz/2015-02/15/content_1900612.htm. Accessed 19 June 2020).

Whiteside, H. (2017) 'The Canada Infrastructure Bank: Private finance as poor alternative'. *Studies in Political Economy*, 98(2): 223–37.

Whiteside, H. (2018a) 'Austerity as epiphenomenon? Public assets before and beyond 2008'. *Cambridge Journal of Regions, Economy and Society*, 11(3): 409–25.

Whiteside, H. (2018b) 'BC's recurrent austerity: Victory unfettered from success'. In: Evans, B.M. and Fanelli, C. (eds), *The Public Sector in the Age of Austerity: Perspectives from Canada's Provinces and Territories*. Montréal, CA: McGill-Queen's University Press, pp 23–47.

Xu, F. (2012) *Looking for Work in Post-Socialist China: Governance, Active Job Seekers and the New Chinese Labour Market*. London: Routledge.

Zuberi, D.M. and Ptashnick, M.B. (2011) 'The deleterious consequences of privatization and outsourcing for hospital support work: The experiences of contracted-out hospital cleaners and dietary aids in Vancouver, Canada'. *Social Science & Medicine*, 72(6): 907–11.

8

Public Sector Reform and Work Restructuring for Firefighters in Scotland

Eva Jendro and Dora Scholarios

Introduction

This chapter examines restructuring in the public services as a policy response to fiscal consolidation pressures. More specifically, it describes restructuring efforts aimed at rationalization and efficiency gains at several levels, including national, organizational, workgroup and job. The case study of Fire and Rescue Services in Scotland illustrates the manifestations of work restructuring at different levels of analysis, and potential consequences for individual experiences of work.

As detailed in Chapter 1, the transformation of the global financial crisis (GFC) into a sovereign debt crisis put public budgets under strain and public expenditure in the spotlight in a significant share of Organisation for Economic Co-operation and Development (OECD) nations. Contraction of public expenditure through cuts and restructuring of public services formed part of the main policy response. Considering the labour-intensive nature of service provision, savings in public sector workforce compensation formed one of the main foci (Glassner and Watt, 2010; Grimshaw et al, 2012), either through reductions in workforce size or through direct decreases in remuneration and benefits (OECD, 2012, p 23).

The combined pressures of identifying parts of the public services that could be (further) cut in a context of increased demand for public services in times of recession, such as for social security and education, arguably further fuelled fiscal retrenchment measures that sought efficiency gains under the banner of 'more with less' (Vaughan-Whitehead, 2013, pp 8, 36; Eurofound, 2015, pp 5–6, 60). As the OECD (2011a, p 9) put it: 'To avoid an excessive curtailing of public services, the state needs to be streamlined and made more efficient.' Consequently, various rationalization efforts involving a restructuring of public services from national level down to the job or workgroup level could be observed as policy responses across Europe. Efficiency gains and cost reductions were key drivers of such restructuring measures.

The focus of this chapter is restructuring as a means of addressing the 'labour problem' of how to enhance efficiency in the public sector (Worrall et al, 2010). It begins by identifying multiple levels where restructuring has occurred, and an analytical framework for the case of the Scottish Fire and Rescue Service. This case illustrates how restructuring has permeated every level of the reform process, from the creation of a nationwide single service to changes in work organization resembling the 'lean' initiatives observed in other parts of the public services (Carter et al, 2013a). The study draws from primary data gathered in interviews with key informants in managerial, human resources (HR) and union roles, interviews with front-line operational 'wholetime' (WT, full time) firefighters (FFs) and focus groups with WT FF crews. The analysis identifies the extent and levels of restructuring resulting from public sector reform, and implications for the experience of work in the public sector.

Multiple levels of public sector restructuring

The label 'restructuring' has been attached to a range of reorganization measures and activities (Eurofound, 2017, p 95). Overall, public sector workplaces across Europe in the years immediately following the implementation of austerity measures were more likely to have experienced restructuring than those in the private sector: 41 per cent of public sector workplaces, as compared to 35 per cent of those in the private sector (Eurofound, 2012, p 59). Although the overall number subsequently reduced, 'substantial restructuring' has remained a feature of organizational life for over 30 per cent of those working in public administration or the health sector (Eurofound, 2017, p 95). While restructuring is not inevitably tied to downsizing efforts, a significant proportion of restructuring measures seem to have effected workforce reductions. Of the workers reporting a significant work-related restructuring or reorganization in the years following the recession, 44 per cent also reported measures aimed at organizational downsizing (Eurofound, 2015, p 37).

Considering that demand for public services on the whole increases in times of economic downturn (OECD, 2011a), restructuring may have been deemed a means for facilitating rationalization efforts in the form of downsizing while simultaneously targeting performance and efficiency improvements (Datta et al, 2010; Alonso et al, 2015). Indeed, after wage cuts to curb government operating expenditure, downsizing or workforce 'right sizing' measures were reported by the vast majority of OECD nations (OECD, 2012, p 22). These measures included the intent to execute or continue with staff reductions through various channels, such as direct job cuts or limits on replacement of retirees according to ratios.

This substantial downsizing trend observed in the years following the recession affected not only central government across the OECD (2015) but also other parts of the public services, such as support functions in education and hospitals. However, according to Tailby (2012), assessing the true scale of austerity-related downsizing is hindered by the difficulty in distinguishing between preceding reforms. Since the initial 'hollowing out of the state' (Bach and Kessler, 2012, p 31) in the early days of New Public Management (NPM), downsizing and outsourcing arguably seem to have become more engrained in the fabric of public sector management. In the following sections we identify the extent of austerity-related reform by considering the levels at which restructuring has taken place.

National-level restructuring

Structural changes to the public sector landscape can be observed in governance arrangements; for example, the introduction of external, inter-agency or internal (quasi) markets, and inter-agency joined-up or partnership working (Bach and Bordogna, 2013; European Commission, 2013). Changes to the numbers, size and duties of public bodies as part of rationalization-driven restructuring efforts are effected through privatization, outsourcing, closures, mergers or a fragmentation of public bodies into smaller units (Eurofound, 2012; Alonso et al, 2015). Privatization measures following the crisis were scarce, implemented only in some EU countries, including the UK and Greece (Grimshaw, 2013; Ioannou, 2013; Eurofound, 2015, pp 86–7). A more significant trend across EU nations was the outsourcing of government 'support' functions, such as cleaning and information technology (IT) services (Eurofound, 2015, p 41).

The merging of public entities as a policy response to the GFC has been mixed. Drawing on data from a survey of public sector executives from 12 European countries, Randma-Liiv and Kickert (2017) found examples in ten of these countries from 2008 to 2013, including the merging of ministries and government departments with varying but largely related remits in Ireland and the Netherlands (O'Connell, 2013; Pollitt and Bouckaert, 2017, p 314). Public sector mergers in the UK and Greece took place both at national level and at the inter-organizational level between the same type of organization, such as hospitals (Ioannou, 2013; Tzannatos and Monogios, 2013; Cabinet Office, 2014). In the UK, the Coalition Government reduced the number of public bodies through closures and mergers from just over 900 by around a third to approximately 600 (Cabinet Office, 2014, p 5). Over 170 public bodies with 'overlapping or similar functions' were identified for merger (Cabinet Office, 2014, p 3). Such rationalization efforts were reportedly associated with more central government coordination and recentralized financial control (Randma-Liiv and Kickert, 2017).

Inter- and intra-organizational-level restructuring

Organizational restructuring in the form of mergers between the same type of organization, such as in the health and education sectors, creates economies of scale that are intended to enhance resource utilization and efficiency (Vaughan-Whitehead, 2013, p 7). As previously mentioned, hospitals in Greece are one example of such organizational amalgamations (Tzannatos and Monogios, 2013). Such mergers further facilitate rationalization measures through the downsizing of support functions and forming a single back office (Randma-Liiv and Kickert, 2017; for UK, see Cabinet Office, 2014).

According to the OECD (2011a), restructuring also was carried out to 'streamline' organizational functions as a means of making savings through reductions in workforce levels and associated expenditure (Vaughan-Whitehead, 2013). Indeed, according to the European Restructuring Monitor, 'internal restructuring' accounted for 'the majority of reports of restructuring to which 7 per cent of job losses were attributable' (Eurofound, 2015, p 15). 'Streamlining' of organizational functions may, for instance, be effected through 'delayering', such as reductions in management or the closure of business units, an increased use of IT or the establishment of 'shared services' (OECD, 2011b; Eurofound, 2015).

Restructuring at workgroup and job level

Restructuring efforts at workgroup or job level have followed recommendations for workforce 'flexibilization'. This concerns flexibility in the utilization of labour within an organization, for instance, through changes to working times such as the increases in working hours observed particularly in Spain, Greece and Ireland (Bach and Bordogna, 2013).

Other flexibilization efforts focus on skills and training (Heyes, 2013). This resonates with work reorganization practices focusing on skills, such as 'high performance work organisation' (HPWO) or 'lean' work practices, which have been observed in some parts of the public services in efforts to enhance efficiency and organizational performance (Carter et al, 2013a; 2013b; Eurofound, 2015, p 97). HPWOs have tended to be more frequently associated with higher-skilled jobs (Harley et al, 2007), whereas 'lean' practices involve broadening the skills palette (Carter et al, 2013a). 'Lean' initiatives, according to Carter et al (2013a), fit with the notion of doing 'more with less'. Multiskilling of front-line roles expands the tasks associated with these roles, thus reducing downtime, while also allowing management to remove positions that have become redundant. A more intensive utilization of fewer workers is expected to generate greater efficiency.

Restructuring and managerial control

Restructuring initiatives tend to be associated with greater control measures or 'formal assessment of work', such as performance targets (Eurofound, 2012, p 64), including within the public sector (Eurofound, 2015, p 97). Some writers have also suggested that a more intensive utilization of labour, or work intensification, is associated with increased surveillance, performance targets and greater individual accountability (Di Nunzio et al, 2009; Thompson, 2010). Carter et al (2013a; 2013b), for example, highlight how 'lean' initiatives, fuelled by performance metrics, increase bureaucracy and workload. Intensification is also found in changes to the pace and amount of work, or extensions of working time (Eurofound, 2012, p 61).

There are some suggestions that 'lean' initiatives effected through new uses of technology can result in beneficial outcomes for individuals (Lindsay et al, 2014). However, restructured workplaces are more likely to be subjected to some form of performance monitoring under tightened managerial control, and this increased control is associated with negative individual outcomes; for example, bullying, bad management behaviour or 'high strain' work, especially in blue–collar occupations (Eurofound, 2012). Restructuring and downsizing are associated with reports of greater work intensity for remaining staff, in particular in public services (Eurofound, 2015, p 97; Harney et al, 2018) and where reductions have led to understaffing and thus redistribution of tasks (Flecker and Hermann, 2011; Eurofound, 2012, p 53). Restructuring efforts under tight (financial) scrutiny also tend to be associated with control and surveillance mechanisms, such as performance measurement and benchmarking practices (Di Nunzio et al, 2009; Flecker and Hermann, 2011, p 537).

Case study context and research approach

Restructuring in the Scottish public sector

The Scottish Fire and Rescue Service (SFRS) case study reflects pressures for reform from both the Scottish devolved government and UK central government. The Scottish budget for public expenditure on devolved matters is tied to decisions made by the UK government in Westminster (Public Services Commission, 2011, pp 9–10). Consequently, the extensive fiscal austerity measures through cutbacks pursued in Westminster translated into the Scottish context, irrespective of the devolved government's views on such economic policy and associated budgetary changes. The Scottish Government consequently embarked on a reform programme to support the cutbacks required to meet the reduced budget (Scottish Government, 2011).

The subsequent policy direction was underpinned by the Christie Commission's recommendations, which argued that 'Scotland's public service landscape [was] unduly cluttered and fragmented', requiring the 'streamlining of public service structures' alongside enhanced control mechanisms, such as improved performance measurement (Public Services Commission, 2011, pp ix–x). In addition, there was a desire to 'improve value for money' by 'embedding an open and rigorous performance culture within Scotland's public services' (Scottish Government, 2011, p 16).

The Scottish Fire and Rescue Service

There were pressures for reform in fire and rescue services prior to the implementation of austerity-related spending cuts in Westminster. Arguments for Fire and Rescue Service (FRS) reform referred to efficiency seeking and change to an 'outdated' service delivery model which failed to respond to local needs (ODPM, 2004). The foundations for the reforms in Scotland in the aftermath of austerity were laid in 2005 through legislative changes to the role of fire brigades to fire *and rescue* services. The Fire (Scotland) Act 2005 provided the first legislated shift away from core firefighting to include preventative activities, such as Home Fire Safety Visits (HFSVs), and (official) expansion of the role of fire services to respond to 'other eventualities' potentially causing a person or the environment (plants, animals, the fabric of buildings) to be harmed, injured, damaged, fall ill or die. Success in reducing the incidence of fires was thought to increase the amount of time FFs would spend idle, thus allowing the introduction of more or new tasks to FFs' working days to ensure an 'optimum use of capacity' (Scottish Government, 2016, p 17). A more intensive utilization of the workforce was thus possible. The findings presented in this chapter correspond with the first half of a two-step programme for organizational change that sought to address this change in incident response in a fiscal cold climate.

In 2017 there were 356 fire stations in Scotland that had remained unchanged since the establishment of the single service in 2013 (SFRS, 2017). The majority of these stations (240) are crewed by retained FFs (on-call FFs with other primary occupations or source of income), whereas 74 are crewed by WT FFs and the remainder by volunteer crews. Overall, on 31 March 2017 the service employed 7,834 staff (SFRS, 2017, p 1), of which 3,645 were WT operational staff, 2,870 retained duty system FFs, 316 volunteer FFs, 165 control room staff and 838 support staff.

Research design

The fieldwork took place in 2017, four years after the nationwide restructuring had established the single FRS. Seven key-informant interviews were conducted within several managerial functions, including senior representatives from HR and the union, in order to gain a more detailed understanding of the reorganization measures and their rationale. As the aim was to link macro-level reform to work reorganization within the labour process, further qualitative enquiry focused on the front line. Seven semi-structured interviews and seven focus groups were conducted with front-line WT FFs. Specifically, attitudes to changes in working patterns, job roles and the nature of job tasks (past changes and those planned under the second reform phase) and the perceived impact of these on the day-to-day experience of work, such as changes in work intensity, were discussed.

In total, 45 participants (38 WT FFs and seven key informants) were recruited, but not all were able to attend for the full duration of each session, owing to callouts. Three focus groups were affected by participants being absent for around half of the duration of the discussion. The numbers of participants in focus groups ranged from four to five FFs, which reflects the crew sizes for appliances (fire engines). Line management (crew and watch managers) forms part of a fire crew and, as such, also participated in focus groups.

The nine fire stations selected were located in the West and East areas in predominantly urban or suburban areas. Two rural fire stations were visited for means of comparison. The focus on more urban areas was dictated by the fact that stations in very rural areas are not manned by WT staff. The sample covered a variety of stations: 'single pump' stations (equipped with just one fire engine) and 'two pump' stations (equipped with two fire engines), with or without specialisms.

Documentary sources from the Scottish Government, Audit Scotland, FBU (Fire Brigades Union) and the SFRS, as well as key informant interviews, provided data for identifying national-level restructuring. Further insights from key-informant interviews then supplemented front-line perspectives to provide data on changes at organizational level as regards management and control mechanisms; workgroup level as regards shift patterns; and ultimately at the job and individual levels in terms of the cascading effects of control mechanisms and changes in staffing.

Findings

Restructuring at the national and inter-/intra-organizational level

The first reorganization phase saw the amalgamation of the eight legacy fire and rescue services into a single organization that became operational in 2013 (Audit Scotland, 2015). In the spirit of 'tackling waste, duplication and inefficiency' (Scottish Government, 2011, p 4), creating a single national Scottish service was seen as effecting savings while at least initially protecting front-line operational staff by reducing duplicate support functions (Audit Scotland, 2015). Efficiency savings emanating from economies of scale in the nationwide service were expected to allow the organization to meet its new budget, which had been reduced by just over 31 per cent as compared to what the eight legacy brigades had previously received combined (Scottish Government, 2011, p 17; Audit Scotland, 2015).

The newly established national single service was transferred from local authority control to the direct control of the Justice wing of the Scottish Government. It was argued that nationally agreed performance measures and a framework for assessment of outcomes of the FRS in Scotland were needed in order to deliver on the national outcomes set by the Scottish Government in 'Scotland Performs' (Audit Scotland, 2011; Scottish Government, 2014). In a cold fiscal climate, it was asserted, this need for developing such measures became ever more pressing. The first *national* performance management framework based on 'high-level targets' and key performance indicators (KPIs) followed, and results were first published in February 2012 (Audit Scotland, 2015, p 11). To this, another tier in performance control was introduced to enable local authorities to still influence the priorities of the service in spite of oversight having been transferred to the Justice Directorate under the Police and Fire Reform (Scotland) Act 2012.

This restructuring at national level was accompanied by intra-organizational restructuring. Back-office functions, such as HR and control room staff, were merged to reduce workforce levels. While support staff arguably had seen the biggest proportional cuts in overall workforce levels post-amalgamation of 24 per cent from 2011 to 2017 (Audit Scotland, 2015), in total numbers WT FFs had experienced the largest reduction. There are now just over 1,000 fewer FFs than in 2010, with reductions mainly from WT staff (FBU, 2017). These reductions occurred through a prolonged recruitment freeze that saw the non-replacement of retirees. While the Chief Fire Officer had maintained the number of fire stations, there were staff shortages among WT FFs (Audit Scotland, 2018).

Furthermore, management structures were revised, seeing the middle-management cadre reduced but also new roles, namely Local Senior Officers (LSOs) and Deputy Assistant Chief Officer, introduced for each Service Delivery Area in the North, West and East. The role of LSO was specifically created to liaise with local authorities in setting priorities and targets in local plans (Scottish Government, 2011, p 17; SFRS, 2018a).

Workgroup-level restructuring

Work patterns saw subtle change in the East and North Service Delivery Areas through a change in shift pattern to the '5 Group Duty System' (5GDS), or '5 Watch Duty System' as it was predominantly still referred to by the front line. The pattern of the new roster was essentially the same as previously, but instead of any one crew member being on leave at any one time, this changed to whole crews taking leave at the same time. This rearrangement of duty patterns allowed the organization to employ the smallest possible number of WT FFs so as to (in theory) just meet the minimum requirement of staff per appliance as agreed with the union. This allowed a reduction of the overall WT FF front-line numbers to be, as one FF put it, 'at bare bones' (F30). The 5GDS disposed of some so-called 'extra bodies' (additional FFs at some stations to buffer sickness absence) in replacing these with annually predetermined 'orange days'. On orange days, FFs could be called in to work to make up their annualized working hours. The FBU had successfully negotiated a 48 hours' notice for orange days. If this notice period was not adhered to, FFs could be *asked* to come in to work on 'overtime', for which they had to receive additional overtime pay, but could not be *required* to come in.

In practice, nearly all respondents from the (sub)urban stations highlighted issues in relation to the smooth running of the system. Several respondents commented that sickness absence levels aggravated staffing issues under this system. While overall the shift patterns per se were seen by the majority of respondents as favourable or as having perks, understaffing as well as poor management and oversight of staffing were sources of frustration across the (sub)urban stations. Due to shortages in staff or no cover being organized ahead of time, second fire appliances from 'two pump' stations were frequently not dispatched to incidents by control room staff (or were taken 'off the run'). Crew members from these appliances were then sent out to other stations, in particular to so-called 'single pump' stations, to cover absences. As one firefighter commented:

> 'It's the way they're basically looking at it [cutting costs] is just cutting jobs, it's why there was a recruitment freeze for quite a while where they got to a real critical point where we were putting appliances off the run [here], four or five every day was [sic] off the run. We now had a load of recruits but … they're not really going to make any much difference.' (F14)

The 5GDS had been introduced in the West some years before the organizational restructuring and rolled out across the North and East of the unified service in early 2017. While in the West staffing issues were mostly seen as a result of understaffing, participants in the East mostly saw these as a result of poor, inexperienced staffing management. With the roll-out of the 5GDS, oversight of staffing at station level was moved to central regional offices.

Further reorganization efforts at the job level were envisaged under the second phase of reform, which saw the service-wide 'transformation' programme. The roll-out of this programme was announced during summer 2017, but stalled owing to discord with the single profession union representing FFs, the FBU. This 'transformation' would see a further widening of the role of the FRS and therefore wider 'multi-skilling' of the front line. A second round of changes to staffing levels, corresponding to fluctuations in 'demand' for services, were also envisaged. Current requirements for staffing levels on appliances would thus be circumvented by introducing smaller vehicles which needed fewer staff. An HR respondent elaborated:

> 'then also we're looking at our demand patterns, you know, because have we got our fire stations in the right places? Have we got the crewing models right for the types of risk that those communities are now facing? [...] Can we be more efficient? Can we use new technologies in a different way to deliver our services differently and therefore be even better value for money?' (Senior HR respondent)

Managerial control

In order to deliver on the goals of enhancing accountability and improving productivity, tightened control mechanisms were evident in two respects. First, emphasis on targets at the group level increased through the reformed and tightened performance frameworks under the increased managerial oversight of newly created management roles (LSOs). Group-level targets would, for instance, relate to HFSV numbers carried out across various parts of the demographic, which then were believed to deliver on higher-level KPIs, such as reductions in accidental dwelling fires. In all but one of the rural stations and throughout the majority of FF interviews/focus groups, issues around targets, in combination with an increase in managerial scrutiny, were described. Some associated this increasing emphasis on targets as a way of 'justifying jobs' or demonstrating 'value for money'.

> 'I guess it all comes down to money as well. It's budget and justifying your job and what you're doing kind of thing.' (F12)

While targets had existed prior to the restructuring in 2013, pressures were widely reported to have increased. Most participating FFs did not mind the activities behind the targets but, rather, commented on how the targets were overseen by middle management. The intensification of performance pressures had given rise to feelings of being undervalued, a drop in morale and greater feelings of frustration where this was associated with poor management behaviour. Targets were perceived as being applied unfairly as they did not take into account long periods of time off or busy spells. Several participants also voiced frustration in accessing households that would benefit the most from target-related activities, such as HFSVs, and dissatisfaction with a sense of having 'to drum up business':

> 'We know that 90 per cent of people have got smoke detectors. Do we need to keep to continue [sic] going out there just because we happen to have included it in one of our KPIs now? Aye, that we have to. So we're a slave to the KPI, a slave to the performance indicator. Not to the actual maybe requirement or need, you know, of the actual activity. [...] but there is a perception of firefighters that we're going through the motions.' (Senior union respondent, F43)

The second area of tighter control reported was through bureaucratic procedures and intensified reporting. This was the most universally negatively discussed issue during interviews and focus groups. The volumes of paperwork expected of line management (crew and watch managers) and increasingly of FFs took up considerable amounts of time. Rules and procedures were perceived as unworkable, restrictive, ill informed and issued in an ad hoc or 'knee jerk' way. An example given by several groups related to the ad hoc instruction to 'do reassurance visits' to flats in all buildings of five or more floors in the fallout of the Grenfell Tower fire in London. This instruction was issued by the Scottish Government, illustrating the changes in governance arrangements. The sheer numbers of visits in city centres were pointed out as this crew manager joked:

> 'everybody sat in this room will be dead before you get two streets done. Hehehe! It is unachievable, it is unachievable.' (F23)

One crew further complained that they had been left with insufficient guidance on what was expected of them in doing such visits, as well as feeling underqualified to effectively 'reassure' inhabitants of multi-storey buildings. Moreover, tightened scrutiny associated with expanded rulesets and procedures may have at times eroded the small amount of discretion that could previously be exerted by the front line.

The majority of respondents at the generally busier (sub)urban stations also criticized managerial oversight of crews' targets or adherence to new rules and procedures. Examples included accounts of constant reprimanding for small mistakes or underperformance (described by around half of participants). The majority of FF participants reported feeling unfairly treated, micro-managed, undervalued and lacking voice.

> 'If we do anything wrong, anything small, we are slapped down like a big stick and that is basically the crux of everything I think.' (F42)

Such unfair treatment and a 'name and shame culture' were acknowledged as action points resulting from a recent cultural audit conducted by the organization (SFRS, 2016: 4).

Work intensity

Line management reported a significant intensification of administrative work under increasing bureaucracy. This was endemic throughout all tiers of management, as illustrated by the following managers:

> 'I would think my workload has increased at least tenfold if not more. Because our reporting mechanisms have changed quite a little bit as well. So if we talk about key performance indicators; that's something I'd never heard of before. But the modern world, everybody wants a statistic and a figure and targets have been set so ... that landscape within the service has changed.' (Key informant, procedure-informing role)

> 'So what should be a two minute job to fill in a tick box to say "this is what's wrong" [...] becomes probably 45 minutes' work.' (F24)

While fire-related incidents had decreased, response to other incidents had increased since 2009–10 (SFRS, 2018b), as well as non-emergency work, such as community engagement. Around a third of FF participants and their line managers felt that the general public perception of 'lazy' FFs was not reflective of their working realities and falsely provided the imperative for yet a further widening of their job role to include more routine tasks – for example, more preventative and computer-based tasks, providing cover for understaffing. These additional tasks also raised a concern that hands-on training quality and frequency had suffered. A firefighter voiced this view as follows:

'it's more about the targets and making sure they're not missed and the training's just — if you get the time, you can do it. Everything else is a priority, that's not the priority for us. But for us it should be.' (F32)

The expansion of tasks associated with the increase in monitoring and control was viewed as excessive. Some felt that collecting numbers in order to produce statistics had become the most important task expected of FFs. Consequently, rather than the intensity of work in terms of its pace and volume being an issue, the intensity of scrutiny experienced under tight performance measurement and bureaucratic procedures was the most significant problem for FFs and line managers alike:

'It's just the gaffer says he's getting e-mails about missed paperwork and somebody's not ticked a box on one page of a training screen and you're like "Oof! All the good stuff I've done hasn't been picked up on? But that one, that one missed box that I've not ticked? Or that one form I filled in wrong? You jobbed all of it?"' (F25)

Understaffing contributed in part to further, if temporary, increases in work intensity that could be observed in (sub)urban fire stations. Staffing shortages had two effects on work intensity. Firstly, where appliances had to 'go off the run' owing to staffing shortages, several respondents noted that the remainder of machines were as a result reportedly busy providing cover for an area. A respondent (F19) described how the remaining pump that was not taken off the run would be so busy providing cover that FFs at that station would jokingly liken being called out once to disappearing in the 'Bermuda Triangle'. The crew was not to be seen again at the station, bouncing from incident to incident.

Secondly, five out of seven focus groups as well as two interviewees further discussed how fewer appliances on the run can potentially intensify stress at incidents when support crews, needed for application of safety procedures, would have to be dispatched from further away. The senior union respondent (F43) as well as some FFs also expressed concern over current procedures becoming unworkable (with a drop in the speed of response anticipated). Reduced staffing models were under discussion at the time of study. Moreover, pumps had to go off the run, due to understaffing and further cuts under austerity. One FF expressed this concern as follows:

'I think one of the biggest issues with the drop [...] is if you do get a job and you need another appliance to show up, there's potential of it coming from further away. So that time difference could actually potentially make a huge difference to the outcome. Not just for anyone that was involved in the fire initially. But to ourselves. 'Cause it's a lot more pressure because we might not have enough bodies there to do the job so being under that extra pressure trying to – will I take more risks?' (F35)

There were also reports by around a third of participants, or most of the crews in (sub)urban locations, of staff shortages having increased involuntary overtime in terms of being relieved at the end of one's shift. However, being offered additional shifts ahead of time was mentioned by several FFs as a good way of earning a little extra. Large increases in overtime, either for calling staff in to cover a whole shift or for hours added on to one's shift until relief could be resourced, were acknowledged as a cost problem by the organization (SFRS, 2018a), suggesting the potential unintended consequences of austerity-inspired staff reduction measures.

Discussion

Organizational restructuring at the national level saw the merging of FRS in Scotland into a single national service. This entailed moving the national service from local authority control to the control of the devolved Scottish Government's Justice wing. A recentralization of control over public entities illustrates the overarching financial imperative to cut public expenditure marking the particular character of public sector reform under austerity (European Commission, 2013; Alonso et al, 2015).

Considering that fire and rescue services as emergency services are deemed essential, the amalgamation of the FRS exemplifies reform that seeks efficiencies at every level where a wholesale outsourcing and privatization of these parts of the public services as an approach to reducing public expenditure is impossible. Moreover, the reform under study has shown how restructuring efforts at the various levels, from the national to the job level, were interdependent in order to deliver on the overarching aim of meeting the reduced budget while attempting to protect services available to the wider population. The merging of the legacy fire services in itself, with the exception of support functions such as HR and IT, would not have allowed for reductions in front-line levels. These relied on the introduction of a new shift pattern to the East and North areas that allowed reductions in front-line WT FFs through 'natural wastage' and a more flexible utilization of the remaining workforce by introducing 'orange days'. Yet factors such as potential miscalculations in recruitment freezes (leading to understaffing in front-line operational FFs), cuts to support functions, the requirement to give 48 hours' notice to call FFs in and sickness absence levels appear to have hindered the roster's ability to deliver cost savings. Cost savings were dampened by the additional pay required by reliance on overtime absence-covering.

The case of the FRS in Scotland confirms previous studies of restructuring for efficiency savings driven by rationalization logics. These have pointed to the negative repercussions of restructuring on the remaining workforce (Carter et al, 2013b; Harney et al, 2018). The study also illustrates the negative effects on front-line staff of the concept of 'doing more with less'. The negative effects of increasing the tasks expected of front-line staff while reducing staffing were to some degree mitigated by the shift pattern, which, in essence, remained intact under the new crewing model. More problematic was the implementation of the roster, with its susceptibility to understaffing and mismanagement.

The study's findings point towards some interlinking effects of higher-level reforms in a fiscal cold climate in which tightened accountability for and oversight of scarce resources appear to have translated into somewhat worsened individual experiences of work. Increased control mechanisms at the workplace level, installed to deliver 'value for money', entailed more tasks at the job level concerned with documenting activities and form filling. As noted elsewhere (Di Nunzio et al, 2009; Flecker and Hermann, 2011, p 537), tightened control mechanisms associated with increases in paperwork, thus reducing downtime, intensified the experience of work for FFs. Line management was also severely affected by the intensification of work. The nature of such changes in administrative, computer-based work and associated mid-managerial behaviour were the focus of concern, rather than the intensification of work itself. For individuals, these issues were associated with unfair treatment and loss of morale.

Conclusion

The aim of this chapter has been to trace the cascading manifestations of macro-level fiscal retrenchment through levels of efficiency-seeking public service restructuring measures at the national level, inter-/intra-organizational level, workgroup and job level. While the study cannot demonstrate causality across levels, the analysis provides a lens for examining the interconnectivity of reorganization measures to effect changes in 'productivity' and, as such, address 'the labour problem' across the various levels. The case of the FRS in Scotland illustrates how reorganization to achieve a more intensive utilization of labour intertwined the creation of a unified national service and leaner staffing models, with changes in the volume and nature of tasks at the job level. The study raises questions about whether reorganization measures can effectively mitigate the impact of fiscal retrenchment while enhancing 'efficiency' in 'labour utilisation'. In this study, it appears that reorganization for more intensive labour utilization has been effective, if perhaps artificially so, given the apparent unintended and less visible consequences of the control mechanisms that have been introduced – for example, overtime costs and low morale. The qualitative value of such increases in 'productivity', therefore, remains in question.

References

Alonso, J.M., Clifton, J. and Díaz-Fuentes, D. (2015) 'Did new public management matter? An empirical analysis of the outsourcing and decentralization effects on public sector size'. *Public Management Review*, 17(5): 643–60.

Audit Scotland (2011) *Response to consultation on the future of the Fire and Rescue Service in Scotland*. Edinburgh.

Audit Scotland (2015) *The Scottish Fire and Rescue Service*. Edinburgh.

Audit Scotland (2018) *Scottish Fire and Rescue Service: An Update*. Edinburgh.

Bach, S. and Bordogna, L. (2013) 'Reframing public service employment relations: The impact of economic crisis and the new EU economic governance'. *European Journal of Industrial Relations*, 19(4): 279–94.

Bach, S. and Kessler, I. (2012) 'Upstream decisions and employee relations under New Labour'. In: *The Modernisation of the Public Services and Employee Relations*. Basingstoke: Palgrave Macmillan, 25–46.

Cabinet Office (2014) *Public Bodies 2014*. London: Cabinet Office.

Carter, B., Danford, A., Howcroft, D., Richardson, H., Smith, A. and Taylor, P. (2013a) 'Taxing times: Lean working and the creation of (in)efficiencies in HM Revenue and Customs'. *Public Administration*, 91(1): 83–97.

Carter, B., Danford, A., Howcroft, D., Richardson, H., Smith, A. and Taylor, P. (2013b) '"Stressed out of my box": Employee experience of lean working and occupational ill-health in clerical work in the UK public sector'. *Work, Employment & Society*, 27(5): 747–67.

Datta, D.K., Guthrie, J.P., Basuil, D. and Pandey, A. (2010) 'Causes and effects of employee downsizing: A review and synthesis'. *Journal of Management*, 36(1): 281–348.

Di Nunzio, D., Hohnen, P., Hasle, P., Torvatn, H. and Øyum, L. (2009) *Impact of Restructuring on Health and Safety and Quality of Work Life*. Leuven: Katholieke Universiteit Leuven. Higher Institute of Labour Studies.

Eurofound (2012) *ERM Report 2012 – After Restructuring: Labour Markets, Working Conditions and Life Satisfaction*. Luxembourg.

Eurofound (2015) *ERM Annual Report 2014: Restructuring in the Public Sector*. Luxembourg.

Eurofound (2017) *Sixth European Working Conditions Survey – Overview Report (2017 update)*. Luxembourg.

European Commission (2013) *Industrial Relations in Europe 2012*. Brussels.

FBU (Fire Brigades Union) (2017) 'Almost one-in-five frontline firefighter jobs cut since 2010'. *Fire and Rescue Service Matters – A Parliamentary Bulletin from the Fire Brigades Union*. 5 July.

Flecker, J. and Hermann, C. (2011) 'The liberalization of public services: Company reactions and consequences for employment and working conditions'. *Economic and Industrial Democracy*, 32(3): 523–44.

Glassner, V. and Watt, A. (2010) 'Cutting wages and employment in the public sector: Smarter fiscal consolidation strategies needed'. *Intereconomics*, 45(4): 212–19.

Grimshaw, D. (2013) 'Austerity, privatization and levelling down: Public sector reforms in the United Kingdom'. In: Vaughan-Whitehead, D. (ed), *Public Sector Shock*. Cheltenham: Edward Elgar Publishing, 576–626.

Grimshaw, D., Rubery, J. and Marino, S. (2012) 'Public sector pay and procurement in Europe during the crisis: Prospects for segmentation, inequalities and social dialogue'. Brussels: European Commission.

Harley, B., Allen, B.C. and Sargent, L.D. (2007) 'High performance work systems and employee experience of work in the service sector: The case of aged care'. *British Journal of Industrial Relations*, 45(3): 607–33.

Harney, B., Fu, N. and Freeney, Y. (2018) 'Balancing tensions: Buffering the impact of organisational restructuring and downsizing on employee well-being'. *Human Resource Management Journal*, 28(2): 235–54.

Heyes, J. (2013) 'Flexicurity in crisis: European labour market policies in a time of austerity'. *European Journal of Industrial Relations*, 19(1): 71–86.

Ioannou, C.A. (2013) 'Greek public service employment relations: A Gordian knot in the era of sovereign default'. *European Journal of Industrial Relations*, 19(4): 295–308.

Lindsay, C., Commander, J., Findlay, P., Bennie, M., Dunlop Corcoran, E. and Van Der Meer, R. (2014) 'Lean, new technologies and employment in public health services: Employees' experiences in the National Health Service'. *The International Journal of Human Resource Management*, 25(21): 1–16.

O'Connell, P. (2013) 'Cautious adjustment in a context of economic collapse: The public sector in the Irish crises'. In: Vaughan-Whitehead, D. (ed), *Public Sector Shock*. Cheltenham: Edward Elgar Publishing, 337–70.

ODPM (Office of the Deputy Prime Minister) (2004) *The Fire and Rescue Service National Framework*. Wetherby: Office of the Deputy Prime Minister.

OECD (Organisation for Economic Co-operation and Development) (2011a) *Government at a Glance 2011*. OECD Publishing.

OECD (2011b) *Public Servants as Partners for Growth: Towards a Stronger Leaner and More Equitable Workforce*. OECD Publishing.

OECD (2012) *Public Sector Compensation in Times of Austerity*. Paris: OECD Publishing.

OECD (2015) *Government at a Glance 2015*. Paris: OECD Publishing.

Pollitt, C. and Bouckaert, G. (2017) *Public Management Reform* (4th edn). Oxford: Oxford University Press.

Public Services Commission (2011) *Commission on the Future Delivery of Public Services*. Edinburgh: Scottish Government.

Randma-Liiv, T. and Kickert, W. (2017) 'The impact of the fiscal crisis on public administration reforms: Comparison of 14 European countries'. *Journal of Comparative Policy Analysis: Research and Practice*, 19(2): 155–72.

Scottish Government (2011) *Renewing Scotland's Public Services: Priorities for Reform in Response to the Christie Commission*. Edinburgh: Scottish Government.

Scottish Government (2014) *One Scotland – The Government's Programme for Scotland 2014–2015*. Edinburgh: Scottish Government.

Scottish Government (2016) *Fire and Rescue Framework for Scotland 2016*. Edinburgh: Scottish Government.

SFRS (Scottish Fire and Rescue Service) (2016) *SFRS Cultural Audit Action Plan 2015–2016*. Cambuslang: Scottish Fire and Rescue Service.

SFRS (2017) *Fire Safety and Organisational Statistics (Scotland) 2016–2017*. Cambuslang: Scottish Fire and Rescue Service.

SFRS (2018a) *Service Delivery Statement of Assurance*. Cambuslang: Scottish Fire and Rescue Service.

SFRS (2018b) *Fire and Rescue Incident Statistics (Scotland) 2017–18*. Cambuslang: Scottish Fire and Rescue Service.

Tailby, S. (2012) 'Public service restructuring in the UK: The case of the English National Health Service'. *Industrial Relations Journal*, 43(5): 448–64.

Thompson, P. (2010) 'The capitalist labour process: Concepts and connections'. *Capital & Class*, 34(1): 7–14.

Tzannatos, Z. and Monogios, Y. (2013) 'Public sector adjustment amidst structural adjustment in Greece: Subordinate, spasmodic and sporadic'. In: Vaughan-Whitehead, D. (ed), *Public Sector Shock*. Cheltenham: Edward Elgar Publishing, 259–99.

Vaughan–Whitehead, D. (2013) 'Public sector shock in Europe: Between structural reforms and quantitative adjustment'. In: Vaughan–Whitehead, D. (ed), *Public Sector Shock*. Cheltenham: Edward Elgar Publishing, 1–42.

Worrall, L., Mather, K. and Seifert, R. (2010) 'Solving the labour problem among professional workers in the UK public sector: Organisation change and performance management'. *Public Organization Review*, 10(2): 117–37.

9

Austerity, Personalized Funding and the Degradation of Care Work: Comparing Scotland's Self-Directed Support Policy and Australia's National Disability Insurance Scheme

Donna Baines and Doug Young

Introduction

This chapter compares and analyses work under two social policies that claim to empower service users, recognize human rights and improve service quality, namely, the Social Care (Self-Directed Support) (Scotland) Act 2013 and Australia's National Disability Insurance Scheme (NDIS) (NDIS Quality and Safeguards Commission, 2018). Although both policies are seen as much-needed steps towards the social inclusion and human rights of people with disabilities, the private-market consumer focus and inadequate funding of these policies pit the rights of service users against the employment rights of care workers, generating a downward spiral in wages and conditions, as well as serious concerns about quality of care. Both policies place customer choice at the heart of care relationships, providing individualized funding packages to eligible individuals for the purchase of needed or wanted services.

These policies emerged during a time of heightened austerity and witnessed considerable concerns on the part of service users that their personalized funding packages were inadequate to their needs and that their views and those of their families and carers were often overlooked (Productivity Commission, 2017; Warr et al, 2017). This has obvious spill-over effects on service organizations, which receive inadequate recompense for services provided, and frequently experience problems with cash flow and shortfall, providing incentives to drive wages down and increase temporary and insecure employment.

In Australia, funding is assigned to the individual in a pay-as-you-go arrangement. This has propelled the rapid emergence of gig-like or casual, on-demand labour markets for individual home care workers in disability care, supplanting long-established, permanent, non-profit employment. Australia's system of employment regulation and sector-wide wage awards seems ill-equipped to protect workers in this new, fragmented context (David and West, 2017).

In Scotland, care organizations are required to pursue cost recovery from the government after individual services have been provided. For Scotland's voluntary sector, the requirement that funded agencies should adopt New Public Management (NPM) practice has resulted in a prevalence of short-term funding contracts, cuts in services, stricter and often confining performance criteria, and the emergence of a 'contract culture' whereby funders determine what type of care is available (Cunningham, 2014). It is ironic that under a policy aimed at consumer empowerment these trends create a greater emphasis on target setting over service users' needs. In addition, a perverse incentive exists, whereby meeting these targets implies that they are adequate and leads to further decline in services and, often, funding (Baines, 2006).

Drawing on 46 in-depth, qualitative interviews in Scotland (27) and Australia (19), the chapter addresses the impact of austerity and personalized funding schemes on terms and conditions of work, as well as on labour markets and work organization. The chapter argues that the austerity state has led these initiatives to restructure a largely publicly funded, non-profit, organization-based workforce into an increasingly privatized, casualized and fragmented one, with few protections for workers or service users and little capacity to realize human rights or employment rights.

Contexts and literature

Disability rights and human rights in individualized funding

An extensive literature confirms that the human and social rights of people with disabilities have been suppressed and marginalized worldwide (Williams, 2014; Howard et al, 2015; Thill, 2015). The social model of disability asserts that society has failed to ensure access to full lives for people with disabilities, and calls for far-reaching changes to advance equity and social inclusion (Howard et al, 2015; Thill, 2015). In Scotland and Australia, individualized models of funding have been presented as the exclusive remedy for the injustices experienced by people with disabilities, although this is only one of many possible options (Kvist and Fritzell, 2011; Williams, 2014; Martinelli, 2017). While disability and human rights movements sought new systems based on an individual's lifetime goals and strengths, the individualized funding model interprets these goals solely through a market lens, with individual care users constructed as consumers empowered through the exercise of consumer choice to purchase care (Productivity Commission, 2011; Brennan et al, 2012, p 378). Within this marketized model, strong incentives exist for employers and service users to reduce costs as far as possible, generating greater precarity for workers and uncertain quality and choice for people with disabilities (Hussein and Manthorpe, 2014; Macdonald et al, 2018). Although conflict could be avoided if governments provided sufficient funding and protections for service users and workers, neoliberal, individualized funding models place the human rights of people with disabilities in opposition to the employment rights of care workers, generating a downward spiral in wages and conditions, and concerns about quality of care, isolation of people with disabilities and back-sliding in terms of rights and protections.

Personalization and individualized funding

Individualized funding is intended to incentivize the development of an array of disability services competing for clients in an open, private market (Cunningham and James, 2014) or a managed market with the government mediating payment through service users (Cortis et al, 2017). Evidence from European countries shows that cash-for-care policies have introduced extensive demands for flexibility, travel between multiple work locations and very short working hours, and may be a cover for deepening austerity policies (Christensen, 2012; Glendinning, 2012; Cunningham and Nickson, 2013).

In Scotland, self-directed support (SDS) is legislated via the Social Care (Self-directed Support) (Scotland) Act 2013, which is designed to encourage greater personalization of services and users' involvement through the increased use of Direct Payments (DPs) and Individual Budgets (IBs) (Kettle, 2015). Via this legislation, service users are presented with one of four options: (1) a DB from the local authority to the service user for support provision; (2) the selection of support by the supported person, but with the practicalities of arrangements being made by the local authority; (3) the selection of support and the practicalities of arrangements being made by the local authority; (4) a combination of the first three options. Additionally, whereas the English and Welsh legislation came into force in 2010, in Scotland the equivalent was not in place until 2013 – directly within the context of austerity. This has resulted in what some authors describe as a lower level of enthusiasm for personalization (Moffatt et al, 2012); others assert that enthusiasm remains high but greater financial constraints are to blame for lower uptake of DP and IB options (Manthorpe et al, 2015). Other explanations for this dynamic include an ideological resistance to the perceived privatization of care (Pearson, 2000; Riddell et al, 2006; UNISON, 2012), and a 'lack of awareness from front-line workers and managers, and the need to invest in advocacy and support' (Rummery et al, 2012, p 7). This view is supported by conclusions drawn from Ridley et al's (2011) report into SDS test-sites in Scotland, which found largely that the approach was hampered by misconceptions of the true purpose of SDS, on the part of both service users and employees. Additionally, Scotland's significantly differing demographics and regionality, partly informed by an urban/rural dichotomy, and differing local authority practices (Craig and Manthorpe, 1999; Cunningham and Nickson, 2013) mean that experiences are far from uniform.

Like personalized funding in the UK, the NDIS in Australia introduces a national system of funding for 'people with permanent and significant disability, their families and carers' (NDIS Act, 2013). This cash-for-care model replaces the organization-based system of funding and allows governments to appear to be responsive to the concerns of people with disabilities that they should be central decision makers in their own lives, while simultaneously reinforcing neoliberalism's commitment to reduced public services through privatization and constrained funding and expenditures (Denniss, 2015; Green et al, 2018). Two forms of disability service under-funding continue under the NDIS: (1) underfunding of services in relation to the needs of people; and (2) underfunding of contracted services (Productivity Commission, 2010, pp 135, 281). This underfunding provides an incentive to pay lower wages (Williams, 2014; Cortis et al, 2017), making it hard to attract or retain workers, removing incentives for workers to upskill and eliminating monies for supervision and training.

The minimum pay and conditions for disability workers are set out in a tripartite labour agreement between government, unions and employers known as the Social, Community, Home Care and Disability Services Award. However, as Cortis et al (2017) argue, pricing has been set too low to meet Award wage minimums, let alone to cover the costs of those employers committed to paying above the Award, meaning that better employers risk insolvency. Under the Award, minimum hours are differentiated, with home care having a minimum engagement period of one hour, as compared to two hours for a disability support worker. This provides an incentive for cash-strapped service users and employers to hire into the category of home care worker rather than disability support worker and has generated calls for further shortening shift minimums to one hour or less for all workers (Macdonald and Charlesworth, 2016). Rather than being organization and group based, much of the work under the NDIS is in people's private homes, as staying at home does not incur travel costs for service users. However, this shifts the work from the public sphere to the private sphere of home and family. As feminist political economy scholars note, care work in the private home is difficult to scrutinize, keeping wages low or non-existent and making it difficult to improve or regulate, and offers little assurance of safety (Meagher and Healy, 2003; Folbre, 2008).

Work under the NDIS is increasingly characterized by assignment of shifts at short notice, multiple employers, multiple job holding, dispersed work sites, no travel pay and short-term work assignments (Macdonald et al, 2018). This signals an important change from largely publicly funded, non-profit-delivered, organization-based employers to a privatized, fragmented, quasi-gig or on-demand economy (Friedman, 2014; van Doorn, 2017). Gig work has thus far been mostly found in the arts, entertainment, delivery services and private domestic work; however, it is increasingly seen in the NDIS (David and West, 2017). In gig economies, employers primarily interface between service users and short-term providers. In Australia, this type of labour market has been instigated and fostered by government policies that interpret the empowerment of services users through a market lens, with built-in incentives to fragment the labour market through low wages and short shifts.

Austerity

The era following the 1980s witnessed a shift from public to private social service delivery (for-profit and non-profit) through government contracting-out and a bolstering of the private market as the solution to all economic and social problems. Referred to as neoliberalism, this set of policies interlaces far-reaching policy changes aimed at shrinking the state, legally mandating balanced budgets, cutting taxes, reducing the regulation of private corporations and creating sustained opportunities for private profit making (Harvey, 2007; Stanford, 2015).

Although Australia did not experience recession after the 2008 financial crisis (Denniss, 2015), it adopted a series of policies that promoted austerity and normalized the notion that sacrifices were necessary in the present, in order to provide for better outcomes in the future (Clayton et al, 2015; Hayes and Moore, 2017). Foremost among these were continued cuts to the public sector and increased contracting out to the non-profit and for-profit sectors. Contracted-out agencies were required to adopt NPM practices with the putative goal of improving performance, increasing efficiencies and providing accountability. Although the economy in Australia remains strong, austerity saturates social and economic policy, ensuring high returns for private business, a rapidly eroding public sphere and diminished protections for workers.

Scotland's experience of austerity is markedly different than that of the rest of the UK (Wallace, 2013). Austerity has intensified marketization in the sector's funding relationships, which have come to be described as increasingly 'arms-length' (Cunningham and James, 2014), with a strong emphasis on NPM-style target setting (Baines et al, 2011). In consequence, terms and conditions of employment have suffered considerably (Cunningham and Nickson, 2011). McKendrick et al (2016) note that austerity has a disproportionate impact on the most disadvantaged and vulnerable, including the predominantly female workforce, and that this dynamic has developed alongside a shift of risk onto the individual. Pilot studies show that local authorities are motivated by cost containment rather than quality, leading to reductions in expenditure under personalization (Ellis, 2007; West, 2013). These government cuts negatively impact on service users as well as on the income security of non-profits providing services. Although neoliberalism and austerity have been studied in many contexts, this chapter explores the effects of these relatively new, individualized social policies on care workers in the context of austerity policies.

Theory

This chapter draws on two sets of theory. The first, feminist political economy theory, is used to clarify how larger economic and political processes and systems shape policy regimes and the interactions of actors at the level of social life, particularly gendered production (paid care work) and reproduction (unpaid care work) (Bedford and Rai, 2010; Peterson, 2012). Feminist political economy will be used to analyse the interplay between larger social policies and the experience at the front lines of care work. We will argue that the content and impact of austerity-linked policies flow across national boundaries and geographies, justifying the postponement of needs today for vague and ill-defined benefits at some point in the future. This narrative advances marketized policies such as individualized and personalized funding, compelling a set of managerialized organizational practices and working conditions and providing the ideological justification for why dispersed people (namely care workers and service users in Scotland and Australia) experience similar work degradation and difficult conditions. The chapter also draws on Labour Process Theory (Thompson and Smith, 2009; Thompson, 2010) to closely analyse the social relations of control and power in the workplace (Thompson and Smith, 2009; Thompson, 2010), including the power of workers and of management to negotiate the conditions of and wages for work. In the context of care work, these shifts include: austerity; precarious work, wages, conditions and work organization; and the gendering of the sector (Aronson and Smith, 2010; Glendinning, 2012; Cunningham et al, 2013).

The studies

The chapter draws on studies in Scotland and Australia. The Scottish data is premised on 27 qualitative, in-depth, semi-structured interviews with 14 workers from a disability organization and 13 from a mental health organization (abbreviated to PDO and MHO, respectively). Interviews were audio-recorded and transcribed in full, allowing for full immersion in the data and the subsequent emergence of a manual coding system (Miles and Huberman, 1994; Auerbach, 2003) from which analysis was conducted. As a means of recruiting participants, two organizations were approached directly with a view to establishing a data set from which comparisons of physical disability and mental health service provision could be made. Interviews with participants were conducted with an interview guide, which included questions on how personalization had impacted on their work, their employer and their service users, and how they perceived this to impact on their own futures and the future of the sector. The gender breakdown of the sample is 58.2 per cent female overall. The sample in the MHO was 69.3 per cent female, which is broadly reflective of the sector at large. The PDO sample was 47.1 per cent female, which reflects the higher representation of males in this sub-sector, possibly owing to perceptions of a requirement for physical strength required for moving and handling (Young, 2018). Length of service varied considerably, from just a few months to over 20 years.

The Australian study involved 19 qualitative, in-depth, semi-structured interviews, using an interview guide, with 19 disability sector workers in one of the early-roll-out regions (the roll-out started in July 2016). The interviews were audio-taped, transcribed and analysed for patterns and themes (Kirby et al, 2006). Research participants were recruited through an open call distributed by unions in the sector and took place in a central location. Interviewees were asked questions regarding changes in their work under the NDIS, challenges, successes and where they saw themselves in the future. The sample was 70 per cent female, which is slightly lower than for the sector as a whole, and all participants had undertaken higher education and/or training. Length of employment ranged from 1.5 to 30 years, with the majority having 8+ years of experience.

Ethics approval was received at the universities and institutions involved. Limitations of the studies include their small sample size, possible bias in their recruitment strategy, and qualitative method, which does not permit generalization but generates insights that may be pertinent in multiple contexts and conditions.

Findings

In this section, themes from the data and the literature are interwoven with exemplar quotes from the data. Similar themes from each country are presented and analysed. Themes from the Australian data include human rights, choice and marketized care; and increased precarity and the gig-like care work. Themes from the Scottish data include the notion of the service user as 'customer'; the relationship between personalization and budgetary cuts; and the increasing fragmentation and precarity. Larger themes that are common across both sets of data include tensions between human rights and marketized care, and the degradation of care work.

Tensions between human rights and marketized care

Underfunding, voice and choice in Australia

Across the board, the Australian research participants and unions expressed strong support for the empowerment, choice and respect for the human rights of people with disabilities. However, most workers also reported that the NDIS "does not feel like it is designed for people with intellectual disabilities". This quote echoed the concerns of all research participants: "These guys we support are the ones that are getting the money taken off them because they can't speak up. It's like a tier system with people with disabilities, and people with intellectual disabilities are on the bottom tier." Other workers concurred: "Our guys have intellectual disabilities, [so] they don't have a voice. They're the ones who're losing out over and over." As will be discussed further later, the NDIS has left many people with underfunded plans (particularly for transportation and activities); less access to advocacy; fewer skilled workers ready and available to work, particularly with people with complex issues; less choice; and more instability. Workers questioned how this underfunded context fit with the concept of 'choice' which is said to underlie the NDIS. As one worker argued, "the service users have less access to services and transportation to and from activities. They are more socially isolated than before and unless they have a really strong parent advocating for them in this really confusing new system, they have no voice and no way to make anything better."

Individualized funding under the NDIS meant that workers were directed to stop working with service users when their inadequate funding packages ran out. Workers found this new philosophy demoralizing and unethical. For example, a support coordinator's manager told her to "drop clients and stop helping them" once their budget had been used up, even when central needs such as housing remained unmet. In a similar vein, another worker was told that she had to stop advocating for service users and working with them when their funding ran low: "My boss said, 'You need to look at things a lot different now. It's about money.'" This same worker and others told us that they felt so torn when they had to "drop clients" who had reached the end of their budgets that they often continued to work with them after hours, off the books and without documenting it. This unpaid work acts as a subsidy to the underfunded NDIS programme, but at considerable risk to the workers, who, ironically, feel that they have no choice but to support those deprived of a voice within the new individualized service system.

Resolving personalization and notions of 'customer' in Scotland

Personalization policies in Scotland have created a need for, as one front-line worker put it, "customer satisfaction" to be used as a measure of performance, but interviewee testimony suggests that the positioning of service users as customers is a challenging prospect. The use of the word 'customer' was certainly regarded as a new phenomenon, and one that required adjustment from workers. In the vast majority of cases, the term 'customer' was discussed in positive terms only in the context of benefit to service users, as in "customer rights" (Service Manager), even where this explicitly intensified work for employees. Evidence suggests that customer terminology was more likely to come up internally, as noted by an Assistant Service Manager: "We don't use it – we wouldn't. Sometimes at a team meeting someone might say, 'oh, God, it seems like they're customers'. Maybe in that sense, but not generally speaking." This demonstrates a dynamic whereby service users are protected from what could be perceived as the negative aspects of a purchaser–provider relationship, such as increased responsibility and accountability, while being allowed to benefit from the positive elements, such as increased choice and discretion. When asked about what he thought of the use of the term, one interviewee asserted that he had "been in too long [...] I find it hard to use the word customer", implying that the shift in direction towards customer-oriented norms and terminology was too great a change for him to acclimatize to.

Several workers objected to the word 'customer' with varying intensity; some felt it didn't accurately capture the relationship between service users and the organisation, and others were offended by the perceived undervaluing of their role. By positioning the service user as 'customer', interviewees perceived an implication that they were being "sold to", which poses a challenge to ideological components of commitment and motivation. While discussing the change at a team meeting, one worker commented, "I remember thinking, 'what have I got into here [...] you need to *sell*?' and I was like, 'Is this sale or is it care? What are we doing?'" This demonstrates a level of confusion and exasperation that was present in many responses. Often, the prospect of "selling" to service users was perceived as being self-serving, opportunistic and directly at odds with the process of support.

Customer sovereignty was regarded as a problematic issue in that workers felt constrained in their ability to challenge unhealthy behaviours such as heavy smoking or inactivity without potentially risking losing a service user's "custom". This results in a situation where the most appropriate course of action for a service user may not be followed. This conflict of interests was discussed by interviewees at all levels of promotion:

> 'The old adage that "the customer is always right" is quite a challenging one, because part of what we are doing is working with people who have very chaotic lives, or who have become stuck in very unhelpful routines, so part of our task is actually

to challenge and confront people, but if you challenge and confront too much, as a customer they might just say "to hell with this – I'm going to go down the road to someone else who's not going to give me such a challenging time".' (Chief Executive Officer)

Another worker noted: "The majority of work we do here, it's long-term stuff. Some have had mental health problems for 40 years, it's not as simple as that to fix it. This customer thing – 'come on over here for six months and I'll do this for you, I'll fix it' – [we can't]."

In other words, the emphasis on short-term contracts seems at odds with the long-term work required for many service users, and the promises required to attract customers may give service users unrealistic expectations with regard to outcomes, which, in turn, intensifies work for employees. It is of significant note that, despite the increase in choice, the majority of service users continue with the service provision that existed prior to the introduction of personalization. Additionally, one of the organizations had a significant number of service users who are non-verbal, posing serious questions about how they might articulate support and care preferences. In consequence, a large number of interviewees demonstrated an uneasiness that customer elements of SDS could be, or appear to be, tokenistic. In order to more fully understand service users' experiences of the new policy, both organizations had begun to gather customer feedback, but reported that this was not to be used for assessing employee performance.

Austerity in Australia

As noted earlier, the NDIS has left many people with underfunded plans. Transportation and activities were particular concerns, alongside less access to advocacy; fewer skilled workers ready and available to work, particularly with people with complex issues; less choice; and more instability. Prior to the NDIS, transportation costs for service users were covered by community agencies or pooled across everyone in the programme, making travel and activities more cost effective. Under the NDIS, each client has their own budget for travel – and for many service users, particularly those outside of the urban core, their travel budgets run out quickly. This is very concerning to clients and staff because choice in activity is meant to be a human rights cornerstone of the NDIS. However, service users often had to forgo activities, due to individualized transportation costs. One worker told us that most of the service users she worked with were allotted funding for 100 kilometres per week. As she explained, "If we stuck rigidly to the hundred kilometres a week, they wouldn't go anywhere hardly. From where we live in […], you can't go anywhere for under 30 or 40 kilometres a trip return. That's just the most basic community access. It gets gobbled up very quickly." Rather than expanded choice, workers noted regretfully, "It's very tight already and they simply can't go out every day."

Research participants also expressed concern that in the private labour market "people with complex needs often struggle finding workers because staff decline to work with them". In the past, staff would be assigned to work with people with complex needs on a rotating basis. Now, often privately hired or on short-term contracts, workers can also refuse to work with particular clients. In this instance, the private labour market is reducing choices and well-being for service users (and the workers who are committed to them), and therefore simultaneously reducing human rights and social care.

Human rights and working conditions were also negatively impacted upon by the revolving door of casual staff, prompted by NDIS underfunding and the short shifts and low wages many employers offered. The constantly changing workforce made for a stressed environment, as new and inexperienced workers had no opportunity to get to know the service users, or their preferences or triggers, meaning that they could unintentionally trigger workplace violence, which was harmful to everyone. One long-time worker related a story in which he had seen violence about to boil over but could not intervene quickly enough with the casual staff to prevent it: "I'm thinking, there's red flags all over the place, back away, give him [the client] some space. But, he didn't so he [the client] kicked nine holes in his bedroom door … it's not self-harm or hurting us but it's still not good because he's under stress and unhappy, and we are wondering what's next."

Most research participants confirmed an increase in workplace violence, but, typical of the sector, they tended to minimize it: "Nothing major, just black eyes, broken noses, the normal sort of things with people just being out their routine, not knowing the support workers and the support workers not knowing clients." As Cortis et al (2018) note, the NDIS does not cover the costs of supervision or training. Not surprisingly, workers identified a lack of training and supervision as the major factors precipitating these dangerous workplace dynamics. However, the revolving-door casual labour market emerging in tandem with the roll-out of the NDIS meant that managers "don't care if the support workers are injured or disheartened. They can always get someone else to take their place; often, they are not trained or have very limited training, and don't stay in the job long anyway."

Austerity in Scotland

The vast majority of interviewees articulated an apprehension that reassessing service users' suitability for personalization-style provision typically resulted in decreases to IBs. All but one of the 27 interviewees stated that they had never seen an increase in funding as a result of personalization, and the one who had seen an increase in funding noted that it was an extremely rare occurrence. Changes in how budgets were allocated under personalization were reported to be premised largely on how support is enumerated, measured and justified, with the unanticipated outcome of reduced funding. Often it was felt that the language of personalization was used to mask this reduction in funding and hours of service. As one service manager reported:

> 'When SDS came about […] it became very much focused in the outcomes for a service user. It's still basically the underlying thing, as comes down to face-to-face hours, but we're not supposed to talk about hours any longer.'

Concern was also expressed in relation to reducing service users' much-needed hours, in that this could cause individuals to go into crisis, after which they would need considerably more support. In this eventuality, not only is reducing funding directly at odds with service users' best interests, it actively costs more. As a service manager noted:

> 'I know one of the individuals I support, she needs 24/7 support and for some reason the council, when they were working out how much they thought she would need, they decided that they would give her everything except for two hours a week. There's no explanation as to why she doesn't need them […] I think it's very irregular how much financial support people get, and you'll have some people who seem to have a lot of funding, which is great, but then you have other people who have very similar needs who don't have the same level of funding and it does seem to be quite random. I mean the two hours seems to be just a little bit petty almost, as if we're not going to give you everything just because [funding has been reduced by two hours].'

This example demonstrates that no explanation for funding cuts is provided to workers, and no criteria on which the decision is based. The opaqueness contributed to frustration and stress for workers and service users.

The degradation of care work

Precarious and gig-like work: Australia

Representing a major shift from secure, permanent employment paid at or above Award levels, the Australian research participants reported that employment had become insecure, precarious and, in many cases, fragmented and gig-like in its impermanence and lack of obligation on the part of employers. In most agencies, except for management, all staff were casual, with many working shifts of two hours or less, in people's homes (which may be dispersed, and travel time is not covered) and with little notice of changes in shifts and schedules. Flexible workforces mean that employers can dismiss staff more easily to cut costs or discipline the workforce and save costs in terms of not paying for sick leave or annual leave. A casualized workforce also makes it easier for employers to schedule short shifts and last-minute shifts to coincide with the needs and desires of service users. As one long-term worker in disability services told us, "They don't want full-time workers. What they say is we need to have flexibility because we don't know, clients could come and go now, it's their choice." Another worker agreed: "Every single person working at my agency is casual and that's the nature of the beast nowadays."

Characteristic of gig economies, short notice of shifts and short shifts were particularly disruptive. As one long-time worker observed, "My stress and fatigue are both way up. I've been living on the phone for shifts, some of which I get less than two hours' notice for." Other workers noted, "all our rosters are electronic" and constantly changing, meaning that workers never "know exactly what shifts you're gonna have that week because something will just randomly change". Workers confirmed that apps notifying workers of their shifts and hours were commonplace, indicating a further shift to an on-demand-work, platform labour market.

As noted previously, gig work and casualization had serious consequences for human rights and the well-being of workers and service users. As a long-term worker noted, "We all know that 'routine is king' in the disability world and swapping up or changing up staff constantly can create challenges for both clients and staff." She continued, "In the past three weeks, I've seen this lead to damage to property from clients and self-harm. Makes the work harder for everyone. Makes it stressful and depressing. Where is service user choice in all this? It's nowhere. We are all in the same boat: the work is harder, and the clients' needs aren't being met!"

Fragmentation of working time and increased precarity: Scotland

In order to accommodate the need for more flexible and personalized services to customers, the Scottish data exhibits distinct moves towards reorganizing working time via the medium of self-managed teams (SMTs). While this is premised on making care more bespoke and reactive for service users, and contains within it the potential to upskill workers, the reality is an intensification of scheduling responsibilities, due to the devolving of 'people management' competencies. Of the tasks ascribed to these SMTs, the most commonly discussed were rotas, sickness absence, holidays and accommodating short-notice changes to hours that resulted from customer choice. Resourcing absences was particularly difficult in one organization, due to some individuals working in multiple SMTs. It was reported that workers were encouraged to take holiday time to cover periods of ill-health, meaning that officially recorded sickness numbers were often misleading. This satisfied the NPM-style targets necessary for funding applications, but did so by informally degrading the experience of employment.

In theory, managers were to oversee any disputes, but no interviewees had experienced this; the negative connotations associated with an unresolved dispute meant that individuals were extremely hesitant to raise any issues with management, who might perceive them as uncommitted or troublesome, which would jeopardize employability and their ability to secure shifts in future. By devolving this responsibility onto workers, organizations created an atmosphere of increased pressures, which meant that workers were less likely to take sick days.

In addition to issues concerning working time, travel time also presented significant challenges, for both workers individually and organizations collectively. Split shifts resulted from the increased choice afforded by SDS and resulted in many service users deciding not to have one eight-hour visit, and instead having, for example, two four-hour shifts, or four two-hour shifts. This significantly increased travel time for the workers affected, the transitioning to and from a new service user or shift, and the amount of unpaid overtime each service user received. Due to both organizations' desires to safeguard continuity of service, the same worker or workers were required to undertake these shifts. Ultimately, this extended the length of time it took workers to perform their contractual obligations; in some instances, in order to work an eight-hour shift, workers could be away from their home for up to 12 hours.

Discussion and conclusions

Although, arguably, Australia is farther down the road in terms of fragmented work, in this chapter we have shown that the operationalization of 'customer choice' has reshaped working conditions for disability care workers in Scotland and Australia and intensified the degradation of work. Supplementing feminist political economy theory, our analysis shows that the content and impact of austerity-linked policies share a similar outcome in terms of the increased vulnerability of workers and service users, and their increased exposure to underfunding and work intensification. Further, in both Scotland and Australia policies of individualized funding provided the impetus to remake a labour market of majority female workers from one with low wages but the possibility for permanent employment and avenues for improving wages and conditions, to one that in Australia is increasingly gig like and precarious, and that in Scotland is characterized by decreasing local authority funding, intensified work for employees and an overall lowering of terms and conditions.

In terms of Labour Process Theory, these austerity-linked changes represent a diminishment in workplace power for care workers. The data confirm that casualized workers tend to feel the need to position themselves favourably for future shifts, and hence are less likely to advocate for themselves or undertake workplace or union activism. This gives employers the upper hand in terms of continuing to degrade workplace conditions and threaten to reduce wages and conditions in the context of very constrained and uncertain funding. Gig-like work in a frequently changing array of service users' private homes means that care workers lack a steady workplace, generally working alone with no opportunity to share knowledge or skills, build a shared analysis and identity or even to connect with others in the organization, except for supervisors by phone calls or texts. This contributes to the demoralization among workers that is present in the data, and sharply reduces opportunities to build workplace-based resistance. As such, it represents a further shift in power to the employer. These ground-changing shifts have been generated by an austerity state with little interest in protections for workers and little capacity to realize human or employment rights.

Our analysis suggests that consumer choice and workers' protections have been set up in competition with each other, with government largely absenting itself from the role of adjudicator or regulator, leaving workers subjected to funding and wage decreases, SMTs, split shifts, short shifts and precarity, alongside many service users who continue to be isolated and excluded. Our analysis also suggests that austerity saturates and co-opts even policy goals that seem beyond debate, such as human rights and choice for people with disabilities, leaving service users and workers more deeply entrenched in pro-market logics and practices.

References

Aronson, J. and Smith, K. (2010). 'Managing restructured social services: Expanding the social?'. *British Journal of Social Work*, 40(2), 530–47.

Auerbach, C.F. (2003) *Qualitative Data: An Introduction to Coding and Analysis*. Qualitative Studies in Psychology. New York: New York University Press.

Baines, D. (2006) 'Forum: Quantitative Indicators: "Whose needs are being served?" Quantitative metrics and the reshaping of social services'. *Studies in Political Economy* 77 Spring, 195–209.

Baines, D., Cunningham, I. and Fraser, H. (2011) 'Constrained by managerialism: Caring as participation in the voluntary social services'. *Economic and Industrial Democracy*, 32(2): 329–52.

Bedford, K. and Rai, S.M. (2010) 'Feminists theorize international political economy'. *Signs: Journal of Women in Culture and Society*, 36(1): 1–18.

Brennan, D., Cass, B., Himmelweit, S. and Szebehely, M. (2012) 'The marketisation of care: Rationales and consequences in Nordic and liberal care regimes'. *Journal of European Social Policy*, 22(4): 377–91.

Christensen, K. (2012) 'Towards sustainable hybrid relationships in cash-for-care systems'. *Disability & Society*, 27(3): 399–412.

Clayton, J., Donovan, C. and Merchant, J. (2015) 'Emotions of austerity: Care and commitment in public service delivery in the North East of England'. *Emotion, Space and Society*, 14, 24–32.

Cortis, N., Macdonald, F., Davidson, B. and Bentham, E. (2017) *Reasonable, Necessary and Valued: Pricing Disability Services for Quality Support and Decent Jobs*. Sydney: Social Policy Research Centre, University of New South Wales.

Cortis, N., Macdonald, F., Davidson, B. and Bentham, E. (2018) 'Underpricing care: A case study of Australia's National Disability Insurance Scheme'. *International Journal of Care and Caring*, 2(4): 587-593.

Craig, G. and Manthorpe, J. (1999) 'Unequal partners? Local government reorganization and the voluntary sector'. *Social Policy & Administration*, 33(1): 55–72.

Cunningham, I. (2014) *Employment Conditions in the Scottish Social Care Voluntary Sector: Impact of Public Funding Constraints in the Context of Economic Recession*. A Report for the Voluntary Sector Social Services Workforce Unit.

Cunningham, I. and James, P. (2014) 'Public service outsourcing and its employment implications in an era of austerity: The case of British social care'. *Competition & Change*, 18(1): 1–19.

Cunningham, I. and Nickson, D. (2011) 'A gathering storm: Re-tendering and the voluntary sector workforce'. *International Journal of Public Sector Management*, 24(7): 662–72.

Cunningham, I. and Nickson, D. (2013) *Public Sector Austerity, Personalisation and the Implications for the Voluntary Sector Workforce*. www.ccpscotland.org/wp-content/uploads/sites/3/2014/02/Public-Sector-Austerity-personalisation-and-the-voluntary-sector-workforce.pdf. Accessed 10 June 2019.

Cunningham, I., Hearne, G. and James, P. (2013) 'Voluntary organisations and marketisation: A dynamic of employment degradation'. *Industrial Relations Journal*, 44(2): 171–88.

David, C. and West, R. (2017) 'NDIS self-management approaches: Opportunities for choice and control or an Uber-style wild west?' *Australian Journal of Social Issues*, 55: 331–46.

Denniss, R. (2015) 'Spreadsheets of power'. *The Monthly*, April: 28–32.

Ellis, K. (2007) 'Direct payments and social work practice: The significance of "street-level bureaucracy" in determining eligibility'. *British Journal of Social Work*, 37: 405–22.

Folbre, N. (2008) 'Reforming care'. *Politics & Society*, 36(3): 373–87.

Friedman, G. (2014). 'Workers without employers: Shadow corporations and the rise of the gig economy'. *Review of Keynesian Economics*, 2(2), 171–88.

Glendinning, C. (2012) 'Home care in England: Markets in the context of under-funding'. *Health & Social Care in the Community*, 20(3): 292–9.

Green, C., Malbon, E., Carey, G., Dickinson, H. and Reeders, D. (2018). *Competition and Collaboration between Service Providers in the NDIS*. Centre for Social Impact, University of New South Wales, Sydney.

Harvey, D. (2007) 'A brief history of neoliberalism'. *Contemporary Sociology: A Journal of Reviews*, 35(5): 529–30.

Hayes, L.J.B. and Moore, S. (2017) 'Care in a time of austerity: The electronic monitoring of homecare workers' time'. *Gender, Work & Organization*, 24(4): 329–44.

Howard, A., Blakemore, T., Johnston, L., Taylor, D. and Dibley, R. (2015) '"I'm not really sure but I hope it's better"': early thoughts of parents and carers in a regional trial site for the Australian National Disability Insurance Scheme'. *Disability & Society*, 30(9): 1365–81.

Hussein, S. and Manthorpe, J. (2014) 'Structural marginalisation among the long-term care workforce in England: Evidence from mixed-effect models of national pay data'. *Ageing & Society*, 34(1): 21–41.

Kettle, M. (2015) *Self-Directed Support: An Exploration of Option 2 in Practice*. Glasgow: Glasgow Caledonian University/P&P.

Kirby, S.L., Greaves, L. and Reid, C. (2006) *Experience Research Social Change: Methods Beyond the Mainstream*. Toronto: University of Toronto Press.

Kvist, J. and Fritzell, J. (eds) (2011) *Changing Social Equality: The Nordic Welfare Model in the 21st Century*. Bristol: Policy Press.

Macdonald, F. and Charlesworth, S. (2016) 'Cash for care under the NDIS: Shaping care workers' working conditions?'. *Journal of Industrial Relations*, 58(5): 627–46.

Macdonald, F., Bentham, E. and Malone, J. (2018) 'Wages, underpayment and unpaid work in marketised social care'. *The Economic and Labour Relations Review*, 29(1): 80–96.

Manthorpe, J., Martineau, S., Ridley, J., Cornes, M., Rosengard, A. and Hunter, S. (2015) 'Embarking on self-directed support in Scotland: A focused scoping review of the literature'. *European Journal of Social Work*, 18(1): 36–50.

Martinelli, F. (2017) 'Social services, welfare states and places: An overview'. In Martinelli, F., Anttonen, A. and Mätzke, M. (eds), *Social Services Disrupted: Changes, Challenges and Policy Implications for Europe in Times of Austerity*. Cheltenham, Edward Elgar Publishing, 11–48.

McKendrick, J.H., Asenova, D., MacRae, C., Reynolds, R., Egan, J., Hastings, A. and Sinclair, S. (2016) 'Conceptualising austerity in Scotland as a risk shift: Ideas and implications'. *Scottish Affairs*, 25(4): 451–78.

Meagher, G. and Healy, K. (2003) 'Caring, controlling, contracting and counting: governments and non-profits in community services'. *Australian Journal of Public Administration*, 62(3): 40-51.

Miles, M.B. and Huberman, A.M. (1994) *Qualitative Data Analysis*. 2nd edn, London: Sage.

Moffatt, S., Higgs, P., Rummery, K. and Jones, I.R. (2012) 'Choice, consumerism and devolution: Growing old in the welfare state(s) of Scotland, Wales and England'. *Ageing & Society*, 32(5): 725–46.

NDIS (National Disability Insurance Scheme) Act (2013). Government of Australia. https://www.legislation.gov.au/Details/C2013A00020

NDIS Quality and Safeguards Commission (2018) 'Legislation, rules and policies'. Government of Australia. https://www.ndiscommission.gov.au/about/legislation-rules-policies.

Pearson, C. (2000) 'Money talks? Competing discourses in the implementation of direct payments'. *Critical Social Policy*, 20(4): 459–77.

Peterson, V.S. (2012). 'Rethinking theory: Inequalities, informalization and feminist quandaries'. *International Feminist Journal of Politics*, 14(1): 5–35.

Productivity Commission (2010) *Contribution of the Not-For-Profit Sector*. Research report. Canberra: Productivity Commission.

Productivity Commission (2011) *Disability Care and Support: Productivity Commission Inquiry Report, volumes 1 and 2.* Report No. 54. Melbourne: Productivity Commission.

Productivity Commission (2017) *National Disability Insurance Scheme (NDIS) – Costs.* https://www.pc.gov.au/inquiries/completed/ndis-costs/report. Accessed 25 October 2018.

Riddell, S., Ahlgren, L., Pearson, C., Williams, V., Watson, N. and MacFarlane, H. (2006) *The Implementation of Direct Payments for People Who Use Care Services.* Health Committee Report to Scottish Parliament, 624. Edinburgh: Scottish Parliament.

Ridley, J., Spandler, H., Rosengard, A., Little, S., Cornes, M., Manthorpe, J., Hunter, S., Kinder, T. and Gray, B. (2011) *Evaluation of Self-directed Support Test Sites in Scotland.* Edinburgh: Scottish Government Social Research.

Rummery, K., Bell, D., Bowes, A., Dawson, A. and Roberts, J.E. (2012) *Counting the Cost of Choice and Control: Evidence for the Costs of Self-directed Support in Scotland.* https://dspace.stir.ac.uk/bitstream/1893/6934/1/counting%20the%20cost%20of%20choice%20and%20control.pdf. Accessed 10 June 2019.

Social Care (Self-Directed Support) (Scotland) Act (2013), www.legislation.gov.uk/asp/2013/1/pdfs/asp_20130001_en.pdf. Accessed 10 June 2019.

Stanford, J. (2015) *Economics for Everyone: A Short Guide to the Economics of Capitalism.* London: Pluto.

Thill, C. (2015) 'Listening for policy change: How the voices of people with disabilities shaped Australia's National Disability Insurance Scheme'. *Disability & Society,* 30(1): 15–28.

Thompson, P. (2010) 'The capitalist labour process: Concepts and connections'. *Capital & Class,* 34(1): 7–14.

Thompson, P. and Smith, C. (2009) 'Labour power and labour process: Contesting the marginality of the sociology of work'. *Sociology,* 43(5): 913–30.

UNISON (2012) *A Fairer Scotland.* www.unison-scotland.org.uk/scotlandsfuture/FairerScotlandNov2012.pdf. Accessed 10 June 2019.

van Doorn, N. (2017) 'Platform labor: On the gendered and racialized exploitation of low-income service work in the "on-demand" economy'. *Information, Communication & Society,* 20(6): 898–914.

Wallace, J. (2013) 'Weathering the Storm? A Look at Small Countries' Public Services in Times of Austerity'. www.carnegieuktrust.org. uk/getattachment/9a28dc44-4c4-4dc6-9e02-fd40749cdc7a/Weathering-the-Storm-Full-Report.aspx.

Warr, D., Dickinson, H., Olney, S., Hargrave, J., Karanikolas, A., Kasidis, V., Katsikis, G., Ozge, J., Peters, D., Wheeler, M. and Wilcox, M. (2017) *Choice, Control and the NDIS. Service Users' Perspectives on Having Choice and Control in the New National Disability Insurance Scheme.* Melbourne: Social Equity Institute, University of Melbourne.

West, K. (2013) 'The grip of personalisation in adult social care: Between managerial domination and fantasy', *Critical Social Policy*, 33(4): 638–57.

Williams, T. (2014) 'The NDIS: What can Australia learn from other countries?'. *New Paradigm*, Summer: 30–33.

Young, D. (2018) *Caring within Constraint: Employment Relations in Voluntary Sector Social Care in the Context of Personalisation, Marketization and Austerity.* Doctoral dissertation, University of Strathclyde.

10

The Rise of Managerialism in the US: Whither Worker Control?

Mimi Abramovitz and Jennifer Zelnick

Introduction: neoliberalism, austerity and the human-service workplace

In both the US and Europe, human-service workers are the 'first responders' for people and communities in need. However, since the late 1980s, the convergence of neoliberal social policy and mounting austerity in this arena have restructured the nature of work and the labour process (Landsbergis, Grzywacz and LaMontagne, 2014; Farnsworth and Irving, 2018). The results have dramatically affected the social relations of production and the capacity of human-service workers and agencies to provide quality care.

Scholars from various disciplines and many countries have studied the impact of neoliberal austerity on the scale and scope of social welfare programmes (Abramovitz, 2014), the hollowing-out of the welfare state (Ehrenreich, 2016) and the slow-down of the economy (Rogowski, 2019). Others have examined its impact on the well-being of different population groups, especially the poor, low-wage workers and service users (Soss, Fording and Schram, 2011). Yet few researchers have examined the impact of neoliberal policies on workers, mostly women, employed in public and non-profit human-service organizations (Baines,

2004; Abramovitz, 2012). We need more information about the ways in which neoliberal austerity has changed work organization, service provision and the working conditions that shape the daily experience of workers and service users in human-service organizations.

This chapter draws on social science literature and our survey of the New York City (NYC) human-service workforce to discuss the impact of neoliberal austerity on the organization of work and the human-service workforce in the US, where women, especially women of colour, predominate. Using the Social Structure of Accumulation (SSA) theory, we (1) explain the rise of neoliberal austerity; (2) identify five neoliberal strategies designed to dismantle the US welfare state; (3) focus on the impact of privatization, a key neoliberal strategy; (4) drill down to show how privatization has transformed the organization of work in public and non-profit human-service agencies; and (5) detail the experience of nearly 3,000 front-line, mostly female, human-service workers in NYC. Neoliberal privatization is most often understood as selling off public assets and/or shifting the responsibility for welfare state programmes – such as Social Security and Medicare – from the public to the private sector. This chapter highlights the understudied operationalization of privatization *within* human-service organizations, also known as New Public Management or managerialism, and the ways in which austerity-driven managerialism falls heavily on women

Background: the rise of privatization and managerialism in the human services

Social structures of accumulation and the rise of neoliberal austerity

Neoliberalism is neither accidental nor simply mean spirited. Rather, the paradigm emerged in the US in the mid-1970s in response to the second economic crisis of the 20th century. SSA theory (Kotz, 2015) explains that such paradigm shifts occur in response to capitalist economic crises. Over time, the institutional arrangements, policies and ideological system paradigms (or SSAs) assembled to address a prior crisis fail to sustain profits, stability and economic growth. The resulting deterioration undermines the institutional structures that had supported the accumulation of capital and the general welfare during the preceding 40 to 50 years. The resolution of the crisis follows a protracted political struggle and leads to a systemic restructuring or a new SSA (Kotz, McDonough and Reich, 1994).

Two such crises occurred in the US during the 20th century. The first crisis – the Great Depression – surfaced in the late 1920s when the laissez-faire institutional structures in place since the 1890s no longer fuelled profits, economic growth and economic security. With the collapse of the economy, the working class, the incipient labour movement and even the national elite blamed their economic woes on the failure of the market economy and demanded that the federal government step in. The resulting New Deal replaced the laissez-faire paradigm with the Keynesian approach that called *for redistributing income downwards and expanding the role of the state* on behalf of the poor and working classes (Kotz, 2015). Drawing on the Western European welfare state models, the main New Deal tactics included higher taxes, more government spending, federalization (shifting responsibility for social welfare from the states to the federal government), deprivatization of social programmes (shifting responsibility for social welfare from the private to the public sector) and supporting popular movements (Abramovitz, 2004/2005). In the end, everyone seemed to agree that in order to 'save capitalism from itself' the US needed a new paradigm based on a more active state. From the 1930s to the mid-1970s the welfare state grew, pressed by the labour, civil rights and women's movements and the begrudging support of the more forward-looking business leaders. The New Deal and Great Society programmes generated both profitable economic growth for business and a higher standard of living for many, but not all, Americans. The changes also benefited many women. They shifted the cost and responsibility of care work from women's unpaid labour in the home to the state. The opening of new jobs to women and persons of colour created a route for upward mobility for these groups, still unwelcomed in the private sector. Some call the post-war period the 'golden era' of capitalism, despite many policies resting on discrimination and institutional racism and sexism (Abramovitz, 2018).

The second major crisis of the 20th century surfaced in the mid-1970s as deindustrialization, globalization and the loss of world power by the US gradually undermined the post-war Keynesian SSA. This time, the national elite blamed the demise of the 'golden era' on 'big government', social movement victories and the behaviour of the 'undeserving' poor (George, 1999; Wacquant, 2009). To restore the economy, they replaced Keynesian social policy with neoliberalism, emphasizing free markets, individualism and fiscal austerity (Harvey, 2005; Caplan and Ricciardelli, 2016). The resulting U-turn gradually undid the New Deal by redistributing income upwards and downsizing the state (Abramovitz, 2018). The various tactics included tax cuts, budget cuts, privatization, devolution and reducing the power of social movements. The reversal of the New Deal and Great Society policies cost many women their public and non-profit sector jobs.

This feminization of austerity also shifted care work from the state back to women in the home (Abramovitz, 2012). At the same time, the Right called for a singular version of 'family values' and a colour-blind social order. Launched by President Reagan in the 1980s, neoliberal policies have been followed by every US administration since then. Only hindsight will tell if Trumpism extends or replaces neoliberalism.

Three stages of privatization in the US welfare state

Neoliberal policies, especially privatization, have transformed the structure, operation and impact of the US welfare state. However, privatization in the US actually evolved through three different, overlapping stages that are rarely analysed as a single trend (Abramovitz and Zelnick, 2016). *Marketization* delivered publicly financed benefits and services through the market; *managerialism* imported business principles into the management of human-service agencies; and *financialization* incorporated investment principles into the financing and growth of human services. This chapter focuses on managerialism.

Managerialism, the second stage of privatization, gained traction in the 1980s. If marketization moved human-service clients and providers into the market, neoliberal managerialism imported the business model (that is, market philosophy and business principles) into human-service organizations (Nightingale and Pindus, 1997; Salamon, 1999). Managerialism assumes that resources are best allocated through the market; that the market allows more consumer choice, lowers programme costs and ensures higher-quality, more productive, efficient, effective and accountable services than government. It calls for using market forces to serve public purposes and insists on running human-service agencies like a business, attending to faster work, measurable outcomes, performance monitoring and other practices that often contribute to the fragmentation, routinization and standardization of services (Harlow et al, 2013). To this end, managerialism adapts Taylorism, an approach to the organization of work developed by Frederick W. Taylor in the US in the early 20th century, to the social service context. Introduced to improve productivity through intensive managerial oversight, Taylorism subdivided jobs into repetitive, standardized and measurable tasks to increase efficiency, reduce labour costs and enable management oversight of the now routinized labour process (Jermier, 1998). Today managerialism, in both the public and non-profit sectors, encourages front-line workers, programme managers and agency directors to maximize productivity, accountability and efficiency. It draws on an intensified use of quantified metrics, standardized procedures and management control (Abramovitz and Zelnick, 2016). Focused on measurable outcomes and evaluation, rather than on the foundation of social work practice (that is, building trust and service-user relationships), neoliberal managerialism rarely references ideals of equality, common good and social justice. It has profound implications for the social relations of production in the human services.

The managerial context: austerity, entrepreneurship, performance

The austerity environment

Managerialism gained ground in human-service agencies at the same time that neoliberal austerity policies such as tax and budget cuts took hold. In the US, federal non-defence discretionary funding – the main source of dollars for human-service programmes – peaked in the 1980s at 5.1 per cent of gross domestic product (GDP). It fell sharply to 3.0 per cent of the GDP in 2018, the same as in 1962, before the war on poverty. Pre-Covid-19, experts projected that this spending stream would drop to a new low of less than 3.0 per cent after 2019 (Center on Budget and Policy Priorities, 2020). The loss of federal support, combined with lower individual and corporate donations, has forced many human-service organizations to consolidate programmes, reduce their services or shut down (Fiscal Policy Institute, 2015), all of which falls heavily on women workers, who comprise the majority of the front-line human-service workforce. To survive, many agencies put their services at risk. A 2019 membership survey by The Alliance: The Voice of Community Nonprofits found that, when faced with a 10 per cent budget cut, agencies would lay off staff, freeze or reduce salaries, reduce staff hours, eliminate programmes, restructure employee benefits, reduce service hours, stop accepting new clients and consider merging. Many agencies also extend credit lines, draw down reserves and otherwise take on debt to make ends meet (Pettijohn et al, 2013). In our 2018 report, *Business as Usual*, we indicate that austerity-driven budget cuts also forced agencies and workers to do 'more-with-less' (Abramovitz and Zelnick, 2018). Respondents reported that their agency was inadequately funded (77.7 per cent), devoted too many resources to keeping the agency afloat (70 per cent) and cut staff and programmes (55 per cent). Eighty-per cent also described their clients as "more stressed", and 90 per cent served clients with "more complex needs". While not attributable just to managerialism, austerity also reduced the likelihood that workers would be in a position to object to practices that might undermine social work's mission and professionalism.

The entrepreneurial environment

Neoliberalism, combined with austerity, pressed agencies to create an entrepreneurial work environment that increasingly relies on market strategies (Hasenfeld and Garrow, 2012). Loss of funding forces agencies to focus on the bottom line, including developing new income sources such as by charging fees, selling products and creating for-profit subsidiaries (Eikenberry and Kluver, 2004). More and more agencies utilize a 'business plan' that identifies their 'product', 'brand' and a 'market niche' (Martin, 2005). This includes adopting business terminology such as retitling their executive director as a chief executive officer, referring to service users as 'customers' or 'consumers', replacing Master of Social Work agency directors with Masters of Business Administration, branding services as 'products', competing for revenue and market share (Salamon, 2012) and otherwise defining social work as an enterprise (O'Sullivan, Considine and Lewis, 2009). In our 2018 report we also note that 36 per cent of the respondents worked in agencies whose director had a business or legal background, and that more men than women occupied top-level positions.

Managerialism's high trust in the market and the business model and low trust in public servants transformed public and non-profit agencies. The growing focus on the bottom line means that agencies increase the number of people seen, emphasize short- over long-term goals regardless of the needs of service users, target services to better-paying clients and otherwise provide services at the lowest cost (Hasenfeld and Garrow, 2012). The introduction of 'lean and mean' management and other techniques associated with Total Quality Management and lean production have reorganized agency work to increase productivity and to manipulate buy-in so as to intensify organizational control of workers (Martin, 1993; Bowen, Omi and Merlino, 2014). In practice, this translates into speed-up, more paper work and real-time technological monitoring of staff. The construction of social services as commodities to be bought and sold has left non-profits to operate in an entrepreneurial context that increasingly rewards discipline, performance and organizational capacity rather than mission, community roots and professional judgement.

The accountability environment

The increased use of non-profit and for-profit agencies to fulfil functions previously performed by government agencies has led funders to press for greater accountability. In the entrepreneurial context, private funders, now often thought of as 'investors', expect their investment to yield positive results and measurable impacts. Government funders require performance-based contracts and 'pay-for-success' reimbursement models that tie payments to attaining specific outcomes. In the past, funders paid non-profit providers for delivering services. Today, reimbursement often follows the successful achievement of pre-set outcomes based on dashboards, scorecards, results frameworks, calculable metrics and formal evaluations. These measurement requirements force agencies to adopt quantifiable outcomes that bypass harder-to-measure qualitative outcomes. Ball (2003) claims that these pressures lead employees to monitor their own performance based on performance metrics, rather than on their professional, personal or social ethics, even when they are aware of the existing conflicts.

Baines et al (2012) argue that such performance management transfers much of the monitoring, evaluation, and resulting self-blame from management to individual workers. Faced with fiscal austerity, the emphasis on performance also encourages agencies to prioritize 'hard' services (that is, employment programmes) over 'soft' services (that is, counselling, advocacy and others) with less easily measured outcomes (Smith, 2017). The literature indicates that the ripple effect of managerialism has transformed the social relations of production in human-service organizations. The incorporation of the business model has restructured the organization of work in ways that risk undermining effective practice. This includes reduced supervision, deskilling the work force, increased use of casual workers, decision making by computers and pay-for-performance contracts (Healy, 2002; Gallina, 2010). The resulting routinization of work further allows funders and managers to press for greater productivity, to control working conditions, to determine the work pace and to force mission change (Baines, 2006). When managerial agencies monitor work, often in real time, workers report that the resulting documentation activities interfere with developing trusting relationships with service users (Lonne, McDonald and Fox, 2004; Baines, 2009). In this work environment, more workers report high stress, ethical dilemmas, health and mental health problems and job dissatisfaction, contributing to the high turnover too common in the human services (Baines, 2006).

Workers' assessment of managerialism

The remainder of this chapter explores how nearly 3,000 front-line NYC human-service workers experienced managerialism and how, in their view, it transformed the social relations of production in public and non-profit human-service organizations. In 2014, in collaboration with six community partners (the National Association of Social Workers-NYC Chapter; the New York City Human Services Council; United Neighborhood Houses;

the Coalition of Behavioral Health Agencies; the Social Service Employees Union Local 371; and the *New York Non-Profit Press*), we initiated the *Human Service Workforce Study: Your Voice Is Needed*. Based on an extensive review of the managerialism literature and discussion with members of partner organizations, we identified 45 indicators of managerialism frequently present in human-service organizations. Our community partners distributed the anonymous, electronic survey to their constituents through their membership lists, websites, internal e-mails and event registration lists. The survey was publicized in the *New York Non-Profit Press* and distributed in waves between January 2014 and June 2015. In 2018 the results were released to the community through a report: *Business as Usual? A Wake-Up Call for the Human Services*. For a complete description of the methods, see Abramovitz and Zelnick (2018). Over 3,000 human-service workers responded to the survey. Some 2,326 met eligibility requirements and provided complete responses to survey questions (Table 10.1). Like the profession, they were generally women (82 per cent) and mirrored the racial diversity of NYC human-service agencies. The majority were highly educated, over half were master's-level trained social workers (56 per cent). While the majority were front-line workers (59 per cent), programme directors and managers were well represented (41 per cent). Respondents worked primarily in the private non-profit sector (70 per cent), and a third belonged to unions – mainly in the public sector (Table 10.1).

Table 10.1: Managerialism survey: demographic and workplace characteristics (n=2,326)

		n (%)
Gender	Female	1,787 (81.9)
	Male	378 (17.3)
	Transgender	6 (0.3)
	Other	12 (0.5)
Race	White	1,181 (54.5)
	Persons of colour	986 (45.5)
Education	≤Bachelors	498 (22.9)
	≥Masters	1,680 (87.1)
	MSW	1,303 (56.0)
Sector	Public	584 (25.1)
	Private non-profit	1,619 (69.7)
	Private for-profit	111 (4.8)
Current position	Front-line workers	1,363 (58.6)
	Programme directors and managers	963 (41.4)
Union member	Yes	676 (31.1)
	No	1,497 (68.9)

Managerialism: prevalence and problems

To represent all viewpoints, we asked respondents if the 45 indicators of managerialism were a 'major problem', 'minor problem', 'not a problem at all', or were not present at their agency ('Doesn't happen here'). Of these 45 indicators, 50 per cent or more of our respondents reported 30 as problematic, indicating that our empirically identified features of managerialism operated in many NYC human-service agencies. These 30 indicators fell into four conceptual clusters that comprise key features of the organization of work dictated by the managerial business model:[1] productivity, accountability, efficiency and standardization (Table 10.2).

The productivity cluster contains five practices related to the pace and volume of work viewed as problematic by 80 per cent or more of the respondents. They include 'too much work', 'not enough staff',

Table 10.2: Indicators of managerialism, by components (n=2,326)

Managerialism indicators by cluster	Problematic n (%)	Not a problem n (%)	n *
Productivity			
Having too much work to do	2,062 (89.4)	245 (10.6)	2,307
Focus on getting more done with same number of staff	1,989 (88.1)	269 (11.9)	2,258
Focus on getting more work done in same amount of time	1,907 (85.2)	332 (14.8)	2,239
Amount of time spent on paperwork	1,913 (83.5)	377 (16.5)	2,290
Having to work too fast	1,857 (81.3)	427 (18.7)	2,284
Accountability			
Time documenting takes time from work with clients	1,794 (79.4)	465 (20.6)	2,259
Measurement does not capture what staff thinks is important	1,688 (77.7)	484 (22.3)	2,172
Too much focus on reporting	1,742 (76.8)	527 (23.2)	2,269
Number of new policies that staff have to carry out	1,658 (76.1)	520 (23.9)	2,178
Staff and funders have different definitions of success	1,556 (73.6)	550 (26.7)	2,115
Too much time spent tracking outcomes	1,547 (70.3)	655 (29.7)	2,202
Too much emphasis on programme results	1,425 (66.3)	725 (33.7)	2,150
Too much reliance on quantifiable performance measures	1,398 (65.6)	734 (34.4)	2,132

(continued)

Table 10.2: Indicators of managerialism, by components (n=2,326) (continued)

Managerialism indicators by cluster	Problematic n (%)	Not a problem n (%)	n *
Efficiency			
Programme is inadequately funded	1,640 (77.6)	473 (22.4)	2,113
Need to increase the number of people seen	1,619 (76.0)	510 (24.0)	2,129
Not enough programme capacity to meet need	1,645 (75.7)	529 (24.3)	2,174
Focus on bottom line interferes with quality of service	1,428 (70.3)	602 (29.7)	2,030
Replace higher-paid with lower-paid staff to do same work	1,080 (58.5)	765 (41.5)	1,845
Too many agency resources used to keep agency funded	1,015 (53.5)	882 (46.5)	1,897
Standardization			
Extent to which work has become routinized	1,466 (68.2)	683 (31.8)	2,149
Not enough time to see the people we serve	1,469 (68.2)	685 (31.8)	2,154
Need to open cases more frequently	1,282 (64.6)	702 (35.4)	1,984
Wait time for services too long	1,108 (60.6)	720 (39.4)	1,828
Emphasis on short term service goals	1,257 (59.5)	855 (40.2)	2,112
Not enough time to assess needs	1,230 (56.8)	936 (43.2)	2,166
People have to meet too many requirements	1,080 (55.7)	858 (44.3)	1,938
Increased use of pre-set/screening question	1,075 (55.6)	860 (44.4)	1,935
No time to build trust with clients	1,160 (54.0)	989 (46.0)	2,149
Use of electronic records to monitor how I use time	1,608 (51.6)	778 (48.4)	1,608
Computers come between staff and clients	1,008 (50.1)	1004 (49.9)	2,012

* n < 2,326 indicates that participants chose 'doesn't happen here' (answer category not shown).

'not enough time', 'too fast a pace' and the perennial 'too much paper work'. The accountability cluster contains nine practices related to the measurement and documentation of performance outcomes. Between 70 per cent and 79 per cent of the respondents said that they spent 'too much time on documentation', 'too much time ... on tracking and reporting', and that the 'measures used do not capture what staff think is important'. Around two-thirds found 'the routinization of work', 'the emphasis on program results or outcomes' and 'reliance on quantifiable performance measures' to be problematic. In contrast, professional ethics mandate that social workers be accountable to service users and community needs rather than to quantified service outcomes (Burton and Van den Broek, 2009).

The efficiency cluster contains six practices related to organizational cost savings. Social workers recognize the trade-off between getting the "biggest bang for the buck" and effective use of agency resources. However, over 70 per cent of the respondents reported as problematic: "inadequate funding" (77.6 per cent), "the need to increase the number of people seen" (75.9 per cent), the agency's "lack of capacity to meet the needs of people served" (75.3 per cent) and its "focus on bottom line" (70.9 per cent). Nearly 60 per cent considered the practice of replacing higher-paid with lower-paid staff as problematic. The standardization cluster includes 11 practices related to the impact of managerialism on relationship building, the foundation of social work and a predictor of positive client outcomes (Norcross and Wampold, 2011). Respondents reported that the managerialism context did not "leave time to serve people in need" (68.2 per cent), "to assess needs" (56.8 per cent) or "to build trust" (54 per cent). Others reported as problematic: that "clients have to meet too many programme requirements" (55.7 per cent), that their agency "used pre-set screening interview tools" (55.6 per cent), monitored their time with electronic records (53.7 per cent), adopted evidence-based practices (50.3 per cent), and that the computer "came between me and my client'" (50.1 per cent).

Managerialism and the labour process

To deepen the understanding of the link between an agency's overall commitment to managerialism and the experience of agency workers, we constructed a score that measured the worker's perception of their agency's 'Commitment to Managerialism' as high, medium or low, representing a continuum of the intensity of work-related problems driven by the managerial business model. We then analysed this 'Commitment to Managerialism' in relation to the social relations of production through variables that captured worker control (autonomy and decision making) and variables that captured management control (monitoring and evaluation). We also examined the impact of managerialism on worker well-being and the extent to which workers coped with managerialism by bending the rules, a form of resistance (Table 10.3).

This analysis of the labour process revealed a troubling trend. Workers employed in agencies with a high commitment to managerialism – the most extreme conditions driven by the business model – were more likely than workers employed in agencies with a low commitment

Table 10.3: Worker and management control reported as problematic, by commitment to managerialism (n=2,326)

| | Commitment to managerialism score* | | | | | |
	High n (%)	Medium n (%)	Low n (%)	n**	df	χ^{2}***
Worker control indicators						
Not enough control over work						
Agree	397 (48.4)	269 (32.8)	154 (18.8)			
Disagree	330 (23.3)	470 (33.2)	614 (43.4)	2,234	2	192.0
Routinization of work						
Problematic	705 (48.1)	530 (36.2)	231 (15.8)			
Not a problem	47 (6.9)	220 (32.2)	416 (60.9)	2,149	2	543.7
Professional autonomy (less professional autonomy)						
Problematic	614 (47.3)	282 (35.6)	221 (17)			
Not a problem	124 (13.9)	462 (31.6)	486 (54.5)	2,189	2	407.2
Not enough say in programme decisions						
Agree	472 (42.1)	349 (31.1)	300 (26.8)			
Disagree	255 (23.0)	395 (35.6)	459 (41.4)	2,230	2	100.9

(continued)

Table 10.3: Worker and management control reported as problematic, by commitment to managerialism (n=2,326) (continued)

	Commitment to managerialism score*					
	High n (%)	Medium n (%)	Low n (%)	n**	df	χ^2***
Management control indicators						
Evaluation of job performance based on client outcomes						
Problematic	433 (57.7)	228 (30.4)	90 (12)			
Not a problem	210 (21.4)	361 (36.8)	410 (41.8)	1,732	2	286.7
Monitor work electronically						
Problematic	449 (54.1)	283 (34.1)	98 (11.8)			
Not a problem	182 (23.4)	265 (34.1)	331 (42.5)	1,608	2	238.7
Evaluation based on management targets						
Problematic	551 (51.4)	376 (35.1)	144 (13.4)			
Not a problem	153 (17.0)	299 (33.3)	446 (49.7)	1,969	2	376.1
Worry about losing job based on programme outcomes						
Agree	198 (49.7)	132 (33.2)	68 (17.1)			
Disagree	527 (28.8)	610 (33.3)	696 (38.0)	2,131	2	86.1

* Low: ≤49; medium: 50–64; high: >65.

** n < 2,326 indicates that participants chose 'doesn't happen here' (answer category not shown).

*** All p values <0.001.

to managerialism to experience management control as problematic (Table 10.3). For example, in the low-managerial agencies, few workers reported loss of professional autonomy as problematic (13.9 per cent), as compared to many more (54.5 per cent) in high-managerial settings. Low-managerial settings also allow workers more voice in decision making. While 43.4 per cent of workers in low-managerial settings reported that they had enough control over their work, only 23.3 per cent in high-managerial agencies did so. Likewise, 41.4 per cent of workers in low-managerial agencies felt that they had enough say in programme decisions, as compared to only 23 per cent in high-managerial agencies. The routinization of work also reduces worker control. Over 48 per cent of workers in high-managerial settings reported routinization as problematic, while only 15 per cent in low-managerial settings did so.

In sharp contrast, management control loomed larger in high-managerial agencies. Workers in high-managerial agencies were troubled by the increased reliance on performance evaluations. More than 54 per cent reported the use of electronic records and data to monitor their time as problematic, as compared to only 11.9 per cent in low-managerial settings. The evaluations of worker performance based on meeting management targets (51.4 per cent versus 13.4 per cent) and based on client success (57.7 per cent versus 12.0 per cent) were also more problematic in high- than in low-managerial agencies. Not surprisingly, more workers (49.7 per cent) in high-managerial settings were worried that such programme evaluations would cost them their job than did their low-managerial counterparts (17.1 per cent).

Impact of managerialism on human-services workers

An agency's 'commitment to managerialism' also affected workers' well-being, reflecting the extent of management or worker control over work and working conditions (Table 10.4).

More workers in high-managerial (53.4 per cent) than in low-managerial agencies (13.3 per cent) reported job stress as problematic. Burnout was also more problematic in high-managerial (38.4 per cent) than in low-managerial agencies (24.6 per cent). Similarly, fewer workers experienced job satisfaction in high-managerial (24.5 per cent) than in low-managerial agencies (41.6 per cent). In contrast 62.2 per cent of workers in low-managerial agencies did not feel that their job was too stressful and only 16.5 per cent of workers in low-managerial agencies reported job dissatisfaction. Not surprisingly, more workers

Table 10.4: Well-being and coping reported as problematic, by commitment to managerialism (n=2,326)

	Commitment to managerialism score*					
	High n (%)	Medium n (%)	Low n (%)	n**	df	χ^2***
Job too stressful						
Often/very often/sometimes	438 (53.4)	273 (33.3)	109 (13.3)			
Almost never/never	70 (11.6)	158 (26.2)	375 (62.2)	1,423	2	420.14
Job satisfaction						
Unsatisfied	338 (52.6)	198 (30.8)	106 (16.6)			
Satisfied	390 (24.5)	542 (34.0)	663 (41.6)	2,237	2	196.80
Turnover						
Problematic	635 (43.3)	522 (35.6)	311 (21.2)			
Not a problem	109 (14.9)	230 (31.4)	394 (53.8)	2,201	2	280.90
Burnout						
Problematic	733 (38.4)	707 (37.0)	469 (24.6)			
Not a problem	21 (6.1)	63 (18.2)	263 (75.8)	2,256	2	360.03

* Low: ≤49; medium: 50–64; high: ≥65.

** n < 2,326 indicates that participants chose 'doesn't happen here' (answer category not shown).

*** All p values <0.001.

in high-managerial settings (43.4 per cent) reported staff turnover as problematic than did those in low-managerial agencies (21.2 per cent).

The association of control and stress with adverse experiences in the high-managerial workplace is underscored by our use of Siegrist's effort reward imbalance (ERI) model, developed to identify stressful work environments (Siegrist et al, 2009). The model suggests that work stress results from a 'mismatch between high workload (high demand) and low control over long-term rewards' (Schnall and Landsbergis, 1994, p 398). Our analysis revealed a significant correlation of moderate strength between our Commitment to Managerialism score and the ERI score (R=.54, p<0.001), indicating a relationship in high-managerial settings between low control over the rewards of work and job stress.

Bending the rules

Many social workers resent loss of control of their working conditions, marked by larger caseloads, faster work pace, standardized practices, loss of professional autonomy and greater surveillance. In response, some resist managerialism informally (Aronson and Smith, 2010). As Hammonds (2019) suggests, when workers are continuously exposed to situations that they cannot control they may cope by slowing their work pace. That is, they take long breaks, make personal calls, use social media and conduct other non-work tasks on work time, and otherwise evade standard work norms so as to reclaim control of their time. Ackroyd and Thompson (2016) refer to such oppositional misbehaviours as informal resistance; Baines and Daly (2015) describes these evasions of control as hidden resistance. That is, when workers lower their performance to leverage more time and resources on behalf of professional values, this push-back, intentionally or not, undercuts managerialism's promise to boost 'productivity', 'accountability' and 'efficiency'. The slowdown, in turn, creates conditions for managerialism to falter (Baines and Daly, 2015), and more generally to expose management, government and/or society as uncaring. We refer to this push-back or resistance as 'bending the rules' (Abramovitz and Zelnick, 2018) (see Table 10.5).

More workers in high-managerial than in low-managerial agencies ignored eligibility requirements (49.8 per cent versus 20.0 per cent), inflated statistics (48.5 per cent versus 20.4 per cent), changed reports to meet measurement demands (44.0 per cent versus 23.9 per cent) and loosely interpreted programme requirements (43.9 per cent versus 23.3 per cent). At the same time, many worked overtime without pay (38.6 per cent versus 26.5 per cent) to ensure that client needs were met.

Table 10.5: Bending the rules, by commitment to managerialism settings (n=2,326)

	Commitment to managerialism score*					
	High n (%)	Medium n (%)	Low n (%)	n**	df	χ^{2}***
Ignored eligibility requirements						
Often/sometimes	281 (49.8)	170 (30.1)	133 (20.0)			
Never	419 (26.3)	553 (34.7)	623 (39.1)	2,159	2	118.1
Inflated statistics						
Often/sometimes	312 (48.5)	200 (31.1)	131 (20.4)			
Never	390 (25.5)	526 (34.4)	611 (40.0)	2,170	2	126.4
Changed reports to meet performance/outcome requirements						
Often/sometimes	402 (44.0)	293 (32.1)	218 (23.9)			
Never	300 (23.9)	430 (34.3)	523 (41.7)	2,166	2	115.8
Loosely interpreted programme requirements						
Often/sometimes	439 (43.9)	327 (32.7)	233 (23.3)			
Never	260 (22.5)	394 (34.0)	504 (43.5)	2,157	2	140.8
Staff worked overtime without pay so that client needs are met						
Often/sometimes	585 (38.6)	528 (34.9)	402 (26.5)			
Never	112 (17.6)	189 (29.6)	337 (52.8)	2,153	2	155.6

* Low: ≤49; medium: 50–64; high: ≥65.

** n < 2,326 indicates that participants chose 'doesn't happen here' (answer category not shown).

*** All p values <0.001.

The latter suggests that in order to fulfil the edict to 'do more with less', managerialism relies on the commitment of individual workers to fill the gap between what is needed and what is provided to fully meet client needs. This capacity to expand resources is rendered possible through the combination of individual self-sacrifice and the managerial expropriation of a worker's commitment to service. Such sacrifice among a largely female workforce exploits the gendered norm of selflessness associated with women's traditional role (Baines, 2010).

Despite the distressing tension between management and worker control described here, large numbers of social workers remain optimistic, though far less so in high-managerial agencies. The overwhelming majority reported that 'their work makes an import contribution to society' (91.9 per cent), that they 'think their work is important' (88.3 per cent) and that 'they believe in their programme' (88.0 per cent). A long-time NYC social worker observed: 'I am very lucky to work for an agency with an unswerving mission of social justice, compassion, and commitment. I have been allowed to be creative in my position. Nearing the end of my career, I believe that my training and work have mattered. A social worker couldn't ask for more.'

Summary and conclusion: another way is possible

Together, austerity and managerialism conjure a perfect storm: austerity cuts resources to the bone, while managerialism promotes 'doing more with less' through 'performance' measures and management control of the labour process. The idea that service quality and cost outcomes can be achieved through managerial control of work organization has a long history. Echoing Taylor, Ford and Deming (Matos and Piros, 2006), managerialism harnesses control of labour processes in the human services through the reorganization of work. This is often driven by government and private service contracts that tie funding to performance outcomes, designed to meet targets within specific time frames and utilizes evidence-based practice models that often standardize professional practice. In the managerial environment human-service agencies cede control (often unwillingly) of their professional and social justice missions to accommodate the pressures of fiscal constraints and the aims of the business model – accountability, productivity and efficiency – achieved through standardized labour processes. Imposed to rationalize austerity, managerialism risks subverting human-service work and workers at all levels.

Given the current high values placed on neoliberalism, the link between quality and performance measurement is seductive. However, our NYC data uncovers serious problems. It reveals a clear and widespread association of managerial goals with employer control of the work process, achieved through a routinization of work, electronic time monitoring, job evaluations based on meeting quantified measures of client success and satisfying management's numerical targets. Loss of workers' control follows greater regulation by management. Work environments highly committed to managerialism evidence loss of workers' decision making, autonomy and overall control. Mirroring the abundance of research that links loss of control with poor workers' health and safety (Laschinger et al, 2001) and job security outcomes (Landsbergis et al, 2014), we found that more workers in high-managerial agencies reported burnouts stress, job dissatisfaction and high staff turnover than did those in low-managerial agencies.

Managerialism appears to exploit human-service workers' skills and commitments to achieve its goals, even as its model of work organization undermines its own goals. The exploitation of labour through managerial techniques has been widely studied (Jermier, 1998). However, human-service sector work in general and care work in particular represent a special case. Work that supports the well-being of vulnerable people who may be traumatized, in crisis, face discrimination or otherwise be marginalized requires specific professional training, unique skills and a strong commitment. It is a testament to human-service workers that many resist the routinization and deskilling of their jobs produced by managerialism. They go above and beyond the call of duty to provide for service users and communities, often working overtime without pay, fudging the numbers, ignoring eligibility rules and otherwise bending the rules. As noted earlier, Baines and Daly (2015) assert that workers slow their work pace, take long breaks and conduct other non-work tasks on work time and otherwise lower their performance in order to reclaim control of their time. She suggests that these types of 'hidden resistance' undercut managerialism's promise to boost 'productivity', 'accountability' and 'efficiency' and otherwise create conditions for managerialism to falter. On the one hand, managerialism takes advantage of its predominantly female workforce. It counts on women to follow prescribed gender norms to selflessly choose or stay in service jobs and work overtime without pay in order to buffer the impact of managerialism's practices on the life chances of service users. On the other hand, by bending the rules to reclaim control of their time, women violate the 'good girl' gender norm that calls for women to be obedient and subservient.

Our data suggests that another way is possible, even if limited by the wider policy context, the lack of funds for human needs and the neoliberal values that demand austerity. Our finding that in low-managerial settings workers had fewer problems with autonomy, a greater say in decision making, less work stress and more sustainable employment extends the large body of theory and research arguing that democratic control of the workplace is an alternative route to quality, worker engagement and successful outcomes.

Note

1 Developed through a 2015 systemic literature review, see Abramovitz and Zelnick (2016).

References

Abramovitz, M. (2004/2005) 'Saving capitalism from itself: Whither the welfare state?' *New England Journal of Public Policy*, 20(1): 6.

Abramovitz, M. (2012) 'Feminization of austerity'. *New Labor Forum*, 21(1): 32–41.

Abramovitz, M. (2014) 'Economic crises, neoliberalism, and the US welfare state: Trends, outcomes and political struggle'. In: Noble, C., Strauss, H. and Littlechild, B. (eds), *Global Social Work Education: Crossing Borders and Blurring Boundaries*, Sydney: Sydney University Press, 225–41.

Abramovitz, M. (2018) 'From the welfare state to the carceral state: Whither social reproduction'. In: Kessler-Harris, A. and Vaudagna, M. (eds), *Democracy and the Welfare State*. New York: Columbia University Press, 195–226.

Abramovitz, M. and Zelnick, J.R. (2016) 'Privatization in the human services: Impact on front lines and the ground floor'. In: Fineman, M., Andersson, U. and Mattsson, T. (eds) *Privatization, Vulnerability, and Social Responsibility*. New York, NY: Routledge, Taylor Francis Group, 182–200.

Abramovitz, M. and Zelnick, J.R. (2018) *Business as Usual? A Wake Up Call for the Human Service*. https://s27588.pcdn.co/wpcontent/uploads/2018/10/report_human_services_workforce.

Ackroyd, S. and Thompson, P. (2016) 'Unruly subjects: Misbehaviour in the workplace'. In: Edgell, S., Gottfried, H. and Granter, E. (eds), *The SAGE Handbook of the Sociology of Work and Employment*. London: SAGE, 185–204.

Aronson, J. and Smith, K. (2010) 'Managing restructured social services: Expanding the social?'. *British Journal of Social Work*, 40: 530–47.

Baines, D. (2004) 'Pro-market, non-market: The dual nature of organizational change in social services delivery'. *Critical Social Policy*, 24(1): 5–29.

Baines, D. (2006) '"If you could change one thing": Social service workers and restructuring'. *Australian Social Work*, 59 (1), 20–34.

Baines, D. (2009) *Resistance as Emotional Labour: The Australian and Canadian Nonprofit Social Services*. McMaster University, Canada. www.academia.edu/3770793/Resistance_as_Emotional_Labour_The_Australian_and_Canadian_Nonprofit_Social_Services.

Baines D. (2010) '"If we don't get back to where we were before": Working in the restructured non-profit social services'. *British Journal of Social Work*, 40(3): 928–45.

Baines, D. and Daly, T. (2015) 'Resisting regulatory rigidities: Lessons from front-line care work'. *Studies in Political Economy: A Socialist Review*, 95, 137–60.

Baines, D., Charlesworth, S., Cunningham, I. and Dassinger, J. (2012) 'Self-monitoring, self-blaming, self-sacrificing workers: Gendered managerialism in the non-profit sector'. *Women's Studies International Forum*, 35(5): 362–71.

Ball, S.J. (2003) 'The teacher's soul and the terrors of performativity'. *Journal of Education Policy*, 18(2): 215.

Bowen, J., Omi, J. and Merlino, J.P. (2014) *Lean Behavioral Health: The Kings County Hospital Story*. Oxford: Oxford University Press.

Burton, J. and Van den Broek, D. (2009) 'Accountable and countable: Information management systems and the bureaucratization of social work'. *British Journal of Social Work*, 39(7): 1326–42.

Caplan, M.A. and Ricciardelli, L. (2016) 'Institutionalizing neoliberalism: 21st-century capitalism, market sprawl, and social policy in the United States'. *Poverty and Public Policy: A Global Journal of Social Security, Income, Aid, and Welfare*, 8(1): 20–38.

Center on Budget and Policy Priorities (2020) *Policy Basics: Non-Defense Discretionary Programs*. https://www.cbpp.org/research/federal-budget/policy-basics-non-defense-discretionary-programs.

Ehrenreich, J. (2016) *Third Wave Capitalism: How Money, Power and the Pursuit of Self Interest Have Imperiled the American Dream*. Ithaca, NY: ILR Press.

Eikenberry, A.M. and Kluver, J.D. (2004) 'The marketization of the nonprofit sector: Civil society at risk?' *Public Administration Review*, 64(2): 132–40.

Farnsworth, K. and Irving, Z. (2018) 'Austerity: Neoliberal dreams come true?'. *Critical Social Policy*, 38(8): 461–81.

Fiscal Policy Institute (2015) *A Fair Wage for Human Service Workers*. http://fiscalpolicy.org/wp-content/uploads/2015/12/15andFunding-Report-Dec2015.pdf.

Gallina, N. (2010) 'Conflict between professional ethics and practice demands: Social workers' perceptions'. *Journal of Social Work Values and Ethics*, 7(2): 1.

George, S. (1999) *A Short History of Neo-Liberalism*. Conference on Economic Sovereignty in a Globalising World, Bangkok. www.tni.org/print/article/short-history-neoliberalism.

Hammonds, B. (2019) *Vicarious Trauma, Perceived Stress, and Self-Care among Social Workers: A Quantitative Analysis*. Available from ProQuest Dissertations & Theses A&I. (2138802021).

Harlow, E., Berg, E., Barry, J. and Chandler, J. (2013) 'Neoliberalism, managerialism and the reconfiguring of social work in Sweden and the United Kingdom'. *Organization*, 20(4): 534–50.

Harvey, D. (2005) *A Brief History of Neoliberalism*. New York: Oxford University Press.

Hasenfeld, Y. and Garrow, E.E. (2012) 'Nonprofit human-service organizations, social rights, and advocacy in a neoliberal welfare state'. *Social Service Review*, 86(2): 295–322.

Healy, K. (2002) 'Managing human services in a market environment: What role for social workers?'. *British Journal of Social Work*, 32(5), 527–40.

Jermier, J.M. (1998) 'Introduction: Critical perspectives on organizational control'. *Administrative Science Quarterly*, 43(2): 235—56.

Kotz, D.M. (2015) *The Rise and Fall of Neoliberal Capitalism* (1st edn). Cambridge, MA: Harvard University Press.

Kotz, D.M., McDonough, T. and Reich, M. (eds) (1994) *Social Structures of Accumulation: The Political Economy of Growth and Crisis*. Cambridge and New York: Cambridge University Press.

Landsbergis, P.A., Grzywacz, J.G. and LaMontagne, A.D. (2014) 'Work organization, job insecurity, and occupational health disparities'. *American Journal of Industrial Medicine*, 57(5): 495–515.

Laschinger, H.K.S., Finegan, J., Shamian, J. and Almost, J. (2001) 'Testing Karasek's Demands-Control Model in restructured healthcare settings: effects of job strain on staff nurses' quality of work life'. *Journal of Nursing Administration*, 31(5): 233–43.

Lonne, B., McDonald, C. and Fox, T. (2004) 'Ethical practice in the contemporary human services'. *Journal of Social Work*, 4(3): 345—67.

Martin, L.L. (1993) *Total Quality Management in Human Service Organizations*. Thousand Oaks, CA: Sage Publications, Inc.

Martin, L. (2005) 'Performance-based contracting for human services: Does it work?'. *Administration in Social Work*, 29(1): 63–77.

Matos, E. and Piros, D. (2006) 'Administrative and work organization theories: From Taylor to current times; influences in health care and nursing'. *Texto & Contexto Enfermagem*, 15(3): 508–14.

Nightingale, D.S. and Pindus, N.M. (1997) *Privatization of Public Social Services: A Background Paper*. Washington, DC: The Urban Institute. https://www.urban.org/research/publication/privatization-public-social-services.

Norcross, J.C. and Wampold, B.E. (2011) 'Evidence-based therapy relationships: Research conclusions and clinical practices'. In Norcross, J.C. (ed), *Psychotherapy Relationships that Work: Evidence-Based Responsiveness* (2nd edn). New York, NY: Oxford University Press, 423–30.

O'Sullivan, S., Considine, M. and Lewis, J.M. (2009) 'John Howard and the neo-liberal agenda: The regulation and reform of Australia's privatised employment services sector between 1996 and 2008'. In: *Australian Political Studies Association (APSA) Conference 2009, Macquarie University, 28–30 September 2009*.

Pettijohn, S.L., Boris, E.T., De Vita, C.J. and Fyffe, S.D. (2013) *Nonprofit-Government Contracts and Grants: Findings from the 2013 National Survey*. Washington, DC: The Urban Institute.

Rogowski, S. (2019) 'Poverty, inequality and social work: The impact of neoliberalism and austerity politics on welfare provision'. *Critical Social Policy*, 39(1): 149–51.

Salamon, L.M. (1999) 'The nonprofit sector at a crossroads: The case of America'. *Voluntas: International Journal of Voluntary & Nonprofit Organizations*, 10(1): 5–23.

Salamon, L.M. (2012) 'The resilient sector: The future of nonprofit America'. In: Salamon, L.M. (ed), *The State of Non-Profit America*. Washington, DC: Brookings Institution Press.

Schnall, P.L. and Landsbergis, P.A. (1994) 'Job strain and cardiovascular disease'. *Annual Review of Public Health*, 15: 381–411.

Siegrist, J., Wege, N., Pühlhofer, F. and Wahrendorf, M. (2009) 'A short generic measure of work stress in the era of globalization: Effort–reward imbalance'. *International Archives of Occupational and Environmental Health*, 82(8):1005–13.

Smith, S.R. (2017) 'The future of nonprofit human services'. *Nonprofit Policy Forum*, 8(4): 369–89.

Soss, J., Fording, R.C. and Schram, S. (2011) *Disciplining the Poor: Neoliberal Paternalism and the Persistent Power of Race*. Chicago: The University of Chicago Press.

The Alliance: The Voice of Community Nonprofits (2019) 'Budget cuts survey. Non-profit survey: Further cuts will devastate those in need'. https://www.aoascc.org/Customer-Content/www/CMS/files/news___stories/Budget-Cuts-Survey_The-Alliance_revised__003_.pdf.

Wacquant, L. (2009) *Punishing the Poor: The Neoliberal Government of Social Insecurity*. Durham, NC: Duke University Press.

11

Austerity and the Irish Non-Profit Voluntary and Community Sector

Pauric O'Rourke

Introduction

Ireland stands as one of the countries most severely affected by the Great Recession (GR) and the Global Financial Crisis (GFC), which necessitated unprecedented remedial measures in the form of a 'bail out' by the three international institutions known collectively as the Troika (International Monetary Fund, the European Central Bank and the European Commission), through promulgation of emergency legislation and the adoption of severe austerity measures (Robbins and Lapsley, 2014). Such interventions impacted on all sectors, including the social economy, with the Irish Non-Profit Voluntary and Community Sector (NPVCS) being forced to do more with less, which had implications for how it did its work and managed its people.

This contribution illustrates one of the themes of this volume's Chapter 1 on how austerity may be framed. In this case, austerity may be interpreted either as a continuation of an established neoliberal ideology or as a not-to-be-wasted opportunity that is unique to a particular era in time (Pierson, 1998; Clarke and Newman, 2012). The economic success of the Irish economy from 1994–2007, better known as the 'Celtic Tiger', was in stark and sudden contrast to the recessionary-fuelled era of 2008 to

2016, in which austerity dominated (Murphy, 2014). This unprecedented period in Irish socioeconomic history placed intense financial pressures on all sectors of the Irish economy as government spending and revenues drastically contracted and taxation increased (Roche et al, 2017). The NPVCS was not immune, given it high dependency on state funding and its close relationship with government in terms of governance, regulation and service contracts.

To provide insight into the dynamics of austerity in the Irish NPVCS context, this chapter draws on a qualitative-based empirical study within the subsector of Physical and Sensory Disabilities (PSD), built around two principal service providers, anonymized as Alpha and Omega. It argues that government funding and service-level agreements (SLAs) created the conduit for New Public Management- (NPM) orientated thinking and practices to enter the sector and exert downward pressures on how it manages people and work. Coincidentally, this conveniently aligned with austerity ideology and gave new impetus to NPM. The findings show strong evidence of NPM-orientated changes in work and human resources management (HRM), propelled by strong isomorphic pressures that had accelerated and intensified during the era of austerity. They enable understanding of NPM and sector–state relations in the unique era of austerity while also shedding new light on how NPM and HRM in the sector interact. The study uses the explanatory lens of institutional theory and labour-process theory to explicate how the state–NPVCS relationship became institutionalized through the isomorphism of NPM and how austerity reinforced and expedited this process.

The Irish non-profit voluntary and community sector

The Irish NVPCS has a long and rich history, growing from purely altruistic and volunteer roots to become a significant socioeconomic force on the Irish landscape and a major employer and contributor to gross domestic product (Donoghue, 2001; Charities Regulatory Authority-Indecon, 2018). In response to economic, social and demographic needs, this sector has grown in scale, scope and diversity, with more than 9,600 registered charities, generating an annual income of €14.5 billion, employing 189,000 people and supported by 300,000 volunteers. Over half of registered charities had an income of less than €250,000 in 2018 and 53 per cent of charity employees were in registered charities supported by some form of government funding (Charities Regulatory Authority-Indecon, 2018). Yet, despite its size and significance, the sector is poorly understood and studied, both nationally and internationally (Third Sector Impact, 2015) – a state of affairs that the new Charities Regulatory Authority is striving to address.

Increasing sectoral convergence and shifting boundaries with the emergence of a mixed economy of care, a growing culture of competition and contracting, value-for-money imperatives and, most recently, austerity pressures, brought new tensions and contradictions to the traditional view of the sector (Hardill and Dwyer, 2011; Department of Health, 2012). The PSD subsector has its own unique set of contingencies and logics and is dominated by non-profit providers, with such organizations having responsibility for 60 per cent of service provision. Four big players dominate this subsector and the majority of funding comes from government (Expert Reference Group on Disability Policy, 2011).

In 2008, the government launched 'Transforming Public Services' (Department of the Taoiseach, 2008), which was a continuation of the public service reform agenda, with a renewed emphasis on costs, efficiencies and shared delivery. The PSD subsector, as a provider of disability services on behalf the state, was included in this reform agenda. It resulted in the *Value for Money and Policy Review of Disability Services in Ireland Report*, which specifically mentioned 'Section 39 Organisations', including the PSD subsector (Department of Health, 2012). This report sought to reconfigure the delivery of disability services and achieve greater value for money for the service user, the service provider and the state via increased monitoring, oversight and accountability. It tightened the contract relationship in the form of an SLA, with more rigorous processes of independent auditing and increasing accountability and transparency. This *Value for Money Report* and the resultant policy initiatives demonstrate strong evidence of NPM-inspired concepts at work, such as client centricity, formalization, standardization, accountability, quality standards and competitive tendering. The latter, coupled with the GFC and public sector austerity of 2008–16 created unprecedented challenges for the NPVCS, with predictions at the time estimating a contraction in funding of 35 per cent and a loss of 11,150 jobs by the end of 2013 (Harvey, 2010). The PSD subsector, like the rest of the sector, entered a new climate of uncertainty in terms of financing, with the threat of further cuts as the recession and austerity deepened.

Literature and theoretical framework

Internationally, the NPVCS has become more professional, business–like, market facing and innovative, with the emergence of new delivery models, contracting technologies and social enterprises (Mohan and Breeze, 2016).

Its relationship with the state has generated specific policy instruments such as competitive tendering, contracting, commissioning and personalization (Cunningham and Nickson, 2011). Such developments could be categorized under the term NPM. Hood (1991) first coined the term NPM, which, as a new concept, was open to many definitions and interpretations, with macro descriptions referring to it as a 'diffuse ideology' (Flynn, 1999, p 27) and micro descriptions referring to it as managerialism (Pollitt, 1990) and market-based public administration (Lan and Rosenbloom, 1992). It raised fundamental questions about the capacity of government to do the 'people's work' (Drucker, 1969).

The adoption of the NPM philosophy marked a paradigm shift in the management of the public service, particularly in work practices and employee relations (Brown, 2004). HRM's centrality to change processes made it a tangible face of public sector reform, articulating this new agenda and linking NPM with HRM reform (Battaglio, 2015). Private and public sector HRM increasingly converged, with the spread of NPM, via the normative and mimetic transplanting of private sector HRM best practice to the public sector, endeavouring to create a high-performance and high-commitment culture (Poole et al, 2006). It involved a devolution of HRM roles and responsibilities to line management, enabling greater discretion and flexibility in an effort to create a more responsive public service.

Emerging new delivery models of public service provision via the NPVCS facilitated the entry of NPM into the third sector, with adverse implications for work and HRM (Cunningham et al, 2013). Literature on HRM in the NPVCS highlights the salience of the state–sector relationship (Parry et al, 2005; Baines et al, 2011). NPM's migration to the NPVCS cultivated formalization of work processes and a focus on measurement. The role of HRM in this process came to the fore in terms of content, function and performance (Kelliher and Parry, 2011). Tracing the impact of such purchaser–provider relationships on people and their work (Cunningham, 2010; Bartram et al, 2017) generated a new line of enquiry examining the changing nature of human resources (HR) in the sector (McCandless, 2011). Focus was placed on how the sector managed change, resourcing, reward management, performance management and employee relations (Kellock et al, 2001; Burt and Scholarios, 2011; Cunningham, 2016). Demands for efficiency and accountability as a prerequisite for government funding resulted in greater formalization of management, including HRM (Suárez, 2011). NPM posed direct challenges to traditional NPVCS workforce attributes, with standardization and formalization divesting traditional attributes such as emotion, discretion and flexibility in favour of efficiency, economies and quality (Clayton, Donovan and Merchant, 2015). Australian studies illustrate how this culminated in greater formalization of HR policies and systems and a standardization of work practices (Charlesworth, 2012). Explicating the interaction of austerity-fuelled NPM and HRM with the NPVCS adds to our understanding of the evolving dynamics and logics of the sector.

The state–sector relationship may be analysed using a variety of frameworks and theories, some of which are reflected in this volume, and include government support theory and Labour Process Theory (Seo, 2016; Cunningham and James, 2017). This study has fixed on institutional theory, isomorphism and Labour Process Theory as an appropriate but not exclusive lens. Institutional theory is premised on the view that organizations are shaped and influenced by the institutional environment that surrounds them (DiMaggio and Powell, 1983). The growing complexity of the external environment triggered change within the NPVCS as such complexity began to be mirrored and mapped onto internal structures of organizations through the process of 'requisite variety' and isomorphism (Lawrence and Lorsch, 1967). Such interaction exerted coercive, normative and mimetic pressures on many organizations within the sector. Coercive institutional pressure stems from legal and governmental sources, while normative institutional pressures arise from cultural and professional expectations. Mimetic institutional pressures stem from the natural business instinct of organizations to imitate one another as a heuristic device to find the most effective technical solution (Subramony, 2006). While institutional theory is complex and multi-stranded, Cunningham (2008) provides strong justifications for applying an institutional theory framework to the NPVCS in that it realistically captures the shifting dynamics and contextual forces at play.

In recognizing the institutional qualities of NPM, this chapter is particularly interested in how the isomorphic concepts and principles of efficiency and value for money recalibrate working conditions in the sector, compounded by the advent of austerity. Labour Process Theory, in turn, sheds light on this dynamic, particularly in areas such as work intensification and skills. Specifically, because it is at the level of the labour process that management will seek to make savings we can, therefore, observe the coercive impact of the institutional pressures of principles such as efficiency and value for money on work and employment (Cunningham, 2008; Baines and Cunningham, 2011).

NPM, HRM, Ireland and the NPVCS

The development of the Irish system of public administration reflects several 'traditions', from Weberian bureaucracy to NPM (Rhodes and

Boyle, 2012, p 43). Public sector reform is central to the latter and has long been on the Irish political agenda (MacCarthaigh, 2017). The Irish approach to public sector change portrays a pattern 'of long periods of inertia, punctuated by occasional bouts of reform, which achieve varying degrees of success' (Hardiman and MacCarthaigh, 2009, p 1). Ireland was considered a slow starter of NPM, as compared to other English-speaking countries, and was described as a 'reluctant reformer' and 'something of an outlier' in its uptake of NPM ideas (Robbins and Lapsley, 2005, p 109, Hardiman, 2010, p 12) until the GR.

The GR and austerity of 2008–16 in Ireland brought a new intensity to the state–non-profit relationship, marking a new era in the evolution of the NPM philosophy (Bach and Bordogna, 2016). It gave new impetus and legitimacy to the principles of NPM, becoming interlaced with a parallel strategy of public sector cuts (Davies, 2011). It accentuated core NPM tenets such as value for money, marketization, private sector managerialism and creating links to a wider neo politico-economic-liberal agenda (Evans and Shields, 2002). The state's close ties with the NPVCS via resource dependencies and obligation contracting and as a shadow employer, combined with the severity of the financial crash, created the 'perfect storm' (Cunningham and James, 2014).

The Anglo-Saxon model of NPM, of 'doing more with less', conveniently aligned with perception among policy makers of Ireland's need to reform. It re-echoed the genesis of NPM, with a crisis in the body state being used by free marketers and libertarians to promote reform of the public sector and the adoption of private sector-like policies and practices. The promulgation of the FEMPI (Financial Emergency Measures in the Public Interest) Acts in 2010 and 2013, at the mandatory behest of the Troika, saw the statutory enforcement of concession-bargaining agreements with public-sector unions. It prompted a new framework for Irish public sector reform, with the successful implementation of three concession agreements, which all contained clauses around reform and a commitment to engage with new work practices (Department of Public Expenditure and Reform, 2014). This 'doing things differently' approach renewed a focus on public sector productivity and performance (Boyle, 2016, p 149). Concessions from vulnerable trade unions resulted in pay, pension and benefit cuts of up to 25 per cent, elimination of old work practices and entitlements, an increase in contracted hours and productivity and a shedding of large numbers of public servants (Geary and Murphy, 2011). There was an 8 per cent drop in public sector employment between 2008 and 2016, despite increases in population and demands for public services (Boyle, 2015).

Any lingering doubts about the effectiveness of NPM (Hyndman and Liguori, 2016) were firmly put to bed during austerity. Indeed, the renewed impetus provided by austerity delivered more and quicker reform than all previous initiatives since the foundation of the Irish state (Roche, 2012). NPM became a central part of the new, austerity-driven reform framework (Comptroller and Auditor General, 2011; Department of Public Expenditure and Reform, 2017; MacCarthaigh, 2017), although there was a reluctance to name it so. The state as chief funder and shadow employer equally imposed such a regime on the NPVCS. Lapsley (2008, p 78) characterized NPM as a 'mechanism of change'. Understanding how organizational change occurs in the non-profit sector is poorly understood (Wilson, 1996). Analysis of the role of NPM in the sector contributes to filling this gap while expanding our understanding of the NPM construct, especially in the Irish context under conditions of austerity, particularly in relation to work and HRM. In sum, this study addresses questions of how environmental and institutional forces of change shaped the evolution of NPM in the Irish NPVCS and how this NPM-inspired change has adversely impacted on work and HR in the sector at a unique and unprecedented time of austerity.

Methodology

This study is part of a wider mixed-methods study, with this qualitative account focused on the management and supervisory level of the PSD subsector. The two case-study organizations, Alpha and Omega, were purposively selected from preliminary informal interviews with a variety of HR directors in the sector and stood out as representative samples of what was happening in the Irish NPVCS in terms of growing complexities and new logics. To optimize potential generalizability, both case studies were in the PSD subsector and are 'Section 39' organizations funded by the HSE (Health Service Executive) under that section of the Irish Health Act 2004. They provide services under contract on behalf of the state and are dependent on government for between 70 and 80 per cent of their funding, with workforces in excess of 1,000 employees. Each has developed and evolved HR functions, with HR directors being members of top management. Both experienced significant change throughout their history, particularly due to recent austerity and public sector retrenchment. They exhibited some of the classic hallmarks of NPM in terms of growing managerialism, commercialization and measurement. In sum, they both presented as organizations that had the evidentiary potential and capacity to showcase the dynamics of austerity in the sector. Table 11.1 shows the schedule of managers and supervisors in both organizations that participated in semi-structured interviews during 2012–13, in which they answered a series of questions in relation to how their growing contractual relationship and dependence on the state funder, the HSE, was adversely impacting on work and HRM in their organizations. The coding tree created from these interviews, is themed around identifying external and internal forces of change. These include austerity imperatives that triggered isomorphic NPM-like changes resulting in greater formalization and standardization of HRM and work practices, and degradation in employment conditions, work quality and employee relations, among others.

Table 11.1: Schedule of qualitative interviews: case studies, Alpha and Omega, 2012–13

Alpha		Omega	
Job title	Number	Job title	Number
CEO	1	CEO	1
Company secretary	1	Director of HR	1
Director of HR	1	HR manager	1
Director of finance	1	Director of services	5
Director of fundraising	1		
Directors of services	3		
Communications manager	1	IT manager	1
Area managers	6	Retail operations manager	1
Service co-ordinator	6	National manager of training	1
Fundraising and retail manager	1	Finance managers	2
		Technology managers	2
Board member	1		
Total:	23	Total:	16

Findings

The influence of austerity-fuelled NPM

Each case study organization, Alpha and Omega, exhibited coercive, normative and mimetic isomorphism as they reacted to NPM-inspired change by progressively adopting greater formality, professionalization and discipline. This was intensified by tighter and more transparent SLAs and funding prerequisites from the HSE and the regulatory inspectorate HIQA (Health Information and Quality Authority):

> 'It [SLA] really gives all the power to the HSE and very little power to the service provider ... It states what the HSE can do and does not state what the service user can do.' (Director of Services at Omega)

Changes to HR under austerity-fuelled NPM

The NPVCS literature recognizes HR as an 'influencing agent' for change (Kellock et al, 2001). In response to NPM-inspired change, both Alpha and Omega developed professional in-house HR functions, meeting the demands of a more professional workforce and the growth of contract relations with the state. They were sufficiently staffed to allow the directors of HR to take a strategic perspective on a number of organizational developments and employee relations issues. The formalization and standardization of work practices through a full suite of HR policies and services, including an Employee Assistance Programme and a web-enabled HR portal, ensured the development of quality standards that could be monitored and measured. NPM also brought cost-effectiveness and efficiency to the fore, which was welcomed by supervisors who wanted greater clarity, transparency and consistency around HR processes and systems.

> '[T]he advantage of the policies and procedures is that there is clarity, there is structure ... If there is an issue I can go to the individual and say this is our disciplinary policy ... these are the standards ... this is what is expected of you.' (Area manager at Omega)

NPM resulted in the development of strong operational and strategic HR approaches, with representation on the highest decision-making forum. The leadership provided by the directors of HR proved instrumental in implementing significant change, as is mirrored in other studies (Cunningham, 2001; Akingbola, 2006). Coercive isomorphic resourcing policies, such as police vetting and employment references, were in evidence at both organizations, necessitating a more systematic approach to recruitment and selection, including of volunteers.

[W]e used to have parents on interview boards, doing an interview for new staff, now you don't ... their engagement has lessened and probably partially because of ... compliance.' (Director of Services at Omega)

Training, learning and development functions progressively developed as a distinct subdivision. The literature identifies the use of such learning and development interventions as a means of successfully changing work behaviours and service quality, and standards and expectations (Carvalho et al, 2016; Dostie and Javdani, 2020). Growing normative isomorphic demands around formal quality standards stemming from the HSE SLA, and external audit process from the quality inspectorate HIQA, brought a greater formality, accountability and traceability to work standards. This was furthered by Alpha's and Omega's pursuit of a formally recognized quality standard.

'[S]taff take the training on board and implement the training and I think that it brings a professionalism to the staff which is shown in how they do things and contributes to quality ...' (Area manager at Alpha)

The adoption of a Level 5 qualification in social care as the basic entry-level credential for the sector helped to rebrand work as a career rather than as stop-gap casual employment, and this positive effect is mirrored in the UK social care sector (Gospel and Lewis, 2011). The entry of credentialed professionals in all areas across the organization has also lifted expectations and shifted the culture and thinking to a stronger managerialist and business outlook rather than purely that of a charity. Such control systems had a restraining influence of the traditional nature of work in the sector, which was particularly felt by employees on front-line delivery.

Alpha and Omega both rolled out a performance management system, which sought to bring about greater accountability on the part of employees and to empower managers to actively manage. Omega implemented an attendance management programme in 2011 that achieved 1,000 hours in savings over the first year. This example of managing and measuring performance and metrification of the HR function also represents a more professional and business-like approach to managing people and processes:

'we all signed up to a new absence management policy ... all managers were trained and then everybody started from a certain date ...' (Director of Services at Omega)

In terms of implementing change, both HR directors spoke of working towards a particular model of HR that was a cross between the traditional welfare role, long associated with the non-profit voluntary sector, and the business partnership role, dominant in the private sector. They acknowledged that it was an evolutionary work in progress, impeded in part by gaps in line-management capability, a pattern that is reflected in the literature (McDermott et al, 2015; McCracken et al, 2017). The ultimate pursuit of a business partnership model was considered fundamental to their work by both HR directors. In gaining legitimacy as an HR function and co-equality at the senior management level, both felt that they were in a better position to implement the changes that NPM and austerity had imposed on their respective organizations:

'the [HR] function has acquired a lot more status and reputation and power … my role is a bit of both driver and facilitator of change …' (HR director at Alpha)

'When I came in … I was very interested in trying to respond to people doing … very difficult jobs and building a welfare model of HR … but I now end up in fire brigade mode and crisis mode, not just now and again but every day.' (HR director at Omega)

This trend is evident in many countries in response to long-standing calls for more educated professionals in the sector, especially at the leadership and management levels (Suarez, 2010).

Pay and working conditions

In terms of their employees, pay and some terms and conditions of employment in both organizations were historically linked with the HSE as 'Section 39' organizations. As the 'shadow employer', who indirectly funded the payroll, the state insisted that the terms of the three concession-bargaining agreements should be passed on to all 'Section 39' organizations, including Alpha and Omega. The enormity of the collapse of the public finances meant a double assault on the NPVCS in terms of both cuts in funding and cuts in pay and conditions. Given the dependency relationship, power imbalance and lack of adequate alternative streams of income, the sector was exposed. This resulted in severe cuts in pay, pension and terms and conditions of employment, and unprecedented actions such as redundancies and job losses (Considine and Dukelow,

2010). This assault was compounded by the introduction of contracting, initially for home care, elderly and disability services, which put further downward pressure on pay and terms and conditions of employment in the sector. This degradation formed part of the implementation of some of the recommendations of the *Value for Money* report, which resulted in Alpha negotiating additional pay cuts for its care assistants. These additional pay cuts, plus cuts in overtime rates and travel allowance, represented a concerted and strategic move by management in both organizations to break the long-established pay-parity links between the public sector and 'Section 39' NPVCS organizations, in an effort to make the sector more competitive against private sector providers. The Irish experience is mirrored in other countries, including the UK and Canada (Cunningham, 2011):

> 'one of the things we have done is that we have agreed a 10 per cent pay reduction with the Personal Assistants ... that means that our pay rates now are much closer to market rates.'
> (HR director at Alpha)

Efficiency and effectiveness imperatives

Austerity brought stronger imperatives to the sector where the logics of efficiency, effectiveness and economies, also known as 'the 3 Es of NPM', became dominant, with the need to do more with less but still maintain, and in some cases increase, service levels. This was further evidenced in the implementation of several initiatives, such as Alpha's becoming a limited company, more stringent reporting requirements, the adoption of quality assurance accreditation as well as the standardization and formalization of policies and practices:

> 'the organisation became a company limited by guarantee ... It brought a huge increase in the financial governance requirements of the organization. The formal legal requirements to produce accounts ... meant you had to have different systems in place.'
> (Director of Services at Omega)

In addition, the scope to subsidize services that were previously underfunded diminished. The application of greater financial discipline meant that some services or ways of working where the organization and its workforce would go the 'extra mile' were diminished:

'we have to break even and we have to be quite disciplined about ... not doing stuff we are not paid for, having service arrangements signed off, making sure we are covering our costs.' (Director of Finance at Alpha)

Technology and work intensification

Technology also began to shape and control work in both organizations, with the introduction of client management systems and mobile devices, which many viewed as a further step in depersonalizing and micro-monitoring their work (Hayes and Moore, 2016):

> 'technology has been a huge area which has developed within the organisation ... PA staff members ... able to record their attendance at each of their service-users electronically, sign it off electronically ...' (Area manager at Alpha)

> 'the new CRM (Client Relationship Management) system has been a pain and a hassle but the analysis you can get out of it now, we are doing analysis that we were never able to do before now.' (Manager of Technology at Omega)

Work intensification, greater monitoring of work and completion of more documentation were also consequences of this move to introduce new technology. The level of bureaucracy and the pressure to deliver more with less were identified as part of NPM-inspired change at both Alpha and Omega. The pilot introduction of smartphones/iPads as time-recording surveillance tools at Alpha and the implementation of a client management data system at Omega both sought efficiencies around service delivery and metrification of outputs:

> 'We have to be efficient ... we have to survive; we have to break even and behave like a business in terms of efficiency ...' (Director of Finance at Alpha)

Intrinsic to the strive towards greater efficiency was a heightened level of work intensification that employees were expected to accept, given the national and organizational crisis:

> 'everyone has toughened up, but that is a national issue ... people have to go the extra mile ... I am multi-tasking,

everyone is multi-tasking. It's a big squeeze ...' (Director of Services at Omega)

Discussion, implications and conclusion

Internationally, the NPVCS's growing relationship with government has impacted on and shaped work and HRM in the sector via NPM-like changes (Akingbola, 2006; Baines et al, 2011). This is equally evidenced in the Irish context, as the two case-study organizations portray. Spotlighting the Irish NPVCS at the unique time of austerity served to highlight tensions and contradictions that lay submerged. Empirically, this study reveals the Irish non-profit sector to be more evolved, sophisticated and complex than common perceptions would indicate, consistent with predicted trends in the literature (Kramer, 2000). Interrogation of the sector through the lens of institutional and Labour Process Theory allowed discovery of how and why NPM-inspired change had impacted on the sector, its work and its people. This brought greater contextual understanding of the Irish NPVCS and its approach to HRM. It also confirmed the continued relevance of NPM (Hyndman and Lapsley, 2016) and offered insights into how this philosophy was applied in an Irish setting under extreme conditions of austerity.

NPM-inspired change has had a real impact on the work, policies and practice of HRM in both organizations, but at a cost. It incrementally brought formalization and standardization to HRM practices and processes and led to the establishment of a professional HR function, with a strategic presence at the top decision-making level (Akingbola, 2013). As a consequence, HR in Alpha and Omega began to look like HR in the public sector, which is not altogether surprising, given its close ties with the HSE (Parry et al, 2005). This is reflected at all stages of the HRM cycle, from resourcing, to learning and development, to employee relations. Such a transformation has been in direct response to institutional and regulatory demands that have made HR governance and compliance a priority, with greater emphasis on performance-related polices.

At the same time, work has become more intensive and discretionary components have been diminished in response to quality and inspectorate standards and strategic expectations. Such developments reflect some of the core characteristics of NPM in terms of infusing greater competition and value for money into the NPVCS as echoed in other nations where the 'dispersed state' has further evolved, such as the UK (Cunningham, 2016) and Australia (McDonald and Charlesworth, 2011). Both organizations adopted a more business-like and market-oriented approach based on performance, cost-efficiency and audit-orientation, all of which are hallmarks of classic NPM with significant adverse implications for HRM and employee relations in the sector. As in other countries, degradation in pay and terms and conditions of employment was the cost that employees pay under the new logics of marketization and austerity (Cunningham et al, 2013).

At a sectoral and policy level, this study raises questions about what kind of NPVCS model Irish society wants and needs, and the sustainability and viability of the current mixed economy of care model (Crowley, 2013). Many countries are asking this question in light of the GFC (Rees and Mullins, 2016). The sector has evolved into a significant socioeconomic force but may be reaching a fork in the road in terms of evaluating the opportunity cost of a full embrace of its 'fourth sector' role as an arm of government service provision. Austerity has brutally exposed the Irish sector's long-recognized Achilles heel of funder capture (Kramer, 1994) in its reliance on one customer, namely the austere state. In light of the ongoing underfunding and restructuring associated with austerity, NPVCS leaders and boards will no doubt continue to struggle to fulfil agency missions and provide reasonable pay and conditions for employees.

References

Akingbola, K. (2006) 'Strategy and HRM in nonprofit organisations: Evidence from Canada'. *Journal of Human Resource Management*, 17(10): 1707–25.

Akingbola, K. (2013) 'A model of strategic nonprofit human resource management'. *Voluntas: International Journal of Voluntary and Nonprofit Organizations*, 24(1): 214–40.

Bach, S. and Bordogna, L. (eds) (2016) *Public Service Management and Employment Relations in Europe: Emerging from the Crisis*. Abingdon: Routledge.

Baines, D. and Cunningham, I. (2011) '"White knuckle care work": Violence, gender and new public management in the voluntary sector'. *Work, Employment & Society*, 25(4): 760–76.

Baines, D., Cunningham, I., Kelliher, C. and Parry, E. (2011) 'Voluntary sector HRM: Examining the influence of government'. *International Journal of Public Sector Management*, 24(7): 650–61.

Bartram, T., Cavanagh, J. and Hoye, R. (2017) 'The growing importance of human resource management in the NGO, volunteer and not-for-profit sectors'. *The International Journal of Human Resource Management*, April (Special Issue): 1–11.

Battaglio, P.R. (2015) *Public Human Resource Management Strategies and Practice in the 21st Century*. Thousand Oaks, CA: CQ Press.

Boyle, R. (2015) *Public Sector Trends 2015*, 17. Dublin: Institute of Public Administration.

Boyle, R. (2016) 'Riding the roller coaster: Ireland's reform of the public service at a time of fiscal crisis'. In: Hammerschmid, G., Van de Walle, S., Andrews, R. and Bezes, P. (eds), *Public Admistration Reforms in Europe: The View From The Top*. Cheltenham: Edward Elgar, 140–50.

Brown, K. (2004) 'Human resource management in the public sector'. *Public Management Review*, 6(3): 303–9.

Burt, E. and Scholarios, D. (2011) 'Recruiting for values in charitable organisations: A comparative perspective'. In: Cunningham, I. and James, P. (eds), *Voluntary Organizations and Public Service Delivery*. London: Routledge, 104–23.

Carvalho, A., Melo, S. and Ferreira, A.P. (2016) 'Training in Portuguese non-profit organizations: The quest towards professionalization'. *International Journal of Training and Development*, 20(1): 78–91.

Charities Regulatory Authority-Indecon (2018) *Social and Economic Impact Report of Registered Irish Charities – 2018*. Dublin: Charities Regulatory Authority and Indecon.

Charlesworth, S. (2012) 'Decent working conditions for care workers? The intersections of employment regulation, the funding market and gender norms'. *Australian Journal of Labour Law*, 25(2): 107–27.

Clarke, J. and Newman, J. (2012) 'The alchemy of austerity'. *Critical Social Policy*, 32(3): 299–319.

Clayton, J., Donovan, C. and Merchant, J. (2015) 'Emotions of austerity: Care and commitment in public service delivery in the North East of England'. *Emotion, Space and Society*, 14(2), 24–32.

Comptroller and Auditor General (2011) *Report of the Comptroller and Auditor General Volume 1*. Dublin: Government of Ireland.

Considine, M. and Dukelow, F. (2010) 'Introduction: Boom to bust, Irish social policy in challenging times'. *Irish Journal of Public Policy*, 2(1): 1–5.

Crowley, N. (2013) 'Lost in austerity: Rethinking the community sector'. *Community Development Journal*, 48(1): 151–7.

Cunningham, I. (2001) 'Why research the voluntary sector?' *Employee Relations*, 23(3): 223–5.

Cunningham, I. (2008) *Employment Relations in the Voluntary Sector*. London: Routledge.

Cunningham, I. (2010) 'The HR function in purchaser–provider relationships: Insights from the UK voluntary sector'. *Human Resource Managment Journal*, 20(2): 189–205.

Cunningham, I. (2011) 'The third sector's provision of public services: Implications for mission and employment conditions'. In: Corby, S. and Symon, G. (eds), *Working for the State: Employment Relations in the Public Services*. Basingstoke: Palgrave Macmillan, 147–65.

Cunningham, I. (2016) 'Non-profits and the 'hollowed out' state: The transformation of working conditions through personalizing social care services during an era of austerity'. *Work, Employment & Society*, 40(4): 649–68.

Cunningham, I. and James, P. (2014) 'Public service outsourcing and its employment implications in an era of austerity: The CASE of British social care'. *Competition and Change*, 18(1): 1–19.

Cunningham, I. and James, P. (2017) 'Analysing public service outsourcing: The value of a regulatory perspective'. *Environment and Planning C: Politics and Space*, 35(6): 958–74.

Cunningham, I. and Nickson, D. (2011) *Personalisation and Its Implications for Work and Employment in the Voluntary Sector*. Glasgow: Scottish Centre for Employment Research, University of Strathclyde Business School.

Cunningham, I., Hearne, G. and James, P. (2013) 'Voluntary organisations and marketisation: A dynamic of employment degradation'. *Industrial Relations Journal*, 44(2): 171–88.

Davies, S. (2011) 'Outsourcing and the voluntary sector: A review of the evolving policy landscape'. In: Cunningham, I. and James, P. (eds), *Voluntary Organizations and Public Service Delivery*. New York: Routledge, 15–36.

Department of Health (2012) *Value for Money and Policy Review of Disability Services in Ireland*. Dublin: Department of Health, Irish Government.

Department of Public Expenditure and Reform (2014) *Public Service Reform Plan 2014–2016*. Dublin: Government Publications.

Department of Public Expenditure and Reform (2017) *Our Public Service 2020 – Development and Innovation*. Dublin: Government Publications.

Department of the Taoiseach (2008) *Transforming Public Services – Citizen Centred – Performance Focused*. Dublin: Government Publications.

DiMaggio, P.J. and Powell, W.W. (1983) 'The iron cage revisited: Institutional isomorphism and collective rationality in organizational fields'. *American Sociological Review*, 48: 147–60.

Donoghue, F. (2001) 'Ireland'. In: Schluter, A., Tehn, V. and Walkenhorst, P. (eds), *Foundations in Europe: Society, Management and Law*. London: Directory of Social Change and Charities Aid Foundation, 34–48.

Dostie, B. and Javdani, M. (2020) 'Not for the profit, but for the training? Gender differences in training in the for-profit and non-profit sectors'. *British Journal of Industrial Relations*, February, 1–15.

Drucker, P. (1969) 'The sickness of government'. *The Public Interest*, 14(Winter): 3–23.

Evans, B. and Shields, J. (2002) 'The third sector: Neo-liberal restructuring, governance and the re-making of state–civil society relationships'. In: Dunn, C. (ed), *The Handbook of Canadian Public Administration*. Toronto and Oxford: Oxford University Press, 236–58.

Expert Reference Group on Disability Policy (2011) *The Future of Disability Policy in Ireland: Report on Disability Policy Review*. Dublin: Department of Health.

Flynn, R. (1999) 'Managerialism, professionalism and quasi-markets'. In: Exworthy, M. and Halford, S. (eds), *Professionals and the New Managerialism in the Public Sector*. Buckingham: Open University Press, 18–36.

Geary, J. and Murphy, A. (2011) 'The reform of public sector pay in Ireland under social pacts'. In: Baglioni, M. and Brendl, B. (eds), *Changing Labour Relations: Between Path Dependency and Global Trends*. Frankfurt: Peter Lang Academic Publishers, 12–32.

Gospel, H. and Lewis, P.A. (2011) 'Who cares about skills? The impact and limits of statutory regulation on qualifications and skills in social care'. *British Journal of Industrial Relations*, 49(4): 601–22.

Hardill, I. and Dwyer, P. (2011) 'Delivering public services in the mixed economy of welfare: Perspectives from the voluntary and community sector in rural England'. *Journal of Social Policy*, 40(01): 157–72.

Hardiman, N. (2010) *Economic Crisis and Public Sector Reform: Lessons from Ireland*. Dublin: UCD.

Hardiman, N. and MacCarthaigh, M. (2009) 'Breaking with or building on the past? Reforming Irish public administration'. In: *Politics, Economy and Society: Irish Developmentalism, 1958–2008*, University College Dublin, 12 March 2009. University College Dublin.

Harvey, B. (2010) *Analysis of the Implications of the 2010 Budget for the Voluntary and Community Sector*. Dublin: IMPACT Trade Union.

Hayes, L.J.B. and Moore, S. (2016) 'Care in a time of austerity: The electronic monitoring of homecare workers' time'. *Gender, Work & Organization*, 24(4): 329–44.

Hood, C. (1991) 'A new public management for all seasons'. *Public Administration*, 69(1): 3–19.

Hyndman, N. and Lapsley, I. (2016) 'New public management: The story continues'. *Financial Accountability & Management*, 32(4): 385–408.

Hyndman, N. and Liguori, M. (2016) 'Public sector reforms: Changing contours on an NPM landscape'. *Financial Accountability & Management*, 32(1): 5–32.

Kelliher, C. and Parry, E. (2011) 'Voluntary sector HRM: Examining the influence of government'. *International Journal of Public Sector Management*, 24(7), 650–61.

Kellock, H.G., Beattie, R., Livingstone, R. and Munro, P. (2001) 'Change, HRM, and the voluntary sector'. *Employee Relations*, 23(3): 240–55.

Kramer, R.M. (1994) 'Voluntary agencies and the contract culture: "Dream or nightmare?"' *Social Service Review*, 68(1): 33–60.

Kramer, R.M. (2000) 'A third sector in the third millennium?' *Voluntas: International Journal of Voluntary and Nonprofit Organizations*, 11(1): 1–23.

Lan, Z.Y. and Rosenbloom, D.H. (1992) 'Public administration in transition' (Editorial). *Public Administration Review*, 52(6): 535–7.

Lapsley, I. (2008) 'The NPM agenda: Back to the future'. *Financial Accountability & Management*, 24(1): 77–96.

Lawrence, P.R. and Lorsch, J.W. (1967) *Organization and Environment: Managing Differentiation and Integration*. Cambridge, MA: Harvard University Press.

MacCarthaigh, M. (2017) *Public Sector Reform in Ireland: Countering Crisis*. Basingstoke: Palgrave Macmillan.

McCandless, A. (2011) *Human Resource Management in Nonprofit Organizations*. London: Routledge.

McCracken, M., O'Kane, P., Brown, T.C. and McCrory, M. (2017) 'Human resource business partner lifecycle model: Exploring how the relationship between HRBPs and their line manager partners evolves'. *Human Resource Management Journal*, 27(1): 58–74.

McDermott, A.M., Fitzgerald, L., Van Gestel, N.M. and Keating, M.A. (2015) 'From bipartite to tripartite devolved HRM in professional service contexts: Evidence from hospitals in three countries'. *Human Resource Management*, 54(5): 813–31.

McDonald, C. and Charlesworth, S. (2011) 'Outsourcing and the Australian nonprofit sector'. In: Cunningham, I. and James, P. (eds) *Voluntary Organisations and Public Service Delivery*. Abingdon: Routledge, 185–201.

Mohan, J. and Breeze, B. (2016) *The Logic of Charity: Great Expectations in Hard Times*. Basingstoke: Palgrave Macmillan.

Murphy, M.P. (2014) 'Ireland: Celtic tiger in austerity – explaining Irish path dependency'. *Journal of Contemporary European Studies*, 22(2): 132–42.

Parry, E., Kelliher, C., Mills, T. and Tyson, S. (2005) 'Comparing HRM in the voluntary and public sectors'. *Personnel Review*, 34(5): 588–602.

Pierson, P. (1998) 'Irresistible forces, immovable objects: Post-industrial welfare states confront permanent austerity'. *Journal of European Public Policy*, 5(4): 539–60.

Pollitt, C. (1990) *Managerialism and the Public Services: The Anglo-American Experience.* Oxford: Basil Blackwell.

Poole, M., Mansfield, R. and Gould-Williams, J. (2006) 'Public and private sector managers over 20 years: A test of the "convergence thesis"'. *Public Administration*, 84(4): 1051–76.

Rees, J. and Mullins, D. (eds) (2016) *The Third Sector Delivering Public Services: Developments, Innovations and Challenges.* Bristol: Policy Press.

Rhodes, M.L. and Boyle, R. (2012) 'Progress and pitfalls in public service reform and performance management in Ireland'. *Administration*, 60(1): 31–59.

Robbins, G. and Lapsley, I. (2005) *NPM and the Irish Public Sector: From Reluctant Reformer to Statutory Codification.* USA: Information Age Publishing.

Robbins, G. and Lapsley, I. (2014) 'The success story of the eurozone crisis? Ireland's austerity measures'. *Public Money & Management*, 34(2): 91–8.

Roche, W. (2012) 'The future of HR in the public sector'. In: *Public Affairs Ireland Annual HR Conference*, Dublin, 27 September.

Roche, W.K., O'Connell, P.J. and Prothero, A. (eds) (2017) *Austerity and Recovery in Ireland: Europe's Poster Child and the Great Recession.* Oxford: Oxford University Press.

Seo, J. (2016) 'Resource dependence patterns and organizational behavior/structure in Korean nonprofit organizations'. *Nonprofit Management and Leadership*, 27(2): 219–36.

Suarez, D.F. (2010) 'Street credentials and management backgrounds: Careers of nonprofit executives in an evolving sector'. *Nonprofit and Voluntary Sector Quarterly*, 39(4): 696–716.

Suárez, D.F. (2011) 'Collaboration and professionalization: The contours of public sector funding for nonprofit organizations'. *Journal of Public Administration Research and Theory*, 21(2), 307–26

Subramony, M. (2006) 'Why organizations adopt some human resource management practices and reject others: An exploraiton of rationales'. *Human Resource Management*, 45(2): 195–210.

Third Sector Impact (2015) 'A Statistical Revolution in Data in the Third Sector in Europe'. Press release. http://thirdsectorimpact.eu/news/a-statistical-revolution-in-data-on-the-third-sector-in-europe/. Accessed 20 July 2016.

Wilson, D.C. (1996) 'How do voluntary agencies manage organisational change?' In: Billis, D. and Harris, M. (eds), *Voluntary Agencies: Challenges of Organisation and Management.* London: Macmillan Education UK, 80–97.

PART IV

Alternatives and Resistance

12

'The most striking progressive achievement in labor and employment policy'? The Scottish Living Wage in Social Care during Austerity

Alina M. Baluch

Introduction

Living wage campaigns command substantial popular support, yet austerity is proving to be a poor bedfellow to their implementation. Recognising that the articulation of austerity is bound by the context of political spaces, governmental formations and constitutional forms in which these policies, programmes and political projects unfold (Clarke, 2017), this chapter seeks to tease out these contingencies of place in the impact of the austerity agenda. To do so, it explores the progressive policy to introduce a living wage to the social care workforce in Scotland.

As a strategy to improve workers' conditions, a living wage endeavours to secure better-than-minimum wages to address the social and economic consequences of low pay. At a time when low-wage earners are experiencing cuts in public services, stagnant real-wage growth and precarious work at the same time as declining union strength, a living wage protects the workforce that is most exposed to market forces as a result of outsourcing and restructuring (McBride and Muirhead,

2016; Parker et al, 2016; Prowse and Fells, 2016). Outsourced social care involves difficult working conditions across multiple sites, with a largely female workforce at the bottom of the wage distribution in a sector plagued by a shortage of workers and high turnover (Howes, 2005). In 2016 the Scottish Government introduced the Scottish Living Wage (SLW) for front-line workers in adult social care in an effort to address cost and quality tensions in the market as well as recruitment and retention difficulties (Cunningham et al, 2018). Intended to relieve the social care sector from a dysfunctional market, the SLW and its implementation present an opportunity to examine the challenges and consequences arising at the intersection of a positive policy initiative and austerity measures.

After briefly outlining the literature on minimum and living wages and on austerity in social care, this chapter presents findings on local authorities' and providers' experiences with SLW implementation. Drawing on interviews with voluntary and private social care providers across Scotland, representatives of lead employer bodies, union officials, commissioning authorities and civil servants, the findings suggest that the re-regulation of pay has, paradoxically, prompted greater insecurity in market relations in social care (Cunningham et al, 2018). Local authorities' experiences highlight several unintended consequences of the policy, including an uneven distribution of funding to poorer payers that disadvantages fair employers, bringing services in-house and making cuts to other services. Thereafter, the chapter discusses the experiences and impact of SLW implementation on social care organizations, such as providers making efficiencies and withdrawing from or declining to enter unviable contracts. The chapter closes with implications for the sustainability of the SLW and service provision in adult social care.

Research on the effects of minimum and living wages

It is first important to distinguish between the UK's National Minimum Wage (NMW) which sets a wage floor (and has since been confusingly retitled the National Living Wage (NLW)), and what is referred to as a 'real' living wage that reflects the amount to sustain an employee and their dependants at a level that is acceptable to society (Prowse et al, 2017). Framed as a moral and social justice issue, the notion of a living wage appeals to human decency, solidarity and underlying concepts of fairness (McBride and Muirhead, 2016). The living wage agenda, as Parker et al (2016, p 3) note, is shaped by 'varied and shifting institutional and political considerations relating to rights at work, poverty reduction and social inclusion'.

Given the local nature of living wage policies, their decentralization allows for wage and benefits mandates to be tailored to local conditions (Freeman, 2005). The UK Living Wage is voluntary, yet the SLW bears similarities to the Living Wage model of a municipal ordinance, best described as a targeted ordinance that affects only a specific group, in this case adult social care workers (McBride and Muirhead, 2016). The SLW in adult social care is an example of sector-specific 'soft' government regulation. Sitting at £9.30/hr (as of April 2020), annual increases are based on the calculation of a Minimum Income Standard made according to the cost of living, which is a figure used by the Living Wage Foundation (LWF). As the accreditation body for employers committed to the living wage, the LWF represents a new actor in determining the pay increases set by the UK government's Low Pay Commission (Prowse et al, 2017).

Significant attention has been devoted to the range of benefits and drawbacks arising from the introduction of a living wage. Studies on Living Wage ordinances from the US and the NMW and the voluntary living wage in the UK provide evidence of improvements to pay levels at the bottom without a significant loss of jobs or working hours, and improvements in morale, work effort and workforce retention and absenteeism (Heyes and Gray, 2001; Fairris, 2005; Fairris and Reich, 2005; Howes, 2005; Luce, 2014; Johnson, 2017). These wage raises, however, are often insufficient to lift workers out of poverty and there is only mixed evidence of second-order ripple effects of wage gains for workers higher up (Freeman, 2005; Reich, Hall and Jacobs, 2005). The NMW has failed to generate this upward pressure on wages in many low-paying sectors, given the wage-compression effect through which the reductions in pay differentials can undermine internal career structures (Grimshaw, 2013).

Research on implementing the voluntary living wage in UK local government against the backdrop of public sector austerity and a pay freeze comes to similar findings, but also highlights its positive impact on procurement and the delivery of services (Prowse and Fells, 2016; Johnson, 2017). Significant wage compression occurred, with trade unions unable to create upward pressure and achieve wider wage gains through bargaining for employers to restore pay differentials. Johnson's research (2017) also points to spill-over effects in relation to procurement processes as wages were increased throughout the supply chain. In relation to social care services, the local authority offset the additional cost of the living wage by renegotiating contracts and rates with external social care providers through the addition of living wage 'clauses'. At the same time, Johnson (2017, p 847) cautions that 'even then progress was slow in tackling low pay in outsourced care for older people'. Prowse and Fells' (2016) work examining this practice of contracting out in a living wage local authority also identifies the tendering process as critical to strengthening the authority's commitment to its living wage policy. The unions played a central role in having sub-contractors indicate how they intended to adopt the living wage in the costings of their tender bids, thereby amplifying union influence into a previously untapped area of the local authority's strategic decision making (Prowse and Fells, 2016).

Evidence remains mixed on whether the NMW and the UK Living Wage lead to the deterioration of employment conditions. On the one hand, managerial responses to higher wages include cuts to hours worked and unsocial-hours enhancements, withdrawal of other benefits, tighter monitoring of staff, reductions in breaks and work intensification (Heyes and Gray, 2001; Machin, Manning and Rahman, 2003; Johnson, 2017). Examining the effect of the NMW in small UK firms, however, Arrowsmith et al (2003) found limited scope to intensify work in order to compensate for increased costs, given the lack of room for manoeuvring in these firms. At the same time, employers' efforts to claw back the cost increase of the NMW included withdrawing breaks and increased recording and monitoring. In contrast, in small to medium-sized UK retail firms adopting the voluntary living wage, these smaller enterprises experience a range of positive impacts, such as improved morale and employee relations and higher productivity (Werner and Lim, 2017).

Turning to research in the care sector, the effects of wage increases are similarly mixed. Machin et al's (2003) study on the impact of introducing the NMW in UK residential care homes found a reduction in wage inequality, yet also evidence that employers responded by cutting the employment and hours of care assistants. Research in the US care sector on the effect of wages on labour-market outcomes found that a near doubling in wages and increases in benefits led to a significant reduction in home care workers leaving the service (Howes, 2005). Howes' study suggests that as a result of the combination of union bargaining and the Living Wage Ordinance, wage and benefit increases improved the retention of individual independent care providers. Further research on the NLW, which was introduced in 2016 and raised the minimum wage (for workers over 25 years), points to a lack of reductions in the number of employees, hours worked, price increases or market exit in care homes in England (Giupponi and Machin, 2018). Instead, the care homes reduced quality and offered more expensive services for residents with complex needs, as is seen in the increase in the proportion of residents requiring specialist care. Giupponi and Machin (2018) conclude that offsetting costs of the NLW in the labour-intensive care sector through deteriorating service quality raises concerns about the sector's ability to ensure standards of quality and safety at the current levels of funding.

Research on austerity in social care

Beyond statutory NMW/NLW legislation, the regulation of pay in social care previously lay with non-state actors in the private and voluntary sectors. With the removal of provisions such as the long-standing Fair Wages Resolution and Schedule 11 of the Employment Protection Act 1975, external social care providers can deviate from the terms and conditions negotiated under collective agreements in the public sector (Cunningham and James, 2017). The subsequent National Care Home Contract covers pay rises in all (private) care homes in Scotland, and the remainder of services (voluntary) are regulated by enterprise bargaining. Without formal external constraints on the wage-setting process, outsourced social care providers possess the (legal) freedom to alter employment conditions in response to financial pressures from local authority funders.

Research has devoted attention to the employment-related consequences of Scottish voluntary sector social care organizations' attempts to deliver a similar or increased level of services and uphold quality standards in the face of austerity-driven reductions in public sector funding settlements. Cunningham et al (2016, p 459) describe the surge in austerity-compelled precarity as: 'funding to nonprofits was increasingly insecure, which, coupled with growing demands for services from under-serviced, vulnerable communities, resulted in a tumbler effect in which precarity operates at multiple levels, amplifying and reinforcing experiences of instability and uncertainty for organizations and the workforce'. Longitudinal analyses suggest that as public expenditure cuts took hold, providers engaged in an ongoing 'race to the bottom' on pay, radically reshaping staff terms and conditions, and made redundancies (Cunningham and James, 2014; 2017). Attempts to reduce costs and increase efficiency were furthermore undertaken in organizations previously paying comparable public sector pay rates by awarding less-than-inflationary rises, introducing pay freezes, removing pay increments or imposing significant pay cuts, thereby ending any alignment with public sector pay scales. Precarity was furthermore observed in Cunningham et al's (2016) study of the impacts of austerity policies on the pay and conditions of employment, indicating a shift from the aforementioned public sector negotiated rates of pay to cuts in wages, sick pay and annual leave at the same time as work intensification in the form of increased weekly working hours. These cuts to terms and conditions under austerity policies meant that workers occupied less powerful positions and, compounded by heavier workloads, point to greater exploitation of the workforce.

By reducing the statutory provision of care services and shifting to commissioning services, local authorities have cut costs dramatically, driven by a combination of market forces and austerity. Bach (2012) describes how scaling back public service provision, and thereby essentially carving out what is left of the social state, and the subsequent increased marketization of public services allows for non-state organizations to replace 'unresponsive' public services. While austerity measures have reduced employment and increased insecurity for the voluntary sector workforce, this is not to suggest that the public sector has emerged unscathed (Bach, 2016). Instead, research shows that, despite support for paying a living wage, local government employers in England respond to cuts by reasserting their right to decide the key terms and conditions of employment locally. These revisions to employment arrangements include cutting sick pay, reducing annual leave, overtime and unsocial hours pay. At the same time, austerity measures have led to reduced employment, including voluntary redundancies, vacancy freezes and delayering through sharing services in English local authorities. In addition, alongside evidence of service withdrawal, there is less frequent provision of statutory services and, in the case of social care, net spending per person was cut by 17 per cent over the period between 2009 and 2015 (Bach and Stroleny, 2014; Bach, 2016). The shrinkage in the size and protective role of the state and the accompanying shift away from systems of employment regulation governing public services represent but one face of austerity. Eroding pay and conditions and increased outsourcing as part of an agenda of encouraging provider diversity (Bach, 2016) go hand in hand with the UK's market-driven approach to low pay and welfare and labour-market policy. Scholars caution, however, that the advance of the 'market' in regulating employment conditions brings the unintended consequence of 'a rapidly growing social welfare budget as governments try to address issues of poverty and the working poor through transfer payments' (Prowse et al, 2017, p 782).

In Scotland, the introduction of the living wage for front-line adult social care workers potentially halts this advance of market-determined pay. This change was prompted by recruitment and retention challenges, due to low pay in the sector in combination with increased workloads and low staff morale (Cunningham and James, 2017). These pressures were occurring at a time of increasing demands on the skills of the workforce through the government's system of mandatory qualifications based on Scottish Vocational Qualifications, the promulgation of 'fitness to practice' standards (SSSC, 2017) and wider policy developments in Scotland such as the personalization of social care and health and social care integration. Together the challenges in recruiting and retaining care workers were leading to growing concerns about the ability of providers to maintain service quality. Seeking to address these issues and correct an increasingly dysfunctional social care market in the voluntary and private sectors, the Scottish Government and the local government representative body (COSLA) therefore jointly agreed that front-line care staff working in publicly funded adult social care should be paid at a minimum the SLW with effect from 1 October 2016. Rather than withdrawal, the state is thereby acting to reconfigure regulatory roles and bucking the trend of reluctance to intervene to regulate pay (Arrowsmith et al, 2003; Parker et al, 2016; Cunningham and James, 2017).

This development followed the defeat of a proposal in May 2014 to add the living wage as a condition to procurement in all Scottish Government contracts to the Procurement Reform (Scotland) Act 2014, although there is the expectation that bidders will demonstrate their willingness and ability to pay the living wage (Prowse and Fells, 2016). Here the growing importance of Scotland's Fair Work agenda provides a favourable public policy setting through which the Scottish Government promotes the adoption of the living wage. The Government's statutory guidance (Scottish Government, 2015) requires all public bodies to abide by best practice fair work procurement guidelines (Fair Work Convention, 2019). In the context of social care, the fair work principles and guidance should be applied by commissioning authorities to consider how a bidder accounts for fair work commitments in their reward, recognition, training and supervision of staff. Yet the guidance remains vague on the responsibilities of the local authority and its capacity to create financial and practice conditions (for example, hourly rate-based competitive tenders and framework agreements) that lead to poor-quality work (Cunningham et al, 2018). Although the inclusion of fair work criteria in procurement guidelines can encourage payment of the living wage by employers, the statutory guidance also emphasises that a failure to pay the living wage 'does not mean that the employer automatically fails to meet fair work standards' (Scottish Government, 2015, p 6). Thus, little is known about how the procurement guidance actually impacts on fair work practices (Fair Work Convention, 2019). As employment regulation is not among the devolved powers in Scotland, the SLW represents a form of 'soft' regulation at best, one that is implemented through processes of tendering.

Implementing the SLW

The implementation of the SLW presents an opportunity to examine the challenges and consequences arising at the intersection of a positive policy initiative and austerity measures for local authorities and outsourced social care providers. Findings are drawn from Cunningham et al's (2018) study, which involved 25 semi-structured interviews: 13 of which were conducted with voluntary and independent sector providers; two sets of group interviews with several voluntary sector providers; five with local authorities, including chief officers and representatives from the Integrated Joint Boards (IJBs) and procurement and finance managers; two with civil servants, including representatives from COSLA; two with representatives of lead bodies of employers (CCPS and Scottish Care); and with a senior trade union representative. Many of these latter interviewees were members of the Implementation Group that was established to oversee and monitor the SLW's introduction and provide joint implementation guidance for health and social care partnerships and providers.

Approaches to SLW funding in the context of austerity

While commissioning and providing services under 'tremendous financial pressures', local authorities are simultaneously implementing the Scottish Government's commitment to the SLW. Councils receive a local government settlement, which includes the annual sum of money for the SLW. This funding is distributed via the National Health Service to the Health and Social Care Partnerships responsible for planning and commissioning services in their area, in the expectation that a process of onward transfer to providers takes place through renegotiation of prices, fees and rates. These partnerships, led by an IJB, take on a hybrid role as the 'contractor provider': commissioning services and delegating the contract to the local authority, who passes the SLW uplift on to outsourced providers. In the context of austerity, local authorities noted the challenges in navigating this circuitous funding route:

> 'initially going through a health board and back through a council, then forward to an IJB who then goes back to the council to fund the providers, was also quite a route for us to go as well, and at a time of financial constraint. Let's just say, I think the angel's share in most areas was taken off that, that then left you in a position where it was quite difficult to actually say, how do we fund the living wage at the same time

as adequately dealing with the capacity issues that we have.'
(Local authority)

Adhering to the principle of local autonomy, councils sought to retain control over their portion of the SLW funding and how the policy is applied to serve their respective populations. Decisions made around the distribution of funds reflected local circumstances and how funding one service was seen as detracting from another (such as education or roads). These constraints were compounded by a failure to account for the expenditure potentially needed to raise pay levels to meet the SLW. Although the local government settlement for each council takes account of various indices (population and geographical factors such as poverty, social deprivation), employer representatives were quick to point out the flaws in the distribution formulae for the SLW as being unrelated to the level of outsourced provision of services and the level of wages within local authority areas:

'If you had an area where in that authority, most social care services are delivered in-house, then they would have got a big pile of money, but they wouldn't have to spend very much, and they could spend it on other things ... if this was about filling a gap in pay in outsourced services, you would think that the distribution would relate to that.' (Lead body representative)

Contracting authorities adopted different approaches to distributing the SLW funding, following the guidance issued by the Implementation Group that oversaw the introduction of the SLW. These approaches ranged from awarding a percentage uplift to all providers, to offering different rates for different kinds of services, paying the difference to bring providers in line with the SLW, asking providers to submit bids for funds or training and information technology investments if already paying this rate, and withholding funding to providers already paying the SLW. Furthermore, given these different mechanisms, councils varied on whether they funded pay differentials, on-costs (national insurance, holidays, sickness benefits, maternity and paternity leave and pension) and the SLW rate for sleepover shifts. Difficulties also arose with implementing inflationary uplifts at the same time as the SLW, as increases in inflation had not been funded for several years.

One outcome was that an uneven distribution of funding emerged, namely towards poorer payers and away from 'fair' employers already paying a living wage, where councils decided to withhold any funding to these latter providers. One respondent explained this blanket approach whereby providers who did not qualify did not receive the uplift:

> 'And it wasn't even that they were penalized, it was just that they didn't effectively qualify. So they're looking at, what's your qualification criteria. We sent out ... a schedule to all of our providers saying, please list out all of your care staff and the rates that you pay them, if it's below £8.25.' (Local authority)

A number of providers perceived that this approach to implementation rewards employers who set wages at the NMW, while penalizing those who paid more. By focusing their resources on those organizations with rates of pay furthest away from the SLW, local authorities undermine efforts to reward staff above the statutory minimum. One respondent recalled the unfairness of receiving nothing for having already rewarded their staff at that level:

> 'For example, in XXX ... do you already pay the Scottish Living Wage? If you do, you're entitled to nothing ... but basically that was it ...we were entitled to none of the uplifts from the additional monies made available by the Scottish Government, and that's still their position.' (Voluntary sector provider)

Other organizations reported foregoing profits (private providers), undergoing restructuring and slimming down central management functions (voluntary sector providers) in order to pay their front-line workforce a wage above the SLW. The unwillingness of several local authorities to provide uplifts led one organization to abandon its policy of paying a rate beyond the SLW:

> 'It's a real bone of contention. Because we think we did the right thing by paying more, sooner and we feel we've been punished for doing it ... we're saying, we're not making that mistake again. You know, we don't have the cash to carry that gap, 'cause we've done it once and it was inordinately expensive.' (Voluntary sector provider)

An unintended consequence of this approach to distributing SLW funding, therefore, is the adverse impact on fair employers and their employment conditions. In some cases, providers were raising the prospect of withdrawing from services in local authorities where no funds were forthcoming.

Consequences for services

Contracting authorities faced numerous dilemmas around service provision, which point to further unexpected outcomes of implementing this progressive policy. These entailed the challenges of providing other council services while meeting the SLW uplifts. Some councils reported making cuts to these services to fund the SLW:

> 'because we have so much of our care externalized [...]. It wasn't enough to cover the cost. [...] So we had to find some resources through savings elsewhere or other funding sources and using that money from there.' (IJB member)

Others reported feeling compelled to make future cuts to other council services. One contracting authority anticipated having to "reduce services somewhere along the line to pay for it" if funding was no longer earmarked for the SLW and partner organizations were no longer required to pass it on to the councils.

More broadly, contracting authorities viewed these challenges around funding the SLW as prompting moves towards service remodelling and work redesign (for example, technology and shared housing support). Citing a need for reform and innovation in the sector, respondents positively viewed the move away from overnight care and towards technology that would monitor service users' well-being at night. Some councils were reportedly already phasing out sleepovers to counteract cost increases. The prospects of the inappropriate removal of sleepovers, however, were raising concerns among providers regarding the safety and quality of service provision to people currently being supported. Providers furthermore expressed reservations about local authorities rushing to introduce technology as a panacea, critiquing both the significant investment this involves and its inappropriateness for some service users.

Greater insecurity in market relations in adult social care

The aforementioned multiple approaches to distributing the funding, delays in payments by local authorities and the unknown implications of the SLW for sleepovers were feeding a climate of uncertainty and financial instability for providers. Providers lacked influence over the timing and the method of implementation, and this uncertainty over payments from local authorities had a detrimental impact on their financial stability. Several smaller organizations reported being temporarily in deficit or anticipating going into deficit because of delays in funding. Not only the small providers, but also large organizations encountered cash-flow problems:

'It had a significant impact on our financial viability ... we carried deficit. We were unable to recoup the finance we required.' (Voluntary sector provider)

Where operating in multiple local authorities, providers experienced fragmented payment dates and numerous difficulties in planning and budgeting for the financial year. Until other local authorities had agreed to pay the SLW, these providers were unable to pay this rate to their front-line workers. Smaller organizations were vocal in the difficulties they faced due to delays in payments from certain local authorities:

'Six months for a small organization is a massive impact. We haven't got those sorts of reserves to just be able to say, well, we'll wait for it to come later.' (Private provider)

Particularly vulnerable was the private sector, given its abundance of small independent organizations. Respondents reported that there were quite a few independent organizations whose survival was thrown into doubt due to delays in receiving funding and significant cash-flow problems.

'It's not what's on paper that shuts an organization down, it's cash flow, and I think that's what hits small organizations ... there could be a whole load of small organizations go to the wall.' (Private provider)

Even larger organizations were depleting their reserves and reducing training budgets, with some providers being reluctant to further exhaust their reserves.

'We're talking about organizations with the economies of scale who could cope with the absence of funded differentials and absence of funded on-costs. So what happened was organizations having to draw reserves, having to reduce and raid training and learning budgets, having to lower dividends.' (Private provider)

Compounding the providers' financial planning difficulties and instability is the intended move of the Scottish Government towards no guarantee of separately identified funds and paying through what was labelled 'business as usual'. Providers noted that this development would bring further insecurity in social care:

> 'I'm appalled ... it worries me greatly. I don't know what next year is going to bring. We need inflationary uplifts. We need it to cover the SLW and other cost increases.' (Voluntary sector provider)

Another unanticipated consequence of this progressive policy is therefore the threats to organizational stability and, in some cases, survival. Identifying a range of negative future consequences if the intended move to 'business as usual' should lead to reduced or no increases, providers anticipated further reductions in sleepovers, as they would be unable to sustain such cover if funding was unavailable. Furthermore, respondents expected making reductions in service provision in order to maintain SLW wage rates:

> 'It'll push some services if we don't get increases to closure. Because services are teetering on a knife edge.' (Voluntary sector provider)

Already providers indicated that some local authorities were no longer negotiating but imposing increases in hourly rates. Respondents expected worsening relations with local authorities as resources shrank and priorities shifted for the latter, but the requirement to pay the SLW remained with the former. In addition, the lack of separately identified money to audit may further encourage local authorities that do not pass on funding to spend it on other priorities.

Making efficiencies

The prospect of not earmarking funding for the SLW functioned as a means of coercing providers to make further efficiencies. Contracting authorities prefer that providers undertake more workplace reforms and efficiencies to assist in paying for the SLW. Civil servants too were opposed to the idea of separately identifying future funding, noting that it removes the responsibility from providers to improve services. These workplace reforms encompassed flattening management layers so as to reduce differentials between different categories of staff. Notwithstanding the job losses these measures might entail, these suggestions exacerbate the already limited prospects for career development in the sector.

Examples of efficiencies being made included providers undertaking a range of pre-austerity and austerity-related rounds of cuts and restructuring that have led to work intensification for team leaders and supervisors. Providers were merging their back offices, stripping out layers of management and investing these resources into their front-line workers. Although there was little evidence of reductions in other terms and conditions to afford the SLW, efficiencies included the additional scrutiny of time taken for administration, learning and development, travel, team meetings and supervision, while also not filling vacancies. Several providers were awaiting forthcoming funding settlements to ascertain if they had sufficient resources to pay the SLW without making cuts to terms and conditions elsewhere:

> 'depending on what happens ...There might be things that go, and that's just to make it [SLW] affordable so that you can provide the service.' (Voluntary sector provider)

In the group interviews, several providers reported that local authorities expected more effort and efficiencies from the workforce in return for the SLW. This expectation was met with objection, as providers felt it exceeds the funders' remit to suggest such reforms:

> 'You can't decide that somebody will deliver something by efficiencies ... we are independent organizations, you can't just write a letter and say this ... Because people can exit this market.' (Provider representative)

Contract withdrawal

A further challenge brought about by the SLW policy is provider withdrawal from unsustainable contracts. Both voluntary sector and independent providers reported handing back services where they were unable to offer the services at the rates or without an uplift for provision in rural areas. No longer deficit-funding services, several organizations declined to submit to local authority tenders where the ceiling in the hourly rate was seen as too low. Relations deteriorated with local authorities that had refused to pay any uplift:

> 'I would say there have been some clear and frank conversations in which both parties are kind of rigid in their positions. I

don't have any more money, I need more money, it's quite intractable there.' (Voluntary sector provider)

The strain on relations led providers to raise the prospect of withdrawing from services, or actually to do so, unless additional funding was available. One contracting authority referred to a provider handing back the service after several fruitless rounds of discussions about making further efficiencies:

'But we would also start off with providers by saying to them, you know, what can we do to try to make things easier for you, and how can we help with efficiencies … So we had all these discussions with that particular provider, but they just really wanted more money. Let's not do things more efficiently, let's just, give us more money. And we can't.' (Contracting authority)

Local authorities responded to contract withdrawal by re-contracting services with other providers based in adjacent local authorities. Furthermore, after one provider handed back a contract, as it was unable to pay its differentials at the rate provided, the contracting authority brought the contract in-house where unit costs were reportedly low enough, given economies of scale:

'one of our providers was not able to work within the financial framework of ours, and that one provider withdrew from the contract that we then brought in-house … because of their differentials, because of their management infrastructure above that, that they couldn't do it.' (Local authority)

Providers noted the opacity regarding how local authorities were determining what it costs to deliver the care being commissioned. Only seldom did funders share and discuss costing formulae with providers. With little opportunity for these costing assumptions to be challenged, providers secured adjustments to them by raising the prospect of withdrawing from services or declining to bid for them. Although this suggests that the market power of providers was influencing how contracts were funded, it also points to the potential for unfair disparities in how particular services or providers are funded (Cunningham et al, 2018).

Constraints on pay regulation

The above context of SLW implementation begins to paint a picture in which employers and local authorities experience a diminished role in regulating pay. This sacrificed control is evident not only in the unpredictable timing of funding and the variation across local authorities in the method of funding, but also in that providers are being directed by an external authority to pay a specific hourly rate, while having no guarantee of consultation over decisions regarding annual increases to the SLW rate. Although contracting authorities still set the hourly rates for social care, their role is being undermined, as they too have no control or input into decisions regarding the annual increases set by the LWF.

At the same time, councils were constrained by collective bargaining in their own in-house services. Market forces have allowed local authorities to cut costs through the outsourcing of services to an extent that they are unable to do with their internal workforce, given that these are still subject to collective bargaining (Cunningham and James, 2017). A number of providers stressed that, despite the pay increases experienced by the outsourced workforce, these will continue to fall behind the conditions of equivalent public sector workers. This pay discrepancy between the internal and external workforce may be exacerbated by government commitments to increase the pay of the former, as well as the continuing strength and influence of unions in the public sector (Cunningham et al, 2018).

Implications for the sustainability of the living wage policy and service provision in the social care sector

Living wage ordinances are hailed as 'the most striking progressive achievement in labor and employment policy' (Fairris and Reich, 2005, p 1). The SLW is one part of the conditions of possibility that frame the national, regional and local articulations of austerity – and resistance to it (Clarke, 2017). As the implementation of this policy initiative demonstrates, however, attempts to mitigate the impact of sustained austerity measures on a vulnerable workforce have undoubtedly met their limits. Despite its progressive roots to improve working conditions and address recruitment and retention issues in the care sector, the unintended consequences of the SLW have exacerbated austerity-compelled precarity. In the aftermath of the Scottish Government's commitment to pay the adult social care workforce a living wage and the potential onset of a 'business as usual' approach, greater insecurity in market relations is evident, including threats to organizational stability and survival in the voluntary sector. Unsurprisingly, its implementation is viewed as a significant transfer of financial responsibility and risk to the sector, further enabling local authorities to pass their funding pressures on to voluntary providers (Cunningham et al, 2018). Against the prospect of continuing austerity, these developments raise several questions around the sustainability of the SLW and adult care services in Scotland.

One question mark looms large over the viability of the SLW policy. Particularly as the forces of austerity meet the waning commitment of the Scottish Government to fund the SLW, the ongoing provision of the SLW is leading to trade-offs with service quality. Providers deliberated contract withdrawal and service closures, with some respondents handing back services that were unviable. Furthermore, the financial sustainability of adult care services is coming under increasing pressure, due to a failure of funding to keep up with the rising costs providers face and the increasing complexity of service users' needs. Some contracting authorities did not award funding for on–costs and inflationary uplifts, and providers struggled to pay differentials, despite having made efficiencies. Providers respond by adopting more market-driven approaches to tendering, including refusal to enter unsustainable contracts, as contracting relationships become increasingly cost based and insecure (Cunningham and James, 2017). It is unlikely that this trend will end once pay increases are to be met from overall Health and Social Care Partnership budgets, raising uncertainty over whether the SLW is sufficiently embedded in practice to be resourced.

The above developments point to the diminishing influence of providers and contracting authorities on employment practices, with the state as a shadow employer (Wolch, 1990) influencing the employment conditions of voluntary and private sector organizations. Bach (2016) similarly notes how austerity measures have also encouraged tighter governmental control of funding and market management, thereby limiting managerial discretion over certain components of HRM. With the SLW, providers surrendered an element of their independence as employers to external bodies, sacrificing control over a substantial part of pay determination. Commissioning authorities too face a loss in control over pay, as the LWF sets these increases. As purchasers, however, local authorities continue to retain their asymmetric monopsonistic position in Scotland's social care market, which affords them considerable discretion over commissioning services (Cunningham and James, 2017). Without the statutory obligations to resource services at a particular level, local authorities introduce increases in resources to providers to pay for the SLW according to what they determine is a 'fair' price for an hour of care – a controversial issue for providers, concerning whether it meets the 'true' cost of care.

Questions also arise over whether an impact is being made on workers' total income. Net take-home pay is anticipated to decrease as sleepover shifts are phased out and employees lose out on universal benefits, echoing caution over whether living wages have a substantive impact on poverty among the working poor (Freeman, 2005; Prowse and Fells, 2016). Prior research on living wage ordinances suggests that, on average, these wage increases are lower than the median wage increase that low-wage earners would otherwise experience from unionization (Luce, 2014). Glaringly absent from the above findings is the role of the unions. Instead, unions feature as a diminished actor in determining pay and other conditions of work alongside the state, employers, service users and workers. Although they are a member of the Implementation Group that issues guidance about approaches to SLW implementation and associated legal issues, the unions emerged as a third wheel, with negotiation and consultation over low pay taken away from the workplace. Further constrained in that they negotiate over pay and conditions for their public sector members, unions must also reconcile their support of a socially just policy that simultaneously undermines employer–union efforts to increase pay at individual enterprise level. The marginalization of the unions confirms previous research on austerity policies in social care that suggests a reduced arena for workers' resistance in which market forces are supplanting internal regulation by collective bargaining (Cunningham et al, 2016; Cunningham and James, 2017).

Adding to ongoing debates on the unintended consequences of a living wage (Fairris and Reich, 2005), this chapter has demonstrated the unexpected outcomes of increasing provider insecurity and the prospect of market exit, despite its being a policy to relieve the social care sector from a dysfunctional market. Furthermore, it has confirmed previous adverse changes to employment conditions (Fairris, 2005; Grimshaw, 2013; Johnson, 2017), as seen in the evidence of squeezed differentials and reduced unsocial hours enhancements. These developments are expected to exacerbate already difficult recruitment and retention problems in the sector. Despite the absence of any large-scale restructuring of other terms and conditions, such as a reduction in training and hours worked, there was also little evidence to support that a living wage forces organizations onto 'high road' HR policies (Reich et al, 2005).

Rather, the Scottish case reveals the vast reach of the austerity agenda and how robustly its neoliberal roots weaken attempts to improve the working conditions of those who are most exposed to market forces. The irony remains that this already vulnerable, largely female workforce might end up financially worse off than before the SLW. Despite its being a policy challenge to austerity measures that aims to create a socially just context and ameliorate the effects of social and economic inequality, its implementation in outsourced social care paradoxically confirms the sheer embeddedness of austerity.

References

Arrowsmith, J., Gilman, M., Edwards, P. and Ram, M. (2003) 'The impact of the National Minimum Wage in small firms'. *British Journal of Industrial Relations*, 41(3): 435–56.

Bach, S. (2012) 'Shrinking the state or the Big Society? Public service employment relations in an era of austerity'. *Industrial Relations Journal*, 43(5): 399–415.

Bach, S. (2016) 'Deprivileging the public sector workforce: Austerity, fragmentation and service withdrawal in Britain'. *The Economics and Labour Relations Review*, 27(1): 11–28.

Bach, S. and Stroleny, A. (2014) 'Restructuring UK local government employment relations: Pay determination and employee participation in tough times'. *Transfer*, 20(3): 343–56.

Clarke, J. (2017) 'Articulating austerity and authoritarianism: Re-imagining moral economies?' In: B. Evans and S. McBride (eds) *Austerity: The Lived Experience*. Toronto: University of Toronto Press, 20–39.

Cunningham, I. and James, P. (2014) 'Public service outsourcing and its employment implications in an era of austerity: The case of British social care'. *Competition and Change*, 18(1): 1–15.

Cunningham, I. and James, P. (2017) 'Analysing public service outsourcing: The value of a regulatory perspective'. *Environment and Planning C: Government and Policy*, 35(6): 958–74.

Cunningham, I., Baines, D., Shields, J. and Lewchuk, W. (2016) 'Austerity policies, "precarity" and the nonprofit workforce: A comparative study of UK and Canada'. *Journal of Industrial Relations*, 58(4): 455–72.

Cunningham, I., Baluch, A., Cullen, A.M. and James, P. (2018) *Implementing the Scottish Living Wage in Adult Social Care*. Edinburgh: CCPS. www.ccpscotland.org/resources/implementing-scottish-living-wage-adult-social-care/.

Fair Work Convention (2019). *Fair Work in Scotland's Social Care Sector 2019*. Edinburgh: The Scottish Government. https://www.fairworkconvention.scot/wp-content/uploads/2018/11/Fair-Work-in-Scotland's-Social-Care-Sector-2019.pdf.

Fairris, D. (2005) 'The impact of living wages on employers: A control group analysis of the Los Angeles Ordinance'. *Industrial Relations: A Journal of Economy and Society*, 44(1): 84–105.

Fairris, D. and Reich, M. (2005) 'The impacts of living wage policies: Introduction to the Special Issue'. *Industrial Relations: A Journal of Economy and Society*, 44(1): 1–13.

Freeman, R. (2005) 'Fighting for other folks' wages: The logic and illogic of living wage campaigns'. *Industrial Relations: A Journal of Economy and Society*, 44(1): 14–31.

Giupponi, G. and Machin, S. (2018) *Changing the Structure of Minimum Wages: Firm Adjustment and Wage Spillovers*. IZA Institute of Labor Economics Discussion Paper No 11474, 1–79.

Grimshaw, D. (ed) (2013) *Minimum Wages, Pay Equity and Comparative Industrial Relations*. London: Routledge.

Heyes, J. and Gray, A. (2001) 'The impact of the National Minimum Wage on the textiles and clothing industry'. *Policy Studies*, 22(2): 83–98.

Howes, C. (2005) 'Living wages and retention of homecare workers in San Francisco'. *Industrial Relations: A Journal of Economy and Society*, 44(1): 139–63.

Johnson, M. (2017) 'Implementing the living wage in UK local government'. *Employee Relations*, 39(6): 840–9.

Luce, S. (2014) 'Living wages, minimum wages, and low-wage workers'. In: Luce, S., Luff, J., McCartin, J., and Milkman, R. (eds) *What Works for Workers? Public Policies and Innovative Strategies for Low-Wage Workers*. New York: Russell Sage Foundation, 215–43.

Machin, S., Manning, A. and Rahman, L. (2003) 'Where the minimum wage bites hard: Introduction of minimum wages to a low wage sector'. *Journal of the European Economic Association*, 1(1): 154–80.

McBride, S. and Muirhead, J. (2016) 'Challenging the low wage economy: Living and other wages'. *Alternate Routes: A Journal of Critical Social Research*, 27: 55–86.

Parker, J., Arrowsmith, J., Fells, R. and Prowse, P. (2016) 'The living wage: Concepts, contexts and future concerns'. *Labour & Industry: A Journal of the Social and Economic Relations of Work*, 26(1): 1–7.

Prowse, P. and Fells, R. (2016) 'The living wage: Policy and practice'. *Industrial Relations Journal*, 47(2): 144–62.

Prowse, P., Fells, R., Arrowsmith, J., Parker, J. and Lopes, A. (2017) Guest editorial. *Employee Relations*, 39(6): 778–84.

Reich, M., Hall, P. and Jacobs, K. (2005) 'Living wage policies at the San Francisco airport: Impacts on workers and businesses'. *Industrial Relations: A Journal of Economy and Society*, 44(1): 106–38.

Scottish Government (2015) *Statutory Guidance on the Selection of Tenderers and Award of Contracts. Addressing Fair Work Practices, including the Living Wage, in Procurement.* Edinburgh: The Scottish Government. https://www.gov.scot/binaries/content/documents/govscot/publications/advice-and-guidance/2015/10/statutory-guidance-selection-tenderers-award-contracts-addressing-fair-work-practices/documents/00486741-pdf/00486741-pdf/govscot%3Adocument/00486741.pdf

SSSC (2017) *Scottish Social Services Council Strategic Plan 2017–2020.* Dundee: SSSC.

Werner, A. and Lim, M. (2017) 'A new living wage contract: Cases in the implementation of the living wage by British SME retailers'. *Employee Relations*, 39(6): 850–62.

Wolch, J. (1990) *The Shadow State: Government and Voluntary Sector in Transition.* New York: Foundation Center.

13

Legislation: A Double-Edged Sword in Union Resistance to Zero-Hours Work – The Case of Ireland

*Juliette MacMahon, Lorraine Ryan, Michelle O'Sullivan,
Jonathan Lavelle, Caroline Murphy, Mike O'Brien,
Tom Turner and Patrick Gunnigle*

Introduction

In industrialized societies unions have traditionally played a key role in regulating the employment relationship and protecting against an unfettered commodification and exploitation of labour. Such exploitation was perceived to pose a threat to workers' fundamental rights to participate as citizens (Bosch, 2004; Standing, 2011). This was largely achieved through the mechanisms of collective bargaining and industrial action, and by lobbying for a floor of rights for workers in the forms of protective legislation.

However, the ability of unions to effectively represent workers (especially through collective bargaining) has been weakened considerably since the 1960s. There has been a combined shift towards globalism, austerity and neoliberalism, exemplified by a rise in liberal market economies (LMEs), of which 'freeing up' of labour markets is a core tenet (Fudge, 2005). LMEs typically adopt labour-market policies that are characterized by a decrease in political support for collective representation of workers and minimal regulation or deregulation of the employment relationship. In tandem with (and probably influenced by) the change to regulatory systems and a weakening of union power, there has been a shift away from the standard employment relationship (SER) (Broughton et al, 2016). The SER is essentially a conceptualization of a traditional model of permanent, full-time, continuous employment (Arnold and Bongiovi, 2013); however, while this model remains dominant in many countries and employment systems, it is widely accepted that the SER is being steadily eroded. What is emerging in its place is a wide range of alternative or non-standard forms of work (Bobeck et al, 2018) that are much more flexible and fragmented in temporal terms. Examples include zero-hours work, gig work and low-hours contracts. According to the European Commission (2017), upwards of 6 million people in the EU are working on an intermittent and on-demand basis. Research indicates that such work has been associated with higher levels of precarity (Kalleberg, 2009; Burgess et al, 2013).

In Ireland, as in other countries, the trade union movement has experienced a steady decline in density (particularly in the private sector) (CSO, 2019). In addition, the collapse of social partnership in Ireland has deprived unions of a position of considerable influence with respect to policy formulation on economic and social issues and veto over many proposals related to the labour market (Donaghey and Teague, 2007, p 39). In an era of weakened power and limited ability to engage in collective bargaining, unions are faced with a particular challenge: how to resist the proliferation of precarious-type contracts in the face of powerful, countervailing discourse that flexibility in the form of non-standard work arrangements is both necessary for economic competitiveness and welcomed by many workers (Rubery and Grimshaw, 2016). According to research (Mrozowicki et al, 2013), unions can choose a number of actions to counter precarious work: to be passive, to use collective bargaining, to engage in industrial action and/or to lobby for protective legislation. Irish unions in the main have favoured two approaches over militant action in tackling non-standard work: firstly, collective bargaining at localized level where they have a presence (for example, in the public sector and pockets of the private sector); and secondly, the pursuit of regulation. Irish unions have had some limited success in some sectors in achieving a curtailment of zero-hours contracts through collective bargaining (see Murphy et al, 2019 for a detailed analysis). However, the main strategy adopted during the period of austerity was to highlight the issue through public campaigning and to seek a legislative response.

In this chapter we examine the effectiveness of legislation pertaining to zero-hours work that was introduced in Ireland mainly as a result of campaigning on the part of trade unions. In our analysis we examine the interconnectedness of various economic/social factors and how this can result in a weakening of the intended outcome of legislation. We argue that, while unions had some success in forcing the enactment of legislation designed to protect zero-hours and low-hours workers, the impact of the legislation has been largely offset by the interaction of opposing actors to influence the construction of the legislation, the ability of employers to bypass its provisions and austerity measures introduced by the government.

The fragmentation of the SER and precarious work

Precarious work has been defined as 'employment that is uncertain, unpredictable and risky from the point of view of the worker' Kalleberg (2009, p 2) and is characterized by low income and limited social benefits and statutory entitlements (Vosko, 2010). Commentators warn that the cumulative effect of an increase in precarious-type work is the creation of a class of outsiders or 'the precariat' (Standing, 2011; Quinlan, 2012). Furthermore, it is argued that precarious work is becoming normalized across countries. Kalleberg (2012, p 428), for instance, argues that the rise in precarity and inequality is not a temporary feature of the business cycle but represents structural transformations, such that bad jobs are no longer vestigial but a central component of employment. Among such structural transformations is the rise of temporal fragmentation, a variant of which is zero-hours work.

Zero-hours work is a particular form of contingent work; and it is truly contingent in that an employer will not undertake to guarantee any hours to the worker but requests them to work 'as and when required' (MacMahon et al, 2017). Many on-call/zero-hours workers fall into the most extreme end of the 'peripheral' spectrum in that they are not accorded any legal employment status. In many jurisdictions, being 'an employee' is a fundamental condition of access to employment rights. Thus, on-call /zero-hours workers exemplify what Standing (2008) refers to as an emergent 'systemic insecurity' whereby much of the risk in the employment relationship is being transferred from employers and the state to individual workers, who must accept risks as part of personal responsibility (Lambert, 2008).

The highly contingent nature of zero-hours work in terms of scheduling and the number of hours required by the employer has a number of negative outcomes for workers. International evidence points clearly to a positive relationship between the rise of such work arrangements and precarity (Vosko, 2010; Kalleberg, 2012). The key consequence is unpredictability for the worker of both hours and, consequently, levels of income. Such unpredictability brings into play the myriad of issues whereby those engaged in zero-hours work have difficulty from temporal and cost aspects in participating in activities associated with citizenship (education, having a family, access to housing, pension planning and so on) (Turner, 2016). Zero-hours workers, as peripheral workers, are also excluded from important benefits of work such as training and development, paid holidays, sick-pay entitlements and family leave entitlements.

The Irish context

The financial crisis and ensuing austerity had a significant impact on the industrial relations landscape in Ireland. A casualty of the crisis was the competitive, corporatist, social partnership model, the emergence of an economy that was more LME-like in its orientation (Schneider and Paunescu, 2012) and a concomitant fall in union density and thus bargaining power. This dismantling of social partnership, aligned with a steady and consistent decline in trade union density to approximately 24 per cent (CSO, 2019), has negatively impacted on any trade union efforts to counteract a diminution in the quality of work, particularly in the private sector. Austerity measures included the reduction of employers' social insurance contributions for low-paid jobs and a shift away from a relatively generous and benign welfare system towards one that has conditionality and sanctions embedded, akin to work-first approaches to welfare in countries such as the US (Murphy, 2016). Another feature of the Irish labour market is enduring low pay for a significant proportion of workers (30 per cent), with women comprising 60 per cent of this cohort. While these workers are concentrated in the accommodation and food sectors, there are cohorts of low-paid workers across all sectors, including the public sector (Collins, 2015). While the SER remained prevalent in Ireland during the crisis there was evidence of a rise in fragmented and variable working time arrangements (O'Sullivan et al, 2015). There had been a steady increase in part-time work before the crisis, but the rate of increase of part-time work rose significantly during the period (CSO, 2019). The nature of part-time work during the financial crisis also changed in this time from more secure part-time employment contracts to two key variants. First was the rise of 'if and when' (no employment status) contracts, which are the same as zero-hours arrangements found in the UK. The second variant of work that emerged was 'low-hours contracts' These are contracts of employment which guarantee only a low number of hours (for instance, four hours a week) and any work given after that is on a totally variable basis and at the discretion of the employer.

Union influence on zero-hours legislation: the 1997 Act

In 1997 a national corporatist system of social partnership was in existence in Ireland and unions enjoyed a powerful and influential position at national policy level (Donaghey and Teague, 2007). During negotiations on a new national agreement, the Irish Congress of Trade Unions demanded that employment legislation be reviewed in light of the growth of atypical work. A section was introduced in the working time legislation to respond to unions' concerns. Thus, on the face of it, it did appear that Ireland was a proactive and early regulator of this form of atypical work, due in no small part to union action. However, as with many things, the devil was in the detail, and a scrutiny of the legislation is informative. Section 18 of the Organisation of Working Time Act 1997 stated that the variant of zero-hours contract that was covered by the legislation is one where there was an obligation on the employee to be available to an employer in a particular week. Should an employer not provide work, the employee was entitled to compensation amounting to 25 per cent of the time they were required to be available or 15 hours' pay, whichever was less. However, section 18 also stated that the protections were not available to those who worked on a more casual basis. This clause was inserted as a result of counter-lobbying by the employers' organizations, notable among them the Irish Hotels Federation (Houses of the Oireachtas, 1997). There was a fundamental problem with this latter condition. By including the words 'contract *of* employment' and excluding work of a 'casual nature', the Act de facto excluded those zero-hours workers who did not enjoy the status of employees engaged under a contract of employment. This provided a potential loophole for employers, who could engage workers on an 'if and when' basis. Essentially, employers would engage workers if and when work became available, but there was no contractual obligation on the worker to accept that work, and no obligation on the employer's side to provide work. There is a plethora of research in both the UK and Ireland that demonstrates that this lack of 'mutuality of obligation' can be fatal to the existence of a contract of employment (Freedland, 2006). Thus, the 1997 legislation, introduced on the back of union demands, was weakened in its construction by countervailing interests. In fact, a regulatory gap was created whereby zero-hours workers on 'if and when' contracts were left exposed. However, it was not until the industrial relations landscape changed during the recession that the implications of the legislative gap became apparent. As our findings demonstrate in the following section, the ability of employers to sidestep the legislation, and the interaction between the legislative gap and austerity measures, had the net effect of neutralizing any potential gains for workers achieved through the union action. Indeed, we would argue that the crafting of the legislation incentivized a move to more casualized employment forms, which, in tandem with austerity measures introduced by the government, had a downward effect on job quality for many workers.

Methodology

The chapter draws on the results of a study conducted by the authors in 2015. The primary method used was 34 qualitative interviews with informed stakeholders (13 employer/business representative organizations, 8 trade unions, 5 government departments/agencies, 4 non-governmental organizations (NGOs) and 4 legal experts). The interviews with NGOs were critical to capturing the voices of groups such as women, youth, migrants and the unemployed. To obtain policy makers' perspectives, the informed stakeholders included government departments with responsibility for the welfare system, public expenditure and education and training, as well as the largest state dispute resolution body and the state labour inspectorate service, responsible for enforcing employment laws. Lastly, interviews were undertaken with the national representative body for the legal profession, for their expertise on employment law on zero-hours work. In total 35 interviews were undertaken with 82 representatives from 31 bodies. Stakeholders with representative capacity/knowledge in the wider labour market were interviewed first and this informed the second round of interviews with sector-specific stakeholders. Secondary data from the Irish Parliament (Houses of the Oireachtas) was also utilized to provide an analysis of the existing legislation introduced in 1997 and the recently enacted Employment (Miscellaneous Provisions) Act 2018.

Findings

The interaction between the legislation and employer practices

First we examine the interaction between the 1997 legislation pertaining to zero-hours work and the action of employers. In our interviews with various legal experts it was routinely observed that it is easy for employers to construct contracts that explicitly state that there is an absence of mutuality on the part of both parties. Indeed, evidence from our study indicated that zero-hours contracts *of* employment that came within the ambit of the legislation were not common in Ireland. However, 'if and when' contracts, with no contractual obligation on either side, were found to be a more common variant of zero-hours work.

In general, such arrangements were found to come under the fall outside the scope of the legislation. A representative of the largest employer organization in Ireland, the Irish Business and Employers' Confederation, acknowledged that very few employers would offer a contract for zero-hours work of the type covered by the legislation. They pointed out that there was no advantage to an employer to do this and incur the risk of paying compensation for unworked hours. It was more economically advantageous for an employer to have a panel of people on 'if and when' contracts, who were not contractually required to be available, and the employer had no obligation to pay someone for unworked hours. Thus, a consequence of the legislation was that it incentivized employers to move away from employing people on one type of zero-hours work (zero-hours contracts of employment) to a more extreme type of zero-hours work ('if and when' contracts), which is more precarious in nature. A representative from the Department of Social Protection also observed:

'So, misclassification of employment is becoming a big issue. Outsourcing, contracting, bogus self-employment – that space is very important to us and it's very dangerous if there's any incidence of it increasing. We're finding that's the big area; zero hours is part of it but the bigger underlying trend that we're finding is contrived self-employment.'

We also found evidence of hybrid contracts whereby a worker would get a contract of employment but for a very low number of hours (for example, three hours). Their remaining access to work would be completely contingent on the needs of the employer on an 'if and when' basis and would also sit outside the provisions of the zero hours legislation.

Our study indicated that 'if and when' contracts are prevalent in certain sectors or certain occupations within sectors in Ireland. They are prevalent across accommodation/food, while hybrid contracts are prevalent among large retail chains. In the education sector, on-call contracts and hybrid contracts are prevalent among second-level school teachers and ancillary staff such as caretakers, secretaries and cleaners, third-level lecturers and adult education teachers. In the health sector, 'if and when' contracts are used on a limited basis in administration, catering and ancillary services, but more widely in intellectual disability and community home care services.

During austerity even the highly unionized public sector was not immune from the use of 'if and when' contracts. As a result of austerity measures, there were severe restrictions on the public sector pay bill up to 2016 (Grummell and Lynch, 2016). Stakeholders across healthcare and education acknowledged that during this time, and as a result of direct recruitment embargos, public sector organizations increased their use of 'if and when' contracts either directly or through agencies. The effect of the 1997 legislation was articulated by a representative of the state Health Services Executive (HSE), who said that the use of zero-hours contracts as provided for in section 18 of the 1997 Act was discouraged (due to compensatory implications) but 'if and when' contracts, whereby a worker did not come under the terms of the Act, were considered a legitimate employment arrangement. While unions had some success in countering this and negotiating restricted use of 'if and when' contracts for workers directly employed by the HSE, they had little or no influence regarding the employment conditions in (mainly non-union) private companies tendering for outsourced services, mainly in the area of domiciliary home care. The use of 'if and when' contracts in private domiciliary care companies was described as 'endemic' by one worker representative. The Migrant Rights Centre of Ireland (MRCI) reported that some migrant workers who are employed as home helps through such organizations often have no guaranteed hours and are given minimal hours: 'enough to keep them dangling but not enough to survive'.

Social insurance incentives

Second, we look at evidence of consequences arising from the interaction between three factors: the regulatory gap around 'if and when'/low-hours contracts, state policy on social insurance and employer practices. In Ireland, employers and employees pay social insurance on wages into a national social insurance fund. The state requires lower employers' contributions for lower-paid jobs. During the economic crisis the government halved employers' social insurance contributions for low-paying jobs, from 8.5 per cent to 4.25 per cent, for two years. The trade union SIPTU argued that this cut was a 'defining factor' motivating employers to hire more people on an 'if and when'/low-hours basis in the accommodation and food sectors. A number of worker representatives whom we interviewed said that this resulted in employers engaging in 'job splitting', that is, dividing one full-time job into two or more low-hours jobs. As such, this represented a direct dismantling of the SER for many workers. While this measure has since been rescinded, those employers engaging people on low pay continue to pay lower social insurance contributions. The current rate for employers is 8.7 per cent for employees earning up to €386 a week and 10.9 per cent for those earning more than €386. Thus, the incentive remains to job-split, and to employ people on a low-hours basis, with part of their contract on an 'if and when' basis.

Welfare provision

Finally, we examine the interaction between the regulatory gap and welfare provision during the austerity period. There are two dimensions here. First, the existing welfare provision for those on zero-hours/low-hours work arrangements, and second, a move towards conditionality in relation to social welfare payments in the Irish context as a result of austerity (Murphy, 2016). All stakeholders in the study noted the importance of welfare benefits existing at the time to people engaged in 'if and when' and low contracted hours work. In Ireland there are two main in-work income supports available. Family Income Supplement (FIS) is a weekly, tax-free payment to families in work on low pay. To qualify, an employee must be in a paid job that is expected to last at least three months, work at least 19 hours per week, have at least one child and earn below particular income thresholds. A second support is the Jobseeker's Scheme, under which a person may gain state assistance if they work three days in a seven-day period and are unemployed for the remaining four days. All of the respondents indicated that workers were generally afraid to go over the hours threshold in a given week, as there was a real risk to them in terms of losing a wide range of non-monetary benefits associated with the Jobseeker's Scheme (such as medical cards and fuel allowance). Given that extra hours were not guaranteed and could be cut, again at the discretion of the employer, taking on extra hours involved serious opportunity costs. A representative from the Department of Social Protection confirmed this:

> 'It is an issue in that if an employer insists on spreading the hours of work over more than three days in seven consecutive days, it's unlikely that the person would be willing to take up that extra hours work on the fourth day, especially if it was only for a small number of hours, because they're going to lose their entitlement.'

For those on FIS, working extra hours could take them over an income limit. Re-accessing these schemes was widely acknowledged to be difficult. Furthermore, for those on low incomes below €352 a week, working extra hours could draw them into having to pay 4 per cent of their income in social insurance contributions as opposed to 0 per cent. At the time of the 2015 study, for those on hybrid contracts employers were under no obligation to regularize into the contract of employment any extra hours regularly worked on an 'if and when' basis. Thus, accepting extra hours represented a risk for workers. In advocating for stronger legislation that would oblige employers to recognize extra hours regularly worked, one union representative described the situation as one that ensnared workers into a 'perverse kind of poverty trap':

> 'You can get to a situation where you don't want extra hours because it will impact on welfare payments. You know there is not a decent job on offer so you are reliant on welfare. It's a perverse type of poverty trap. It's all interactional with welfare/ entitlements and poverty traps.'

In relation to conditionality, Murphy (2016) found that Ireland had moved from a system where there was a reluctance to apply benefit sanctions to job seekers to one where conditionality had become the norm. In interviews, the Department of Social Protection noted that people on unemployment benefit would normally lose their benefits if they refused job offers 'without just cause'. Trade unions and NGOs believed that people felt increasingly pressured by the social welfare system to accept insecure work with non-guaranteed or low hours. The National Youth Council of Ireland argued that there had been a shift towards increased sanctions and conditions attached to unemployment benefit since the economic crisis and that young people felt impelled to accept low-quality jobs or risk losing welfare entitlements.

The net outcome of weak legislation for workers

Representatives from trade unions and the four NGOs interviewed were highly critical of 'if and when' contracts, considering them to be precarious jobs that transfer the risk of business onto employees:

> 'Minimum commitment from employer demanding maximum flexibility from the employee. You can see that this is a one-way system with the advantage to the employer.'

It was also asserted that the regulatory gap, combined with a lack of representation for employees and the austerity measures outlined earlier, pushed the frontier of control of the labour process very firmly back in favour of management and that employers made use of that control. Examples cited included cutting hours, changing the pattern of hours so that access to supplementary welfare entitlements was affected and not giving references to people leaving:

'It's an unfair employment relationship – you make yourself totally available and they offer the bare minimum and that then translates into an unequal power relationship and the possibility of abuses of power. Hours can be used as a disciplinary mechanism.'

'There is churn in the jobs which suits employers as people do not rise up the pay scales. Even if they do last and they are on the highest rate of pay – then their hours will be cut to the minimum guaranteed hours and their hours will be shifted to new entrants on min wage. We have complaints from members on the top pay scale that they are being managed out. Their hours are being cut to the minimum.'

If workers challenged employers, raised a grievance or refused work in a given week, the variable or hybrid nature of their contracts meant that employers could schedule hours in a highly variable pattern that might render the worker in question ineligible for social welfare income supports. In the retail sector one union official observed:

'It's predominantly females in these sectors who are constrained by childcare. They have no choice but to accept hours and low pay and keep the head down [stay silent] for fear their hours will be changed.'

The idea that workers could exercise choice and refuse work when it suited them was also widely challenged, with people being 'penalized for not being available for work', according to the Irish National Organisation of Unemployed (INOU).

Why, then, do workers accept such work? Employer groups argued that on-call contracts suited many people, such as women with caring responsibilities, students and older people, and represented a stepping-stone for people to more secure and higher-paid employment:

'Advantages for workers are the availability of some form of work, may suit a particular lifestyle, may provide an opening into a particular sector. Low-hours contracts can provide stability. They are not necessarily low paid. They can be very positive. It's a foot in the door – so I don't have a gap in my CV.'

Unsurprisingly, trade unions and NGOs had a conflicting perspective. In their view, the majority of individuals accept these so-called 'if and when' and hybrid contracts because of a lack of alternatives. Across the board, workers' representatives challenged the assertion that zero-hours work was a stepping-stone to more secure work, arguing instead that zero-hours hours and low-hours work was trapping people into long-term 'dead end' jobs in which they received little or no career-enhancing training from employers and could not commit to education, due to the unpredictability of hours and an inability to afford it. The INOU had this view:

'It's not a stepping-stone if you don't get the hours you need. It's not a stepping-stone if you don't feel free to take the time to look for other work. In fact, they can become cul-de-sacs.'

Across all sectors the financial uncertainty for on-call workers was highlighted. Issues identified included access to bank loans/mortgages, as this is normally conditional on having a contract of employment. Lack of predictability was also highlighted as a barrier to childcare arrangements for on-call workers, as most childcare providers will accept only full-day payments and require notice. A representative from the MRCI identified childcare as a particular issue for migrants and disputed the idea that zero-hours work suited people with childcare obligations. Other issues identified by workers' groups were inability to commit to family occasions and pension poverty:

'You need security and structure to manage childcare. So, to say unpredictable zero hours suits people with families is wrong. People need a steady income to build a life for progression. It's impossible for them to build a career. There is no provision for flexible childcare here. Migrants do not have family networks here to pick up the slack.'

Union campaign for legislative revision

The research detailed in the previous sections was conducted in 2015. Following the publication of the zero-hours study, there was a concerted campaign by trade unions, NGOs and opposition political parties to bring about a change in existing legislation regulating zero-hours work. This resulted in a very public debate conducted across national media and other fora. Unions questioned the existing situation with respect to the sustainability of the Irish economy and wider social issues in the medium to long term. In a strategically astute move the ICTU launched their Charter for Fair Work in the run-up to the 2016 general election. This charter advocated that workers have a right to security of hours and income and called for an end to low-hours and zero-hours contracts and precarious work practice.

Largely as a result of union campaigning, the Employment (Miscellaneous Provisions) Act 2018 was enacted in March 2019. The Act increases the compensation that formerly existed under the 1997 Act where a zero-hours employee is required to be available for work but is not provided with work. This is now calculated at three times the national minimum wage rate. However, the 2018 Act contains the exact same clause as the previous 1997 legislation, excluding from the provisions of the Act work that is deemed to be 'casual'. This means that employers can continue to avoid the terms of the legislation by simply inserting non-mutuality-of-obligation clauses into contracts, or clauses explicitly deeming the work as casual. Thus, the situation for zero-hours workers who fell outside the scope of the provisions of section 18 of the Organisation of Working Time Act 1997 does not look set to improve under the 2018 Act. On the contrary, we argue, the legislation may merely embed the current exclusion of these workers from access to protective legislation and will further contribute to the erosion of the SER in Ireland.

On a more positive note, the Act does introduce new 'banded hours' provision. Employees on low-hours contracts who regularly work a greater number of hours than those named in their contract will be entitled to have their contract changed to reflect the reality of their situation. This should provide a route into more stable employment for low-hours employees who have contracts of employment. The banded hours provision is largely based on a model that was negotiated through collective bargaining in specific unionized large retailers in Ireland (notably Primark and Tesco). Here we must exercise a note of caution, however, as the law has not been tested with respect to the banded hours provision to date.

Discussion and conclusion

In Ireland the unions have played an instrumental role in effectively forcing the Irish government's hand to introduce legislation relating to zero-hours work, first as a condition of continuing social partnership in 1997 and subsequently as part of a concerted public campaign in 2016, approaching a general election. However, in assessing legislation it is important to examine the effects of that legislation, both in its interpretation by the courts in relation to protecting those whom it professes to protect and in its relationship to the wider industrial relations and economic context in which it is embedded. Our study adopted a multifaceted framework of analysis. In so doing it found that when the legislation was truly needed by workers (post the onset of the 2009 recession as employers began to utilize zero-hours work arrangements to a greater extent) the legislation was found wanting in its construction and thus weak in protecting zero-hours workers and low-hours workers. We found evidence of employers utilizing a clause relating to casual work in the legislation to avoid coming within its ambit. Indeed, we would argue that the net effect of the legislation introduced in 1997 was to contribute to a greater proliferation of more casual, on-call work arrangements by employers who did not wish to be constrained by the compensatory provisions of the legislation. Employers took actions to hire workers on an 'if and when' basis, but without a contractual obligation to be available for work. They also utilized hybrid contracts – essentially a mix of low number of guaranteed hours and variable hours given at the discretion of the employer. Evidence indicated that such contracts have become embedded in certain sectors such as hospitality, care work and the retail sector, at the expense of traditional SERs. On a broader basis, we examined the effects of the interaction of the weak legislative provision with measures introduced during the austerity period. The effect of these interactions was to effectively trap workers into low-paid, insecure jobs and extend the reach of managerial control.

While the unions were successful in their campaign to have legislation enacted in 2018 which revised existing legislation on zero-hours work, the centre-right government trenchantly refused to change the casual clause (Houses of the Oireachtas debates, 2018). As a result, zero-hours workers employed on 'if and when' contracts remain vulnerable. More effective may be the section of the 2018 Act relating to 'banded hours', which may provide more stable working conditions for employees on low-hours contracts of employment and which may incentivize such workers to move away from dependence on social welfare supplementary benefits. However, a bleaker alternative prospect would be that this legislation as a whole may incentivize employers to move away from low-hours contracts, which now have conditions attached, and move to a greater use of more precarious 'if and when' contracts. As Fredman and Fudge (2016) assert, 'the regulated (here employers) will seek the less regulated format, just as water will find its way around barriers to run downhill' (Fredman and Fudge, 2016, p 248). This highlights a conundrum for unions in relying on piecemeal changes to statutory legislation to resolve high-stakes issues such as low-cost labour. While a recognized advantage of legislation in a time of weak representation is that it covers all workers regardless of union presence, a key limitation from the union perspective is that once legislation is enacted it can lock unions in, and the process to change it can be costly and onerous. Thus, unforeseen and unintended consequences can emerge that act against their interest. This has been seen to be the case on the zero-hours issue in Ireland, where employers and their representatives have a strong interest in counter-lobbying and sidestepping the legislation. Ideally, we have previously argued (Murphy et al, 2019), collective bargaining presents a more effective way to curtail precarious-type work, and this has been demonstrated in the few agreements that unions have achieved in some parts of some sectors in Ireland. Collective agreements allow unions the flexibility to adapt to new circumstances and to renegotiate agreements as the need arises. However, in the current industrial relations landscape this option is not realistic, especially in the private sector where unions have a very limited presence/voice. Thus, the current strategy of the Irish unions is probably the best that can be hoped for in the current economic and political climate.

However, a third option (also legislative) is suggested here. That is that unions may need to adopt a higher-level strategy than seeking to achieve statutory legislation that operates within the current accepted legal definition of a contract of employment and instead challenge the fitness for purpose of the actual concept of a contract of employment. In this they would join their voices to a number of eminent legal scholars (Freedland, 2006; Collins, 2018) who challenge a 'concept of employment that was useful in the middle of the 20th century [but] is now outdated and hard to apply to the various kinds of networks and precarious arrangements through which work is performed' (Collins, 2018). These scholars have asserted that creating statutory legislation within the current legal concept of employment is no longer useful. They argue that what is needed to combat the rise of fragmented and casualized work is a fundamental reconceptualizing of the legal taxonomy of the employment relationship (Davidov, 2011). For instance, commentators such as Freedland (2006) have argued that protective legislation should not be contingent on the existence of a contract of employment but should be expanded to include all workers who contract for the personal execution of work. Other legal scholars have argued that, for workers deemed casual, courts should not rely on the test for mutuality but, rather, should base decisions on a reasonable expectation by the worker that the work will continue, due to a record of regular and continuous work with the employer (Keane, 2014). However, authors in this field acknowledge that recent jurisprudence indicates that there is little appetite, as of yet, to deviate into such uncharted territory in the legislative sphere (Freedland and Prassl, 2017). Nonetheless, it may be a long-term strategy for unions to consider in the absence of a likely return to a strong collective bargaining base.

References

Arnold, D. and Bongiovi, J.R. (2013) 'Precarious informalizing and flexible work: transforming concepts and understandings'. *American Behavioural Scientist*, 57(3): 289–308.

Bobeck, A., Pembroke, S. and Wickham, J. (2018) *Living with Uncertainty: The Social Implications of Precarious Work*. Dublin: TASC.

Bosch, G. (2004) 'The standard employment relationship in the information society'. *Concepts and Transformation*, 9(3), pp 231–48.

Broughton, A., Green, M., Rickard, C. et al (2016) *Precarious Employment in Europe: Patterns, Trends and Policy Strategies*. Brussels: European Parliament.

Burgess, J., Connell, J. and Winterton, J. (2013) 'Vulnerable workers, precarious work and the role of trade unions and HRM'. *The International Journal of Human Resource Management*, 24(22): 4083–93.

CSO (Central Statistics Office) (2019) *Employees Aged 15 Years and Over Classified by Sex and Whether They Are Members of a Trade Union*. https://www.cso.ie/en/statistics/labourmarket/labourforcesurveytimeseries/.

Collins, H. (2018) 'A missed opportunity of a unified test for employment status'. *UK Labour Law Blog*, 31 July. https://wordpress.com/view/uklabourlawblog.com.

Collins, M.L. (2015) *Earnings and Low Pay in the Republic of Ireland: A Profile and Some Policy Issues*. Dublin: NERI (Nevin Economic Research Institute).

Davidov, G. (2011) 'Re-matching labour laws with their purpose'. In: Davidov, G. and Langreille, B. (eds), *The Idea of Labour Law*. Oxford: Oxford University Press, 179–189.

Donaghey, J. and Teague, P. (2007) 'The mixed fortunes of Irish unions: Living with the paradoxes of social partnership'. *Journal of Labor Research*, 28(1): 19–41.

European Commission (2017) *Proposal of the Commission and the Council for a Directive on Transparent and Predictable Working Conditions*. Brussels: European Commission.

Fredman, S. and Fudge, J. (2016) 'The contract of employment and gendered work'. In: Freedland, M. (ed), *The Contract of Employment*. Oxford: Oxford University Press, 231–52.

Freedland, M. (2006) 'From the contract of employment to the personal work nexus'. *Industrial Law Journal*, 35: 1–29.

Freedland, M. and Prassl, J. (2017) *Employees, Workers and the Sharing Economy: Changing Practices and Changing Concepts in the United Kingdom*. Oxford Legal Research Paper Series, 19/2017.

Fudge, J. (2005) 'After industrial citizenship: Market citizenship or citizenship at work?' *Relations industrielles*, 60(4): 631–56. doi:10.7202/012338ar.

Grummell, B. and Lynch, K. (2016) 'New managerialism: A political project in Irish education'. In: *The Irish Welfare State in the Twenty-First Century*. London: Palgrave Macmillan, 215–35.

Houses of the Oireachtas debates:

Houses of the Oireachtas (1997) *Select Committee on Enterprise and Small Business Debate. Section 18*, 26 February. Dublin: Houses of the Oireachtas.

  Organisation of Working Time Act 1997, (Act 20 of 1997) Organisation of Working Time Bill 1996 (Bill 52 of 1996) Debates. www.oireachtas.ie/en/bills/bill/1996/52/?tab=debates.

  Seanad Eireann, 4 December 2018, debate on the Employment Provisions Miscellaneous Bill 2017. https://www.oireachtas.ie/en/debates/debate/seanad/2018-12-04/12/.

  Various sections of other debates on The Employment Provisions Miscellaneous Bill 2017. https://www.oireachtas.ie/en/bills/bill/2017/147/?tab=debates.

Kalleberg, A.L. (2009) 'Precarious work, insecure workers: Employment relations in transition'. *American Sociological Review*, 74(1): 1–22.

Kalleberg, A.L. (2012) 'Job quality and precarious work: Clarifications, controversies, and challenges'. *Work and Occupations*, 39: 427–48.

Keane, E. (2014) 'Providing access to job security legislation for intermittent workers', *Kings Law Journal*, (25): 332–9.

Lambert, S. (2008) 'Passing the buck: Labour flexibility practices that transfer risk onto hourly workers'. *Human Relations*, 61(9): 1203–27.

MacMahon, J., O'Sullivan, M., Turner, T., Ryan, L., Lavelle, J., Murphy, C., O'Brien, M. and Gunnigle, G. (2017) 'Zero hours work and the role of the law in Ireland'. In: Ahlberg, K. and Bruun, N. (eds), The New Foundations of Labour Law. Frankfurt: Peter Lang Publishing, 148–63.

Mrozowicki, A., Roosalu, T. and Senčar, T.B. (2013) 'Precarious work in the retail sector in Estonia, Poland and Slovenia: Trade union responses in a time of economic crisis'. *Transfer: European Review of Labour and Research*, 19(2): 267–78.

Murphy, C., Turner, T., O'Sullivan, M., MacMahon, J., Lavelle, J., Ryan, L., Gunnigle, P. and O'Brien, M. (2019) 'Trade union responses to zero hours work in Ireland'. *Industrial Relations Journal*, 50(5–6): 468–85.

Murphy, M.P. (2016) 'Low road or high road? The post-crisis trajectory of Irish activation'. *Critical Social Policy*, 36(3): 432–52.

O'Sullivan, M., Turner, T., MacMahon, J., Ryan, L., Lavelle J., Murphy, C., O'Brien, M. and Gunnigle, P. (2015) *A Study of the Prevalence of Zero Hours Contracts among Irish Employers and Its Impact on Employees*. Dublin: Department of Jobs, Enterprise and Innovation.

Quinlan, M. (2012) 'The "pre-invention" of precarious employment: The changing world of work in context'. *The Economic and Labour Relations Review*, 23(4): 3–24.

Rubery, J. and Grimshaw, D. (2016) 'Precarious work and the commodification of the employment relationship: the case of zero hours in the UK and mini jobs in Germany'. *Den Arbeitsmarkt verstehen, um ihn zu gestalten*. Wiesbaden: Springer VS, 239–54.

Schneider, M.R. and Paunescu, M. (2012) 'Changing varieties of capitalism and revealed comparative advantages from 1990 to 2005: A test of the Hall and Soskice claims'. *Socio-Economic Review*, 10(4): 731–53.

Standing, G. (2008) 'Economic insecurity and global casualization: Threat or promise'. *Social Indicators Research*, 88(1): 15–30.

Standing, G. (2011) *The Precariat: The New Dangerous Class*. London and New York: Bloomsbury Academic.

Turner, B.S. (2016) 'We are all denizens now: On the erosion of citizenship'. *Citizenship Studies*, 20(6–7): 679–92.

Vosko, L. (2010) *Managing the Margins: Gender, Citizenship, and the International Regulation of Precarious Employment*. Oxford: Oxford University Press.

14

Moral Projects and Compromise Resistance: Resisting Uncaring in Non-Profit Care Work

Donna Baines

Debates about workplace resistance and dissent are a central aspect of Labour Process Theory (Burawoy, 1979; Thompson, 1997; Thompson and Smith, 2017). This chapter focuses on care work in the non-profit social services (NPSS), and argues that resistance in this sector is a series of compromises and moral projects.[1] With the objective of extending Labour Process Theory and commenting on resistance in the context of austerity, this chapter draws on qualitative data and on Ackroyd and Thompson's (1999; 2013) three-part analytic frame (described in more detail later) exploring the dynamics of resistance and dissent in care work.

The NPSS is funded largely by government and grew dramatically under welfare state contracting out (Cunningham, 2008; Eikenberry, 2009). It provides support and care services to a range of populations such as the elderly, young, people with disabilities and people with mental health issues. Agencies come in a variety of sizes, from very small (one or two employees) to very large (1,000+ workers), and some operate as regional or national non-profit chains.

Mirroring the contradictory relations of the austerity-linked, contracted-out state that funds most non-profit care in Canada, workplace resistance and dissent in the NPSS is an unstable equilibrium that can legitimize austerity, act as a catalyst to undermine it, or both. NPSS staff members often have altruistic/social justice identities outside of the workplace, and they seek these values in the organization's mission, work content and workplace relationships. Workers' personal values often form the bedrock on which oppositional identities and practices are built, enhanced, frustrated and circumscribed, or a combination of all these factors simultaneously (Van Til, 2009; Nickel and Eikenberry, 2016). Most workers assume that altruistic values and identities will be held in common by fellow employees and managers, and seek ways to bond with others in the workplace around this presumed shared identity. In addition, they often educate and mobilize each other around ongoing political and social understandings of social justice and care (Aronson and Smith, 2010; 2011). This shared, oppositional analysis can extend beyond the workplace to analyses of the larger society and the ways that unjust relations are seen to be active in the workplace. Many of these unjust relations are argued to operate through the long arm of state funding, the austere conditions that state funding contracts force onto agencies and the social relations of inequity and injustice that many workers believe undergird larger society (Baines et al, 2014).

Within the workplace, the altruistic/social justice individual and shared identity(ies) can be harnessed to extract significant amounts of paid and unpaid labour from workers (Nickson et al, 2008; Van Til, 2009). Simultaneously, however, they can be turned against the employer if the employer is seen as not contributing sufficiently to social justice. In that case, the altruistic/social justice individual and shared identity(ies) become forms of resistance. Agencies' missions and workers' commitment to client populations are argued to buffer the negative impacts of New Public Management (NPM)[2] and other forms of managerialism, providing legitimacy for workers' expression of personal and professional values on the job and reinforcing their sense of themselves as linked to larger moral or social justice projects (Eikenberry, 2009; Salamon, 2010).

Labour Process theorists Ackroyd and Thompson (1999; 2013; see also Ackroyd, 2012) assert that although much of the literature focuses extensively on formal external forms of self-organization and resistance (such as unionization, legislation and industrial relations procedures), two additional forms of autonomous worker activity also build and reinforce collective identities. They are internal informal (forms of self-expression and expressions of identity) and external informal (recalcitrance and work limitation, pilferage and group ritualistic and ceremonial actions). These overlap significantly in unionized workplaces and are often drawn upon in external formal activities. All of these actions are forms of intentional worker self-organization, that is, they operate autonomously, outside of management control, often challenging the raw edges, if not the main content, of that control. In NPSS workplaces, these three forms of worker activity overlap to produce individuals and groupings of workers who are prepared to resist not only management, but also external funding bodies, governments and the larger 'uncaring' society. As such, these resistance activities also challenge the frontiers and boundaries of workplaces, demonstrating workers' sense of how the larger world of socioeconomic policy interacts with and shapes the workplace.

A significant body of literature confirms that resistance strategies are widespread in the NPSS and often include unionization and unpaid care work. While unionization as a form of resistance is well accepted in the literature (Charlesworth, 2010; Baines et al, 2012; Daly and Armstrong, 2016), claims that unpaid work is also a form of meaningful resistance have been disputed and recast as self-exploitation that benefits management and legitimizes constraint measures such as those associated with austerity. Arguing that workers make intentional trade-offs between self-exploitation (unpaid work) and care of others, which take the form of 'compromise resistance', this chapter attempts to extend Labour Process Theory in the area of resistance and dissent in care work. It draws on data from earlier studies of care work in the non-profit care sector and, using the dimensions of external formal, internal informal and external informal forms of dissent/resistant behaviour, explores the following two questions. Do workers' dissent and resistance strategies promote their interests, or management's, or both? Do these strategies act as a catalyst for change inside and/or outside the workplace, or do they legitimize constraint, or both?

The exploration begins with a discussion of the contexts, followed by a theory section about Labour Process Theory. The largest section of the chapter interweaves Ackroyd and Thompson's three-part analytic frame with five themes pulled from the qualitative data that form the 'evidence' for this chapter. These five themes are moral projects; unpaid work and gifts; using work time and resources for non-work activities; work limitation; and social unionism.

Contexts

The NPSS is a unique sector, putatively operating outside the profit motive and the public sector, pivoting on an ethos of civil society, altruism and social justice (Cunningham, 2008; Nickson et al, 2008; Baines and Daly, 2015). During the era of the contracted-out government, the NPSS grew rapidly as welfare states were downsized and shifted public service provision to non-profit and for-profit providers (Nickel and Eikenberry,

2016; Salamon, 2010). Seeking value for money, increasingly austere government contracts demanded strict adherence to outcome measures and required the use of metrics associated with competitive performance management models, such as NPM. Labour Process Theory tends to view NPM as a set of processes and logics that standardize work practices in an effort to elicit best practices and eliminate waste and inefficiency (Cunningham, 2008; Armstrong et al, 2016; Daly and Armstrong, 2016). Standardization and NPM have not been well received by the NPSS workforce, and are often equally disliked by more progressive management (Van Til, 2009; Nickel and Eikenberry, 2016). In large part, this is because of NPM's tendency to reduce or eliminate practices of, and opportunities for, the difficult-to-quantify, open-ended, unscripted, social justice-engaged ways of working. Instead, tightly scripted and quantified care is promoted, with work documented regularly to confirm that it is completed in a timely and efficient manner (Aronson and Smith, 2011; Baines et al, 2014). Practices associated with social justice are thus reduced or removed altogether with considerable autonomy and discretion.

The NPSS is a highly gendered sector in which women comprise the majority of low-paid workers, struggling service users and unpaid volunteers. Management, workers and the larger society tend to expect that the predominantly female staff members will work well beyond their paid hours in ways that are not dissimilar to expectations of boundless female care work in the home and community (Themudo, 2009; Charlesworth, 2010). These naturalized associations of women and care work make it difficult to improve wages or conditions, and often mean that resistance includes some aspect of care for others. Aptheker (1989) argues that, for many women, resistance is shaped by the social conditions of their lives and the discourses and spaces available to them. Resistance in highly gendered contexts, such as the NPSS, often looks different and contains different aspects than resistance in other, less gendered contexts. For example, resistance often reflects the values base of those continuing to work in the sector and targets an uncaring society and government in addition to employers. Analysis and research need to be highly attuned to the finer points of these differences.

Theory

This chapter draws on Labour Process Theory, in particular Labour Process Theory concerning resistance and dissent in care work. Labour Process Theory finds its roots in the work of Braverman (1974) and the subsequent debates concerning autonomy, agency, skill, management control and the dialectics of control and resistance (Burawoy, 1979; Pollert, 1981; Edwards and Scullion, 1982; Knights and Willmott, 1989). Resistance is generally seen as the pursuit of greater autonomy in response to management's attempts to exert control in the workplace. Both formal and informal resistance involve group or individual self-organization, also referred to as the autonomous organization of workers, outside of management control and approval (Burawoy, 1979; Edwards, 1986).

Formal resistance includes unionization; activities that are within industrial relations procedures, such as unionization or other forms of worker representation; and formal political and legal processes. Informal resistance is sometimes seen as less important and is often called misbehaviour (Ackroyd, 2012; Ackroyd and Thompson, 2013) in the management literature, where these activities are generally viewed as individual deviance or character flaws. However, Ackroyd and Thompson (1999; 2013) assert the social character and importance of informal resistance. They view it as 'an impulse to take control rather than always be the subject of control', and a way to expand individual and group autonomy (Ackroyd and Thompson, 2013, p 23). For the purposes of this chapter, misbehaviour, dissent and resistance will be viewed as a package of overlapping but separable activities aimed at claiming and reclaiming workers' identities and control within the workplace. Not all of these strategies actually attain greater control – they are often partial or non-successes – but they remain activities at least nominally outside of explicit management control. This chapter uses the following two terms: 'dissent', or the spread and invocation of oppositional discourses; 'resistance', or the formal and informal practices that challenge management's control and attempt to regain autonomy in the workplace.

In terms of informal self-organization and resistance, as Ackroyd (2012) comments, even if they are not active participants, most members of an organization tend to be aware of misbehaviour and act either in complicity or in collusion. Management may tolerate various forms of informal resistance/misbehaviour in the hopes that it will go away, or that management tolerance will elicit flexibility and tolerance from workers. However, the disciplining of individual workers, in the hopes that making an example of one person will deter others, confirms that management is keenly aware of misbehaviour's social nature (Ackroyd and Thompson, 2013).

Ackroyd and Thompson (2013) argue further that dissent, or various ways that workers fail to approve official views and propose alternatives, is a new area for significant misbehaviour, particularly in the highly controlled contemporary, professional and quasi-professional workplace. In this battle of ideas, and battle for loyalty in the workplace, speech acts hold considerable power, as demonstrated by libel, slander and hate-speech laws in the larger society. Dissent activities often shift workers' view of management, recasting management as greedy, petty and/or ineffectual, making it more difficult for management to exert control and discipline.

The use of emotions in the service transaction has been analysed extensively in Labour Process Theory (Guy et al, 2008; Bolton, 2009; Brook, 2009; Baines, 2011; Hochschild, 2012). Traditionally, emotional labour has been seen as a way to speed up the service encounter by requiring that workers use emotions and emotional content to control the service user or customer (Hochschild, 2012). In the highly gendered arena of care work (such as social services, nursing, childcare and eldercare), emotional labour is simultaneously a form of management control and the main source of meaning and satisfaction for workers. Workers often guard emotional content and labour against management control and encroachment, insisting, as does Sharon Bolton (2009), that emotional labour is an open-ended, philanthropic gift that cannot be quantified and rationalized.[3] Bolton (2009) and others (Maconachie, 2005; Guy et al, 2008) argue that, as an area of contestation between management and workers, emotional labour needs to be understood as an integral part of the labour process. Baines (2011) has taken this analysis a step further, arguing that forms of formal resistance (for example, social unionism) and informal resistance (for example, bending rules for service users, coaching service users in how to advocate for themselves against the agency, undertaking unpaid work, subsidizing the workplace with goods from home, joining committees and coalitions to fight cutbacks at the agency and in the sector) constitute a particular form of resistance unique to care work. Adding to Bolton's conceptualization of some forms of care as given freely or philanthropically with no expectation of reciprocity, Baines (2011) uses the term 'gift-solidarity' to argue that care workers' resistance strategies are a form of emotional labour, sustaining meaning and identities for workers, and sustaining collective, social bonds between and among service users, workers and communities.

Workers cannot always accomplish these forms of emotion work/resistance within paid hours and so they regularly extend their working days in various ways, subsidizing the agency with their unpaid labour while simultaneously building dissent and oppositional activities within the workplace. Employers depend on unpaid care work to extend the services they provide in austere conditions, even though the meanings and degree of resistance ascribed to these actions may differ between managers and various groups of workers. The line between self-exploitation and self-empowerment in this unpaid care/resistance nexus is thin, contradictory and unstable, as well as under-researched. This chapter now turns to these dynamics.

The studies

The chapter draws on two sets of data collected as part of larger, international studies of the shifting relations of care work. One study used international, qualitative case studies (interviews at all levels of the agencies, participant observations and review of publicly available documents) to compare NPSS agencies in four liberal welfare states (Esping-Andersen, 2000; Scruggs and Allan, 2008), namely Canada, Australia, New Zealand and Scotland. All NPSS agencies studied were similar, large-sized, multi-service, multi-site agencies providing a range of social services, including housing, addictions services, food, budgeting and income support, child and family services, elder supports, policy analysis and referrals. They received the majority of their funding through government contracts. The second data set is drawn from a subset of a large international, qualitative study (interviews at all levels of the agency, participant observations, review of documents) exploring promising practices in non-profit long-term residential care in six countries in the global North, namely Canada, the US, the UK, Germany, Sweden and Norway. The data from the long-term care study used in this article is only from Canada and the US. All care homes were non-profit, medium sized (more than 100 and fewer than 200 employees) and located in large urban centres.

In all case studies, interviews and observation sites were selected through criterion sampling and snowball sampling (DeWalt, 2007; Glesne, 2011). In-depth, audio-recorded, verbatim-transcribed, semi-structured interviews took place with a broad cross-section of players in agencies, including managers, front-line staff, union representatives and executives. Research themes that shaped data collection included changes that staff had experienced in the last few years; reasons for working and staying in the social services; changes that staff would like to see; advice staff that would give to others; and their experience of working in this environment. Participant observations were naturalistic and involved a mix of interaction and informal discussions with agency workers, service users and others present at the project. Data was analysed through a constant comparison method until themes were identified and patterns discerned (DeWalt, 2007).

Non-profit care work and resistance

Five main themes are discussed in this section: moral projects; unpaid work and gifts; using work time and resources for non-work activities;

work limitation; and social unionism. It is assumed that gender and the gendered expectation of elastic and boundless care operate in the background of these themes as principle aspects of the forms and strategies of resistance, along with a naturalized expectation of the overwhelmingly female workforce. Exemplar quotes are presented, although considerably more data exist to confirm the findings. The concepts of external formal, internal informal and external informal resistance are woven through the analysis of the five themes.

Moral projects and resistance strategies

As noted earlier, the predominantly female workforce tends to seek jobs and remain in the NPSS sector because of the opportunity to express social justice/altruistic values on the job; in essence, to be part of a moral project, using skills on behalf of and/or in solidarity with those in need. Echoing the words of many research participants, a senior social service worker noted that "I came to (the agency) because of its reputation for social justice". Social justice/altruistic values are usually assumed to be shared, to some degree, with others in the workplace, including management. This can take the form of commitment to the mission of the agency.

Missions tend to be worded in terms of fairly lofty long-term goals such as equality, fairness, social justice and participation, and this appeals to those across a wide spectrum of political and social commitments. Missions can be used as a rallying point when workers and managers feel that social justice content is slipping. One senior social services manager referred to the agency's drift away from broader community involvement by commenting that "We need to get back to what our mission really means for us and the whole community". Missions and the values they reflect can also be used to buffer challenging circumstances. For example, one worker commented on low wages and a lack of benefits by saying that "If you haven't got meaning in these jobs, what else have you got?". In addition, agency missions provided NPSS workers and managers with an official, if not actualized, mandate for collective social justice strategies on behalf of service users and communities. When managers failed to live up to this mandate, some workers used it as evidence of management's low skill, duplicity and/or incapacity to live up to the agency's moral project.

Discussions about how social justice/altruism operate or should operate within the workplace and larger society tend to be a topic of informal, ongoing, open-ended discussion and shared analysis and identity within

NPSS workplaces. As one long-term, part-time social service worker noted, "everyone who works here is very progressive. We always talk about everything and learn from each other." This practice of discussion and debate on social issues operates as a conduit for mobilization, and means that dissent and resistance strategies can emerge spontaneously outside of management-controlled pathways and can spread quickly when workers feel disappointed in management's conduct. Informal, open-ended staff discussions are not the exclusive pathway for building opposition, as union leadership might also foster dissenting debate. In most cases, these two mechanisms overlap and, in Ackroyd and Thompson's (1999; 2013) analysis, operate as internal informal rituals, building mutual self-esteem and shared oppositional identities, strategies and tactics.

The data analysed in this chapter show that dissenting conversations turned into union mobilization when workers developed extensive narratives and justifications for their disenchantment with management. For example, in one social service workplace, unionized workers voted in favour of strike action when management continuously refused to provide benefits to part-time workers, despite agency policy briefs condemning growing precarity, austerity and poverty in the larger society. The data also show that most workers believed that management would agree that part-time workers deserved better treatment and would find a solution.[4] Workers and some managers expressed surprise that management was willing to escalate the dispute to the point that workers eventually felt compelled to go out on strike. "People were angry, they were upset, the comments that we heard were 'how could management let this happen?'" This dissent and disappointment continued after the end of the six-day strike. As one front-line worker told us, "[The agency] had a staff party after the strike; lots of people didn't come because they were offended. They didn't want to deal with management." A progressive senior manager told us that on the first few days back at work after the strike, a number of her staff members – "the nicest, gentlest, most pleasant people you've ever met" – refused to look at or speak to her, and she knew that something significant had shifted in agency relationships.

An unintended outcome of the strike was building stronger oppositional identities and analysis on the picket line because it provided a mechanism for workers to get to know people from other parts of the agency. One long-term worker said that "One of the best parts of walking the line was you could actually have the conversations about structural issues in a way that we can't do during work." These interactions on the picket line counteracted the fragmentation typical of NPM, in which different parts of a single agency rarely have contact with each other or know what other programmes and workers are doing. As such, interactions like those on the picket line unintentionally provide new moments and spaces for formal and informal resistance strategies. They also provide opportunities for the further development of collective and individual oppositional identities and analyses.

In the example analysed here, internal informal practices of social debate and shared identity building influenced formal external practices bolstering the union's interest in, and capacity for, challenging management. They provided a moral storyline that motivated the unionized workforce.

Unpaid work and gifts

When they felt that justice was not being served, most NPSS workers' sense that they were part of a moral project of defending and expanding social justice gave them a certain amount of latitude to create their own meanings and feel entitled to condemn and critique management, funders, government and the larger society. This sense of values–based indignation also gave workers the moral upper hand when management appeared to be unwilling or incapable of living up to social justice/altruism values in workplace practices and/or within the larger society. This dynamic can make it difficult for managers to discipline workers or to regain moral authority when workers believe management has failed. Disciplinary actions may be viewed as confirmation that management is harsh, unreasonable and inept.

This dynamic operated, in particular, when workers regularly and publicly undertook the aforementioned highly gender-linked practice of unpaid care work on the job – working through coffee breaks and lunch hours, staying late, taking work home, coming in on weekends and taking clients home for birthday parties or weekend barbeques. Managers often found it difficult to discipline workers who everyone knew worked more hours than they were paid for, particularly when this overwork involved significant components of care and altruism.

In part, the majority female workers were resisting the stripping-out of care content in their everyday work processes by caring more during work hours and after work hours, and by taking care work home and to the community. The workers were using work and non–work spaces to reclaim social connections with co–workers and services users that were not regimented by tightly scripted time schemes, government metrics and information technology packages. In effect, they stepped outside the control of management and broke the thread of uncaring fostered by outcome measures and inadequate funding for social care. Instead, they developed relationships that were not merely technical and outcome directed.

Doing unpaid work is an intentional strategy that tends to be viewed as a trade-off between self-exploitation and trying to maintain a sense of integrity in the work and the workplace. It is generally viewed by workers as a necessary compromise that is often accompanied by counter-narratives and oppositional identities. As one worker quipped, "the wages are terrible here anyway so why not work even more hours for no pay if it means you can keep a programme afloat or keep someone from having to put their kids to bed hungry".

In general, these practices were internal informal activities because the individual workers undertook them in tandem with their personal and professional values. The practices also had an external informal aspect in that they were a widely known and accepted performance of care and altruism, and a disregard for the pecuniary concerns of funders and management and the boundaries of the agency. As such, they helped to build shared oppositional identities and narratives. The lines between internal informal and external informal blend in the performance of unpaid care work because this practice contributes both to the individual's sense of integrity and identity and the larger work culture of compromise and resistance strategies.

As noted earlier, Bolton (2009) and others (Guy et al, 2008; Brook, 2009; Baines, 2011) in the emotional labour literature have argued that these kinds of care work, whether they take place within a paid or unpaid context, are philanthropic gifts characterized by open-ended, unscripted, relationship-based interactions that serve as an interactive source of meaning between the provider and recipient, and a source of identity for the predominantly female workforce undertaking the work. These identities are generally shared in the care work examined in this chapter, through the discussion conduits and mobilization elements described earlier, giving a collective aspect to this emotional labour. Moreover, the recipients of this resistance were both individual service users and a presumed generalized other, in the sense of Richard Titmuss (2001) – one of the principle architects of the British welfare state – that the recipient of the gift is not known or important to the giver. Rather, a benefit to the greater social good is presumed, and motivates the giver. This gives a collective and social character to the emotional labour saturating the resistance of care workers, or what Baines (2011) has called a solidaristic-philanthropic gift.

There is another aspect to this question of gifts because some managers recognized that NPSS workers were providing a gift to the agency and sector by working for lower wages than they would receive in the public or private sectors. Referring to why it was difficult to retain care staff, a senior manager told us that "they can't afford to keep working at $30,000 a year when you can get $60,000 somewhere else. So, there's a bit of a gift factor." Workers were aware of this "gift" factor and spoke of being able to work in the NPSS because of their partner's wages: "If I was the sole breadwinner, I couldn't probably afford to work here." On the other hand, a single worker with no dependants noted that "If I had a family, there is no way I could afford to keep working here". The former situation presumes female dependence on a male wage and provides a way for employers to rationalize low pay, while the latter creates retention and recruitment issues. Both presuppose a naturalized female preoccupation with providing infinite, elastic care regardless of pay or conditions of work. However, gift factors can contain elements of oppositional identity and the potential for dissent and mobilization strategies. As Table 14.1 shows, these practices operate as internal informal activities, building oppositional identities, but also as external informal activities, contributing to shared identities and counter-narratives of non-profit care workers as people prepared to trade off their own time in order to sustain their personal and professional values and integrity.

Table 14.1: Resistance and dissent strategies

Practice	External formal	Internal formal	External informal
Moral projects		X	X
Unpaid work		X	X
Work resources for non-work		X	X
Work limitations			X
Social unionism	X	X	X

Using work time and resources for non-work activities

The data show that some workers simultaneously undertake unpaid overtime and use work time and resources for non-work activities. Workers sometimes justify this reclamation of time by viewing these activities as job content that restructuring and cutbacks have eliminated: "I used to get to do all this stuff [community mobilization] on the job, but we don't have time for it anymore and the government won't fund it. But, I can't just pull the plug and tell people 'my job won't pay me to do this anymore, so go away'." Workers also justified these activities by citing their importance to larger social justice causes and the broader society (the generalized other): "We can't wait out this period of conservative politics and watch people suffer. We have to try to make things better."

Some misuse of work time included using work time or work resources to organize and attend community and political meetings; write research, policy and campaign materials; use agency computers and copiers to make materials for social and political campaigns; and communicate, network and mobilize using agency e-mail and Twitter accounts and phones. Workers often felt that they had collusion or tolerance from at least some managers regarding these activities. As one young worker told us, "I was in one weekend with a friend copying campaign materials and my boss walked in. Like … it was really obvious. I thought I was in for it, but all she said was that I shouldn't work too long 'cause it was nice outside for a change and I shouldn't miss it."

Some workers also encouraged service users to advocate against the agency when the agency violated its own policies or mission, and sometimes workers joined picket lines and protests at the agency or in the community. In some instances, workers joined with activist groups that managers and directors felt were too political and inappropriate. In the latter case, unless their participation was too obvious and too public, workers told us that managers "pretended" not to see them: "I kinda tried to catch my supervisor's eye when she walked into work; I had nothing to hide. But she studiously avoided eye contact, though she said 'hi' to a couple of our clients who were also out there." In another example, a worker who gave a dissenting interview to the media was reprimanded by management, but then found an unexpected ally on the board of directors – an ex-social worker who felt that the interview was justified, defended the rights of staff to engage in political action, and told the board to "back off". In another case, a young worker was disciplined for arriving (barely) late for work, rather than for participating in the controversial protest that resulted in her being barely late for work.

These practices of time reclamation and resource misuse/repurposing represent internal informal activities that build workers' sense of themselves as social actors and people operating in tandem with their social consciences and values. They also act as a way for workers to separate themselves from the directives and priorities of the employer, confirming their dissenting identities. The public nature of many of these actions involves an element of performance, providing role models and examples for other staff to discuss, critique and emulate. As such, these actions operate as an external informal mechanism (see Table 14.1), shaping and building the shared identity of workers inside and outside the workplace and inside and outside formal mechanisms of resistance. These practices operate simultaneously at the internal informal level, building individuals' sense of themselves as different from the demands of management, and as people who will take risks for their values.

Work limitations

Not all of the resistance and dissent strategies were replete with moral and symbolic content. Some workers sniggered at running jokes that made no sense to the researchers but seemed to knit the workers together.[5] Other workers took part in classic work-avoidance strategies such as taking lengthy breaks and failing to complete assigned tasks. Sometimes these forms of informal resistance involved collusion from co-workers and tolerance from supervisors. In one study site, some workers were observed going on very long breaks. On one particular shift the registered nurse (RN) in charge repeatedly asked the other staff where a particular worker was. The workers shrugged and said she "must be on break". Eventually, the RN told a worker to go find her and tell her to get back to work. The worker said "OK", but after moving out of the RN's sight, she quietly went back to her own work.

Some workers preferred to work shifts where supervision was thin and their work was less controlled. Two front-line workers demonstrated a shared understanding, and possibly identity, noting that "lots of the staff don't like working morning shift because all the bosses are around", whereas in the evening and the night shift, "you're on your own and you can do what you want without anyone looking over your shoulder all the time".

Although documentation and recording outcome measures were emphasized as pivotal to the ongoing funding of the agencies, workers sometimes left documentation incomplete. This is seen as a major problem by many managers. As one manager complained, documenting is "the most important thing staff does on a shift", but "they let anything get in their way". The front-line staff felt that the most important aspect of their job was that they "cared about the service users" and that documentation took too much time away from doing this. Most of this relationship-based, open-ended, unscripted care could not be documented in the narrow metrics of outcome targets and, like care work in the home, it was rendered invisible in the documentary practices of the state and workplace. Supervisors told us that they phoned workers at home after hours and told them to come back to work to complete their documentation. Coming to work outside of paid hours to finish work was very unpopular with workers. A senior worker reflected the sentiments of many when she commented that "they can wait 'til Monday or the next day. It's no big deal. But they [managers] act like the world is gonna fall apart." These kinds of practices represent forms of individual, unconnected acts of disengagement and the formation of dissenting identities (and strategies) that lack the moral content of some of the strategies discussed earlier. These practices act largely as internal informal activities (see Table 14.1) that let workers distance themselves from the priorities of management and try to "get away with" leaving documentation work incomplete, despite the importance attached to it by managers and funders.

Social unionism

Unions in the NPSS were viewed by some care workers as an external mechanism for increasing their participation and decision making in the workplace. Many of these workers reported that they were union activists in order to "have a voice" in the workplace, and to recapture some of the autonomy and opportunities for social justice and relationship-based care work that they felt they had lost under NPM and constraint (see also Daly and Armstrong, 2016; Baines et al, 2017). Fortunately, the dominant model of unionism in the NPSS is social unionism, which, as Robinson (1993) argues, operates in a unique way in Canada, unfolding within a 'moral economy' in which members are attracted, retained and mobilized by invoking 'the importance of moral commitments of labour-movement members, leaders, and supporters' (Robinson, 1993, p 24). This moral project overlaps comfortably with the moral projects at play in the NPSS workforce, agency missions and work content.

There are numerous examples in the NPSS of workplace-based union bodies, known as locals, modifying their formal, bureaucratic structures or running parallel structures to accommodate workers' comfort with more horizontal, participatory formations and existing informal debate of social issues (Baines, 2010). Briskin (2013) calls these practices 'post heroic' because they emphasize leadership models that are inclusive and encourage shared leadership and the widest possible involvement. Some union locals took on or joined social justice projects outside the workplace, publicly staking their ground as caring people who tried to build a fairer society and as being involved in the everyday struggles of the communities they served. When union activism was framed as a moral project, it was more appealing to workers, and it was more difficult for management to attack or discredit the union. At the same time, it cast management's lack of action on social issues and distrust of unions as regressive and captured by neoliberal small-mindedness. The activities represent a mutually reinforcing overlap of external formal, internal informal and external informal practices because they build shared identities, moral projects and analysis within the union, as well as within the workplace and individual (see Table 14.1).

Discussion and conclusions

Earlier, the question was asked whether workers' dissent and resistance strategies promote their interests, management's interests, or both, and whether those strategies act as a catalyst for change, legitimize constraint, or both. For those outside of the care-work debate, the fact that some care workers see unpaid work as a form of dissent and resistance is often viewed as a form of false consciousness and a set of actions that expand management's capacity to deal with inadequate resources. As such, working to extend the agency's capacity to provide care can be seen to confirm that austerity policies are legitimate and that claims that service users and communities will suffer are based on unfounded hysteria. Drawing on new and previously published qualitative data from the author's studies of care work, this chapter has argued that unpaid work may unintentionally lend credibility to the claims that austerity-embracing policies are working and workable. Simultaneously and principally, however, unpaid work is a form of dissent, builds dissent and is a central part of the moral projects that workers use to analyse and critique their work, the agencies they work for, social policy and larger social relations.

This dissent distances workers from management priorities and hegemony. The data also suggest that many workers view unpaid work as a trade-off compromise in which they choose to work additional unpaid time in order to meet higher goals of care for others in an increasingly uncaring society. In other words, the workers gain a sense of integrity and of fighting back against uncaring, while at the same time they lose some of their time and energy. As such, this unpaid work can be seen as compromise resistance or an unstable balancing of moral projects, oppositional identities, counter-narratives and self-exploitation.

The data show further that many workers ascribe dissenting and oppositional meanings to unpaid work as an act of pushing back at jobs that have been managerialized and increasingly preclude the social justice/altruistic practices that workers find meaningful for themselves and others. Unpaid work and the often-symbolic moral projects that saturate it contribute to the building of individual and shared dissenting identities and can lead to more formal and organized forms of resistance, such as strikes, as well as various kinds of informal resistance within and beyond the workplace. These actions and identities take place outside of management's control and explicit agendas. Perhaps most importantly, unpaid work can shift the balance of moral power in a workplace, making it difficult for management to discipline workers who are known to work well beyond their prescribed hours and outcome targets. It also makes it difficult to denigrate unions known to be socially involved and caring.

Unpaid work is not the only practice that contributes to moral projects in a NPSS workplace. The informal process of debating and discussing social issues and values extends shared analyses and identities. These practices also serve as a pre-existing conduit for more formal dissent when opinion coalesces around a particular moment of real or perceived management failure to live up to the mission or values of the agency and greater social justice.

Workers also use agency resources and work time to undertake practices that they feel should be part of their jobs, or once were part of their jobs, such as advocacy, community organising, writing policy briefs and building oppositional campaigns. The data suggest that management often quietly supports or tolerates these actions, perhaps sharing the same social justice values and frustrations with the managerialized workplace and/or hoping that workers will extend the same tolerance and flexibility to management. More formal resistance practices, such as building social unionist locals with structures and practices modified to fit the participatory values of the workers, are built from these same notions of moral projects and the need to resist uncaring practices inside and outside the workplace.

This chapter has shown that the lines between external formal, internal informal and external informal resistance are fairly porous, overlapping and mutually reinforcing. Table 14.1 shows that resistance and dissent practices cluster in the categories of internal informal and external informal, with only social unionism drawing explicitly on formal external forms of worker self-organization. This underscores the importance of informal worker self-organization in care workplaces. The care content, willingness to trade self-exploitation for caring outcomes and the possibilities these practices create for further dissent, shared identities and counter-narratives suggest a link between the notion of unending care expected of women and of gendered work environments such as the NPSS. This suggests that informal workers' self-organization has a strongly gendered character in certain contexts, such as care work, and that this phenomenon certainly merits further research and exploration. The overlap of the three forms of worker self-organization in social unionism – which is itself embedded in and inseparable from the gendered context, practices, identities and resistance strategies in care work – suggests the importance of understanding workers' self-organization strategies holistically rather than by analysing only the formal external aspects.

The chapter has also suggested that the line between resistance, dissent, promoting management's interests and unintentionally legitimizing constraint agendas can be thin and contested. In the context of care practices reduced to narrow metrics, resistance often seems to be largely a battle of ideas and a struggle for the space in which to care about service users and communities. If resistance is the pursuit of greater autonomy in the workplace, then workers who participate in these types of dissent can be seen to operate intentionally at the frontier of management control. The strategies, involving aspects of a moral project, erode the overarching legitimacy of uncaring funding constraint and management control. They form examples of what Briskin (2011) calls the politicization of care, in which managerialized and rationalized care is rejected alongside naturalized notions of women as inherently and centrally responsible for care. Care is reconstituted and reclaimed as a collective responsibility. In the context of austerity, these activities may form the backbone of a larger project of resistance if, through this murky struggle, workers can carve out symbolic and moral space for further dissent, oppositional meanings and identities. Like the unstable equilibrium that characterizes the contemporary state, this struggle for space, meanings and compromise resistance also seems to reflect the successes and failures of past struggles, as well as opportunities inherent in everyday struggles to provide care, debate social issues and sustain social justice-engaged meaning in constrained and managerialized NPSS workplaces.

Notes

[1] The term 'moral projects' is used here to designate value-driven projects and decisions. Although it frequently contains social justice content, it can be highly individualistic, of a religious or spiritual nature and/or an action that makes the actor feel virtuous in that she or he is living in tandem with her or his values.

[2] NPM is a public sector management model that draws on private sector notions of competitive performance management, outcome measures and cost-saving. It was introduced across public and non-profit sectors from the mid-1980s onwards as part of neoliberal restructuring and downsizing of the welfare state.

[3] Bolton uses the term 'philanthropic' to describe a freely given gift with no expectation of reciprocity. She differentiates this kind of giving/caring from 'charity', which expects some form of recognition and spiritual or corporeal recognition and reward.

[4] Kelly's (1998) classic article identifies six elements of union mobilization: emergence of a sense of widely shared injustice in the workplace, where workers reject the status quo; the capacity to attribute blame, and liability for a solution, to the employer; a sense that collective action can make a difference; the presence of a collective organization for workers to join and provide resources for their concerns; assessments that the cost of such actions (employer reprisals) will be small; and the existence of a core of activists/leaders who can construct and maintain the sense of injustice, identity and cohesion in the face of counter-mobilization strategies from management. These elements were all present in the example discussed in this chapter.

[5] Humour seen as a form of resistance/misbehaviour may not be aligned with management goals for time use and identity. See Ackroyd and Thompson (1999; 2013).

References

Ackroyd, S. (2012) 'Even more misbehaviour: What has happened in the last twenty years?'. *Advances in Industrial and Labor Relations*, 19(4): 1–28.

Ackroyd, S. and Thompson, P. (1999) *Organizational Misbehaviour*. London, UK: Sage.

Ackroyd, S. and Thompson, P. (2013) 'Remapping resistance and misbehaviour'. Paper presented at the Work, Employment and Society Conference, Warwick University, Warwick, 3–5 September.

Aptheker, B. (1989) *Tapestries of Life: Women's Work, Women's Consciousness, and the Meaning of Daily Experience*. Massachusetts: University of Massachusetts Press.

Armstrong, P., Armstrong, H. and MacLeod, K.K. (2016) 'The threats of privatization to security in long-term residential care'. *Ageing International*, 41(1): 99–116.

Aronson, J. and Smith, K. (2010) 'Managing restructured social services: Expanding the social?' *British Journal of Social Work*, 40: 530–47.

Aronson, J. and Smith, K. (2011) 'Identity work and critical social service management: Balancing on a tightrope?' *British Journal of Social Work*, 41(): 432–48.

Baines, D. (2010) 'Neoliberal restructuring/activism, participation and social unionism in the nonprofit social services'. *Nonprofit and Voluntary Sector Quarterly*, 39(1): 10–28.

Baines, D. (2011) 'Resistance as emotional work: The Australian and Canadian non-profit social services'. *Industrial Relations Journal*, 42(2): 139–56.

Baines, D. and Daly, T. (2015). 'Resisting regulatory rigidities: Lessons from front-line care work'. *Studies in Political Economy*, 95(1): 137–60.

Baines, D., Cunningham, I. and Shields, J. (2017) 'Filling the gaps with unpaid, formal and coerced work in the nonprofit sector'. *Critical Social Policy*. doi: 10.1177/0261018317693128.

Baines, D., Charlesworth, S. and Cunningham, I. (2014) 'Fragmented outcomes: International comparisons of gender, managerialism and union strategies in the nonprofit sector'. *Journal of Industrial Relations*, 56(1): 24–42.

Baines, D., Charlesworth, S., Cunningham, I. and Dassinger, J. (2012) 'Self-monitoring, self-blaming, self-sacrificing workers: Gendered Managerialism in the non-profit sector'. *Women's Studies International Forum*, 35(5): 362–71.

Bolton, S.C. (2009) 'Getting to the heart of the emotional labour process: A reply to Brook'. *Work, Employment and Society*, 23(3): 549–60.

Braverman, H. (1974) *Labour and Monopoly Capital: The Degradation of Work in the Twentieth Century*. New York: Monthly Review Press.

Briskin, L. (2013) 'Nurse militancy and strike action'. *Workers of the World International Journal on Strikes and Social Conflicts*, 1(2): 105–34.

Briskin, L. (2011) 'Union renewal, postheroic leadership and women's organizing: Crossing discourses, reframing debates'. *Labour Studies Journal*, 36(4): 508–37.

Brook, P. (2009) 'The alienated heart: Hochschild's "emotional labour" thesis and the anticapitalist politics of alienation'. *Capital and Class*, 33(2): 7–31.

Burawoy, M. (1979) *Manufacturing Consent: Changes in the Labour Process under Monopoly Capitalism*. Chicago: Chicago University Press.

Charlesworth, S. (2010) 'The regulation of paid care workers' wages and conditions in the non-profit sector: A Toronto case study'. *Relations Industrielles/Industrial Relations*, 65(3): 380–99.

Cunningham, I. (2008) *Employment Relations in the Voluntary Sector*. London: Routledge.

Daly, T. and Armstrong, P. (2016) 'Liminal and invisible long-term care labour: Precarity in the face of austerity'. *Journal of Industrial Relations*, 58(4): 473–90.

DeWalt, K.M. (2007) *Participant Observation: A Guide for Fieldworkers*. Walnut Creek: AltaMira Press.

Edwards, P. (1986) *Conflict at Work*. Oxford: Blackwell Press.

Edwards, P. and Scullion, H. (1982) *The Social Organization of Industrial Conflict*. Oxford: Blackwell Press.

Eikenberry, A. (2009) 'Refusing the market. A democratic discourse for voluntary and nonprofit organizations'. *Nonprofit and Voluntary Sector Quarterly*, 38(4): 582–96.

Esping-Andersen, G. (2000) 'Interview on postindustrialism and the future of the welfare state'. *Work, Employment and Society*, 14(4): 757–69.

Glesne, C. (2011) *Becoming Qualitative Researchers*. White Plains, NY: Longman.

Guy, M., Newman, M.A., and Mastracci, S.H. (2008) *Emotional Labor: Putting the Service in Public Service*. Armonk, NY: M.E. Sharpe.

Hochschild, A.R. (2012) *The Managed Heart: Commercialization of Human Feeling*. Los Angeles: University of California Press.

Kelly, J. (1998) *Mobilisation, Collectivism and Long Waves*. London: Routledge.

Knights, D. and Willmott, H. (1989) 'Power and subjectivity at work: From degradation to subjugation in social relations'. *Sociology*, 23(4): 535–58.

Maconachie, G. (2005) 'Emotional suppression to regulated empathy: from one face of control to another'. *Labour and Industry*, 16(1): 43–58.

Nickel, P.M. and Eikenberry, A.M. (2016) 'Knowing and governing: The mapping of the nonprofit and voluntary sector as statecraft'. *VOLUNTAS: International Journal of Voluntary and Nonprofit Organizations*, 27(1): 392–408.

Nickson, D., Warhust, C., Dutton, E., and Hurrell, S. (2008) 'A job to believe in: Recruitment in the Scottish voluntary sector'. *Human Resource Management Journal*, 18(1): 20–35.

Pollert, A. (1981) *Girls, Wives, Factory Lives*. London: Macmillan.

Robinson, I. (1993) 'Economistic unionism in crisis: The origins, consequences and prospects of divergence in labour-movement characteristics'. In: Jenson, J. and Mahon, R. (eds), *The Challenge of Restructuring: North American Labour Movements Respond*. Philadelphia: Temple University Press, 19–47.

Salamon, L. (2010) 'Putting the civil society sector on the economic map of the world'. *Annals of Public and Cooperative Economics*, 81(2): 167–210.

Scruggs, L.A. and Allan, J.P. (2008) 'Social stratification and welfare regimes for the twenty-first century: Revisiting the three worlds of welfare capitalism'. *World Politics*, 60(4): 642–64.

Themudo, N. (2009) 'Gender and the nonprofit sector'. *Nonprofit and Voluntary Sector Quarterly*, 38(4): 663–83.

Thompson, P. (1997) *Nature of Work: An Introduction to Debates on the Labour Process*. London: Palgrave MacMillan.

Thompson, P. and Smith, C. (eds) (2017) *Working Life: Renewing Labour Process Analysis*. London: Palgrave Macmillan.

Titmuss, R. (2001) *Welfare and Wellbeing: Richard Titmuss's Contribution to Social Policy*. Cambridge, MA: MIT Press.

Van Til, J. (2009) 'A paradigm shift in third sector theory and practice: Refreshing the wellsprings of democratic capacity'. *American Behavioral Scientist*, 52(7): 1069–81.

15

Austerity, Resistance and the Labour Movement

Helen Blakely and Steve Davies

Introduction

This chapter draws on a research study carried out with UNI Global Union (the Global Union Federation for unions representing workers in private sector service industries). A total of 58 interviews were undertaken with officials and activists of UNI Global and their affiliates from around the world with a view to investigating union responses to the changing world of work. This chapter briefly outlines three of the 25 cases from this study of union resistance: namely, Sindicatul IT Timişoara in Romania; Sindicato de Trabajadores de la Empresa Teleperformance de a República Dóminicana in the Dominican Republic; and the Retail, Wholesale and Department Store Union in the US. It will focus on new forms of unionism for the 21st century. The chapter begins with a brief outline of the challenges faced by unions in the context of austerity and then moves on to examine the cases, which reflect a range of union activity: from elements of social movement and community-based unionism with little immediate 'pay off', to forms of unionism that have secured collective bargaining agreements and transformative increases in membership.

The world of work is changing rapidly and, while there are important geographical variations, a number of global trends present challenges to trade unions. The major changes in political economy that have taken place since the 1970s – the emphasis on the dominance of the market and,

301

by association, trade liberalization, de-regulation and financialization – have become the accepted economic 'common sense' around the world. In this context, employment relationships that diverge from standard forms, for example, temporary, part-time and agency employment, as well as bogus self-employment, are on the rise in developed economies (ILO, 2016). This comes at a time when standard forms of employment remain unattainable for many working within the informal economy elsewhere. This work is associated with lower wages, reduced social protection, income insecurity and poorer working conditions, as well as challenges over rights to unionize and engage in collective bargaining (Eurofound, 2013). These developments in the world of work take place against a context of rapid and far-reaching technological change that has aided outsourcing, offshoring and the fragmentation of production processes locally, regionally and globally.

While many of these trends predate austerity, it is undeniable that post-2008 retrenchment policies have exacerbated them. Blyth (2013, p 2) defines austerity as:

> a form of voluntary deflation in which the economy adjusts through the reduction of wages, prices, and public spending to restore competitiveness, which is (supposedly) best achieved by cutting the state's budget, debts and deficits. Doing so, its advocates believe, will inspire 'business confidence' since the government will neither be 'crowding-out' the market for investment by sucking up all the available capital through the issuance of debt, nor adding to the nation's already 'too big' debt.

Austerity and the policies associated with it are often assumed to affect primarily the public sector, in terms of both the public services provided and those workers that provide them. What is obscured by this rather limited perspective is the impact that austerity has on labour as a whole, including those who work in the private sector. The long-term squeeze on public spending as a response to 'unaffordable' social programmes has both direct and indirect impacts on private sector workers' pay and conditions, undermining the collective bargaining position of those who are organized and further individualizing those who are not.

Austerity is nothing new for many of the countries of the global South, having had such policies imposed upon them by the International Monetary Fund and the World Bank during the debt crises of the 1970s (Plehwe et al, 2019). However, the breadth and depth of the current adoption of policies of austerity in the global North – with attendant implications for policy and impact in the global South – is unprecedented in the period since the Second World War. It is also clear that, rather than understanding cuts in public spending and a general shrinking of the state as an episodic response to economic crisis, some governments appear committed to a policy of 'permanent austerity' (Streeck, 2017, p 84). The public sector was formerly an exemplar in pay, conditions and pensions, creating a positive effect on employment conditions in the private sector in many countries. Today the push to lower public sector production and service costs, through wage cuts and the 'reform' of 'over-generous' pensions for example, undermines any supposed pressure on private sector companies to act as 'model employers'. It also eases labour–market competition for private sector employers as the public sector increasingly adopts those practices prevalent within the private sector. While the state in its many forms remains a major source of funding for the private sector, austerity means that contractors to the state are expected to provide the same (or more) for less. Inevitably this affects the quality of service, but, in particular, the pressure is felt by the employees in deteriorating pay, conditions and job security.

Austerity-linked cuts in the welfare state represent a reduction in the social wage for all workers in a range of different areas. The impact on the lower-paid is inevitably greater, since they have less disposable income and so are less able to exercise 'choice' in procuring services such as healthcare, education, transport, childcare or support for the elderly. They are also more likely to suffer detriment in relation to the social security entitlements paid to those in work – those 'working poor' in need of welfare relief to achieve sustainable earnings. Cuts in public spending have a cost to all workers in the sense that they may have to do without, try to provide the service themselves, pay for supplements to reduced services or buy privately provided services that were previously offered by the public sector for free. Expectations of the terms and conditions of work may also be lowered, as austerity is often accompanied by state-facilitated changes in the labour market, including the dismantling of large bargaining units where they exist and the growth of precarious work practices. There is a close relationship between the reduction of expenditure in the public sector and regulatory oversight of labour–market conditions, and an expansion in precarious work and deteriorating pay and conditions (McKay et al, 2012; Hudson-Sharp and Runge, 2017).

In the context of a hostile environment for collective organization across the globe, trade union membership and density has declined. In May 2019 the Organisation for Economic Co-operation and Development (OECD) released figures show that 'Trade Union membership in OECD countries has dropped to 16 per cent of workers on average, from about 30 per cent in 1985' (OECD, 2019). A combination of market-focused economic policies and the rise of politically antipathetic governments that see unions as a restraint on the efficient working of free markets have been key determinants of this trend. In this context, the labour movement is tasked with organizing a labour force that is more diverse, disconnected and fragmented than that of the mid-20th century. Consequently, workers require new configurations and formations of collective representation and organization if unions are to remain relevant and representative.

Such workers present the labour movement with a challenge that is common to the cases of union organizing that will be considered in this chapter, in that while their need is great, they have traditionally proved difficult to organize. A further shared feature of the cases we consider is the multi-scalar nature of the challenge that each union faced at the workplace, employer, national and international level, which necessitated an associated multi-scalar response from the union. What Beverley Silver (2003) terms the 'hyper mobility of capital' – as opposed to the relative immobility of labour – creates significant issues for unions seeking collective bargaining agreements. Luce (2014, p 199) argues that the response of unions has to scale up and to broaden out: to 'reframe their struggles as broader movements'. Evans (2008, p 298) points out that 'Every system of domination generates its own distinctive set of opportunities for challenge and transformation, and neo-liberal globalization is no exception.' He urges the use of 'the tools created by generic globalization' (Evans, 2008, p 298) and cites the Global Union Federations, the range of labour-oriented NGOs (which exist at national level and also often as part of transnational networks) and the changed attitudes of national unions toward global solidarity as three factors that offer hope for effective union action against global capital.

While unions possess and deploy various different types of power resources and strategic capabilities to enact change (see Levesque and Murray, 2010), this chapter focuses on two salient dimensions. First, we focus on the extent to which the union is embedded in a network through links to other local, national and global unions, community groups and social movements. For example, a union may have links with unions covering the same sector or with unions with the same employer; a union may also have links that are galvanized by issues beyond the workplace. The ways in which, and under what circumstances, such networks can leverage power are important here. The implications of the different types of activity undertaken by each of the actors involved, as well as how any forms of coordinated action are negotiated, are of interest here. Second, we consider the strategic capability of unions to act at multiple levels, and in multiple spaces over time. The development of 'glocal' actions, that is, those which are simultaneously both global and local, is particularly significant (Murray, 2017), as is the ability to integrate bottom-up and top-down approaches (Voss and Sherman, 2000) and to coordinate and collaborate across boundaries through transnational forms of solidarity. Each of these is a noteworthy feature of the exemplars discussed here.

Sindicatul IT Timişoara: Romania

Outsourcing is a commonly used strategy available to a multinational company to reduce labour costs, and Romania has emerged as one of Europe's most significant outsourcing destinations in the information technology (IT) sector. The functions that are outsourced may vary across companies, with what were once regarded as 'core' functions increasingly likely to be outsourced (Holtgrewe and Schörpf, 2017). Within Romania outsourcing companies are concentrated in particular places, and in 2009 a French member of Alcatel-Lucent's European Works Council discovered that the company had plans to outsource approximately one-third of the IT workforce of its Romanian subsidiary to Wipro in one such place, Timişoara. The member, having witnessed the deterioration in the quality of employment for French workers once IT functions were outsourced, passed the information on to a Romanian co-worker. In response, and despite the lack of a strong tradition of union organizing among IT workers in Romania, the imminent prospect of outsourcing prompted workers in Timişoara to unionize. As Alcatel-Lucent's outsourcing of maintenance services to Wipro was a global strategy, which it was anticipated would prove difficult to resist locally, the union Sindicatul IT Timişoara (SITT) was formed, with the explicit intention of preserving current working conditions by negotiating a collective agreement with Alcatel-Lucent in Romania.

SITT entered into negotiations with Alcatel-Lucent with the guidance of Cartel Alfa,[1] the National Trade Union Confederation of Romania, UNI Global and the Alcatel-Lucent European Works Council. Unusually for Romania, SITT also hired a legal team to help negotiate the collective agreement (Trif and Stoiciu, 2017). In support of the negotiations, SITT organized strike action to protest against the proposed changes, and a collective agreement was signed prior to outsourcing in 2010. The union drew on EU regulation, specifically the Acquired Rights Directive (covering the transfer of undertakings) to ensure that the collective agreement protected outsourced workers' working conditions – at least at the point of transfer. This decision led to SITT being recognized in the destination company and outsourced workers retaining their membership. At this point the union decided to become the 'voice of all the IT workers at least in Timişoara regionally, but also nationally. And we decided ... to unionize not only companies that would outsource workers, but all the IT companies in the sector.' (SITT organizer).

However, subsequent changes in Romanian labour law in 2011, and specifically the increase in the threshold for union recognition at company level to 50 per cent +1 of the total workforce, presented SITT with difficulties. While workers in Timişoara were unionized, the number of non-unionized workers in other cities meant that the union did not have the necessary 50 per cent +1 membership. The result was that SITT lost legal recognition, and: "just as we expected, the company cancelled almost all workers' rights won back in 2009" (SITT organizer).

In response, SITT focused efforts on organizing the workforce outside of Timişoara. One element of the strategy was an open re-evaluation of the membership dues, whereby potential members were asked how much they thought was reasonable to pay. Another was the advertisement of running membership totals during the campaign in the workplace: "You would have people saying 'I want to be the plus one', the worker that would assure the legal threshold" (SITT organizer). SITT went on to secure legal recognition in both Wipro and Alcatel-Lucent companies. The collective agreements with both companies were renegotiated in 2012 and 2013, although concession bargaining in Wipro led to some deterioration in pay, terms and conditions. The story continued in 2014, when Alcatel-Lucent outsourced workers to professional services company Accenture. Again, through collective bargaining SITT secured largely the same working conditions for the outsourced workers. The union also managed to recruit new members from the outsourced Accenture workforce in Timişoara, where a tradition of unionization was developing.

In 2015 SITT met with UNI Global to develop an organizing strategy to enable the union to bargain at a sectoral level, which included the development of an activist training programme across the three companies (Alcatel-Lucent, Wipro and Accenture). In 2017 the focus turned to organizing a fourth company, Atos Romania. SITT's strategy was to build on their image and visibility in Timişoara, as within Atos there were workers who had been members of SITT in the past. SITT's activists were also meeting workers face to face in Atos sites across Romania, as well as recruiting the company's employee representatives, who provided opportunities for union communications with significant numbers of workers via conference calls. During the final phase of the campaign, UNI Global and tens of its affiliated unions wrote to Atos Romania, congratulating them on SITT's presence in the company.

SITT currently represents more than 3,000 employees, working for a number of IT companies, with a union density of over 65 per cent, and is currently developing a long-term strategy for sector-level negotiations. SITT organized and mobilized atypical workers, relatively young IT workers vulnerable to outsourcing, as their predominant members. This is in stark contrast to the general trends in the composition of union membership (Heery, 2009). For the most part the union is taking a largely geographical, as opposed to employer-based, approach to organizing workers from different companies. This strategy emerged in response to a particular type of fragmentation, whereby workers from a number of companies, located in the same workplace, *can* join the same union. This form of mobile union membership, which travels with the worker from one employer to the next, is an interesting development (and unusual in Romania), not least because it affirms the importance of face-to-face interactions between members and leaders in close geographical proximity to each other. The case also demonstrates that trade unions can make use of established bargaining structures, positions and processes, and existing supra-national regulatory frameworks, to deal with new challenges and secure new agreements in new contexts.

SITT has benefited from a multi-scalar approach with the input of well-established institutions, like the European Works Council, and UNI Global Union and its affiliates. It began as a single-employer, single-city organization, but, using the institutional opportunities offered by the European legislation, and the networks and support offered at national and international levels through affiliation to Cartel Alfa and UNI Global, it was able to expand to create a national organization operating in several different companies. In most of the global North there has been a sustained campaign of government political hostility to trade unionism since the beginning of the 1980s and the elections of Thatcher in the UK and Reagan in the US. Sissons (2010, p 281) describes this as the 'undermining of the "legitimacy power" of trade unions and collective bargaining'. In Romania, the additional problem faced by any emergent trade union is a scepticism or, at best, indifference from potential members because of the legacy of the Stalinist period in which 'unions' were a part of the one-party state. This is not unique to Romania; it is a widespread problem across the countries of the former Soviet bloc (Hoffer, 2018). SITT has overcome this through face-to-face recruitment, deployment of forms of direct action and skilful use of institutional opportunities, which shows that a combination of traditional and new approaches to union organization and worker mobilization can be effective in the contemporary era, even in Eastern Europe.

Sindicato de Trabajadores de la Empresa Teleperformance de a República Dóminicana: Dominican Republic

The Dominican Republic has become a regional hub for the contact centre industry, which is renowned for low pay and precarious employment, and, specifically, a key site for Teleperformance – the world's largest provider of outsourced contact centre services. With 300,000 employees in 80 countries around the world (Teleperformance, 2019), the company has an established presence in the country. Historically, most of the workers in the contact centre industry, and Teleperformance specifically, have been unorganized by trade unions, but the workers at Teleperformance in the Dominican Republic at least have made significant attempts to change that reality. Specifically, a new union, Sindicato de Trabajadores de la Empresa Teleperformance de a República Dóminicana (SITRATEL), or the Union of Teleperformance Workers in the Dominican Republic, was established in 2016, with the support of UNI Global and the Dominican Republic's union federation, FEDOTRAZONAS. SITRATEL is an affiliate of FEDOTRAZONAS, a body that traditionally represented unions in the Dominican Republic's textile industry. Over time, and as the textile industry moved overseas, FEDOTRAZONAS has focused its efforts increasingly on those new industries coming to the Dominican Republic, including those forms of employment associated with off-shoring trends within the global contact centre sector.

Organizing workers in the global contact centre sector is challenging, due to the dynamics of a competitive-tendering process where clients seek to lower costs:

> 'When you organize workers, you will typically face a lot of very anti-union behaviour. Clients drive down the prices to the contact centre companies through the tendering process meaning some contracts have quite low margins. So, when contact centre companies see a union they think they'll make them uncompetitive because their competitors don't have a union.' (UNI Global official)

Unsurprisingly, Teleperformance did prove to be a hostile environment for union organizing and the company deployed a number of 'union busting' tactics. For example, trade union leaders were subject to legal action to lift protections against firing them and the company attempted to remove the workers' right to organize by deregistering the union in the courts. The union also found it challenging to inflict reputational damage on the company in the absence of a distinctive Teleperformance brand identity. Despite its significance as a global employer, the company operates largely 'under the radar' and is a relatively unknown entity in the public sphere.

In response, the campaign for union recognition built relationships with some of Teleperformance's clients, encouraging them to take responsibility for their supply chain and allow workers to organize. The strong union presence within some of these client companies, as well as the development of relationships with those unions with a presence in Teleperformance workplaces around the world, became a key source of leverage. This UNI Global Teleperformance Alliance of unions was activated in various ways during the campaign. One example included the dissemination of a collective, open letter addressing the chief executive officer of Teleperformance, calling for him to respect human and labour rights, including the right to join a union. Another involved a UNI Global affiliate, the Communications Workers of America (CWA), which has a collective agreement with AT&T (one of Teleperformance's most significant customers). The CWA led a delegation of American workers from AT&T to investigate working conditions at Teleperformance and meet with local trade unionists. The CWA sent a letter of protest to both AT&T and Teleperformance management about the poor treatment of the Teleperformance employees serving AT&T customers, and sought to educate their membership through solidarity missions and social media activity (UNI Global, 2019a).

As a result of this type of concerted campaigning, in 2018 Teleperformance, their Dominican union SITRATEL and FEDOTRAZONAS, signed an agreement for union recognition that allows for freedom of association to be respected in the Dominican Republic. Under the agreement, Teleperformance and SITRATEL are bound to the following: the company will be neutral with regard to union membership and respect workers' right to freedom of association; Teleperformance will provide paid time off for union representatives to talk to employees about union membership; and there will be a space at the induction of new employees to explain the benefits of union membership (UNI Global, 2018). Since the agreement was signed in April 2018, almost 1,000 workers have joined the union, meaning that SITRATEL now represents a majority of Teleperformance workers in the country (UNI Global, 2019b).

In the context of the fragmentation of company supply chains and the decrease in the coverage of collective bargaining, organizing down the value chain has become increasingly important. Efforts are invariably hampered by the fact that outsourcing is typical in countries where there is no sector-level collective bargaining. It is notable that SITRATEL in the Dominican Republic is a *new* union. In an increasingly fragmented economy it may well be that successful unions are new unions, with new leaders, ready to adopt new strategies. What SITRATEL achieved here was to ally the organizing of workers at workplace level with a series of other actions that engaged other actors at national and international levels. Within the Dominican Republic they had the assistance of the union federation FEDOTRAZONAS. As a result of the federation being affiliated to the Global Union Federation, UNI Global, they were able to work with the international network of unions created by UNI Global within the company – the UNI Global Teleperformance Alliance of unions. Through this network they were able to contact unions in companies that were customers of Teleperformance, one of which was the US union that represents workers in Teleperformance's client AT&T. Lacking any 'institutional embeddedness' within their own country, SITRATEL were able to tap into the institutional embeddedness of a sister union in a different country in order to place indirect pressure on the employer through one of its major customers. The representations to AT&T made by the American affiliate of UNI Global (the CWA) and this union's high-profile visit to the Dominican Republic proved impossible for Teleperformance to ignore.

Retail, Wholesale and Department Store Union: US

The difficulties of building union organization in the US are well known: a trying legal situation, frequently hostile employers and an anti-union political atmosphere. Add to this the nature of employment practices prevalent within the retail sector (for example, low pay and insecure employment) and it is unsurprising that, in 2014, the Retail, Wholesale and Department Store Union (RWDSU) felt that a new approach was needed to recruit workers to the union in the fashion retail industry in New York. In recent decades, employers in this industry, including Zara and H&M, have become key players in 'fast fashion'. Their competitiveness relies on monitoring and keeping pace with the latest consumer trends, and the attendant rapid design, production and sale of stock. In the US it is not uncommon for retail workers in this industry to be subject to very poor working conditions, including 'just-in-time' scheduling, the growth of part-time hours and the payment of relatively low wages, meaning that one characteristic of fast-fashion workplaces is the high turnover of retail staff. This context poses a huge challenge for unions seeking to recruit, organize and mobilize workers.

To combat the low union density and poor conditions in retail in New York, and in the absence of a collective agreement at the time, in 2005 the RWDSU created a worker centre[2] called the Retail Action Project (RAP) that any retail worker can join, whether in a unionized company or not, for mutual aid and support. In 2014, as the numbers of Zara workers joining RAP grew, a group of RAP members who worked at Zara and were looking for ways to improve their working conditions launched the #ChangeZara campaign. This campaign was founded on two key sources of leverage: the Global Framework Agreement that Inditex, Zara's parent company had signed with UNI Global, and a grassroots strategy supported by RAP.

RWDSU is an affiliate of UNI Global and the leverage that this relationship provided with the company was viewed as instrumental to the campaign. The reason why the Zara campaign happened was "because of the UNI Global Union and Inditex global framework agreement that existed" (RWDSU officer). This framework agreement committed Inditex to allowing freedom of association, including access, neutrality and card check in Zara's workplaces. Discussions around the implementation of the agreement, and the devolution of a US protocol, began before the grassroots campaign started in earnest. Indeed, it was the very existence of the global framework agreement, and the failure of social dialogue to ensure Zara's adherence to it, that prompted the grassroots campaign.

While it was the global framework agreement that created the opportunity for RWDSU's campaign, "it became pretty clear ... that unless there was greater pressure from the ground, there would not be any movement" (RWDSU officer). RAP's approach to the campaign was to engage with retail workers on the ground, listen to their issues and support them to fight for improvements. Having undertaken this form of outreach work – the canvassing and recruitment of Zara workers regarding their concerns – over a number of years prior to the campaign meant that RAP were already aware of the issues that these workers faced. Over time, increasing numbers of Zara workers not only joined RAP but also participated in their leadership training programme:

'It really works to engage retail workers in general and educate them and involve them in understanding the power dynamics they work within. And to try and change that power dynamic so that it would improve their rights as workers, and as part of the community.' (RWDSU officer)

Through the training, workers learned more about their role in the global retail industry, as well as about the labour movement and campaigning for social justice more broadly. Crucially, workers, even if only a minority, learned how to identify workplace issues and how to organize their co-workers to take action. Specifically, increasing numbers of Zara workers drew on their right to concerted activity under federal law, and workplace activist committees formed across multiple sites. In turn, by petitioning their employer and holding public rallies, Zara workers began to draw attention to the differences in working conditions between US retail workers and those of their European counterparts who are unionized, such as access to social protection and representation at work. Workers also called into question practices at the store level that were incompatible with the company's global culture and stated business philosophy. In 2014, Zara agreed to increase the number of full-time positions, end on-call shifts and increase wages, as well as to recognize the RWDSU. A protocol of the global framework agreement was submitted for Manhattan and over 1,000 workers in eight Zara stores became unionized as a result. The union extended its reach into other Zara stores, and in 2019 announced that it now represents approximately 2,000 employees with the company in the New York area (UFCW, 2019).

The Change Zara campaign was not an example of traditional, local union organizing. Rather, it was a 'brand pressure' campaign urging Inditex to implement a global framework agreement in its subsidiary, Zara. In this way the union was able to overcome the challenges of unionizing in the retail sector:

> 'we were able galvanize the interest of ... activist committees in each store in New York City without the greater, overwhelming impossibility of trying to get 50 plus 1 per cent support from the workplace when literally every month you're seeing 100 per cent turnover, so with what army can we actually do that?' (RWDSU officer)

It is important to note that the global framework agreement, and its related stipulations of access, neutrality and card check, were a lever in this process of unionization. But ensuring commitment to the implementation of the lever is only half of the story:

> 'The other half is actually having workers signed up for the union. All that ground activity really helped to foster the result that we wanted, once the protocol was signed and once the protocol was implemented ... once the vote time came up there was no store that got less than 98 per cent worker support to join the union.' (RWDSU officer)

An important component of the success of the organizing effort was the development of an effective worker–engagement strategy in the context of the neutrality agreement by RWDSU and RWDSU Local 1102. The organizing effort that was employed at Zara once the neutrality agreement was in effect was different from the kinds of campaigns that are typically run in the US. This effort required a refined outreach approach that would work in the context of the company's neutrality and the limited time allotted for worker engagement. The case of the Zara campaign points to the importance of a multipronged approach to unionization, which takes advantage of the institutional opportunities available without neglecting the engagement and organization of workers on the ground, which can be strategically harnessed.

Reflections

We began by asking how unions are responding to the contemporary world of work, defined by an era of austerity, a background of changes in the composition of the economy and a broader programme of neoliberal reform and technological advancement. Essentially, each of the cases discussed here saw unions grappling with establishing effective representation: either by building on past success and growing an existing union in new ways; or by building a new union to tackle emerging, contemporary challenges on new terrain. In the case of RWDSU in the US and its highly effective Zara campaigning, new approaches within established organizations were developed. In contrast, SITT in Romania and SITRATEL in the Dominican Republic were working in uncharted territory and creating new unions. In each case, the capacity of workers, through their union, to counter the inherently asymmetrical power relationship within the workplace involved recognizing the need to augment current workplace power in order to enhance future workplace power. All three unions found themselves dealing with employers that operate at workplace, company, national and international levels. An uneven power relationship is laid bare in these cases: these workforces did not occupy positions within a traditionally well-organized sector, nor did they possess any kind of militant labour movement tradition. Nevertheless, each case demonstrates that unions can possess and deploy various different types of power resources and strategic capabilities to enact change (see Levesque and Murray, 2010). Luce's (2014, p 175) observation is very pertinent to our study. She notes, 'Neoliberalism has brought a host of new challenges and intensified existing ones, requiring labor leaders to think strategically and creatively about how to take advantage of opportunities to organize.'

We began by explaining that our focus is on two dimensions – both relevant to Luce's comments. We looked at the degree to which our three unions were embedded in networks linked to other local, national and global unions, community groups and social movements. These varied (although each union shared an affiliation with the Global Union Federation, UNI Global). SITT in Romania had an institutional link within a European Works Council, together with links at national and international levels. SITRATEL developed bilateral links with an American sister union (through UNI Global) as well as with the national federation. Faced with a hostile employer, the RWDSU created a labour NGO to assist workers whom it could not yet represent as a union, utilized a global framework agreement between UNI Global and the employer's parent company and subsequently built a union at workplace level. We examined the unions' capacity to deploy resources and strategic capabilities effectively (Levesque and Murray, 2010), whether they were able to act at multiple levels and in multiple spaces over time, such as the attempt to utilize the supply chain (Luce, 2014) as was done in the case of Teleperformance. All three unions explicitly recognized the international dimensions of their campaigns and developed what Murray (2017) calls 'glocal' actions, that is, those which are simultaneously both global and local and assume particular significance in the context of globalization.

The unions in our study operate on a multi-scalar basis, operating at local, national and international levels within their own union and the wider labour movement, as well as building coalitions of influence and protest (Frege et al, 2004) closer to home through community alliances of various types. They have used institutional power resources of the state – local, national and supra-national – in order to move towards effective representation. Of course, different political opportunity structures emerge for unions in different contexts in relation to industry, sector and place, for example. Each of these unions took advantage of institutional opportunities at various levels: for instance, the formation of SITT in Romania within the French transnational company Alcatel-Lucent would probably not have been created without the information shared by a French European Works Council (EWC) member with their Romanian counterpart. This case not only suggests that more favourable negotiating conditions exist when outsourcing arises in a company with a 'home' country – in this case France, with a tradition of unionization (Trif and Stoiciu, 2017) – but also shows how the new Romanian union, SITT, was able to utilize the terms of European legislation (the Acquired Rights Directive) and the structures of the EWC as a communication and lobbying instrument. The SITRADEL case shows the possibilities of organizing down the value chain. The union was able to leverage networks available to it through its international affiliation to UNI Global. So, although there was neither a national agreement in the Dominican Republic nor a global agreement with the employer, it was possible to apply pressure via a client of the employer (in a different country) because the client had a union agreement with a well-organized union. A number of unions have drawn on global agreements signed by a Global Union Federation (in our case studies, UNI Global) to advance their position at a national level, as was the case with RWDSU in the US. This union demonstrated that the value of global framework agreements lies in their enforcement on the ground.

All three cases show the broader lesson of the necessity of developing approaches that are both 'bottom up' and 'top down' (Voss and Sherman, 2000), illustrating that 'rank-and-file mobilization is best understood not as an alternative to but rather as complementary – and indeed integral – to the success of top-down strategic campaigns' (Milkman, 2006, p 25). They show that the capacity to coordinate and collaborate across boundaries through transnational forms of solidarity is an important strength. Crucially, this is often the work of a small but critical number of activists, working together in different spaces and at different scales (Kelly, 1998). For example, the RWDSU in the US recognized that in some circumstances there is not necessarily an immediate payoff for the union in terms of membership, dues paid or collective agreements. Instead, the broad community and political campaigning with workers in Zara in New York prepared the ground for future union organization. The RWDSU created the RAP – essentially a pro-labour NGO – as a body focused on educating workers and bringing them together as forerunner to their introduction to the union itself, thus demonstrating a leadership role in civil society, campaigning for benefits beyond its own membership. By its work with RAP, the RWDSU was embracing the role of a social actor in the local community as well as a prospective bargaining agent in the workplace (Tattersall, 2005). This approach is described by Heery and Adler (2003, p 61) as 'a broadening of union purpose' associated with 'new organizing' in the US and the UK. It includes workplace issues but sees the importance of extending beyond the workplace and acting for a broader constituency, and 'in the most developed cases has embraced community coalitions' (Heery and Adler, 2003, p 62).[3]

These cases show the role of union agency in transforming difficult situations into opportunities for union growth and bargaining gains. By learning from organizing practices elsewhere and through the use of combined and complementary strategies, unions have been able to draw upon, strengthen and create new sources of power to find direct and indirect routes to sustainable gains. These efforts to build and harness power to defend and extend workers' interests in the workplace and beyond demonstrate that it is often the application of traditional methods and ideas in a new context that provides a breakthrough in uncharted territory. The extent to which these cases can be seen as indicative of the revitalization of the labour movement in the contemporary era remains unclear. It is significant that our interest here is on sectors that are hostile to trade unionism historically, and on workers that unions have traditionally found hard to organize, largely due to the precarious nature of the work and the fragmentation of the workforce. As yet, although there have been transformational increases in trade union membership in our specific examples, there is no indication of any broader such increases either within or across the sectors of employment covered here. However, it is clear that the labour movement is rethinking the way in which it approaches organizing workers, devising new repertoires of action that are beginning to establish a presence in organizing workers once considered beyond reach.

Notes

[1] At the time, company unions could get legal recognition by affiliation to a legally recognized federation, hence SITT joined the metalworkers' federation (as IT traditionally was linked to it) and they were affiliated to Cartel Alfa, one of the national union confederations, which is how Cartel Alfa became involved.

[2] 'Worker centers are community-based and community-led organizations that create a safe space where workers organize and build power' (Bobo and Pabellon, 2016, p 4).

[3] 'Community unionism' as a form of social movement unionism has been extensively researched (for example, Wills, 2001; Wills and Simms, 2004; Tattersall, 2006; 2008; McBride and Greenwood, 2009).

References

Blyth, M. (2013) *Austerity: The History of a Dangerous Idea.* New York: Oxford University Press.

Bobo, K. and Pabellon, M.C. (2016) *The Worker Center Handbook: A Practical Guide to Starting and Building the New Labor Movement.* Ithaca, NY: Cornell University Press.

Eurofound (2013) *Impact of the Crisis on Working Conditions in Europe.* Brussels: European Foundation for the Improvement of Living and Working Conditions. https://www.eurofound.europa.eu/sites/default/files/ef_files/docs/ewco/tn1212025s/tn1212025s.pdf. Accessed 18 June 2020.

Evans, P. (2008) 'Is an alternative globalization possible?'. *Politics and Society*, 36(2): 271–305.

Frege, C.M., Heery, E. and Turner, L. (2004) 'The new solidarity? Coalition building in five countries'. In: Frege, C.M. and Kelly, J. (eds), *Varieties of Unionism: Strategies for Union Revitalisation in a Global Economy.* Oxford: Oxford University Press, 137–58.

Heery, E. (2009) 'Trade unions and contingent labour: Scale and method'. *Cambridge Journal of Regions, Economy and Society,* 2(3): 429–42.

Heery, E. and Adler, L. (2003) 'Organizing the Unorganized'. In: Frege, C. and Kelly, J. (eds), *Varieties of Unionism: Strategies for Union Revitalization in a Globalizing Economy.* Oxford: Oxford University Press, 45–70.

Hoffer, F. (2018) 'So who's transforming whom?' In: Traub-Merz, R and Pringle, T. (eds), *Trade Unions in Transition: From Command to Market Economies.* Berlin: Friedrich-Ebert-Stiftung, 433–448.

Holtgrewe, U. and Schörpf, P. (2017) *Understanding the Impact of Outsourcing in the ICT Sector to Strengthen the Capacity of Workers' Organisations to Address Labour Market Changes and to Improve Social Dialogue.* Vienna: FORBA/ ZSI. https://www.forba.at/wp-content/uploads/2018/11/1251-FB_10_2016_Final_Report.pdf. Accessed 18 June 2020.

Hudson-Sharp, N. and Runge, J. (2017) *International Trends in Insecure Work: A Report for the Trades Union Congress.* London: National Institute of Economic and Social Research.

ILO (International Labour Organization) (2016) *A Challenging Future for the Employment Relationship: Time for affirmation or alternatives?* The Future of Work Centenary Series, Issue 3. Geneva: ILO. https://www. ilo.org/wcmsp5/groups/public/---dgreports/---dcomm/documents/ publication/wcms_534115.pdf. Accessed 18 June 2020..

Kelly, J. (1998) *Rethinking Industrial Relations: Mobilization, Collectivism and Long Waves.* London: Routledge.

Levesque, C. and Murray, G. (2010) 'Understanding union power: Resources and capabilities for renewing union capacity'. *Transfer: European Review of Labour and Research,* 16(3): 333–50.

Luce, S. (2014) *Labor Movements: Global Perspectives.* Cambridge: Polity Press.

McBride, J. and Greenwood, I. (eds) (2009) *Community Unionism: A Comparative Analysis of Concepts and Contexts.* Basingstoke: Palgrave Macmillan.

McKay, S., Jefferys, S., Paraksevopolou, A. and Keles, J. (2012) *Study on Precarious Work and Social Rights.* Report for the European Commission. London: Working Lives Research Institute, London Metropolitan University.

Milkman, R. (2006) *L.A. Story.* New York: Russell Sage Foundation.

Murray, G. (2017) 'Union renewal: What can we learn from three decades of research?'. *Transfer: European Review of Labour and Research,* 23(1): 9–29.

OECD (Organisation for Economic Co-operation and Development) (2019) Trade Union membership. 3 May. https://twitter.com/OECD/status/1123875322653442048. Accessed 18 June 2020.

Plehwe, D., Neujeffski, M., McBride, S. and Evans, B. (2019) *Austerity: 12 Myths Exposed*. Falkensee, Germany: SE Publishing.

Silver, B. (2003) *Forces of Labor: Workers' Movements and Globalization since 1870*. Cambridge: Cambridge University Press.

Sissons, K. (2010) *Employment Relations Matters*. Cornell University ILR School Research Studies and Reports, 1 January.

Streeck, W. (2017) *How Will Capitalism End?* London: Verso.

Tattersall, A. (2005) 'There is power in Coalition: A framework for assessing how and when union–community coalitions are effective and enhance union power'. *Labour & Industry*, 16(2): 97–112.

Tattersall, A. (2006) 'Bringing the community in: Possibilities for public sector union success through community unionism'. *International Journal of Human Resources Development and Management*, 6(2–4): 186–99.

Tattersall, A. (2008) 'Coalitions and community unionism'. *Journal of Organizational Change Management*, 21(4): 415–32.

Teleperformance (2019) Our locations across the world. https://www.teleperformance.com/en-us/who-we-are/about-us. Accessed 18 June 2020.

Trif, A. and Stoiciu, V. (2017) 'Turning crisis into opportunity: Innovation within the Romanian trade union movement'. In: Bernaciak, M. and Kahancová, M. (eds), *Innovative Union Practices in Central-Eastern Europe*. Brussels: European Trade Union Institute, 161–78.

UFCW (2019) 'Growing number of New York Zara workers join RWDSU/UFCW'. 10 June. http://forlocals.ufcw.org/2019/06/10/growing-number-of-new-york-zara-workers-join-rwdsu-ufcw/. Accessed 18 June 2020.

UNI Global (2018) 'Teleperformance recognises labour union in Dominican Republic'. 19 April. https://www.uniglobalunion.org/news/teleperformance-recognises-labour-union-dominican-republic. Accessed 18 June 2020.

UNI Global (2019a) 'Contact center worker organizing is making the outsourced economy a fairer one'. 28 August. https://www.uniglobalunion.org/news/contact-center-worker-organizing-making-outsourced-economy-a-fairer-one. Accessed 18 June 2020.

UNI Global (2019b) 'UNI ICTS gives first-ever excellence in organizing awards to SITT, SITRATEL-FEDOTRAZONAS, and GPEU'. 27 August. https://www.uniglobalunion.org/news/uni-icts-gives-first-ever-excellence-organizing-awards-sitt-sitratel-fedotrazonas-and-gpeu. Accessed 18 June 2020.

Voss, K. and Sherman, R. (2000) 'Breaking the iron law of oligarchy: Union revitalisation in the American labor movement'. *American Journal of Sociology*, 106(2): 303–49.

Wills, J. (2001) 'Community unionism and trade union renewal in the UK: Moving beyond the fragments at last?'. *Transactions of the Institute of British Geographers*, 26(4): 465–83.

Wills, J. and Simms, M. (2004) 'Building reciprocal community unionism in the UK'. *Capital & Class*, 28(1): 59–84.

16

Afterword:
Final Word and the Path Forward
– Is the Myth of Austerity
Giving Way to the Myth of
the Robots Taking the Jobs?

Jill Rubery

The premise on which austerity is founded is that markets should take over responsibilities from the state (Grimshaw and Rubery, 2012; Farnsworth and Irving, 2018) and therefore more responsibility should be placed on people to self-provision through wage employment or through unpaid labour. This is argued to be good for the economy, as in a globalized world employers would resist paying higher taxes. Under a low-tax regime and with access to an enlarged and flexible labour supply, existing employers would expand employment and new entrepreneurs would spring up to offer opportunities to work for all, provided no one was too choosy about what the work was or when, where or for how long they had to do it.

In the period since 2010, when austerity mania took over government policies fuelled by media calls to balance the books, a great deal has happened and a new mythology is emerging to replace the austerity mythology of perfectly functioning markets offering an alternative to state welfare systems. Instead of promising as much employment as we want, provided we are not fussy about conditions or security, the new mythology is the need to adjust to the demands of the unstoppable force of technology, which may result in mass destruction of jobs, and even the end of work as we know it (Frey and Osborne, 2017). The implications of how this forecast of a work Armageddon fits with the austerity agenda and the role of the state have not yet been fully thought through by politicians and those setting the international policy agenda. If, instead of offering self-provisioning through work as the means of survival, the predictions of mass job destruction are taken seriously, then there is no credibility to the argument that there is no need for state intervention in the labour market and social system. No one is seriously suggesting a smooth transition to, for example, full employment around a shorter working week under the impact of the artificial intelligence and digitalization revolution. To enable people to provide for themselves, some degree of state intervention will be needed to ensure a redistribution of work and resources, otherwise governments can expect to face the political discontent that would come from mass unemployment supported by benefits that have been cut to the bone under austerity. There is some recognition that this new debate changes the context for employment policy, as witnessed in the development of a new Organisation for Economic Co-operation and Development (OECD) Jobs Strategy that places less emphasis on deregulation and more on job quality and inclusion; but the legacy of the neoliberal flexibility agenda is still intertwined with this new approach (Janssen, 2019; McBride and Watson, 2019). The key issues raised by this new scenario have yet to be properly considered: are we coming to the end of austerity, and was it therefore simply a phase in both capitalist and welfare state development? How will governments change their rhetoric in relation to 'work first' and 'scroungers' if the predictions of mass displacement are even only half realized? Is there any likelihood of a rebirth of democratically based solutions to the problems of distribution of income and social protection, or might we see a continuing erosion of democracy itself?

To take a step back from this potential Armageddon, we should first go back to the emergence of austerity after the financial crisis to consider its origins and its underlying premises. We can then trace the connections between austerity and the market-focused labour-market policies under austerity and identify the forms of resistance and the contradictions within the austerity model. In the analysis that follows, we draw mainly on the UK example as one of the most sustained examples of explicit and voluntary endorsement of austerity, that is, austerity that was not mandated by international authorities.

The second section of the following analysis returns to the issues of new technologies and considers the implications for the next phase of technological innovation and current policy approaches to labour markets.

The extent to which this is a new scenario or in fact an extension of austerity is also considered. The section calls for more radical solutions than are currently considered if the dystopian scenarios of no jobs and no welfare are to be avoided, with all the implications that they present for our political systems and future. Of course, at the same time we also consider the predictions related to new technologies to be yet another phase of 'project fear' (not about Brexit this time, but a project to keep the working classes in their place). The problem, though, is which mythology is better – the austerity work first and work-till-you-drop mantra, or the end of work as we know it in the new technology era?

The austerity phase: how work was key to promoting and legitimizing austerity

The adoption of austerity policies from 2010 onwards in response to the conversion of the financial crisis into a sovereign debt crisis was legitimized on the basis of a number of key assumptions. The first was that balancing the books of the nation–state was similar to balancing the books of a household, requiring thrift and doing without, thereby scotching the Keynesian notion of reducing debt through growth so as to generate higher tax revenues. The second assumption was that the state had become over-bloated and was supporting idlers and those with vested interests, to the detriment of hard-working people and entrepreneurs. The fact that the 'overspend' in public finances was primarily due to bailing out the profligacies of the 'entrepreneurial', excessive risk-taking financial sector (Skidelsky, 2018) was thereby hidden under the carpet and the notion of not spending above what one could afford was rammed home. The premise that it was both possible and desirable to 'shrink the state' depended upon the further proposition that self-provisioning into old age through wage work was achievable. This was premised on the notion that the volume of work available would be sufficient, provided the labour market was made even more flexible and entrepreneurs were freed from the burden of taxes, as higher taxes purportedly squeezed out employment opportunities. It is through this last proposition that the case for 'permanent' austerity became critically tied to the labour market and employment opportunities. For the most part, the role of the state in supporting the social reproduction of labour was not directly referred to, thereby distracting attention from the clear negative implications for those undertaking most of the social reproduction work, namely women (Karamessini and Rubery, 2013). However, the implicit assumption was either that the women could do more unpaid work to compensate for seriously reduced services or that, through hard work in the wage-labour market, people could purchase private services and make provision for retirement. This reliance on wage work to replace the state's functions in support of social reproduction also freed governments to start to expand public expenditure again without the main focus being on restoring cuts to the benefits or public services supporting individuals and families. Thus, austerity in relation to welfare support could be considered permanent, even if the overall goals of shrinking the state may fail.

Some bumps in the road for the austerity project

Even though austerity has been the policy objective of choice since 2010 in the UK, this does not mean that the objectives of austerity have been fully realized. The most 'successful' part of austerity has been the growth in employment, apparently indicating that the imperative to find work of whatever quality has been understood and acted upon. The twin pincers of frozen benefits and a punitive sanction regime has made reliance on benefits alone very difficult, and the accompanying growth in low-wage and low-productivity employment (including part-time self-employment) under austerity has also led to 'added worker effects' at the household level (IFS, 2018) – that is, when married women increase their labour supply when their husbands become unemployed. This effect assumes that married women are secondary workers with a less permanent attachment to the labour market than their partners.

The result, despite the added worker impacts, has been the most serious and prolonged squeeze on living standards since the 19th century (TUC, 2018), leading to a huge rise in poverty, particularly in-work poverty, and affecting large numbers of children (Just Fair, 2018). While these effects can be argued to be intended, they also indicate that the employment boom has not provided much capacity for self-provisioning, with many people turning to food banks to get by as well as being unable to purchase private services or save for retirement.

Indeed, one of the major problems of austerity from the point of view of the government was that the increasingly poor employment on offer raised the costs of maintaining support for low-income households. This prompted more major cuts to the level of support offered, pushing more people into deeper poverty. To sweeten the pill, this was accompanied by a significant increase in the minimum wage, which compromised the policy of not imposing new constraints on employers. However, the rolling-out of the new in-work benefit system Universal Credit (UC) that provided a flexible benefit according to wages earned handed employers additional opportunities to duck responsibilities for maintaining minimum living standards. Under UC, employers can vary hours of available work, even of their regular employees, and expect the state to provide some financial compensation. Although opportunities for employers to vary hours at will can be seen as an objective of labour-market flexibility, there is a case for governments of all persuasions to be careful about what they wish for. When it comes to the welfare bill, an increase in the number of precarious jobs is likely to increase the burden on the state even under austerity measures, unless those employed can be expected to rely on family members (for example, women and young people). However, the erosion of male wages also makes this strategy unlikely to meet with success. The government has sought to deal with this problem by reducing the minimum benefit floor and reintroducing responsibilities on benefit recipients to get a proper job – that is, a job with guaranteed full-time hours. Here we can see the clear contradictions between the notion of self-provisioning through work and the granting of moral authority to employers to renege on guaranteed hours and wages even in apparently 'full-time' jobs.

The less-than-rosy labour market, even for those in the middle deciles, is also causing problems for the strategy of making young people pay for their post-secondary education through fees of £9,000-plus a year. The loans for fees were to be paid off at a 9 per cent tax above a given earnings threshold and written off after 30 years, but recent estimates found that only 19 per cent were likely to have paid off their loans by this point.[1] This scheme design failed to consider the fact that many graduates, particularly women, get stuck in poor-quality and part-time jobs, for even if they could extend their working time and earnings the prospect of a further 9 per cent tax plus higher child-care charges is a rather poor incentive. New proposals are under discussion for the government to reduce thresholds for repayment and lengthen the repayment time from 30 to 40 years, policies that, if implemented, will mainly hit the less well-off graduates and women.

A further problem for the state is that employers are increasingly shirking their newly ascribed responsibilities. Not only are they failing to provide job opportunities for the increasingly sick, disabled and older workers deemed fit to work by the benefit system, but also, when charged to provide the public services that used to come under the responsibility of the state, they fail in many and often spectacular ways. Thus, whether it is the train franchisees walking away from contracts,[2] the chains of care homes declaring bankruptcy after being stripped of their real estate assets by private equity owners[3] or the outsourcing companies going bankrupt after prioritizing shareholders over obligations to pension funds,[4] the performance of private sector companies in delivering public services has often been lamentable. Meanwhile, responsibility for public services and for filling gaps in social protection provisions still, from the perspective of the public and also often the law, stops with the government. Thus, the government had to guarantee that no elderly person would end up on the street when Southern Cross care homes went bust.[5] The government was obliged to take rail franchises back under public control to keep the railways running and was required to bail out insolvent pension funds when outsourcing companies prioritized dividends to shareholders and went bust. There was also the knotty problem of what to do about children when there are increasing imperatives on both parents, as well as on single parents, to enter paid employment. These imperatives included household budgetary concerns and the increasingly enforced sanctions on anyone not actively seeking work. This issue led to an out-of-character offer of 30 hours' free childcare for working parents of three-year-olds, induced in part by competition with the Labour Party in the 2015 election campaign, fuelled by concerns that the Conservatives were losing women's votes (OECD, 2017).

Thus, even under austerity neither the private sector nor the labour market has delivered all that the state requires, in large part because of the contradictions within austerity policy itself. Allowing for ever more flexible labour markets does not provide a context in which wage work can be relied upon as a safety net to reduce the need for state support. Instead, as in the new UC regulations, the government has effectively reinvented the full-time regular job by requiring recipients of UC to do all they can to secure a minimum of 35 hours of work, but at the same time facilitating employers' use of more insecure and variable hours of work.

The contradictions of austerity and the intended impact on the living standards of the working classes have led both to some socially progressive resistance movements – for example, in the form of living-wage campaigns – and to more locally focused resistance to the degradation of employment – for example in Greater Manchester Combined Authority's employment charter campaign[6] and Scotland's Fairer Scotland Action Plan.[7] More significant, however, is the rise of populist political movements in many Western countries, fuelled by discontent but led often by far-right politicians who may champion relaxing some of the austerity rules in the name of populist policies. However, their agendas are far from those of restoring rights and resources to the working classes, and it is in this context that we now need to consider the current and potential impact of the emerging propaganda that the robots are finally coming.

Austerity and the rise of the robots

Predictions that nearly half of all jobs are at risk (Frey and Osborne, 2017) should, in principle, provide a wake-up call to those policy makers still promoting social planning based on work first and work till you die. Do we really want to raise the retirement age to 75 (see recent suggestions from Centre for Social Justice[8]) if many in their 30s and 40s are being thrown out of work? The current hype about the impact of new technology may in many senses be a further continuation of 'project fear' – that is, to raise the threat of impoverishment so as to induce compliance with whatever capitalism wants to do. Already the rhetoric around the robot threat places responsibility on the individual for being inflexible or lacking the motivation to reskill. Even so, the need for reconsidering the plausibility of the 'everyone should work and forever mantra' that underpinned policy in the austerity phase might become obvious if mass unemployment were to return.

Of course, the threat from robots to jobs may not be on the scale predicted, and many low-level jobs may continue to be too poorly paid for mechanization to be worthwhile. But policy makers cannot have it both ways; if the population is to prepare for robots, then the government also needs to prepare for what it will do if there does appear to be a significant reduction in available wage work. If wage work opportunities are to decline, it is also the case that the key problems already identifiable in the post-austerity society and economy would come to a head, causing at the very least a major financial crisis. For example, the high levels of debt incurred since the financial crisis can only be sustained if people are able to stay in work; this applies also to the housing market, on which the stability of the British economy still relies. If there is a shortage of wage work, then the UC system of topping-up living standards will prove fiscally unsustainable, particularly if earners lose their employment or find themselves confined to precarious work, offering variable and too few hours to meet subsistence needs. Furthermore, any expectation that individuals would have the capacity and motivation to retrain once their jobs or profession disappeared is at odds with the current system of financing higher education, where the fees assume that this education would set someone up for life in a good, stable job or career.

What is clear is that, under the current policy trajectories where employers have been increasingly freed of obligations towards their workforces, the outcome of the next technological revolution is likely to result in employers absorbing most of the productivity gains and employees being left to compete for a dwindling number of decent jobs. Any seismic shift in the way economies and labour markets operate should also provide opportunities for new political movements to seize control and reshape the future. The biggest danger here is that this political space will be occupied by right-wing populists. Right-wing populist policies are likely to include restrictions on globalization in order to fuel the racist fears that it is people from outside, not the capitalists, who are stealing jobs. However, this will come at the cost of freedoms, protections and democratic rights. Hence, it is essential for progressives to consider what kind of alternative can be offered in the wake of concerns about the take-over by robots. Clearly, this is a time to counter the current obsessions that the cause of political problems lies in the welfare scroungers on society and to instead provide an alternative vision of how society and employment can be organized. Three main alternative progressive visions have been offered, and each merits consideration. These include the end-of-work scenario associated with universal basic income; the direct alternative, namely establishing the state as the employer of last resort under a universal job-guarantee fund; and a move towards a more equal sharing of wage work and income, in part also to facilitate a more equal sharing of unpaid care work.

The most talked-about option in the future of work debates is the universal basic income (UBI) solution to permanent job shortage and as a means to end the coercive control of the unemployed under the austerity period. While the latter objective is welcome, this only requires a change of approach to the unemployed, not an abandonment of work as a core life activity. There are several major problems with the basic income proposal. These include first, how it is to be funded at a level where it offers genuine choices to citizens whether to work or not; if funded below that level, it is likely to encourage the further growth of more casual and precarious work forms (Rubery et al, 2018). Even if introduced at a generous level, the programme would be vulnerable to cutbacks in the level of the UBI with changes of government, particularly if there were a return to austerity. Furthermore, it would be likely to reinforce the gender division of labour between wage and non-wage work (Smith and Shanahan, 2018). Perhaps the main reason to be wary of this policy is the fact that some right-wing think-tanks[9] and political parties, and even the World Bank (2018), are beginning to consider and even advocate the measure – as a means to reduce employment rights and shrink responsibilities for social protection to the provision of a low basic income. This does not mean that rights to basic support independent of work record should not be part of a progressive agenda, but it may be best to focus on a basic income for those who clearly need support outside work, for example a citizens' pension and a basic income for children so as to reduce the risk of child poverty.

The second approach, a guaranteed job provided by the public sector as an employer of last resort, takes a directly opposite perspective to UBI, by regarding access to work as essential for human dignity. It is also in line with Beveridge's view that idleness is one of the great giants to be vanquished (Beveridge, 1944), not only because of the effect on self-esteem and living standards but also because of the lost productive time that it implies. Job guarantees have been used in countries outside the OECD, in India and Argentina for example, but they are now also being considered by US presidential candidates such as Bernie Sanders. One advantage of such a system is that they provide a means of stabilizing economies in a way that ensures a positive impact on employment (Skidelsky, 2019), as the links between monetary and fiscal expansion and employment multipliers are uncertain and may take a long time to take effect. There are two major and interlinked drawbacks to this agenda; first, the impact for those taking up these jobs depends on the political context, namely whether the objective is to give people opportunities for gainful work or if the aim is to discipline the workforce and end the apparent 'something for nothing culture' that is cited as a critique of traditional unemployment benefits. The growing climate crisis plus the clear under-provision of public services, particularly care, following nine years of austerity means that there are plenty of possible and socially worthwhile activities to which extra staff could be deployed. A key issue is the level of payment – this would probably have to be above the benefit level, but where these are low the scope for low-wage exploitation is high. In Hungary, the large public works programme associated with the populist Orban government pays participants much less than the minimum wage and the unemployed are forced to participate after only 90 days of joblessness.[10] However, the second major issue is whether these publicly paid for jobs act as substitutes for properly paid public sector service jobs and thereby undermine both the level and the professionalization of public sector service provision. There would in any case be a clear need to expand the size of the managerial and professional public service jobs, including training departments to provide the organizational and technical support to manage an expansion of untrained public sector workers. A job-guarantee scheme would thus not be a simple policy to enact and would need careful planning and the development of high-trust relations with existing public sector staff in order to avoid fears that their own jobs would be at risk. Nevertheless, as with the UBI approach, there are elements of this policy that should be included in any progressive agenda to replace austerity and the fatalistic end-of-work scenarios, particularly in the context of the climate and care crises. In contrast to the UBI approach, the job-guarantee approach assumes that it is better for these new community needs to be serviced by people who have paid jobs rather than by unpaid volunteers, funded by basic income. Choice between these two approaches is thus highly dependent on attitudes towards whether a potential 'end to work' is to be celebrated or regretted.

As again with UBI, a key issue is not the policy measure itself but the context in which it is implemented and the underlying aspirations of the policy makers. This of course applies to all policies, but it may be better to aim for policies that become embedded in social practices in both the workplace and the home, so as to make changes somewhat more difficult to reverse. This could apply to the third type of progressive policies being mooted, namely a work-sharing policy, in some versions aligned with Nancy Fraser's (1994) vision of a universal carer, universal breadwinner model of society, where everyone is in work and everyone is a carer. This would involve a Polanyian re-embedding of the market within society, but with a gender-equality twist to the societal arrangements (Fraser, 2012). This means going beyond the Trades Union Congress's call for a four-day week, to a more gender-equal call for flexible and shorter hours to enable equal work and equal caring. This approach would potentially reduce open unemployment, share both work and income more equally and help to dissolve the gender divide in work and care roles. This, in my view, is by far the most progressive vision, as it offers possibilities both for time for work and for time for both care and other activities (particularly in periods when care responsibilities are low). It therefore combines the key demands of UBI supporters to expand opportunities for activities beyond wage work and those of the job-guarantee proponents to keep wage work as a positive activity for citizens (Kamerāde et al, 2019). Of course, a work-sharing approach can and should be combined with various elements of both the basic income and the job-guarantee schemes. This could include, for example, providing a UBI for children (to reduce pressure to increase hours and wages so as to pay for the costs of children) and for those who have retired, and also expanding the range of activities within the public sector in order to address the climate and care crises. Many of those who are primary carers can currently manage to work only short hours, but under a general shorter working policy many might be able to increase their hours towards 30, due to better support for care from partners.

However, a move towards shorter working hours would require major changes in employment arrangements, which would need to be mandated by the state even if campaigned for and negotiated through social movements and trade unions. It would involve redistribution of high-quality work and income and would therefore be likely to be contested by people with and used to considerable power in society. These anticipated obstacles should not, however, deflect attention from what the goals of a progressive policy agenda need to be. Furthermore, if this change led to a new social norm that we should all be both earners and carers, it might be more difficult for this change to be reversed by a new government with a different political agenda. This change in social norms and associated mindsets is perhaps more important than a strict focus on hours of work itself, as many jobs are increasingly undertaken in non-standard work situations, including the home and outside of any standard hours of work. The opportunities to remain connected to work and to engage in virtual working make the number of hours spent on particular jobs difficult to both monitor and control. However, a change of mindset is important in order to reduce workloads even in these types of jobs. Instead of minimizing staffing levels, companies need to be encouraged to job-share and promote team working rather than individual responsibilities for activities or clients, so as to allow people to turn off work-related activities and pass the responsibility on, as well as encouraging clients and managers to expect responses only within specified time frames. Sectors, companies and individuals may need to find their own route to shorter working hours, but the important issue is to start the process.

Most importantly, all progressive visions for the next technological revolution require a reversal of the trend to reduced regulation of employers that is absolving them of responsibilities. We need more societal control in order to fund social protection, change employment patterns to fit with the universal carer/universal breadwinner model and ensure that not all the productivity gains from new technologies are siphoned off by capital. This will require a change in the international governance order as well as at the national level. To hope for these changes may be utopian, but, in the light of the dystopian predictions, we need a new vision of what we should be striving towards. The debate on UBI has been around a long time and has only just started to be taken seriously; we can expect a similar long haul for a more egalitarian joint carer and breadwinner society, but we still have to start the debate.

Notes

1 https://www.bbc.co.uk/news/education-48459910.
2 https://www.theguardian.com/politics/2018/may/16/east-coast-rail-line-to-be-temporarily-renationalised-virgin-stagecoach.
3 https://www.theguardian.com/business/2011/jul/16/southern-cross-incurable-sick-business-model.
4 https://www.theguardian.com/money/2018/jan/16/after-carillion-how-many-firms-can-the-pensions-lifeboat-rescue.
5 https://www.bloomberg.com/news/articles/2011–06–01/cameron-guarantees-care-for-elderly-in-southern-cross-homes.

6   https://www.greatermanchester-ca.gov.uk/what-we-do/economy/greater-manchester-good-employment-charter/.
7   https://www.gov.scot/publications/fairer-scotland-action-plan/pages/7/.
8   https://www.centreforsocialjustice.org.uk/core/wp-content/uploads/2019/08/CSJJ7421-Ageing-Report-190815-WEB.pdf.
9   https://www.independent.co.uk/voices/universal-basic-income-adam-smith-institute-austerity-libertarian-a8167701.html.
10 https://www.socialeurope.eu/inside-hungarys-work-based-society.

References

Beveridge, W. (1944) *Full Employment in a Free Society*. London: Allen and Unwin.

Farnsworth, K. and Irving, Z. (2018) 'Austerity: Neoliberal dreams come true?' *Critical Social Policy*, 38(3): 461–81.

Fraser, N. (1994) 'After the family wage: Gender equity and the welfare state'. *Political Theory*, 22(4): 591–618.

Fraser, N. (2012) *Can Society Be Commodities All the Way Down? Polanyian Reflections on Capitalist Crisis*. Fondation Maison des Sciences de l'homme No 18. www.msh-paris.fr/en/news/news/article/can-society-be-commodities-all-the-way-down-polanyian-reflections-on-capitalist-crisis/.

Frey, C. and Osborne, A. (2017) 'The future of employment: How susceptible are jobs to computerisation?'. *Technological Forecasting and Social Change*, 114: 254–80.

Grimshaw, D. and Rubery, J. (2012) 'The end of the UK's liberal collectivist social model? The implications of the coalition government's policy during the austerity crisis'. *Cambridge Journal of Economics*, 36(1): 105–26.

IFS (Institute for Fiscal Studies) (2018) *Living Standards, Poverty and Inequality in the UK 2018*. London: Institute for Fiscal Studies.

Janssen, R. (2019) 'The revised OECD Jobs Strategy and labour market flexibility: a double-handed narrative'. *Transfer*, 25(2): 221–7.

Just Fair (2018) *Visit by the UN Special Rapporteur on Extreme Poverty and Human Rights, Philip Alston, to the UK from 5 to 16 November 2018. Written submission*. http://justfair.org.uk/wp-content/uploads/2018/09/Just_Fair_15_Alston_Submission-FINAL.pdf. Accessed 20 June 2019.

Kamerāde, D., Wang, S., Burchell, B., Balderson, S. and Coutts, A. (2019) 'A shorter working week for everyone: How much paid work is needed for mental health and well-being?'. *Social Science & Medicine*, 112353, https://doi.org/10.1016/j.socscimed.2019.06.006.

Karamessini, M. and Rubery, J. (2013) *Women and Austerity*. London: Routledge.

McBride, S. and Watson, J. (2019) 'Reviewing the 2018 OECD Jobs Strategy: Anything new under the sun?'. *Transfer*, 25(2): 165–80.

OECD (Organisation for Economic Co-operation and Development) Directorate for Financial and Enterprise Affairs Working Group on Bribery in International Business Transactions (2017) *The United Kingdom Phase 4 Report*. http://www.oecd.org/officialdocuments/publicdisplay documentpdf/?cote=DAF/WGB(2017)3/FINAL&docLanguage=En

Rubery, J., Grimshaw, D., Keizer, A. and Johnson, M. (2018) 'Challenges and contradictions in the "normalising" of precarious work'. *Work, Employment & Society*, 32(3): 509–27.

Skidelsky, R. (2018) 'Ten years on from the financial crash, we need to get ready for another one'. *The Guardian*, 12 September. https://www.theguardian.com/commentisfree/2018/sep/12/crash-2008-financial-crisis-austerity-inequality.

Skidelsky, R. (2019) 'The case for a guaranteed job'. https://robertskidelsky.com/2019/08/16/the-case-for-a-guaranteed-job/.

Smith, M. and Shanahan, G. (2018) 'Is a basic income the solution to persistent inequalities faced by women?'. *The Conversation*, 7 March. http://theconversation.com/is-a-basic-income-the-solution-to-persistent-inequalities-faced-by-women-92939.

TUC (Trades Union Congress) (2018) '17-year wage squeeze the worst in two hundred years'. *TUC Blog*, 11 May. https://www.tuc.org.uk/blogs/17-year-wage-squeeze-worst-two-hundred-years. Accessed 20 June 2019.

World Bank (2018) *World Development Report 2019: The Changing Nature of Work*. Washington, DC: World Bank.

Index

Note: page numbers in italic type refer to Figures;
those in bold type refer to Tables.